Covenant and Civil Society

Daniel J. Elazar

Covenant and Civil Society

The Constitutional Matrix of Modern Democracy

...

THE COVENANT TRADITION IN POLITICS
VOLUME IV

Transaction Publishers
New Brunswick (U.S.A.) and London (U.K.)

Copyright © 1998 by Transaction Publishers, New Brunswick, New Jersey.

Preparation of this book for publication was made possible through the Milken Library of Jewish Public Affairs, funded by the Milken Family Foundation.

Library of Congress Catalog Number: 97-49240
ISBN: 1-56000-311-1
Printed in the United States of America

Library of Congress Cataloging-in-Publication Data

Elazar, Daniel Judah.
    Covenant and civil society : the constitutional matrix of modern democracy / Daniel J. Elazar.
        p. cm. — (The covenant tradition in politics ; v. 4)
    Includes bibliographical references and index.
    ISBN 1-56000-311-1 (alk. paper)
    1. Civil society—History. 2. Covenants—Political aspects. 3. Democracy—History. I. Title. II. Series: Elazar, Daniel Judah. Covenant tradition in politics ; v. 4.
BL65.P7E43   1995 vol. 4
[JC336]
301—dc21
                                                            97-49240
                                                            CIP

This book is dedicated to Jonathan and Ruti.
May their lives together be all that is good.

Contents

Preface   ix

Introduction   1

Part I: Covenant: From Commonwealth to Civil Society

1. Prologue: Toward a Civil Constitutionalism   7
2. Covenant and the New Political Science   31
3. Britain: From Whiggism to Liberalism   59
4. From Tocqueville to Personalism: Covenant and its Displacement in Post-Revolutionary European Thought   81
5. Four Twentieth-Century Federalist Thinkers   101

Part II: Covenant and the Age of State-Building

6. Europe: Modern Nationalism and the Covenant Tradition   117
7. The Covenant Motif in Modern Revolutions   141
8. Revolutions: Cooperative, Collectivist, and Coercive   161
9. Swiss Exceptionalism: Communal and Liberal Democracy   177

Part III: Covenant and Constitutionalism

10. Constitutionalism: The Modern Expression of the Covenantal Tradition   197
11. The Three Dimensions of the Constitution   215
12. The Covenant Tradition and Rights   239

Part IV: Present and Future

13. The Decline and Possible Revival of Covenant in Our Times   265
14. Toward a World Covenantal Network   291
15. Covenant, Republicanism, and Democracy   317
16. Where Does This Bring Us?   341

Excursus 1. The Language of Covenant   361

Excursus 2. The Biblical Covenant as the Foundation of Justice, Obligations and Rights   375

Index   383

Preface

This, the fourth of the quartet of volumes on the Covenant Tradition in Politics completes the discussion begun in *Covenant and Polity in Biblical Israel* which explored the origins of the covenant tradition in the Bible and its subsequent expression in the Jewish political tradition. The second volume, *Covenant and Commonwealth*, continued the exploration by focusing on the premodern European experience, from the days of ancient Greece and Rome through the rise of Christianity and culminating in the Protestant Reformation. The third volume, *Covenant and Constitionalism,* focused on the extension of the covenant tradition to what was for Europeans, the "New World," discovered at the end of the fifteenth century and settled over the next 500 years. In this volume we will explore the efforts to introduce covenant models derived from the covenant tradition in the Old World during the modern epoch and some efforts, both intentional and unintentional, to revive the covenant tradition or its derivatives in the postwar world. Needless to say, all these explorations are no more than partial, touching upon important highlights—indicators of the covenant tradition, its manifestations and derivatives. No one is more conscoius of what has been omitted and what has been insufficiently explained than this writer. My apologies to my readers for those deficiencies. My only hope is that what is discussed and the framework within which it is presented will be helpful in encouraging others to continue the exploration which I have tried to begin, perhaps to find ways to utilize the covenantal tradition in the never-ending effort of improving our world and the life within it.

Once again, I wish to express my deepest thanks to the Earhart Foundation of Ann Arbor, Michigan, its president, David Kennedy, its secretary and director of programs, Dr. Antony T. Sullivan, and its former president, Richard Ware, for the very tangible encouragement and assistance they have provided me over the years of this effort, and the understanding that accompanied it. Deepest thanks, too, to the institutions with which I have been associated and their staffs, who have been enormously helpful, indeed indispensible: the Center for the Study of Federalism at Temple University in Philadelphia, Pennsylvania; the Jerusalem Center for Public Affairs in Jerusalem, Israel; the Department of Political Studies at Bar-Ilan University in Ramat Gan, Israel. All three have also provided support for this project: the Jerusalem Center through the Milken Library of Jewish Public Affairs, and the Bar-Ilan Department of Political Studies through the Senator Norman M. Paterson Chair in Intergovernmental Relations. They have my deepest gratitude. My sincere thanks also to the Milken Family Foundation for its support for the publication of this book through the Jerusalem Center.

I would like to especially thank Mark Ami-El, publications coordinator of the Jerusalem Center for his vital role in bringing this book to publication, and Deborah Gerber and my other research assistants in both the Philadelphia and Jerusalem centers for their contribution to its final preparations. The final stages of the research for this volume benefitted from the collections of the Weidener Library at Harvard University, where I was a visitor in 1993–1994, one of the world's major repositories of European and American covenantal materials as befits a university with Harvard's origins.

A project of the magnitude of this one requires considerable support from many sources, but no support is more extensive or more critical than that provided by one's own family. My wife Harriet and my children were everything that one could possibly expect in this connection and even more, making it possible for me to live and work in a way most conducive to beginning this undertaking, staying with it, and finally bringing it to a proper conclusion. My love for them is inexpressible as is my gratitude.

In have learned much about covenantal manifestations and expressions from colleagues with whom I have participated in Liberty Fund Colloquia, hence I would be remiss if I did not express my deep gratitude to Liberty Fund, its founder Pierre Goodrich, its board and staff for making those experiences possible.

Special thanks to my good friend Irving Louis Horowitz, founder and guiding spirit of Transaction Publishers, Mary Curtis, Transaction's present publisher, and Laurence Mintz, my editor for these four volumes, for their support, encouragement, and contributions to the improvement of the final project. I owe them a great debt.

I have benefitted from the work of so many who have gone before me and from whom I have learned. My apologies to those whom I have failed to acknowledge. Needless to say, any errors are my own and I accept responsibility for them.

DJE
Jerusalem
5757–1997

Introduction

The settlement of new worlds by bearers of the covenant tradition in politics (see volume 3, *Covenant and Constitutionalism*) gave those settlers an unparalleled opportunity to build societies on the covenantal model or as close to it as they could, given the pressures of the environment and parallel traditions borne by other settlers. The bearers of those same covenantal ideas who remained came into conflict with the bearers of the rival ideas of hierarchy and oligarchy. The stage for that conflict was set in the two centuries before the opening of the modern epoch.

In the seventeenth century, with the revival of the idea of covenant as a powerful force, the covenantal idea had had a certain success in those countries reshaped by the Protestant Reformation in its Reformed Protestant (sometimes called Calvinist) version, or where earlier oath and pact societies had existed. Both were found on continental Europe and the British Isles in the borderlands on both sides of the line that had once divided the areas under Roman control from the lands of the barbarian tribes more than a thousand years earlier. Initially they were submerged by Christianity and the political regimes with which the church allied itself as described in volume 2 of this series. In other parts of Europe, however, the covenantal tradition was distinctly a minority one, if it existed at all, and was submerged by one or another of the hierarchical traditions. Thus, in Europe, even more than in the New Worlds, covenantalism confronted major barriers that could only be overcome to some degree.

Governmentally, the modern epoch was preeminently an epoch of statism. Modern states arose to replace the feudal complexities of medieval Europe and Asia and the tribal complexities of Africa and the Americas to establish states as the fundamental arenas within which all the other struggles of modernity took place. Statism triumphed for many reasons, but probably the most important was that the first states—France, Spain, and England—that emerged were powerful entities that could defend themselves and win wars against other, more fragmented polities such as Germany, Italy, and the Netherlands. In the end, the leaders of the latter felt the need to transform those polities into states for self-protection.

Most states were consolidated by strong royal rulers functioning within hierarchies that they or their predecessors had established. In most, the crown was even reified so that the king was referred to by the name of the embryonic

1

state. Statism succeeded because modern states seemed to demand hierarchical frameworks and both mobilized and concentrated their power through such frameworks to mobilize military strength vis-a-vis their neighbors through the centralization of power within the state.

Hierarchy is the exact opposite of what covenantal polities are all about. The latter emphasize equality and power-sharing instead of hierarchy and centralization. To the degree that some polities were covenantal they tended to be federal, just as to the degree that the modern states were hierarchical they tended to be centralized. Even after the kings themselves lost their powers and their authority was transferred to the parliamentary institutions of the reified state, the hierarchical pyramid was simply transformed into a center-periphery model with the state dominated by a single center occupied by its elite with the remainder of the population located on the peripheries. At most the peripheries could influence who was chosen to govern in the center, but the center functioning very much like the top of the pyramid in the earlier hierarchies and only a bit more subject to popular will, even if there were pro forma elections on a regular basis. The center-periphery model thus continued to differ from the covenantal one in this critical respect.

The statist model and its rival, the federalist model, both had their philosophic champions at the very beginning of the modern epoch. Jean Bodin spoke in the name of statism, and Johannes Althusius, in the name of federalism. Both laid out rather comprehensive models of the ideal polity from their perspectives.[1]

Bodin's philosophy triumphed in the realities of statism while that of Althusius was left to be advocated by a few mavericks or specialists who continued to argue for an Althusian-style polity rather than a reified state.

As European influence and power spread throughout the world, and the Americas, Africa, and Asia were colonized by the European powers, they brought with them their statist approach which, except where the British trod and federal systems took root, became the dominant pattern for state-building when the era of decolonization began and the European powers were expelled or withdrew of their own accord. Thus the whole world was divided into a system of states, most of which followed the models of European statism.

Meanwhile, in Europe the first revolutions of modernity rejected royal absolutism and attempted to transfer power to the people. In doing so they left the reified state in place, so that it soon became the actual repository of the power which was exercised by the state bureaucracy. In some cases, acceptable messages of covenantalism, namely covenanting and constitutionalism, were introduced as formal coverings of the reality. In time, however, they began to acquire a meaning of their own.

Meanwhile, the people came up with other devices to introduce covenantal principles into their now modernized, reified states in Europe. Now they are slowly being introduced in the other Old Worlds of Africa and Asia. Latin

America, that part of the New World settled in late medieval times before the dawn of the modern epoch, has remained locked in a struggle between hierarchical and covenantal forces, a struggle which has lasted with greater or lesser intensity throughout the modern epoch. Only after World War II did the tide begin to turn toward covenantal models and even then only in a limited manner.

The history and meaning of these struggles is our concern in the following pages. The outcome is of concern not only for students of the process but for all of us who are concerned with the regimes in which we find ourselves or to which we have access.

In the end, as the modern epoch unfolded, certain key ideas of the covenantal tradition that could express the essence of that tradition translated into the realities of the political arena did score major successes to become the norm for modern democratic republicanism. These included: (1) the idea that political society is a human artifact established through political compact either in conjunction with or in the wake of the founding of civil society through some form of pact or covenant; (2) the transformation of the old principle of constitutionalism into new and eminently practical forms of constitutional design and politics that introduced real constitutions with enforceable characteristics to shape the governance of real polities, thereby translating paper theories of constitutionalism that had been essentially unenforceable in the Middle Ages into enforceable constitutions and constitutional systems; (3) the idea of popular sovereignty (presented as "under God"), whereby the people could covenant or compact with each other and form their own constitutions and polities accordingly; (4) where covenantalism was strong yet not strong enough to replace other models of polity-building, the development of consociational and cooperative forms of political and social organization within existing hierarchical frameworks to give it expression.

These ideas and the institutions they represented penetrated most parts of Europe with difficulty and required the entire modern epoch to do so. The changes were accompanied by various revolutions, the most important of which in the short term fostered hierarchical modifications of hierarchical models rather than new covenantal models. In a number of cases, authoritarian and totalitarian backlashes developed that rejected covenantal principles totally. Yet in the end, the basic principles and institutions outlined above have come close to triumphing throughout Europe, if unevenly.

The ultimate extension of covenantal ideas and institutions is the true success of the revolutions of modern Europe. While in some ways aided by those revolutions usually deemed important, it is a success that not only transcends those revolutions but in certain respects counters them with a very different model. This volume is devoted to the exploration of those ideas and institutions, and the struggles to develop them in the Old World, especially in modern and early postmodern Europe. Best read in conjunction with the three earlier volumes of this series, it does stand alone.

Covenantal arrangements make political society possible on a more equitable basis than any other kinds of arrangements. They also make possible the establishment of a new whole that preserves the integrities of its constituent parts while developing a new integrity of its own based on the coming together of those parts. This aspect of the covenantal process is now being extended worldwide, on a globalized basis. This has been done by secularizing both the process and the outcome, albeit without satisfying the needs that a more religious approach satisfied in the past or gives promise of satisfying through covenantal religion in the future.

Note

1. See Daniel J. Elazar, *Covenant and Commonwealth: Europe from Christian Separation through the Protestant Reformation,* Volume II of *The Covenant Tradition in Politics* (New Brunswick: Transaction Publishers, 1995), ch. 16.

Part I

Covenant:
From Commonwealth
to Civil Society

Part I

Covenant,
From Commonwealth
to Civil Society

1

Prologue: Toward a Civil Constitutionalism

The cleavage between the modern and premodern epochs is generally acknowledged. We may argue over the extent of the cleavage and the degree of continuity across the premodern-modern divide, but the fact that the cleavage was and is a reality for most people who have undergone modernization has been well-documented. Nevertheless, covenant is one of those concepts and its tradition one of the cultures that did manage to cross the divide and survive; transformed, indeed, but in the process having an enormous influence on the shaping of the modern epoch, especially in its political dimension, and continuing to compel certain populations or at the very least to serve as the rock of refuge to which they return for reinvigoration in times of need. It is no less important to recall that the political transformations of modernity were initiated by and achieved their greatest success in those countries where the covenantal tradition had been strongest, particularly Switzerland, the Netherlands, Scotland and England, and the United States.

Circumstantial evidence alone would suggest that there should have been a connection between the covenant tradition and modern constitutionalism. That evidence is strengthened by the record, which shows real connections, and also by the results. Indeed, the most successful results, even from the perspective of the first modernists, came when the tradition of the covenantal commonwealth and that of modern civil society found common ground and served as mutual modifiers, as in the founding of the United States.[1] Moreover, the record of constitutionalism in those countries and polities without a covenantal tradition is so sharply different as to suggest the same. This book seeks to tell the story of the crossing of that gap and its consequences, and to analyze the results and present status of the covenant tradition in Western, now increasingly world, politics.

To do so we must look at covenant in all its many dimensions, as generator of theory, as fundament of culture, as ideological manifestation, as shaper of institutions, and as influence on behavior within the matrix constructed by all, many, or some of the foregoing. Covenant theory and practice had its greatest flowering in the Bible and its second greatest during the Protestant Reformation as the basis for Reformed Protestantism.[2] It may be at the beginning of its third great revival today, early in the postmodern epoch.

7

Although we can uncover the beginnings of covenant theory, ideology, and institutions in the Bible and Biblical Israel, the ultimate origins of covenantal cultural predispositions, especially political culture, and behavior remain unclear. Even the most careful investigation fails to uncover those origins beyond certain elements in Mesopotamian culture with any certitude. Even the lines of continuity of covenantal culture or political culture tend to be obscured for certain times and in certain places. What we have pieced together from the past is a kind of incomplete puzzle where many of the pieces are still missing or, if not ultimately missing, have yet to be uncovered. In the modern epoch, the problem is less one of missing pieces than of inadequate information regarding the many pieces that we have, often because they have been reported to us without addressing the covenantal dimension, either taking it for granted or considering it unimportant. In such cases, only a return to the most original sources can help us, and it has not been possible to do so in all cases.

Covenant, Compact, Contract

A covenant is a morally informed agreement or pact based upon voluntary consent and mutual oaths or promises, witnessed by the relevant higher authority, between peoples or parties having independent though not necessarily equal status, that provides for joint action or obligation to achieve defined ends (limited or comprehensive) under conditions of mutual respect which protect the individual integrities of all the parties to it. Every covenant involves consenting, promising, and agreeing. Most are meant to be of unlimited duration, if not perpetual. Covenants can bind any number of partners for a variety of purposes, but in their essence they are political in that their bonds are used principally to establish bodies political and social.

Covenant is tied in an ambiguous relationship to two related terms, compact and contract. On the one hand, both compacts and contracts are derived from covenant, and sometimes the terms are even used interchangeably. On the other hand, there are very real differences between the three which need clarification.

Both *covenants* and their derivative, *compacts*, differ from *contracts* in that the first two are constitutional or public and the last private in character. As such, covenantal or compactual obligations are broadly reciprocal. Those bound by one or the other are obligated to respond to one another beyond the letter of the law rather than to limit their obligations to the narrowest contractual requirements. Hence, covenants and compacts are inherently designed to be flexible in certain respects as well as firm in others. As expressions of private law, contracts tend to be interpreted as narrowly as possible so as to limit the obligation of the contracting parties to what is explicitly mandated by the contract itself.

A covenant differs from a compact in that its morally binding dimension takes precedence over its legal dimension. In its heart of hearts, a covenant is an agreement in which a transcendent moral force, traditionally God, is a party, usually a direct party, to or guarantor of a particular relationship; whereas, when the term compact is used, a moral force is only indirectly involved. A compact, based as it is on mutual pledges rather than the guarantees of a higher authority, rests more heavily on a legal though still ethical grounding for its politics. In other words, compact is a secular phenomenon. This is historically verifiable by examining the shift in terminology that took place in the seventeenth and eighteenth centuries. While those who saw the hand of God in political affairs in the United States continued to use the term covenant, those who sought a secular grounding for politics turned to the term compact. While the distinction is not always used with strict clarity, it does appear consistently. The issue was further complicated by Rousseau and his followers who talked about the social contract, a highly secularized concept which, even when applied for public purposes, never develops the same level of moral obligation as either covenant or compact.

Covenant is also related to constitutionalism. Normally, a covenant precedes a constitution and establishes the people or body which then proceeds to adopt a constitution of government for itself. Thus, a constitution involves the implementation of a prior covenant—an effectuation or translation of a prior covenant into an actual frame or structure of government. The constitution may include a restatement or reaffirmation of the original covenant, as does the Massachusetts Constitution of 1780, but that is optional.

Although perhaps more difficult than tracing covenantal ideas expressed in political thought, covenant as ideology is more easily identifiable since ideology is a very public form of theory. Covenant-as-culture persists even when it is not necessarily recognized as such, while covenantal ideology had its ups and downs in the modern epoch. It was strong in the mid-seventeenth century in the British Isles, the Low Countries, and in the American colonies; again at the time of the American Revolution; and periodically thereafter in covenant-based civil societies, but never again during the modern epoch did it achieve the same status.

One of the tests of the presence of the covenantal dimension is to be found in the institutions that developed within the covenantal matrix, particularly in matters of their institutional governance and culture. These, indeed, can be identified throughout the epoch. Even if the larger environment is less covenantal, institutions remain carriers, at least until some massive change comes to transform them. Thus the behavior of people functioning within those institutions, particularly their political behavior, is a clear manifestation of covenant where it exists. Less easy to identify than institutions, nevertheless political behavior can be studied sufficiently well in most cases.

Covenant entered the modern epoch as a manifestation of Reformed Protestantism and in every respect it was tied to the rise and fall of Puritanism and
the residues Puritanism left in certain parts of the world. Reformed Protestantism had two principal sources: one was in Ulrich Zwingli, Heinrich
Bullinger, and their colleagues and disciples in Zurich and the Rhineland,
principally in the German-speaking territories of Switzerland and western
Germany. The other was the product of John Calvin and his associates and
students in Geneva. Calvin came on the scene after Zwingli had been killed
and Calvin's doctrines rapidly became the most influential in the Reformed
Protestant world.

As these influences affected the Huguenots in France, the Netherlanders,
the Scots, and the English Puritans as well as the Puritans in British North
America, in matters theological Calvinism was the stronger influence, but in
matters political the influence of Zwingli and Bullinger was the greater. While
every nation influenced by Reformed Protestantism developed its own synthesis of the two, the most influential synthesis in the world was that formed
by the English Puritans. In no small measure, this was because of the power
of first England and then its successor, Great Britain, in the world as the greatest
power from the mid-seventeenth century until nearly the end of the modern
epoch, with influence that stretched far beyond its tight little island. That
influence was further increased by the fact that the Puritans fought, and in the
short term won, a civil war in England itself which not only brought them to
power in their own country, but enabled them to conquer Scotland and Ireland, and settle a good part of British North America as well.

Religiously based covenantal thinking undoubtedly reached its most sophisticated level of development under Reformed Protestantism and most
particularly Puritanism, finding major expression on the European continent,
in the British Isles, and in New England where it had lasting impact on subsequent generations, even after the Puritan commonwealths had passed from
history, to be replaced by modern, secularized civil societies. Only at major
historical intervals has a movement had as much impact as Reformed Protestantism has had on the history of the world.

Nevertheless, the kind of integral society that was required to maintain
Reformed Protestantism came under great assault in the seventeenth century.
Ultimately it was brought down in favor of a far more heterogeneous world
view, in part because the demands of Puritanism, and Reformed Protestantism in general, on flawed individuals were too high. For better or for worse,
most people did not want to live Puritan lives, seeing Puritanism as far too
serious, demanding, and unsatisfying. Moreover, those who saw Puritanism
as an appropriate way of life often could not personally sustain its demands
and hence were perceived by others to be hypocrites.

Thus we had a paradox. On one hand, Reformed Protestantism developed
very important and compelling theories, ideologies, and cultures supporting

liberty and equality, two of the principal political aspirations of the modern epoch, but the Reformed way to achieve them required institutions insufficiently broad or free and behavior of an impossibly high standard to be realized by the vast majority of people. It remained for the new science of politics and its developers and exponents, who began with a very secular, if equally pessimistic, approach to human nature (the development of which Reformed Protestantism actually facilitated) to provide not only a bridge but a more satisfying framework for political theory and practice, both of which drew on covenant ideas in new ways.

The New Political Philosophy

The first steps toward the new science of politics were taken through the new political philosophy, the philosophic revolution brought by Hobbes, Spinoza, and Locke. All three were products of covenanted commonwealths and all three developed systems of political thought that moved people from covenanted commonwealths to their modern equivalents, constitutional civil societies. The new political philosophy began by breaking with traditional conceptions of human nature which held that the good was as much a part of human nature as other elements and that humans would naturally strive for the good if circumstances permitted that side of human nature to flourish. From a philosophic perspective, premodern theories saw natural law as overarching the entire human enterprise, built into the very foundations of the world or humanity and including all of the ideal aspirations of humankind. This overarching character was also manifested in Christian theology, which indeed was grounded in a synthesis between natural law and Divine revelation, first developed by the Jewish thinker Philo of Alexandria for Jews living at the time of Jesus and subsequently embraced by the Church and its theologians. Thus it was not difficult for the Protestant reformers to go back to what, for them, was the Old Testament and still remain within an overarching system which believed that the good could be brought out in humans because it was within them by virtue of their very nature or by Divine grace, or both.

It was this edifice that was demolished by the new political philosophy, which held that the psychology of individual humans, grounded in human passions, provided the foundations for human nature, not some overarching system that included virtue; that humans had certain elemental rights by virtue of their being humans that could only be protected by the establishment of civil society, through which order could be maintained to protect the weak against the strong and strong individuals against the combination of many weak ones against them. Grounded in methodological individualism, this new political philosophy viewed individual human beings not only as the building blocks of the social order but as radically independent from one another except insofar as they chose to or felt the necessity to combine, which the political philosophers themselves believed they would inevitably do for sheer survival if for no other reason.

To effect their combination, the new political philosophers drew upon covenant ideas put forward by Reformed Protestantism, but in a secularized way. Hobbes, indeed, secularized the very term "covenant," apparently seeing within it the moral dimension and the importance of that dimension to make covenants work in an otherwise highly individualistic world.[4] Thus Hobbes, who has come down to us with a reputation as the most "pessimistic" of the new philosophers of the seventeenth century, actually rested his philosophy, especially in its political dimension, on relatively high moral expectations. Spinoza and Locke, on the other hand, moved from the term "covenant" to "political compact" to highlight a morality based upon human mutuality rather than even a putative Divine connection. Of course, Hobbes had the same idea but thought that he could keep the term which so clearly expressed the moral dimension of pacting that he had in mind.

Despite this, however, covenant continued to mean a pact between humans either with a transcendent power or under its aegis until it later was transformed into the idea of a contract that was binding only morally and not legally enforceable—its meaning today in the business world. Spinoza, indeed, tries hard to avoid even discussing the matter, except historically, preferring to concentrate on other issues such as the rejection of revelation in favor of rational knowledge of natural right.[5] One might argue that this could be understood as stemming from his particular background as a Jew from a Marrano family, and the questions that it led him to raise. Those questions led him to be more interested in directly confronting the problem of Divine revelation and the necessity for its replacement by a system of rational philosophy than either Hobbes or Locke.

Locke was sufficiently a product of his late Puritan environment to seek to incorporate some of its major premises and methodologies into his new, more secularized, version of political philosophy. He felt the need to undermine Divine revelation only insofar as it seemed to protect the Divine right of patriarchal monarchy, which he did very thoroughly in his *First Treatise on Government* but which also was not very difficult, given the thrust of Scripture away from patriarchy in any case.[6] For Locke, however, as in the Bible, humans organized themselves around morally grounded and reinforced pacts. God became, at most, a guarantor for those human pacts rather than a partner in them.[7] With those developments in mind, Locke could then enlist much of Puritan political thought in his cause, albeit in secularized form.

What was common to all three of these philosophers was a very realistic psychology, one that made no moral demands on humanity other than those perceived to be in their self-interest. The full consequences of this shift would not be known for another three hundred years—until the tenth generation after its occurrence—when it became an agent of extreme secularism as well as republicanism. While the latter is what particularly concerns us here, we cannot understand it unless we understand the former as well, for while all three and the lesser philosophic lights of the seventeenth century who travelled the same path preferred to refer to political society as a commonwealth, by the end of the century they had introduced the term "civil society," which added a new, more secular and heterogeneous dimension to the commonwealth.

The idea of civil society explicitly or implicitly secularized the commonwealth in two ways, by grounding society in a civil rather than a Divine order, and by resting it on the private lives of individuals that were modified only by the agreement of those selfsame individuals to surrender some of their privately held power (which after all was authoritative in this view of the world) to one or another collectivity, either a public nongovernmental association or a far more binding governmental association that became the framing institution of the civil society. Since both of these were private decisions to establish and maintain collectivities, the private was primary, even though for those philosophers the public domain was absolutely necessary for the protection of life, the advancement of liberty, the ownership of property, and the pursuit of happiness. For them, the commonwealth was no longer the Puritan commonwealth resting on Divine guidance defined and established by covenants, the original of which rested on human partnership with God, but was a civil society based upon political and social compacts, entered into by human beings with or without Divine protection on the basis of mutual pledges to be sustained by the power of the new collectivity derived from the moral commitments of the mutual pledging. The essence of covenanting was preserved but with a new grounding and more limited purposes.

The New Science of Politics

This, in turn, led to the new science of politics. The process of translating the new political philosophy into effective institutions of government became the province of the exponents of the new science of politics. That took more time. By the end of the seventeenth century, the new political philosophy had already become the cutting edge if not the regnant philosophy for Western Europe and the British Isles in one form or another. It took longer for the new science of politics to make its mark, in practice, after the change in theory. Indeed, not until the end of the eighteenth century, could it be said to have done so.

The task of the new science of politics was multifaceted. Not only would it have to translate abstract theories of the origins and foundations of the polity into operational ones but it had to secure sufficient penetration and spread of those theories among the publics which would have to make practical governing decisions. Those philosophic theories, once translated, became the cornerstones of eighteenth-century theories of republicanism, revolution, liberty and equality, federalism and rights, inter alia.

To some extent those theories necessarily had to become ideologies, accessible in simpler form to wider circles of people. As such, they could begin to penetrate the political cultures of those same publics and at the same time influence the design of new institutions to make them operational. Those institutions, in time, had a profound effect on the political behavior of those who lived within them.

The key to the successful movement from the new political philosophy to the new science of politics was the modern idea and practice of constitutionalism, itself derived in its essence from the Reformation covenantal political tradition rather than from premodern constitutionalism which rested on medieval monarchic or aristocratic political philosophy and politics. Constitutionalism involved the translation and concretization of the ideas of the new political philosophy into the civil institutions of the new polity. Modern constitutionalism was essentially an eighteenth-century invention, although its beginnings had appeared in the seventeenth. It received its fullest embodiment in the Constitution of the United States of America.

Several things stood out as marking the new constitutionalism.[8] One, it was limited, seeking only to frame governments for civil societies, unlike ancient constitutionalism which sought to construct the basic rules for comprehensive ways of life in religiously grounded commonwealths meant to be homogeneous with regard to beliefs and norms, and practices expressing both.[9] Two, it was designed to protect the principles of the new political philosophy, especially those addressed to the issue of individual rights. Three, it was to draw its source of authority principally from the people it served. This was made manifest by directly involving the people in the writing and adoption of constitutions in a concrete expression of their sovereign powers. Four, it was to establish appropriate institutions for achieving the constitutional goals of the new political philosophy, including representative republican government, separation of powers and checks and balances, rights protections, and in the most prominent cases, federalism.[10]

The crowning constitutional achievement of the new science of politics was to be found in the constitutional order established in the United States of America, first in the individual states, then for the United States as a whole through the Articles of Confederation and finally through the federal Constitution of 1787, which was ratified and went into effect in 1789.[11] That constitution embodied all of the elements called for by the new science of politics and set both a model and a standard for the rest of the world, remaining just that even today, more than two centuries later. Moreover, the commentaries on that constitution, beginning with *The Federalist*, explicate it explicitly in terms of the new science of politics and have made it possible for subsequent generations to learn how the two are connected.

One of the most important achievements of the American founding era was the resynthesis of the two great strands of political theory and practice of the previous 250 years. Not only were the ideas of the new political philosophy and its science of politics so important, but as many observers, foremost among them Alexis de Tocqueville, have recognized, they were integrated with the ideas of the Puritan commonwealth. Indeed, one of the principal ways in which we can see how closely those two sets of ideas could be harmonized operationally without doing terrible injustice to them intellectually was through the way that they were amalgamated in the American founding.

Many, if not most, of the British colonies in North America had been founded on a covenantal basis, most while the idea of the Puritan commonwealth was still regnant in England and Scotland. This was especially true of the New England colonies, which formed a concentration of political and intellectual power not exceeded anywhere else in the world for these purposes. In them, as Tocqueville put it, the spirit of religion and the spirit of liberty could walk hand in hand not only with each other but with the idea of civil society because of a particular convergence of circumstances.

Indeed, even those aspects of eighteenth-century constitutionalism which would have been very difficult for partisans of the Puritan commonwealth of previous centuries to accept, for example, formal separation of church and state and the granting or allowance of equal participation by "Jews, Turks and infidels," that is to say, those not fully within the ambit of the Christian commonwealth, had become acceptable because of federalism. Theorists of American constitutional understanding could distinguish between establishment of religion by the federal government (the First Amendment begins "Congress shall make no law...") while leaving to the people of the several states to decide whether or not religion should be established within their states.[12] The multiplicity of sects made it impossible to maintain an established church in all but a handful of states, without seriously infringing upon the rights of other powerful religious bodies in the civil society. Moreover, by the late eighteenth century in the United States all parties had come to the conclusion that it was necessary to protect individuals against government encroachment on their rights. Even the seemingly most benign and responsible government was an ever-present danger in this regard because it could get out of hand unless appropriately restricted, first by a constitution, then by appropriate institutions established by that constitution, and finally by the political culture and behavior of the people involved.

All of these lessons had come out of the covenantal tradition, which has always called for humans' involvement in their own governance, even vis-a-vis God, and for appropriate protections for what we today refer to as human rights within the framework of the commonwealth. In other words, the design of the covenanted commonwealth required republican institutions and non-hierarchical relationships between the institutions and those they served. The covenantal ideas of self-government, local control within a common federal (in the sense of its original meaning of covenantal) constitution, and individual liberty within the context of a community all had to be adapted to a more secular world.

The Puritan idea of federal liberty went a long way toward providing all but those who placed themselves outside of civil society by virtue of their actions with the protections they required to live. Moreover, the synthesis between religion and civil society achieved in the new United States suggested that humans could have the benefits of privacy and privatization within the framework of proper government that civil society provided while still retaining most of the moral dimensions of commonwealth that right religion provided. While this civil commonwealth would not be as morally demanding as the Puritan commonwealth, it would be morally demanding enough and at the same time would provide for greater individual choice and self-expression. Not only that, but all this could be guaranteed by appropriate constitutions of government.

Through the eighteenth century all philosophers as well as practical politicians believed that government was invariably necessary, that authoritative framing institutions were needed which could use coercive powers at least against those who broke the political compact or covenant. It was only in the nineteenth century that the idea of the automatic society arose, societies that no longer had to be civil but could rely upon such automatic mechanisms as the market, the goodness of man, the march of history, or whatever. By that time, modern constitutionalism was sufficiently established to cope with that theoretical delusion in practice, albeit at some cost. Most important from our perspective, proper constitutions involved humans coming together and establishing pacts that were not only enforceable in practice but that were sustained by the moral commitment of the compacting or covenanting parties. In this way the covenant tradition was transformed into the semi-secular one.

This felicitous synthesis remained the dominant characteristic of American life until well into the twentieth century. After World War I it began to be undermined, however, a process which continued until it collapsed as the dominant synthesis during the climax of the first post-World War II generation, the first generation of the postmodern epoch, in the 1960s. The postmodern epoch, then, has had to confront an unprecedented situation of its own which requires discussion on its own terms.

From Federal Theology to Federal Philosophy

The root political idea of the modern epoch was the idea of civil society, initially the modern manifestation of the Reformed Protestant commonwealth of late medieval times. Whereas that commonwealth was motivated by a theopolitical covenant and the vision that grew out of it, sought solidarity based upon the normative demands of that covenant, and saw the polity as an educator of the citizenry; civil society developed out of the political compact, a secularized version of covenant that led to the development of the modern, secular, pluralistic state. Increasingly, the modern polity became a state designed to provide security and services to its inhabitants rather than to motivate them by a compelling vision that obligated them in some way. In place of solidarity came an emphasis on individualism and individual self-expression. In place of normative demands came latitudinarianism and then permissiveness. In place of a sense of the commonwealth as an organism, perhaps divided among camps with somewhat different definitions of their common vision, civil society ultimately sought to accommodate overlapping cultures, pursuing different visions. The polity did not seek to educate but to be neutral regarding the value (and values) of those various cultures.

The full flowering of this relativistic social order was not achieved by civil society until the end of the modern epoch, just as the classic covenanted commonwealth was not achieved until the end of the previous one. Indeed, a civil society of this kind did not become fully operative until the second generation of the postmodern epoch, but when it did, it could be seen as the fulfillment of the modern project, even if many earlier moderns would hardly have recognized it.

The contrast between the civil society and commonwealth models is portrayed in Figure 1.1. In practice, the two models survived as models in the public mind, parallel to one another through most of the modern epoch, although in theory the civil society model had become the dominant one by the end of the seventeenth century or, at the very latest, the middle of the eighteenth. It was the ability of both models to share sufficient similarities in practice at the end of the eighteenth century, in the new United States and elsewhere, that enabled their respective adherents to work together to build modern constitutional and democratic republicanism.

In the twentieth century, however, what was left of the commonwealth model was undermined by social and cultural changes in Western society. In a sense this is ironic, since the idea of *civil* society had been replaced in theory by the idea of "society" in the nineteenth century. In continental Europe government was redefined as the state separated from society, and in the Anglo-American world the ideas of liberal democracy replaced those of civil society.

The new possibilities for individualism enhanced by technological change gave impetus to the further breakdown of the system of obligations, heavily religious, that lay at the base of the liberal democratic commonwealth forged out of the synthesis between the two models in the late eighteenth century. The nineteenth-century abandonment of the civil dimension of civil society further opened the door to these developments. The idea of covenant was replaced in the late eighteenth and nineteenth centuries by the idea of social contract, an idea that was far less demanding and far more a matter of agreements among individuals in society on a contractual basis without the moral backing of either covenant or compact.

The sixteenth-century Protestant religious reformers believed that they were at an important historical juncture that required a new road map. Having broken with the past and the religious tradition they had inherited, they sensed the need to develop new ideas of history, especially about God's will and man's destiny. This was, moreover, a general sentiment shared by secular thinkers as well. As Machiavelli suggested, the church had endeavored to bring history to a halt and to obliterate the truth of what had come before.

This effort to introduce a new sensibility had two dimensions. The theological federalists returned to the history of the Hebrew Bible (to them the Old Testament) first to understand God's plan of salvation and then God's principles of political and social organization. Beginning with the Renaissance, secular philosophers returned to the classics of Greece and Rome, which, like the Bible, were retranslated for modern purposes. Most of the philosophers, great and small, also consulted the Bible; some, such as Erasmus, retranslated that too.[13]

By trying to understand the past and how the ancient Israelites, Greeks, and Romans had gone wrong, the modern philosophers and theologians sought to exercise greater control over their present and future. While the philosophers finally rejected the classical Greco-Roman systems, most of the political philosophers did not outwardly reject the Bible; in part, because they would have been persecuted for doing so.[14] Instead, they deliberately reinterpreted, retranslated, misquoted, and adapted the Bible for their own purposes (and were often persecuted anyway). Spinoza, Hobbes, and Locke, for example, demonstrate a thorough knowledge of the Bible and skillful use of it to support their teachings.

The result was yet a third separation in the history of the covenant idea in politics: the development of a secular politics, that is to say, a politics that did not rely upon a divine base for its justification or source of authority, to follow on the earlier separations, first of Christianity from Judaism and then of Protestantism from Catholicism. While continuing to acknowledge God's sovereignty, the seventeenth-century political philosophers made the exercise of His authority unnecessary to maintain the commonwealth. While continuing to acknowledge the importance of religion in the maintenance of morality and social norms, in their thought they transformed organized religion into an instrument of civil society rather than vice versa.

In effect this turned biblical tradition on its head, just as the political philosophers, by emphasizing natural right over natural law stood classical philosophy on its head, replacing earlier ideas of natural law as the overarching law of the universe in which the good and the real were one and the same, and embracing instead man's nature—good, bad, or indifferent—as having to be the foundation of both reality and philosophy. In time, the individual rather than society became the measure of all things, and individual rights the measure of political things. The polity in which individual and society were integrated as one gave way to the concept of civil society, in which public and private spheres were separate.[15]

The one biblical concept which could be readily carried into the new political philosophy was covenant. Given its theo-political character in ancient Israel, it could be disconnected from direct reliance on God with relative ease. Theologians could ponder the covenants between God and man, thereby giving solace to citizens and providing a civil religious basis for civic obligation, while philosophers could ponder the covenants among men, thereby bringing peace and security to citizens and providing a consensual basis for civic obligation.[16]

There is also an interesting parallel here. The theologians were certain of the eternal steadfastness of God's covenant in this scheme for the redemption of man from the punishment of death after the Fall which resulted from man's violation of God's commandment. The new political scientists were equally certain of at least the long-term stability of their civil compactual rescue of men from the omnipresent fact of death in the state of nature which results from both man's deliberate and accidental inability to follow natural law. If the theological federalists regarded the new Covenant of Grace as having solved man's basic spiritual problem, the exponents of the new political science regarded their new covenant of civil society as having solved man's basic political problems.

The New Political Vocabulary

By the end of the sixteenth century, the dissemination of federal ideas by Reformed Protestants had been so forceful and successful that it had generated a new language or vocabulary of covenant throughout most of western Europe. The Latin words *foedus, pactum* or *pactio, confederatio, contractus,* and *consocentio* had become common currency. In English, covenant and such covenant-related terms as pact, compact, contract, charter, convention, combination, congregation, constitution, treaty, league, bargain, agreement, and presbyterian were ever more common in religious and political discourse.

By the end of the first quarter of the seventeenth century, federal theologians had developed not only a thorough system of covenant theology, but also a full conception of covenant as the basis for republican political theory. All of these served the emerging modernist vision of civil society as being the product of free human will as expressed through voluntary consent and agreement rather than conquest or a mystical natural evolution into an organic whole.

As Lord Acton, a Roman Catholic, once said, modern democracy derives more from the realities of congregationalism (the predominant form of church organization of the Puritans) than from the political thought of ancient Athens.[17] To a great extent this is accurate both from an intellectual and practical standpoint. Intellectually, the principles of federal theology that gave rise to congregationalism fostered republican and democratic ideas. Practically, local congregations served as schools of self-government, while the presbyterian (the alternate system of the other Reformed Protestants) system of nationwide organization served as a model of federal republicanism. In the process, the concepts of covenant and compact and their consequences underwent a number of changes, though their essential core, the idea of voluntary mutual agreement and pledging for public purpose of social and political order, remained central to these various philosophic approaches.

Althusius: The First Federal Theorist

Johannes Althusius (1557–1638) was the first major philosopher to utilize covenant in order to develop a modern pact-rooted political theory. He was not only the first systematic federal theorist but served as a bridge between the late medieval theopolitics of the Reformation and the political philosophy of the modern epoch. While a devout Reformed Protestant of the Swiss-German school, who drew heavily on the Bible for the evidence to support his systematic theory, he was at the same time a trained jurist and by his own definition a political scientist in the modern sense. His career in public administration brought him to serve very successfully as the Syndic of Emden in northern Germany. As such he was almost the ideal synthesis of both the theoretical and practical worlds, and his works reveal that.[18]

Althusius's ability to achieve these two syntheses, which was apparently viewed as unusual by subsequent moderns, has led to considerable misunderstanding of his work, some claiming that he is the first modern federalist and others that he is no more than a late medieval corporatist. In my opinion, the truth is that he was a true original who could see the advantages and disadvantages of both modernism and medieval corporatism and used federalism to bridge the two and provide what might be referred to, in a paraphrase of *The Federalist*, as federal remedies for both medieval and modern diseases.

Althusius was born in Hesse near the city of Herborn in western Germany. He received a doctorate in civil and ecclesiastical law at the University of Basel in 1586, then taught at Herborn. In both places, he was associated with Dutch, German, and Swiss theologians who developed covenant ideas. Gierke regarded his major political work, the *Politica Methodice Digesta* (1603), as the first systematic treatise on politics since the ancients.[19] Harold Laski and Carl Friedrich viewed Althusius as an important watershed in the development of modern political theory, especially modern federalism.[20]

For Althusius, the commonwealth is a "consociation of consociations" and covenant is the proper foundation for all adult relationships within it, beginning with marriage. Marriage is the primary human association which arises from mutual sympathy and mutual need. While marriage is a natural association in the Aristotelian sense, any particular marriage is a voluntary association constituted in a covenantal manner for mutual assistance, advantage, and responsibility. Covenant is the means by which individuals, and then groups, voluntarily consent to enter into relationships and agree to terms of association as well as the basic unit of human governance and economic production. Most importantly, ties of familial affection and mutuality help to maintain a communitarian rather than individualistic orientation among citizens.

In turn, Althusius treated families rather than individuals as the fundamental unit of the commonwealth. Families are consociated through covenants into professional corporations, guilds, and estates which serve their wider socioeconomic needs and exercise governing responsibilities with regard to their basic socioeconomic tasks and relationships. Families, together with these voluntary associations, constitute the private sector of civil society. Unlike Hobbes and Locke, who construed individuals as existing alone in a state of nature prior to civil society, Althusius construed individuals as being already voluntary members of a dense network of relatively pacific and cooperative associations of mutual aid. In this respect, Althusius retained much of the biblical view of covenant as a mix of kinship and consent.

The public sector, or commonwealth, is also a compound association consisting of towns, provinces, and then the commonwealth as a whole. Towns and cities are covenanted associations of guilds and professional corporations; provinces are covenanted associations of towns and rural estates; and the universal commonwealth is a covenanted association of provinces and large cities. Each of these larger associations arises from mutual sympathy and mutual need among the smaller associations who create the larger ones and delegate authority to them to perform area-wide functions which are beyond the scope and capacity of the smaller associations. Hence, the arrangement is quintessentially federal. The system is a matrix, not a pyramid; power originates in the smaller units and sovereignty is shared among the various associations.

Althusius developed his federal theory, in part, in response to theories of absolute, indivisible sovereignty being advanced by the French philosopher Jean Bodin (1530-1596) and others. Although Bodin also regarded the family as the building block of the commonwealth; he treated sovereignty as arising from humans rather than God, holding that the people through their families transfer this sovereignty to a single person or group in an unlimited manner. As a result, this theory lends itself to both royal and "democratic" absolutism.[21] In Europe, the Althusian idea that sovereignty can be shared among covenanted partners was a revolutionary conception of the commonwealth that contradicted traditional organic and hierarchic understandings of the right order of things.

Philosophers and Jurists Try to Save the Holy Roman Empire

It is no coincidence that Jean Bodin, who developed the doctrine of modern political sovereignty, also denied the existence of the *res publica Christiana* upon which the medieval political order rested. Bodin claimed that there was no universal political authority after the end of the Roman Empire, that the individual states were completely independent externally and internally. He even went so far as to claim that the Roman *ius gentium* could not be the basis of international relations since it was based upon the idea of a common universal polity and did not reflect the way the world was structured around independent entities. This began the movement to the modern state system, according to which politically sovereign states possessing full external independence and internal concentrations of power became the only acceptable political systems. All polities that did not conform to this model were to Bodin "irregular" or at worst merely systems of states, in other words, alliances.

Left out of this system were the Holy Roman Empire, Switzerland, and the United Provinces of the Netherlands. Switzerland and the United Provinces already were confederations with covenantal bases, but the future of the Holy Roman Empire, a confederal arrangement with a secular pactual base and a hierarchical religious one, was very much in doubt. The political thought of Althusius was a direct challenge to Bodin and Bodinian principles in an effort to provide a covenantally rooted theory upon which to base the political reformation of the Holy Roman Empire.

After Althusius, the two most important figures in that effort were Gottfried Wilhelm Baron von Leibnitz (1646–1716) and Ludolph Hugo (1630–1704). The first was a librarian by profession and the second the official historian of the Duchy of Hanover at the heart of the Holy Roman Empire. Leibnitz, who is better remembered in history as a mathematician, was also a philosopher learned in history, law, and science. He also was the first president of the Prussian Academy.

The proximate target of their thinking was the thought of Samuel Pufendorf (1632–1694), one of the pioneer international lawyers of the modern school who wrote *De Jure, Naturae et Gentium*. Pufendorf, although following the then accepted idea of the political compact, held that the governmental political entity thereby established was the nation-state and that the international "system" was comprised of nation-states as the repositories of sovereign powers.[22]

In Pufendorf's view, on the one hand no member state of a confederation had to go along with majority decisions of the confederated states and, on the other hand, the other members could wage war against it to force it to do so, vitiating the whole ideal of federalism, which was to estabish a system of constitutionalized interstate relations based on negotiation and comity that would prevent either the former eventuality or the latter necessity. Pufendorf's became the predominant continental European view of federalism. For example, in Diderot's famous *Encyclopedie*, the fullest expression of French Enlightenment thought, the entry on federalism, entitled *etats composees* (compound states) and written by Chevalier des Jaucourt completely followed Pufendorf.

Hugo and Leibnitz, on the other hand, were able to think federal rather than statist,[23] hence they continued the Althusian covenantal tradition. Hugo published his book *De Statu Regionum Germaniae* in 1661, in which he presents a theory of federalism in discussing the status of the region. While Hugo's argument begins from medieval premises, he soon moves on to modern ones and even draws carefully designed distinctions between confederal leagues, decentralized unitary governments, and what subsequently were called federations.[24]

The first is based on alliances such as the Achean League. The Roman Empire is the model of the second. "There were lower special administrations, not really separate political societies, whose magistrates were nothing more than the servants of the emperor." The third he referred to as "double government" and a territorial division of powers, "When the civil power is somehow divided between the highest and the lower governments, so that the higher manages those things pertaining to the commonwealth there, the lower those things pertaining to the welfare of the individual regions."[25]

According to Hugo, "while the regional states are still subject to the empire, their power is still universal and wide enough to seem to take something from the highest power." This was to become the typical German approach to federalism or constitutionalized power-sharing, but within a hierarchical framework. It continues even today in the German and Austrian federal systems.

Hugo wrote primarily as a statesman; he was not a philosopher. Hence his discussion is almost entirely governmental in the way of such discussions of federalism in the twentieth century. This meant that philosophers paid him no attention and his views disappeared from sight until Gierke somewhat resurrected them literarily in the nineteenth century. Leibnitz, on the other hand, may be considered the greatest German philosopher before Kant to bring to bear a philosophic perspective on political affairs. Federalism is only a small part of his body of work.

Leibnitz may have been even more interested in restoring the Holy Roman Empire and the reunited Catholic Church of Christendom than Hugo. But he was a modern nonetheless who, like Hugo, was able to escape the Bodinian idea of statism. His analysis was not framed in terms of sovereignty but in terms of limited government, a federal, and hence covenantal, idea. Sovereignty was secondary, subordinate to what Leibnitz and others termed *majestas*, the traditional usage for the repository of authority of the universal empire.[26] Sovereignty for Leibnitz was at most a comparative matter, indicating a degree of authority rather than an indivisible center. It has to do primarily with the actual exercise of power by a "master of the territory" through "treaties, arms, and alliances." Leibnitz further declared: "It matters not whether he [the sovereign] holds his lands as a fief, nor whether he recognizes the majesty of the leader, provided that he be master at home and that he cannot be disturbed except by arms." Germans referred to this as "territorial superiority." Leibnitz's definition of *majestas*, "the right to command without being subject to commands," came with the caveat that "sovereignty does not exclude the obedience that one owes to the orders of a spiritual or temporal leader." He sought to remove sovereignty from states and invest it in universals. Leibnitz directly addressed the Hobbesian definition of sovereignty and critically at that: "If we listen to Hobbes there will be nothing in our land but out and out anarchy."[27]

Leibnitz understood the dynamic and realistic dimensions of his definition, saying that "when the supreme power is divided, many dissensions can arise; even wars, if everyone holds stubbornly to his own opinion." He argues that experience shows that "men usually hold to some middle road, so as not to commit everything to hazard by their obstinacy,"[28] suggesting that in both Poland and the United Provinces of the Netherlands, where nobles or towns [enabled] veto power, the "prudence and moderation of the whole most matters to turn out well enough." Riley says, "Political life in general, he thought, was not made possible by 'mandates through the plentitude of power,' but by 'negotiations and discussions.'"[29]

Hobbes, to Leibnitz, demonstrates that his theories can work "only in that state whose king is God, whom alone one can trust in all things."[30] Leibnitz distinguished between confederacies that were closer to the international lawyers' theories of federalism, and unions which his theory described. His sense of the realities of power and political dynamics was good but his anti-sovereignty theory was rendered outdated by the demands of the political powers of the times, who looked to other philosophers for justification, not content with the limits that the medieval empire and Leibnitz would have imposed upon them. Thus events rapidly overtook Leibnitz's thought. The emergence of states such as Prussia, Bavaria, and Saxony from within the declining Holy Roman Empire reinforced the state system and the philosophies that supported it and displaced those who would have saved the imperial system even on more modern grounds.

These theorists of the Holy Roman Empire not only grounded their theories in the realia of government far than the more famous political philosophers but also were close to the many leagues and confederations that came into existence within the weakened Holy Roman Empire at the end of the Middle Ages. While the legal and jurisprudential terminology used at the time did not identify them as such, for those theorists who were trying to build a new federal theory of the empire, those confederacies were at the very least suggestive of what might be.[31]

It was only in the early seventeenth century that they were able to begin to develop an independent theory of constitutional law for the empire, breaking with the Roman law patterns of the Middle Ages. This new constitutional law drew upon Germanic as well as Roman sources and more contemporary materials as well. The founder of this new constitutional law was Dominicus Arumaeus (1579–1673), who published five volumes of monographs and dissertations which he or his colleagues wrote under the title *Discursus Academici de Juro Publico* between 1616 and 1623. He was joined by Johann Limnaeus (1592–1663), who wrote the first comprehensive and systematic commentary on the constitution of the empire proper, *Jus Publicum Imperii Romani Germanici,* which he published in three volumes in Strasbourg between 1629 and 1632. At the same time, Hermann Conring (1606–1681) proved that Roman law had been introduced into Germany only since the fifteenth century.[32]

Another constitutional lawyer of the time was Ripolitus Alapide (1605–1678), a pseudonym for Philipp Bogislaus von Chemnitz who published *De Ratione Status en Imperio Nostro Romano-Germanico* in 1640. In it he accepted the modern concept of sovereignty but did so entirely on Germanic principles. Meanwhile, acceptance of Bodin's doctrine of sovereignty was spreading and conflicting with the alternate concept of *majestas* which was related to the universal empire rather than individual states. So in 1648 the Peace of Westphalia essentially ended the empire's constitutional development by passing powers to those of its constituent states who sought them, thereby enabling them to assert their authority over the next century as well. Thus political or juridical theories designed to strengthen imperial federalism had nowhere to go in practice.[33]

Moreover, those who continued to try to develop imperial theories of constitutional law remained under the influence of Aristotle so that they did not adopt the new political science which, in the years after 1648, rapidly became accepted. Althusius, the precursor of these theorists, came closest to breaking out of those Aristotelian medieval limitations and some would argue that he did, but his successors did not follow his lead and hence his breakthrough withered. Even where his influence in other respects can be found, the closest any of them came to federal ideas was in the idea of *landeshoheit* or territorial supremacy with regard to certain governmental activities, a concept advanced, inter alia, by J. Lampadius (1593–1649)[34] that could be combined with *conjunctim,* that is to say, a share in the empire's *summum majestus* as members of the imperial diet, a concept advanced by B.C. Carpzov (1595–1666), a jurist of the time.[35]

Ludolph Hugo was a student of Conring's. He already began to cross the threshold to modernity by elaborating more precisely and systematically on the idea of the *civitas composita* (compound polity) initially advanced by Christoph Besold (1577–1638), a jurist who wrote much on legal and ecclesiastical subjects.[36]

Besold in turn had taken the idea from P.H. Hoenonius (1556–1640), who taught law at Herborn (Althusius's alma mater) and published his *Disputationum Politicarum Liber,* which relied heavily on Althusius.[37] Gierke says that Hoenonius can be seen as "following Althusius throughout."[38] Hoenonius distinguished between the *res publica simplex* consisting of one state and the *res publica composita,* just as Althusius does. Hugo then picked up on the idea and used it as one of the fundamental bases of his theory. Eulau suggests that "Hugo seemed well aware of the constitutional differences between federalism and decentralization: if the territorial authorities are merely officials of the 'super-states' and obey its orders, the states would be nothing but provinces; the German territories, however, although subordinate to the Empire as a whole, are independent and must therefore be regarded as real states."[39]

Ludolph Hugo, indeed, was the first to explicitly distinguish between federalism and decentralization and between federation and confederation. In doing so, he broke out of the Aristotelian mold and entered the Althusian, primarily concerned with the practicalities of relationships, structures, and powers, taking the Holy Roman Empire as it was and trying to improve it rather than trying to understand how it came to be or on what philosophic basis it should be reconstituted. Thus Eulau writes: "Hugo did not want to write a treatise on the constitution of the Empire, but on territorial constitutions; and secondly,... he did not write a heated political pamphlet as did most of his contemporaries, but a learned dissertation."[40]

Gierke, in his book on Althusius, states that, whatever Hugo's limitations, after him "the concept of the composite state never disappeared again completely from political science."[41] Nevertheless, neither was he successful in shaking the statist foundations of continental European political thought. Even those who commented on his works did so in such a way that they returned to the conventional wisdom.

Leibnitz, by focusing on sovereignty as well as the empire's constitution, carried the discussion of imperial federalism further without necessarily contributing to the larger questions of covenant theory. Leibnitz distinguished between a *confoederatio* and a *unio*, explaining the difference as the same as between a *societas*, a body accidently composed of individuals who remain individuals, and a *collegium*, a new civil person with a corporate personality. In private law, the decisions of a *societas* require unanimity, while those of a *collegium*, also called a *corpus*, may be made by majority vote, bringing us close to the operational issues involved in covenant theory. Implicit in these discussions, especially those of Hugo and Leibnitz, was the idea of political covenant or compact, especially when their discussions are contrasted with that of Pufendorf, who had remained faithful to the conventional wisdom and saw such linkages among states as merely contractual. Moreover, by using the term *foedus* to describe the systems they were addressing, they give us a clear clue and image of the covenantal character of their thought.

In the eighteenth century, Christian Thomasius (1655–1728), a jurist who bitterly opposed Aristotle and scholasticism and founded a school of political science that continued for several generations, emphasized the compactual basis of the federal relationship rather than issues of sovereignty.[42] He and his school kept alive the discussions of federalism until they moved back on stage toward the end of the century. It may be said that at least as long as political scientists and jurists wrote in Latin, which was the case on the continent at least until the mid-eighteenth century, the use of the term *foedus* or related terms kept the idea of covenant prominently in mind for all those who wrote on the subject of the political organization of composite polities.

Althusian Echoes

While Althusius emerged a distant second to Bodin in the early modern struggle of statism versus federalism, his influence continued in a minor but not insignificant way through the seventeenth century and into the eighteenth, especially among the jurists but also among certain political theorists of the Holy Roman Empire who sought federal solutions to the problems of reforming Germany, by then virtually synonymous with the extent of the Empire that survived. Students of Althusius's writings carried on his federalist political scientific reinterpretation of the covenant tradition as it had been reformulated through Reformed Protestantism. They not only crossed the bridge that he built but tried to build a continuation of it over the next chasm. Although they were not successful, they did succeed in transmitting the Althusian tradition from generation to generation among that small minority who rejected modern statism and sought a different—federalist—path.

Ultimately, the tradition they passed on was to resurface, primarily as an intellectual one, in nineteenth-century Germany (see chapter 4). Some of that thinking may even have carried over into the German Bund of the nineteenth century, the last of the modern confederations. But in the end nationalism and statism proved to be policies too seductive. They transformed Germany into a federation founded on statist principles modified by the necessities of reality and then, in the twentieth century, into a totally anticovenantal Nazism, the totalitarian antithesis of all that Althusius had sought to teach. Perhaps the only link between the two was the puzzling thought of Carl Schmitt who began as a federalist and ended up a defender of Nazism.[43]

Yet even as Carl Schmitt was perverting German federal thought, Carl Friedrich, another great German political scientist and theorist, was escaping to the United States where at Harvard University he reestablished the Althusian line. In 1935 Friedrich published the *Politica Methodice Digesta* in its original Latin with a long introduction in English. While in that introduction Friedrich emphasized the organic rather than the federalist dimensions of Althusian thought, perhaps influenced by the totalitarian turn of so many of Germany's philosophers, he himself carried on the Althusian federalist tradition, communicating it to a new generation in the United States and the world, one that stood ready to pick up the reins of political thought, analysis, and action after the Nazi state and ideology collapsed in the *Gotterdammerung* of World War II. They were to teach or otherwise find their way to a new postmodern federalism in the generation following the war and begin the process of replacing or significantly modifying the statist paradigm with a federalist one.

Meanwhile, back in the eighteenth century, another branch of Althusian thought crossed the Rhine into France. Those two countries were so different yet so alike (different in their response to demands for national unity and political organization; alike in their striving for the hierarchical administration of their governments and in their appetites for world power). Certainly in France, Althusian federalism could not replace Bodinian statism, but in a line that extends from Montesquieu through Benjamin Constant to Tocqueville, Proudhon and into the twentieth century with emergence of the post-World War I integral federalists and on into the post-World War II personalists, exemplified by Alexandre Marc, Denis de Rougement, and Robert Aron, the ideas similar to those of Althusian federalism were developed, preserved and modified, always having at least one or more articulate advocates. Something of a synthesis of the two actually can be found in the theo-political thought of Martin Buber, a German Jew who was drawn to Personalism in the interwar period. Althusian ideas were to resurface after World War II in concrete ways, especially in advocacy of European federalism and at least some of them found a home in the theories associated with the establishment of the European Union.

Notes

1. Daniel J. Elazar, *Covenant and Constitutionalism* (New Brunswick, N.J.: Transaction Publishers, 1996).
2. Daniel J. Elazar, *Covenant and Polity in Biblical Israel: Biblical Foundations and Jewish Expressions* (New Brunswick, N.J.: Transaction Publishers, 1995), and Daniel J. Elazar, *Covenant and Commonwealth: The Covenantal Tradition from Christian Separation Through the Protestant Reformation* (New Brunswick, N.J.: Transaction Publishers, 1996).
3. G. R. Driver and John C. Miles, eds., *The Babylonian Laws* (Oxford: Claredon Press, 1952); E. A. Speiser, *Oriental and Biblical Studies: Collected Writings of E. A. Speiser*, J. J. Finkelstein and Moshe Greenberg, eds., (Philadelphia: University of Pennsylvania Press, 1967); *Eretz-Israel: Archaeological, Historical and Geographic Studies*, vol. 5 (Jerusalem: Israel Exploration Society and the Hebrew University, 1958); Reuven Yaron, *The Laws of Eshnunna*, second edition (Jerusalem-Leiden: Magnes and Brill, 1988); *The Histories of Herodotus*, E. H. Blakeney, ed. (New York: Dutton, 1964).
4. Thomas Hobbes, *Leviathan*, Michael Oakeshott, ed. (New York: Macmillan, 1962).
5. Baruch Spinoza, *Tractatus Theologico-Politicus*, Samuel Shirley, ed. (New York: E.J. Brill, 1991).
6. John Locke, "First Treatise on Government", *Two Treatises of Government*, Peter Laslett, ed. (New York: Cambridge University Press, 1988), pp. 141–263.
7. John Locke, "Second Treatise on Government", *Two Treatises of Government*, Peter Laslett, ed. (New York: Cambridge University Press, 1988), pp. 265–428.
8. Leo Strauss, *Liberalism: Ancient and Modern* (New York: Basic Books, 1968); Daniel J. Elazar, "Deuteronomy as Israel's Ancient Constitution: Some Preliminary Reflections," *Jewish Political Science Review*, vol. 4, no. 1.

9. Daniel J. Elazar, *Covenant and Polity in Biblical Israel* (New Brunswick, N.J.: Transaction Publishers, 1994); Aaron Wildavsky, *The Nursing Father: Moses as a Political Leader* (Tuscaloosa: University of Alabama Press, 1984).
10. Vincent Ostrom, *American Federalism: Constitutiong a Self-Governing Society*, (San Francisco, Cal.: Institute for Contemporary Studies, 1991).
11. Vincent Ostrom, *Political Theory of a Compound Republic*, second edition (Lincoln: University of Nebraska Press, 1987); Martin Diamond, "Democracy and the Federalist-A Reconsideration of the Framer's Intent," *American Political Science Review*, March 1959, pp. 52–68; Donald Lutz, *The Origins of American Constitutionalism*, (Baton Rouge: Louisiana State University Press, 1988).
12. John Witte, "The Essential Rights and Liberties of Religion in the American Constitutional Experiment," *Notre Dame Law Review*, vol. 71, no. 3 (1996).
13. Leo Strauss, *Hobbes*, ed. Keith C. Brown (Oxford: Blackwell, 1965).
14. Cf., for example, Leo Strauss, *Persecution and the Art of Writing* (Chicago: University of Chicago Press, 1988) and *Natural Right and History* (Chicago: University of Chicago Press, 1953).
15. Strauss, *Natural Right and History*.
16. Elazar, *Covenant and Polity; idem., Covenant and Commonwealth: The Covenantal Tradition from Christian Separation Through the Protestant Reformation* (New Brunswick, N.J.: Transaction Publishers, 1995).
17. Lord Acton, *Essays on Freedom and Power* (New York: Meridien, 1955); *Lectures on the French Revolution* (London: Macmillan, 1910); *Lectures on Modern History* (London: Collins, 1966).
18. Johannes Althusius, *Politica*, edited and translated by Frederick S. Carney (Indianapolis, Ind.: Liberty Fund, 1995).
19. Otto von Gierke, *Johannes Althusius und die Entwicklung der Naturrechtlichen Staatstheorien*, 3rd ed. (Breslau: M. and H. Marcus, 1902).
20. Harold Laski, *The Rise of European Liberalism* (London: G. Allen and Unwin, 1936); Carl Friedrich, *Constitutional Government and Democracy* (Waltham, Mass: Blaisdell, 1968).
21. Jean Bodin, *Six Books of the Commonwealth* (Cambridge, Mass.: Harvard University Press, 1962); Julian Harold Franklin, *Jean Bodin and the Rise of Absolutist Theory* (Cambridge: Cambridge University Press, 1973).
22. Samuel Freiherr von Pufendorf, *De Jure Naturae et Gentium Trans Libre Acto*, translated by C.H. and W.A. Oldfather (Oxford, Clarendon Press, 1934).
22. Patrick Riley, "Three Seventeenth Century German Theorists of Federalism," *Publius*, vol. 6, no. 3 (Summer 1976), pp. 10–11.
24. Ludolph Hugo, *De Statu Regionum Germaniae* (Helmstadt: Sumptibus Hammianis, 1708); Reily, "Three German Theorists," p. 64.
25. Hugo, section 8, quoted in Riley, "Three German Theorists," p. 23.
26. Gottfreid Wilhelm Leibnitz, *Entretien de Philarete et D'eugene* (1677) in *Oeuvres de Leibnitz*, edited by A. Foucher de Careil, vol. 6 (Paris: Firmin Didot Freres, 1865), p. 347.
27. Riley, "Three German Theorists," p. 69.
28. Patrick Reily, *The Political Writings of Leibnitz* (Cambridge: Cambridge University Press, 1972), pp. 46–47.
29. Riley, "Three German Theorists," p. 28.
30. Reily, *Leibnitz*, pp. 47–48.
31. See Heinz H.F. Eulau, "Theories of Federalism under the Holy Roman Empire," *American Political Science Review*, vol. 35, no. 4 (August 1941).
32. Hermann Conring, *De origine juris germanici commentarius historicus* (Helmstadii: Henningi Mulleri, 1643).

33. Eulau, "Theories of Federalism."
34. J. Lampadius, *De republica Romano-Germanica liber unus* (Helmstadii: Hennigi Mulleri, 1671). Otto von Gierke, *Das Deutsche Gnossenschaftsrecht,* trans. by Ernst Barker as *Natural Law and the Theory of Society 1500–1800* (Cambridge: Cambridge University Press, 1950).
35. B.C. Carpzov, *Commentarius in legem regiam Germanorum: sive capitulationem imperatorium* (Lipsae: Sumptibus Tobiae Riesens, typi, exscribebat Johannes Bauer, 1651).
36. Besold's works are discussed in Gierke, *Genossenschaftsrecht,* and briefly in Eulau.
37. P.H. Hoenonius, *Disputationum Politicarum Liber,* 3rd ed. (Herborn, 1615).
38. Gierke, *Johannes Althusius und die entwidklung der Naturrechtlichen Staatstheorien,* 3rd ed. (Breslau: M. and H. Marcus, 1902); Gierke, *Genossenschaftsrecht,* vol. 4.
39. Eulau, "Theories of Federalism." Eulau in turn relies on S. Brie, *Der Bundessataat* (Leipzig, 1874), pp. 17–20.
40. Eulau, "Theories of Federalism."
41. Gierke, *Althusius,* p. 246.
42. Eulau, "Theories of Federalism," p. 20. See Carl Schmitt, "The Constitutional Theory of Federation," *Telos,* no. 91 (Spring 1992):26–56.

2

Covenant and the New Political Science

Hobbes: A Radically New Covenant

The idea of covenant initially was secularized in the second half of the seventeenth century by Thomas Hobbes, Benedict Spinoza, and John Locke, the principal founders of the "new political science" based on political compact. Although these philosophers are usually located in the secular stream of thought and treated as being indebted not to theology but to classical political science, medieval political ideas, and Machiavelli, it is difficult to avoid the conclusion that their political teachings were strongly and decisively influenced by the language and ideas of covenant that dominated English, Jewish, and Dutch religious and political discourse during their lifetimes. Furthermore, all three explicitly rejected classical and medieval political science as being unrealistic and ultimately oppressive.

Ironically, Hobbes, Spinoza, and Locke, the three great secularizers, brought Western political philosophy back to the Bible, that is to say, to a direct confrontation with the biblical text rather than viewing it through the accepted interpretations of the church. In their efforts to grapple directly with the plain text itself they taught their readers how to go back to that text for political understanding and the necessity to do so. Spinoza, indeed, even is credited with inventing modern biblical criticism to aid him and his readers in that endeavor.

When in need of traditional authorities, all three men cited the Bible more than the Greeks and Romans, apparently perceiving its very different political premises as more promising for compactual republicanism. True, they did this in order to subvert the conventional understanding and traditional belief in the biblical text. In the short term, much of what they taught could only be understood through esoteric reading while they presented an apparently different teaching exoterically.

Spinoza was the great exception in the sense that his teaching was more plainly visible than the others and he was attacked accordingly. Hobbes and Locke were attacked by perceptive readers who disagreed with them on these points. Among the friends and acquaintances of all three, and even family members, in the case of Spinoza, were many individuals associated with covenant thought, including Jews, Dutch Reformed Protestants, and Puritans. Moreover, both Hobbes and Spinoza formulated their compactual theories during the apogee of the Dutch Calvinist, Scottish Covenanter, and English Puritan movements. Locke did so at the time of the Glorious Revolution.

Unlike today, when theology often imitates philosophy and sociology, theology was still the queen of the sciences and a rigorous intellectual enterprise in the seventeenth century. Philosophy had to work through and around it. Indeed, much like the Reformed theologians who translated the Bible along the lines of their teachings so as to alter the language of discourse as well as popular conceptions of church and society, philosophers and scientists mounted a major effort during this period to secularize language along the lines of their teachings and findings. In addition, just as the Puritans endeavored to make theology speak English, Hobbes especially was concerned with making philosophy speak English.[1]

Hobbes, like Locke, has often been labelled in contemporary political science as a "social contract theorist." This is a total misreading of Hobbesian ideas through the prism of Jacobin thought which draws heavily on the Rousseauian social contract. Hobbes, however, had a different and more sophisticated orientation which he used to express his ideas and misleading simplifications distract us from understanding them.

Hobbes very deliberately used the term "covenant" as his root term. Often, even those who have been careful to adhere to Hobbes' own language and have referred to his use of covenant have tended to miss the deliberate character of that use and have seen it rather as an attempt to cover his revolutionary ideas with terms of normal usage during the Golden Age of English Puritanism. In fact, Hobbes carefully distinguished between contract, which he referred to as "the mutual transferring of right" in an immediate sense, and covenant, a pact that initiates continuing relationships of trust which, in contemporary economic language, will change the covenanting parties' calculations of risk. As Hobbes himself put it:

> There is a difference between transferring of right to the thing; and transferring or translation, that is delivery of the thing itself. For the thing may be delivered together with the translation of the right; as in buying and selling with ready money; or exchange of goods, or lands, and it may be delivered sometime after....
> Again, one of the contractors, may deliver the thing contracted for on his part, and leave the other to perform his part at some determinate time after, and in the mean time be trusted.... [This]...is called PACT, or COVENANT: or both parts may contract now, to perform hereafter; in which cases, he that is to perform in time to come, being trusted, his performance is called keeping a promise, or faith; and a failing of performance if it be voluntary, a violation of faith."[2]

In this way did Hobbes distinguish between covenants and contracts, emphasizing the moral dimension that must adhere to all covenants and which has the consequence of promoting long-term relationships through the fostering of trust to enable the terms of the pact to be made operational. Hobbes understood that "the bonds of words are too weak to bridle men's ambitions, averice, anger, and the other passions," especially in "the conditions of mere nature." Hence, relationships maintained by trust established by covenants are needed.[3]

Covenants can work because of the threat of anticipatory violence, but the threat alone is not enough. There must be a covenantal framework to offer a promise as well. The kinds of relationships that Hobbes sees as necessary for civil peace cannot be attained through contracts, but only through covenants. Covenant makes civil justice possible. It is necessary because even though civil justice must fit into the natural order and replicate natural justice, it is an artifact that needs to be established by humanity. That is done through covenants.

Covenants must be maintained voluntarily, whether by those who initiate them from the state of nature or those who maintain them thereafter from within civil societies. The latter keep their covenants when there is security of performance on both sides. Those securities are indeed in accordance with reason. To prevent the war of all against all one needs "the help of confederates."[4]

As Hobbes put it,

For the question is not of promises mutual, where there is no security of performance on either side; as when there is no civil power erected over the parties promising; for such promises are no covenants; but either where one of the parties has performed already; or where there is a power to make him perform; there is the question whether it be against reason, that is, against the benefit of the other to perform, or not. And I say it is not against reason. For the manifestation whereof, we are to consider; first, that when a man doth a thing, which notwithstanding any thing can be foreseen, and reckoned on, tendeth to his own destruction, howsoever some accident which he could not expect, arriving may turn it to his benefit; yet such events to not make it reasonably or wisely done. Secondly, that in a condition of war, wherein every man to every man, for want of a common power to keep them all in awe, is an enemy, there is no man who can hope by his own strength, or wit, to defend himself from destruction, without the help of confederates; where every one expects the same defence by the confederation, that any one else does; and therefore he which declares he thinks it reason to deceive those that help him, can in reason expect no other means of safety, than what can be had from his own single power. He therefore that breaketh his covenant, and consequently declareth that he thinks he may with reason do so, cannot be received into any society, that unite themselves for peace and defence, but by the error of them that receive him; nor when he is received, be retained in it, without seeing the danger of their error; which errors a man cannot reasonably reckon upon as the means of his security; and therefore if he be left, or cast out of society, he perisheth; and if he live in society, it is by the errors of other men, which he could not foresee, nor reckon upon; and consequently against the reason of his preservation.[5]

In other words, in a state of nature the individual is subject to the war of all against all and needs confederates in order to survive. To have such confederates there must be reciprocity and one who deceives one's confederates will

soon be detected. When detected, they can no longer count on their confederates to protect them, so it is only rational not to defect. To covenant means to
trust. Yet covenants are needed to produce trust. Hence we have the paradox
that to have covenants, trust is necessary, yet prior to covenants trust is lacking.
Thus at some point there must be the political equivalent of the Kierkegaardian
"leap of faith" to begin the covenanting process, just as religious covenants
required a leap of faith on the part of humans to believe in God. With that leap
it is possible to covenant and to establish commonwealths. Hobbes again:

> A *commonwealth* is said to be *instituted* when a *multitude* of men do agree, and
> *covenant, every one, with every one,* that to whatsoever *man,* or *assembly of men*
> shall be given by the major part, the *right* to *present* the person of them all, that is
> to say, to be their *representative;* every one, as well he that *voted for it,* as he that
> *voted against it,* shall *authorize* all the actons and judgments, of that man, or
> assembly of men, in the same manner, as if they were his own, to the end, to live
> peaceably amongst themselves, and be protected against other men.[6]

Once he established this basis for civil society, Hobbes turned his attention from covenants and the maintenance of civil order to authority and indeed absolute authority as needed for the maintenance of civil order. Whatever
the other deficiencies of taking the one path rather than the other, it did lead
Hobbes to define liberty in terms similar to the definition of federal liberty
only with a human sovereign rather than a transcendant one. That is all the
difference in the world, of course.[7]

Covenants can change expectations and hence alter risk calculations. As
such they are the breath of life to the civil order. In this respect covenants are
human creations that are extensions of God's natural creation. Hobbes puts it
this way:

> The only way to erect such a common power...is to confer all their power and
> strength upon one man, or upon one assembly of men, that may reduce all their
> wills, by plurality of voices, unto one will...to appoint one man...to bear their
> person...and acknowledge himself to be author of whatsoever he that so beareth
> their person shall act, in those things which concern the common peace and safety;
> and therin to submit their wills, every one to his will, and their judgments, to his
> judgment. *This is more than consent, or concord; it is a real unity of them all, in
> one and the same person, made by covenant of every man with every man.* [my
> italics]...as if every man should say to every man, *I authorize and give up my
> right of governing myself, to this man...on this condition, that though give up they
> right to him, and authorize all his actions in like manner.* This done, the multitude
> so united in one person, is called a COMMONWEALTH.... This is the generation
> of that great LEVIATHAN, or rather, to speak more reverently, of that *mortal god,*
> to which we owe under the *immortal God,* our peace and defence.[8]

In short, covenants are human art in the way that nature is Divine art. In all
of this Hobbes refers explicitly to the Hebraic covenanting tradition as described in the Bible, especially the covenant with Abraham.[9]

From that tradition he drew his understanding that covenants could serve as the foundation for civil rule only when they are made by consent of the parties.

In *Leviathan* (1651) Hobbes used the term *covenant* as the centerpiece of his political system and defined a commonwealth as "one person, of whose acts a great multitude, by mutual covenants one with another, have made themselves everyone the author, to the end he may use the strength and means of them all as he shall think expedient for their peace and common defense."[10] Hobbes may have used covenant rather than another term to signify the formation of civil society through voluntary consent rooted in mutual commitment because he was influenced by the Puritans, who were often termed "precisians," and because the word was common to the language of his day. It has been suggested that he may also have employed the term as a cosmetic device to render more acceptable a teaching that he knew would be distasteful to and be taken as atheistic by many of his Christian countrymen but, as we have seen, that is very doubtful.

A more likely possibility is that Hobbes used covenant to signify a tighter, more enduring civil bond than that suggested by such terms as contract, treaty, or agreement. While Hobbes is in many respects a thoroughgoing secularist, he is also a strong link in the chain of covenant theory. He begins with a basic computational logic reduced to a single summary rule: *"Do not that to another, which thou wouldst not have done to thyself"* (his emphasis).[11] This, of course, is the Golden Rule, but stated in its negative formulation, in the manner of the Jewish political tradition, in terms almost exactly the same as those used by Hillel the Elder, a great rabbinic, that is, a post-biblical, Jewish sage. Moreover, just as Hillel the Elder uses this rule as the basis for normative inquiry into the Torah, stating that this is the whole of the Torah, all the rest is commentary, so too does Hobbes see it as providing a method of normative inquiry for, in Vincent Ostrom's words, "computing the basic structure of order in human societies."[12]

With this rule in place, we have a basis for controlling individual passions and self-love, which we do through our covenants, which establish a community of relationships in forms that Ostrom refers to as "shared standards of value that serve as criteria for choice in human societies."[13] Moreover, Hobbes formulates his covenants to establish and maintain conditions of peace. Thus he reaffirms the indissoluble biblical connection between *brit* (covenant) and *shalom* (peace). That is because, for both the Bible and Hobbes, peace can only be maintained through law and law can only exist through covenant.

Hobbes could disconnect the idea of covenant from God and translate it into a wholly secular, humanistic concept of a binding promise. Moreover, the idea of voluntary self-obligation contained in covenant held out the possibility of a stronger and more enduring civil tie than other forms of obedience to government based on conquest or organic development. This is well reflected in Hobbes's list of natural laws:

1. To seek peace, and follow it.
2. By all means we can, to defend ourselves.
3. That men perform their covenants made.
4. That a man which receiveth benefit from another of mere grace, endeavor that he which giveth it, have no reasonable cause to repent him of his good will.
5. That every man strive to accommodate himself to the rest.
6. That upon caution of the future time, a man ought to pardon the offences past of them that repenting, desire it.
7. That in revenges, men look not at the greatness of the evil past, but the greatness of the good to follow.
8. That no man by deed, word, countenance, or gesture, declare hatred, or contempt of another.
9. That every man acknowledge another for his equal by nature.
10. That at the entrances into conditions of peace, no man require to reserve to himself any right which he is not content should be reserved to every one of the rest.
11. If a man be trusted to judge between man and man, that he deal equally between them.
12. That such things as cannot be divided, be enjoyed in common, if it can be; and if the quality of the thing permit, without stint; otherwise proportionably to the number of them that have right.
13. That the entire right; or else, making the use alternate, the first possession be determined by lot.
14. That all men that mediate peace, be allowed safe conduct.
15. That they that are at controversy, submit their right to the judgement of an arbitrator.

Each is an article of agreement—a covenant—to which humans initially aspire in their search for peace and security, according to Hobbes, who ultimately clothes (or cloaks) his ideas in Scriptural-Christian justification. I would suggest that Hobbes ultimately believed in Christianity, at least as he understood it. The predominant opinion among modern scholars (most of whom are themselves secular) is that he did not, that what he seemed to clothe, in reality he cloaked. We may never know, but we can know that his covenants of peace could be strictly civil. On the other hand, by their content alone it is evident that he does not see them as merely part of a social contract. They are *covenants*, that is, they involve mutual promising sustained by a moral framework. He is enormously dubious of the possibility of erecting such a moral framework and certainly of sustaining it on its own. Consequently, he sees what *The Federalist* would later term in another context "auxiliary precautions" as necessary, even more than auxiliary.

On the other hand, just as he sees moral promises as insufficient by themselves and in need of interest, properly directed, to sustain them, so, it seems, he sees that self-interest needs to be within a moral framework. Whether Hobbes saw this in the context of Christianity, some kind of natural religion, or a more civil and secular morality we cannot say. One does not have the feeling that he was a particularly religious person in his spirit so it may not have mattered much to him. Whatever was the dominant moral system was fine, as long as it was suitable to control the less pleasant realities of self-interest and thereby sustain the covenantal system he proposed.

In the face of all the arguments to the contrary, from Hobbes's day to our own, seeing Hobbes as an atheist, at best in disguise, A.P. Martinich, in a recent book, has argued that Hobbes's theism is vital to understand the coherence of his political philosophy.[14] As we have seen, Hobbes requires that humans escape from the state of nature in order to survive. The ability to escape from the state of nature depends upon the human capacity to enter into covenants. Martinich argues that covenants for Hobbes were impossible without laws commanded by God using His power, which humans cannot resist. This is what Martinich refers to as a Divine command theory of morality, widespread in the premodern West as elsewhere. For Hobbes, the Divine commands are confined to establishing the requirement of and framework for human covenanting. By reducing the Divine commandment to this one, Hobbes comes as close as he believes possible to eliminating the command theory of morality and making it possible, even necessary, for humans to reflect, choose and act to take command of their own situation, but that one irreducible Divine command remains. Thus Martinich argues that Hobbes requires a theistic basis for his entire structure. Whatever Hobbes may have thought in his heart-of-hearts, the Hobbes received by the world not only founds his policy on Martinich's dictum but claims to be more of a believer than that, indeed, to be a Christian who spends the last half of *Leviathan* explaining his thought in biblical terms. If too many people today only read the first two books of *Leviathan*, it would do well for them to read the last two as well.

Spinoza and Secular Liberal Civil Society

Asking a somewhat different question without rejecting the spirit of the times, Baruch (Benedict) Spinoza (1632–1677) shared Hobbes's covenantal tradition but in its original Jewish version. Because of that, Spinoza was both more deeply conversant with its biblical roots and more leery of its possible application to the world in which he lived. A Jew from Amsterdam, his parents were Marranos who had escaped from the Iberian Peninsula, where their family had been forced to convert to Catholicism and had to preserve their Judaism secretly. The Netherlands in those days was a haven for such persecuted Jews as part of the opposition of both to Spain and Catholicism. Holland, indeed, was the first state in Western Europe to admit Jews to equal status and to develop a multireligious society based on civic principles. Indeed, the ruling authorities, who were themselves Calvinists, were more tolerant toward Jews than they were to the Christian Arminians in their midst. The latter, as advocates of a non-Calvinist Reformed Protestant theology, were considered heretics by the regime, while the Jews were just of a different religion.

Spinoza was an early convert from Judaism to philosophy, that is to say, he recognized that Judaism as a religion and the religions that grew out of it were based on Divine revelation, which he rejected as the foundation for human knowledge, while philosophy was based on reason, the foundation he sought for himself and for others. A belief in reason as against revelation served Spinoza's political purposes as well, since in principle it opened the door to establishing political society on strictly civil (as distinct from religious) principles, thereby making it possible for Jews and Christians to be equally citizens, one of Spinoza's major aspirations. In that sense, Spinoza was the first modern Jew, certainly the first modern Jewish philosopher, who sought to rebuild European society on modern principles. To do this required the secularization of society, a detachment of state and religion, that is, the end of the Christian commonwealth, either in its universalist Catholic dimension or its particularistic Protestant one.

In Spinoza's lifetime, the first steps in the detachment of religion and state took place in the larger society to conclude the Reformation-initiated wars of religion. They were embodied in the Treaty of Westphalia in 1648. Religion remained established in every polity but was removed as a legitimate reason for interstate wars in Europe. Spinoza was engaged in the parallel construction of a philosophic rationale for all of this.

In order to construct that rationale, Spinoza had to discredit the Bible as the most important source of political ideas for the general world. The Reformation had restored the Bible to an exclusive position that earlier it had had to share with Greek and Roman philosophy. Therefore, Spinoza's greatest political work, the *Tractatus Theologico Politicus*, is, in the main, an effort to demonstrate that biblical teaching was valid only for the ancient Israelites and their commonwealth and had no intrinsic validity for any other peoples. This inevitably led to a denigration of the covenantal dimension in his writings in consideration of his other purpose, namely, the grounding of civil society in religious neutrality for the sake of promoting the possibility of religious pluralism or, better, secularism within it.

All of the major political philosophers of the seventeenth century devoted approximately half of their major political works to the problem of the Bible and how to confront it through the new political philosophy. That in itself is testimony as to how important the Bible was in the political thought of their day. All of them were in some respects able to rely on the Bible as a support for their rejection of Classical political thought and in some respects had to denigrate and diminish the authority of the Bible for the sake of other parts of their modern political thought. The Bible provided excellent support for a human nature derived from human psychology, from the real nature of man rather than the ideal. Yet the Bible also commanded men to follow God in the search for the improvement of the weaknesses in their nature, something that the political philosophers wanted to achieve through human agency alone (despite the best protestations of piety made necessary by the times). Spinoza was certainly no less of this school than Hobbes or Locke and indeed may have been more so since he had to discredit the Bible in the eyes of Jews as well as Christians.

Like Hobbes, Spinoza begins with a realistic view of human nature as a bundle of passions and interests, more often base than noble. Reading his *Political Tractate,* in which he summarizes his understandings of human nature and politics, one senses that in writing it, he must have recalled the famous Talmudic dictum: "Pray for the welfare of the government, for if not for the fear of it each man would swallow his neighbor alive (*Pirkei Avot*, ch. 3, mishnah 2). Thus he erects his politics on a realistic psychology.

Spinoza seems to accept the prevailing view in his circles that the polity is founded on a political compact, a view no doubt as much influenced by the political understanding of the Reformed Protestant Dutch as Hobbes was influenced by regnant Puritan thought in England, and both ideologies were influenced by the Bible, a direct influence on Spinoza himself. Nevertheless, Spinoza seems to view human linkage as more natural and the compact more a matter of political organization than the establishment of society itself. Here, too, he is true to his Jewish background, which views living in society as what we might call a natural arrangement rather than a conventional one, and is much less radically individualistic than his English counterparts. All told, however, he pays little attention to the origins of civil society, focusing more on its organization for human protection and advancement.

Nevertheless, Spinoza, too, felt the necessity to rely upon the idea of a political covenant, compact, or contract to establish the political order. Although he played down the idea of an original document to establish social connections among individuals in families, viewing those as natural, he did indicate acceptance of the idea that a political covenant or compact was needed to establish what he already termed the state in the manner of continental European thought. The state could offer the advantages of civil society that Spinoza held to be vitally necessary, feeling the need for those responsible for the maintenance of order to have coercive powers at their disposal to do so.

While Spinoza does not emphasize the role of covenant in his direct discussions of the subject, in his discussion of the ancient Israelite polity he provides his readers with a teaching that enables them to fathom his concerns in this area. In doing so, he rests his thought on Maimonides's understanding

Covenant and Civil Society

that humans are naturally social and need society for their development, but they also are the least capable of living in society among all creatures. In his eyes, this basic contradiction leads to the necessity for government and politics. Spinoza agrees and goes a step further, holding that it is also the justification for democracy, to overcome this contradiction at least sufficiently to maintain political society.

Spinoza further holds that there is no natural morality, that what humans mean by "natural rights" are really the powers that they possess by nature; that is to say, whatever they can do, they have a natural right to do. This is a Hobbesian formulation if there ever was one. For Spinoza, as for Hobbes, this makes it absolutely necessary for human beings to establish covenants and compacts through which they will relinquish some portion of their rights, that is to say, their powers, to a collectivity, the polity and its rulers.

Spinoza further understands that in order to achieve this humans must consent to doing so. He goes further; the need for this consensus is not just for a consensual act but a continuing consensus with continuing ways and means for people to affirm their consent and understand that they are doing so. It may be that this, too, comes from Spinoza's background in the Jewish tradition in that Judaism provides numerous acts of renewing consent, from prayer three times a day to annual reaffirmation on Shavuot, the traditional anniversary of the giving of the Torah at Sinai.

Moreover, there are limits to humans' ability to relinquish their rights or powers. Those limits are also natural. They cannot limit their powers beyond what nature will allow. So, for example, it is impossible to relinquish the right to one's thoughts. Even the meanest (in the sense of lowest and most miserable) human being can and will think about what is good for him and there is no way to make him relinquish or to limit that power of thought even by his own consent.

Thus, for Spinoza, morality is founded on consent and through covenanting. The federal and constitutional implications of his ideas are present within those ideas and are recognizable upon contemplation of them. That is to say, were one-time consent all that was needed, one would not need constitutions and constitutionalism. Constitutions provide the basis for continuing consent by establishing the principles and providing the ways and means to translate them into practice through popular consent. In this way Spinoza lays a philosophic grounding for modern constitutional republicanism.

Spinoza seeks consent through people consenting with one another, but it is equally possible, as he himself admits, to do so in the biblical manner, that is, through people consenting to a covenant with God, who thereby establishes the constitution for them that meets the same criteria. The morality established by those covenants and constitutions is a federal morality in the original sense of the term "federal"; that is to say, it is based upon covenant and does not have, nor can it have, any other basis than covenant and consent.

Others have argued that there must be a natural morality, that is to say, a moral order built into nature in order to have covenants; there have to be people who are naturally moral, or morally capable, and who seek to establish that morality for larger publics or for humanity as a whole on that basis through covenant. Spinoza would not agree.

Nor would the Bible. In it, God is the source for establishing covenantal morality, that is, He provides the moral principles to which people agree by covenant. People may be naturally free, but once they are covenanted their freedom consists of being free to live up to the terms of their covenants. Otherwise they are outside the law or outlaws. Spinoza recognizes this by allowing governments greater power of coercion in the public sphere than they would otherwise be entitled to in order to maintain public order in civil society.

Since Spinoza wrote in Latin, the word that he uses to describe this process is "obey." People obey authority, whether governments or pacts or God. Read carefully, however, one sees that the term that Spinoza has in mind is not the Latin word for obedience but the biblical Hebrew word for hearkening, *shamoa*, which means to hear and to act accordingly, as a result of reasoned choice and consent (or what Alexander Hamilton later referred to in *Federalist, no. 1* as "reflection and choice."[15] Coming as he did out of the Jewish tradition and its biblically based political ideas and culture, Spinoza thought of the act of what Christians call obedience as a matter of hearkening. Even though he rejected what for him were the limitations of that tradition, he retained the imprint of its culture on his thought.

In this way, too, Spinoza served a bridging function, reintroducing the biblical political tradition grounded in covenant into a modern, secularizing world in such a way that it did not immediately rest upon God's providence and thus could be translated into modern terms. The requirement that there be continuing consent further served to open the door to modern constitutionalism as the vehicle for assuring that continuing consent. While Spinoza saw himself as secular, his resynthesis of biblical and classical political thought also contributed to making it possible for both modern Jews and modern Christians to rest their thinking on the base that he provided.

Spinoza's understanding of the essence of religion played the same bridging function based upon Hebrew and biblical ideas and norms. While Spinoza himself may have denied the ultimate rational truth of religion and expressed that denial in his esoteric teaching, at the very least he understood that for most people in the world, even the generally enlightened public who molded opinion in the polity but who were not and would not ever be philosophers, religion was politically necessary and perhaps even absolutely necessary. As such, it was true even if not rationally true.[16]

Religion, for Spinoza, was the means for their moral salvation (*salus*). He suggested that blessedness (*beatitudo*) is a higher form of salvation and candidates for achieving it are very few indeed. Therefore he did not continue his discussion of it. For moral salvation, then, people need religion, but they need the essence of religion, not its particularized accretions in particular cultures or communities. (Hence Spinoza could deny the validity of biblical laws for mankind in general on the grounds that they were designed for the Israelites, indeed, the ancient Israelites at that.)

What, then, is the essence of religion? The pursuit of justice and charity (*iustitia et caritas*). That pursuit is salvation for all but the tiny few who can be blessed.

> Faith demands goodness rather than truth, but it is good and a means to salvation only because of the obedience which it inspires, and, consequently, that it is obedience alone which makes man a believer. Hence it is not necessarily the man who produces the best arguments who displays the best faith, but he who produces the best works of justice and charity." (*Theological-Political Tractate*, ch. 14).

Indeed, Spinoza's fifth proposition of the universal faith is "worship of God and obedience to him consists solely in justice and charity (or love) toward one's neighbor."

Spinoza's parenthetical insertion gives us a very important clue to what he means by justice and charity and most particularly by charity or *caritas*. What we have before us is nothing other than the biblical Hebrew phrase *tzedakah v'hesed*; *tzedakah* as justice in the largest sense, and *hesed* as covenant love (following Snaith's translation), or as this writer would translate it, "loving covenantal obligation." Indeed, Spinoza, in elaborating on a definition of *caritas*, reaches the same definition.

So in the end Spinoza draws upon the Bible for the basic premises of universal religion but not that part of the Bible devoted to the detailed laws given by God and Moses to the Jewish people but on the essence which God, Moses, and the prophets speak of to the people on different occasions. Moreover, that essence is covenantal. Spinoza further defines what it means to be just as being obedient to God. If we correctly understand his understanding of obedience as hearkening, to be just is to hearken to God, that is, to fulfill one's potential as a covenanted being. If charity for Spinoza indeed is *hesed*, then the second part of the phrase has to do with fulfilling one's obligations as a covenanted being toward one's fellows; or phrased more concisely, justice is essentially fulfilling one's covenantal obligations to God and charity, fulfilling those obligations to one's fellows.[17]

In the last analysis, Spinoza is seemingly unfair to the idea of covenant because he is so close to it. He alone of the great philosophers of his time had a direct experience with the original covenantal tradition, that of the Bible and the Jewish people, and for reasons of personal preference rejected that tradition and attempted with no little success to found a new, more secular, tradition in its place. The first modern Jew, he was a major architect of the new political philosophy, because even more than Hobbes needed security in

England, Spinoza needed acceptance in the larger world. In another sense, however, Spinoza invented a new covenant based on a moral commitment so as to be able to abandon the old tradition, presented by him as parochial, on behalf of a new one presented as universal. That was as much an act of covenanting as any other that took place in the seventeenth century.

Spinoza did serve, even if unintentionally, as one of the bridging figures between the older covenantal tradition and modernity. Like Hobbes and Locke, his careful treatment of the Bible to make his points gave his readers and subsequent generations a chance to do the same from a nontraditional perspective. Spinoza even shows them the necessity of confronting biblical political thought and with it the covenantal tradition from outside of the religious tradition.

Spinoza used the word "covenant" only in reference to its usage in the Bible as a theo-political term and was hardly an advocate of a broader use of the term. Moreover, his reluctance to emphasize the compact theory of politics and his apparent leaning toward a more organic view of the origins of civil society kept him from seeking any alternate term. Nevertheless, by taking the Bible seriously and in laying the foundations for modernity and modern democracy, Spinoza became an influence on subsequent generations of moderns. He did so because he wanted to make the world safe for philosophy or, more accurately, science and philosophy. Scientists and philosophers had to have lives that were both tranquil and unrestricted for science and philosophy. Both stability and freedom were prerequisites for doing that, and he saw democracy as providing both the most stable and the freest of regimes.

On the other hand, a very good case can be made that Spinoza thought that in matters of the polity and its governance, rulers did indeed have the right to apply restrictions if they were necessary for the survival and health of the polity, including fostering religious myths and political or social restrictions that, while not necessarily true or just in the philosophic or scientific sense, were ultimately true in that they enabled civil society to survive. This Spinozistic approach was the one that actually took hold in the modern world and was sustained throughout most of the modern world wherever democracy took root until the end of the modern epoch. This, indeed, may have been his most practical contribution to the transformation of the covenantal tradition. Only the totalitarian polities whose rulers wanted to control everything or those polities that retained too much premodern character and did not become modern democracies did not follow Spinoza's lead.

Locke: An Optimistic Civil Compact

The relationship between political philosophy and current events was not diminished by John Locke. Quite to the contrary, his two-part *Treatise on Civil Government* was written to defend the principles of the Glorious Revolution of 1688. In them, he subtly shifted the philosophic understanding of those principles for the careful reader.[18]

On the surface, Locke defended the biblical basis of political authority even as he emphasized the covenantal rather than the patriarchal understanding of biblical ideas on the subject of the relation between rulers and ruled. In this he followed the understanding of the Hebrew Bible as I demonstrate in *Covenant and Polity in Biblical Israel* (volume 1 of this series). Indeed, one may read the Book of Genesis through the beginning of the Book of Exodus as a record of biblical experimentation with and rejection of the hierarchical model, first unrefined for an epoch (from Adam to Noah) then defined by covenant (from Noah to Abraham), and then brought into a firmer covenantal system in the epoch of the patriarchs (Abraham, Isaac, and Jacob). According to Genesis, its decline was already noticeable in the days of Jacob but, most especially, from the days of Jacob's children, especially his son Joseph. As Wildavsky has demonstrated, Joseph represented the worst possible degradation of the use of power in the Divine framework.[19]

This led God to shift from a patriarchal to an organic model which also did not work and served only as a transitional stage. God ultimately adopted a covenantal model, embodied in the persona and activities of Moses, the binary opposite of Joseph in his use of power, to set the Israelites on a better path and the political tradition in Western politics on covenantal foundations.

Locke presented his position in contrast to that of Filmer's hierarchical thesis.[20] Following through on that, he emphasized the contractual binding of king and people in his own time. Locke's first and second treatises can easily be read by the broad public on that level alone, but a more subtle reading suggests that Locke, without repudiating the utility of biblical authority, replaces it with the authority of human reasoning alone, and without rejecting the contract between king and people makes it subsidiary to an original political compact between individuals to establish civil society in the first place, thereby making all rulers, in Locke's terms, only "fiduciary powers to act for certain ends."[21]

In a sense, Locke returns to the earlier Sophist-Epicurean view of civil society as limited in its role since it is instituted to secure the rights of individuals better than they can be secured in a state of nature. On the other hand, there is a moral dimension, more Whiggish than Puritan, lurking behind Locke's proto-utilitarianism. If the first task of the commonwealth is to promote life, it also has some responsibility for promoting the good life.

Locke, who also used language carefully, preferred the terms *compact*, *contract*, and *constitution*. This usage comported perhaps, with Locke's more limited view of government, more commercial view of civil society, and more hospitable view of the right of public resistance to tyranny. Locke wrote at a time when many Englishmen, including Puritans, were weary of the struggles for religious conformity and the kind of comprehensive, leviathan-like government needed to enforce it. Accordingly, Locke thoroughly secularized government by separating church and state and by counseling toleration, and thereby diversity.[22] Like the Puritans, he defined religion as a voluntary association of believers; but unlike the Puritans, he confined religion to the private sector. For the churches, this was the price of toleration; religion had to relinquish its juristic claims on civil society.

No longer a community of the faithful engaged in the Lord's work, civil society was to be a commercial association of individuals engaged in private enterprise. If individuals could not love their neighbors covenantally as fellow Christians, they could at least love their neighbors contractually as potential consumers and business partners. In this respect, Locke was closer to the secular side of Puritanism which had begun to come to the fore as the religious side spent itself. Many of the more commercial constituents of Puritanism desired a sure and stable society held together by contracts enforced by the rule of law promulgated by a constitutionally elected government having limited powers. This is part of the background of Locke's conception of the primary duty of government, namely, "the Regulating and Preserving of Property."[23] Although Locke is often criticized for elevating possessive individualism to the highest place, his teachings were, in part, a response to the insecurity of property and cavalier violations of contracts by social superiors during his day. That human beings have the freedom to establish and, then, the moral obligation to abide by their covenants, compacts, contracts, and constitutions is the central teaching of both Locke and Hobbes. Any other arrangement is neither free nor just in their view.

Covenant lent itself to secularization and modern needs as compact because the latter seemingly could be divorced from God and grounded in human will. Furthermore, the idea of a social or political compact had been considered by classical political science but rejected in favor of natural law. It was not, therefore, foreign to philosophy and could be adapted to it under new ground rules. To do so, Hobbes and Locke transformed classical natural law and, at the same time, opened the option that God or any transcendent power could be removed as an essential agent in human affairs. This had the effect of leaving humans alone in what Hobbes and Locke regarded as a state of nature, seemingly without any external standard of the right order of things or external source of obligation. Instead, they suggested that standards of right and obligation could be derived only from individual desires and reason. However, because reason and desire are rooted in the drive for self-preservation, human beings come into conflict and find themselves in a state of continual war, and thereby insecurity, so long as there is no effective sovereign among them. Under such circumstances, reason tells individuals that it is to their advantage to enter into agreements and formulate articles of peace among themselves. By such covenants or social compacts, humans create civil society and establish forms of government to enforce their own promises to each other.

In secularizing covenant, however, Hobbes and Locke rendered it much more individualistic than communitarian; and, thereby, more contractual. The key element is mutual self-interest and advantage. Whereas Reformed churchmen entered covenants to save their souls, secular citizens entered compacts to save their skins.

Hobbes and Locke also discarded the various federal approaches to political organization developed by the Reformed theologians-cum-statesmen and Althusius. Instead, their secular compact united the whole people of a nation into a single body and sovereignty. The federal idea of multiple local, provincial, and nationwide compacts creating multiple polities and governing bodies as well as dispersed majorities was replaced by a single compact and the rule of a single majority. As such, this limited the applicability of these theories to the circumstances of such polities as the United States.

In subsequent generations, Hobbes frequently was undervalued as a seminal political philosopher, no doubt because his operational conclusions for the political system were apparently so absolutist, reinforcing the Divine right of kings with a natural right of kings unlimited by other institutions or authority. At the same time, the influence of Locke was overvalued, in all likelihood because, while those were not his views, they could be adapted to the statist and centralist tendencies of many nineteenth and twentieth century intellectuals who on the one hand sought liberty, privacy, and greater equality in a democratic centralized republican state that could be seen as responsive to the popular will, but in fact could concentrate power as the governors of the state willed.

More recently, scholars have shown that the conventional wisdom regarding both men has erred.[24] The major contribution of both lay in their destruction of the classical framework and substitution of another that was more favorable toward secular civil democratic republicanism. Hobbes had another dimension as well, one that goes beyond his own operational conclusions that most democrats reject to offer a compactual approach to the maintenance of civil peace that offers us many possibilities and deserves our continued attention.

Montesquieu: The Bridge to Federalism

The post-Hobbesian bridge between covenant and federalism was built by Montesquieu. While Hobbes emphasized unitary rule, preferring a monarch but recognizing that unitary rule was also possible in a single assembly, Montesquieu clearly understood that a single assembly of all, a direct democracy, ran the risk and the almost certain consequence of institutional failure as a result of the usurpation of authority by its leaders. This was later formulated by Robert Michel as the iron law of oligarchy.[25]

Montesquieu formulated a theory of confederation as an answer to this problem and also as an answer to the other problem of government, namely that of external security. As he put it, "if a republic be small, it is destroyed by foreign force. If it be large, it is ruined by internal imperfection."[26] By confederating a group of small republics, a large enough entity would be established to repel foreign invaders while at the same time the balance of forces within the confederation should offer the possibility to overcome the internal corruptions of individual members. For the authors of *The Federalist*, Montesquieu's theory was insufficient because of the confederate nature of his polity. Only a Madisonian extended republic could deal with both of these problems, but Montesquieu did build the first major and widely recognized bridge between the new political philosophy and federalism.

Montesquieu may have done so on the basis of civil society as a political compact, but he certainly did not emphasize that aspect. He placed his emphasis instead on the political compact that united small states as confederates within a larger framework, reflecting his primary interest. Montesquieu wrote at the height of informed public acceptance of the compact theory at a time when virtually all political philosophers espoused it. David Hume's challenge to it had not yet developed widespread influence, whereas men like Hugo Grotius and Samuel Pufendorf extended it into every political sphere. True, what they had espoused, especially in the case of Pufendorf, was well removed from the religious basis of the original covenant idea and was thoroughly secularized as political compact although its exponents paid lip service to the framework which God had provided for it. Compact could be taken for granted as the conventional wisdom and the attention to it be devoted to its applications in different spheres of political life as Montesquieu did.

Montesquieu was probably the first great political philosopher since Aristotle to have a truly comparative perspective of humanity and to develop his political philosophy accordingly. By his time, Western knowledge of the world had become broad enough to bring Westerners into contact and acquaintance with other radically different civilizations on every continent and essentially in every part of every continent. Thus without losing the awareness of human essences, Montesquieu could contemplate those essences as they are filtered through the physical circumstances and social conditions of humans wherever they might be. While this could have led to a stark relativism, Montesquieu instead developed philosophic canons for judging the laws of a given people as better or worse. He is more relativistic when it comes to understanding the norms behind the laws and the political configurations that emerge from those laws.

Montesquieu has become conventionally famous for his emphasis on the virtues of small democratic republics associated through rather tight confederations, with their own regimes secured through separation of powers. His efforts to combine virtue, political liberty, and religion are reminiscent in many ways of Althusius. Indeed, his deviation from the English advocates of civil society in the seventeenth century is along Althusian lines. To what extent he knew of or was influenced by Althusius in any direct way we cannot say, but there is reason to suspect at least an indirect connection if not a direct one.

Herder, the Bridge to Nationalism

If Montesquieu was the bridge from political compact theory to federalism, the much lesser-known Johann Gottfried Herder (1744–1803) performed much the same function in bridging between political compact theory and the nationalism that was to appear after the French Revolution and especially in the nineteenth century. Herder did so through a comprehensive system of political philosophy which he anchored in Jewish history. For him, the ability of the Jews to survive was by combining kinship and consent, that is to say, by being bound by their covenant with God, which takes the form of law, and the facts of their common ancestry and heritage. For Herder this combination was demonstrably the ideal for nationalism, precisely because it sustained the Jews and enabled them to survive not only as individuals but as a clearly distinct nation almost from what was then perceived of as the beginning of time.[27]

Herder's discovery of the Jews came out of his own personal religious background. He was at one time a student of the Hebrew Bible and came early to the conclusion that the Bible was not merely a religious but also a political work. For that matter, he understood that Hebrew poetry also had a strong religious dimension and he published a book on that subject, *Vom Geist der Ebraischen Poesie*, in 1783. In that innocent sounding volume Herder was able to expound his political ideas more fully than he was in his directly political works which were censored.

Basically, Herder saw ancient Israel as a people with its own distinct national character. Moses was the founder of their nation, which he did by uniting twelve independent republics, the way in which Herder referred to the tribes. He saw Moses' handiwork as the establishment of a federal system, which Herder compares to the Swiss Confederation.

Herder attributes the Hebrew national character to five principal historical determinants: (1) the land as the people's common heritage; (2) the law of the constitution as a covenant freely entered into; (3) a common language and a common folklore tradition; (4) the emphasis on family cohesion fostered and perpetuated by; (5) a deeply ingrained reverance for the forefathers, that is, a felicitous combination of kinship and consent that has survived exile and dispersion.

Herder referred to the ancient Israelite political system as a nomocracy where the rule of law was supreme. The Mosaic constitution, indeed, was a political document and Moses, the oldest and wisest of legislators, could subordinate himself to the needs of his nation. As far as the covenant was concerned, Herder saw it as a flexible rather than a rigid document that could be altered to suit changing circumstances and was from the days of Moses onward.

Herder saw in the Mosaic covenant an alternative to the natural law tradition which viewed the ancient Israelite constitution as basically a declaration of individual rights. He saw that the main task of the Mosaic constitution was the establishment of a free people which, because it was governed as a republic, eliminated the danger of arbitrariness that could interfere with individual rights. Consequently, for Herder, the introduction of kingship was a vitiation of these basic protections.

Herder identified good government with impersonal government, in which the community determines who governs on a regular basis. The Israelite republic, like any good republic, was backed up by a public, nongovernmental sector of voluntary associations that also served the nation. Government became principally a matter of cooperation among the various elements within the communal polity. It did not serve a "state."

Herder's appreciation of ancient Israel as the ideal polity was because it fit the commonwealth model, even though it had pluralistic elements already associated with the civil society model. In this respect his model was more in the tradition of Althusius than of Spinoza or Locke. As a supporter of the commonwealth model he saw the Jews of his time as legitimately separate. While he was among the supporters of their emancipation, he did not seek their assimilation, seeing it as both presumptuous and futile. As he put it,

the [Jewish] people remain therefore also in Europe, in our part of the globe, an alien Asiatic nation, who [in]extricably tied by its own confession to that ancient law that has been given to it under distant skies...since Israel regards itself in its prayers as a people distinct from all other peoples, how could it be judged differently by the other nations?"[28]

Herder was one of the early proto-Zionists, seeing that only the Jews' return to their land and resurrection of their commonwealth could be the means for their achieving full freedom and fulfillment. Moreover, he suggested that the Jews could get world support if they would present their problem as a political one on the world stage, precisely the program that Theodor Herzl, the founder of modern Zionism, was to advocate a century later. Even if not all Jews would return to Zion, if a sufficient number did to restore the people's collective political rights, the others could live in the diaspora as individuals with civil rights and could be recognized as doing so legitimately.

In a very real sense Herder was the culmination of the political compact tradition, resynthesizing it with an organic dimension. Herder's concepts of nationalism included more of an organic dimension than had been common up to that time. While not genetic or racist, it was based upon issues of language or culture which to him, were the true sources of differences in national character. In doing so he followed more in the spirit of Althusius than any of the earlier moderns, which may be one reason why he has generally been neglected. Another, of course, was that as a German his thought was submerged in other Germanic ideas of a less attractive kind that were to gain currency in the nineteenth century.

Rousseau: The Despotism of the Social Contract

The Lockean liberal political compact was challenged in the mid-eighteenth century by the absolutist social contract theory of Jean Jacques Rousseau. A son of the Genevan republic, itself a major manifestation of the covenantal tradition of Reformed Protestantism, Rousseau in many respects can be seen as carrying on aspects of the tradition of John Calvin by providing a covenantal basis for absolute secular rule in the name of higher principles, in Rousseau's case the general will of the people rather than Calvin's divine will of a gracious God. The people became Rousseau's secularized divinity.

On the surface, Rousseau's was the most democratic of systems or so it seemed. Rousseau at least understood its limitations in the sense that he advocated his system only for city republics like Geneva, small polities where all the people could assemble to collectively determine their general will. But in fact, because of the holistic nature of his theory he opened the way to what J.L. Talmon and others have referred to as totalitarian democracy, a useful oxymoron.[29] As it turned out, Rousseauian theories were not used in the small republics, especially not in his native Geneva, but were first tried in revolutionary France, at the time the largest state in Europe outside of Russia. There the people could not assemble except symbolically. (In the early stages of the revolution, the revolutionaries actually did establish a Day of the Covenant in which the citizens of Paris were invited to assemble in the name of all of France on the Champs de Mars, first to affirm and subsequently to renew the new social contract which was viewed as binding the French.

Moreover, it was not easy to discover the general will, since, in fact, the federalist theory developed in the United States (of which more below) was more accurate in projecting society as composed of many different "factions," (in today's terms, interests) with every majority in fact a transient coalition of minorities. Thus the revolutionaries had to find another way to determine the general will and decided that they were best capable of doing so themselves. Jacobinism was born out of Rousseauian doctrine, with its idea that self-selected revolutionary leaders were best equipped to understand the true interests of the people, to identify the general will, and then to force the people to accept their diagnosis and program.

The line from Jacobinism to Napoleonic rule to twentieth-century totalitarian democracy, whether Bolshevik or National Socialist, has been demonstrated by numerous students of the subject and should be clear enough. In the process, the social contract has either been lost or has survived as a fiction of what the Bolsheviks came to call "democratic centralism," that is to say, an initial device establishing a regime and transferring power to the revolutionary cadre, where it was to remain solidly entrenched and generally misused, only demonstrating once again how easy it is to misuse ideas.

The foregoing paragraphs do not do full justice to the relationship between the Rousseauian social contract and the covenantal tradition in its secular form. Nor is there any claim here to have done full justice to Rousseau's thought in general. Rousseau's social contract may have had its origins in the conventional wisdom of the time but its direction was very different, at one and the same time more private and more collective than the more public yet more relaxed dimensions of the covenantal tradition. Some scholars, such as Catherine Zuckert, have argued that in the early to mid-nineteenth-century United States, when covenantal thought still influenced, albeit in a diminishing way, intellectual circles, Rousseauian thought stepped in to fill a certain vacuum caused by the diminution of the American theopolitical tradition.[30] This writer does not agree with her conclusions, but her arguments must be taken seriously.

Nevertheless, Rousseau's use of contract, it seems to this writer, is a good example of the difference between covenant and compact, on one hand, and contract, on the other. The widespread acceptance of the Rousseauian term is in part a simple matter of imprecision. More than that it reflects the widespread acceptance of Rousseauan ideas through Jacobinism and its various heirs in nineteenth- and twentieth-century thought.

Even if Jacobinism and its successors failed as operational ideologies, their ideas have left a very heavy residue among many intellectuals and academics and their opinion-maker students. They found the idea of a social contract more attractive because of its Rousseauian secular meaning rather than the idea of covenant with its religious overtones. Moreover, it seems to have been aesthetically more satisfying. Even the idea of compact which, as applied, for example, by the Federalists; seemed, to them, to be "messier." That is to say, it did not provide a neat hierarchical structure for democracy which could allow the sense of "refined" order and dominance that they craved. They wanted things to be neat and directed from the top (where they saw themselves well-positioned) and easy to identify without much effort because they were so directed (or were presumed to be). Thus the more federal models of a democracy, even based on a secular political compact, which might have been more effective in practice but required more effort to follow and control, were thus less attractive.

The Jacobins and their supporters miss the point entirely. Republican liberty can live only if it is a bit messy—a little chaos is necessary for democracy to live and breath.[31] This may be a condemnation or at the very least a serious criticism of those academics and intellectuals, but it is nevertheless the reality. This tells us much about the pursuit of power by those who claim to favor democracy but embrace ideologies whose implementation requires coercive powers.

Nor should we underestimate the degree to which the attraction to Jacobinism is an aesthetic one. That is to say, it is based on a sense of what looks and feels good rather than one based upon serious and systematic investigation and judgment.

Another reason for that attraction relates to the way that a certain kind of privatism closely identified with individualism has overwhelmed the sense of community solidarity and the idea of a people living within the framework of a covenant or political compact to which they are bound. As society moved towards greater privatization of the nongovernmental spheres of civil society and the idea that every person could do as he or she pleased as long as it did not hurt others (a very problematic idea as we shall see later), the idea that individuals were bound together and to the polity by contract, essentially a private arrangement, was at least implicitly encouraged since being bound by covenant or compact would bring with it obligations that many individuals were loathe to take on.

In the last analysis, Rousseau was ambivalent about federalism. After all, he was Swiss and in the Swiss pattern disliked both the material ostentation and the territorial scope of large states. Although his particular kind of small community did not lend itself to federal connections, he saw their use and necessity, recognizing that while small states would have the virtues of avoiding excessive wealth and cosmopolitanism and could be modest, they could also be swallowed up unless they banded together for protection in a manner similar to what Montesquieu suggested. Thus he, too, leaned to confederation rather than federation. The spirit of nationalism should be vested in small states which he saw, prefiguring the Jacobins desire for everything to be political, as of an appropriate size to be very political. Larger states were insufficiently political in his mind. If one's politics were the politics of a city, one could be dependent on the city, that is to say, more "public." Otherwise, one had to be more independent and private.[32]

Benjamin Constant: Swiss but not Rousseauan

Like Rousseau, Benjamin Constant was a Swiss by birth who achieved his standing because of his connection with the French Revolution.[33] Whereas his countryman Rousseau laid the prerevolutionary intellectual foundations for much of the revolution-generated government, Constant, having witnessed the excesses of the revolution, especially government terror in the name of democracy and civic republican virtue, reformulated the eighteenth-century principles which later became known as liberalism in the effort to make those revolutionary excesses impossible because they were philosophically unjustifiable.[34] Constant stood in contrast to Rousseau regarding the issue of sovereignty, rejecting not only the idea of the general will but also its absolute notion of sovereignty as endangering basic human rights. As Constant put it:

"On the contrary there is a part of human existence which, by necessity, remains individual and independent and which by right is outside any social competence."[35] Constant further concluded that Rousseau's *Contract Social* "so often invoked on behalf of freedom, has been made into an auxilliary of all kinds of despotism."[36]

Like Montesquieu, Constant saw sovereignty limited by public opinion and, perhaps more important, by "the distribution and balance of powers."

Constant's theoretical redefinition of sovereignty made federalism possible. The "new kind of federalism" which he propagated could be defined as follows: "the direction of the business of everyone pertains to everyone, I mean, the representatives and to their delegates. That which is of interest only to a fraction must be decided by this fraction; what has a relation only to the individual should be submitted to no one but the individual."[37]

As we now know, this is a very simplistic definition, disregarding the problem of externalities, but it is a definition of national federalism rather than interstate confederalism. In that sense it is closer to the federalism of Althusius than to that of Montesquieu. Constant's federalism, moreover, is closer to the contemporary European formulation of subsidiarity than it is to the American idea of a multiplicity of political compacts. Still, his is the first unequivocal expression of the federal idea in modern French thought. In it, his Swiss background shows. Ralph Nelson describes Constant's thought as "concrete where the theorists of the eighteenth century Enlightenment were abstract, concerned with the local as they were concerned with the national...Constant was for tradition as they were for innovation."[38] Constant also visualized and advocated a political federation for Europe more in the spirit of the European Union than of the early twentieth century movement for a United States of Europe.

Like his predecessors, Constant understood the great political and social difference between the modern and previous epochs based on the degree of unity of purpose around which political communities could be organized, rejecting both the Aristotelian and the Christian commonwealths on the grounds that they did not provide the degree of separation between public and private spheres which was necessary for modern liberty. For him a strong private sphere that would be nonpolitical was vital in order to have a political sphere that would protect human liberty. Constant, like many of his contemporaries, essentially argues that the private nonpolitical sphere is best anchored in commerce, not in virtue, enabling the establishment of a modern commercial society framed by a strong and responsible government but essentially prior to it. In other words, he sought a society based on contract rather than covenant or compact, to translate matters into the terms of this discussion.

As that modern project has unfolded, it has, for good and other reasons, overcome its adversaries. In the nineteenth and twentieth centuries we might say that premodern politics struck back in modern guise through the advocacy of socialism, communism, fascism, Nazism, or their variants, all rejections of the modern divisions of civil society on behalf of renewed organic societies but based on what were essentially the modern innovations of collectivism and populism. The most reactionary of these challenged the democratic republics based on modern constitutionalism in the twentieth century and were beaten to end the modern epoch. In the first generations of the postmodern epoch, modern liberalism triumphed over the efforts to restore organic systems because the market worked better and was able to demonstrate that it satisfied more wants in an already highly individualized society which had become so as a result of modernism, but, of course, this is a perennial struggle and the matter is never decided once and for all.

Kant: Contract as a Rational Fiction

Immanuel Kant (1724–1804) accepted the Rousseauan idea of the social contract but, in the Kantian way, elaborated upon it to make it part of his comprehensive philosophy. In his *Rechstslehre*, (p. ii, para. 47), he put it in the following manner:

> The act by which a people is represented as constituting itself into a state, is termed the original contract. This is properly only an outward mode of representing the idea by which the rightfulness of the process of organizing the constitution may be made conceivable. According to this representation, all and each of the people give up their external freedom in order to receive it immediately again as members of a commonwealth. The commonwealth is the people viewed as united altogether into a state. And thus it is not to be said that the individual in the state has sacrificed a part of his inborn external freedom for a particular purpose; but he has abandoned his wild lawless freedom wholly, in order to find all his proper freedom again entire and undiminished, but in the form of a regulated order of dependence, that is, in a civil state regulated by laws of right. This relation of dependence thus arises out of his own regulative law-giving will.

Like Rousseau, Kant makes it clear that the social contract is a philosophic fiction:

> The original contract is merely an idea of reason; but it has undoubtedly a practical reality. For it ought to bind every legislator by the condition that he shall enact such laws as might have arisen from the united will of the people; and it will likewise be binding upon every subject, in so far as he will be a citizen, so that he shall regard the law as if he had consented to it of his own will.

While Kant does not emphasize the sovereignty of the people, certainly not in the way that Rousseau does, in *Zum Ewigen Frieden* (p. 89) he states that: "The republican constitution is the only which arises out of the idea of the original compact upon which all the rightful legislation of a people is founded." Thus, toward the end of the eighteenth century, at the time of the

Americans' experimentation with modern constitutions in their states and on
a federal basis, Kant gave philosophic expression to what would be the new
basic expression of the idea of covenant; namely, modern constitutions and
constitutionalism, through which the people of the world's several politically
sovereign states would, through their representatives, come together and consent to articles of agreement embodied in a constitution which translated the
principles embodied in those articles, either declared outright (as in the early
American state constitutions) or implicit in the documents (as in the Articles
of Confederation and the U.S. federal Constitution), into frames of government which specified how those principles would be embodied in institutions
and activated through those institutions.

This basic idea had already surfaced a century and a half earlier, in practice, in the British colonies of North America (see chapter 4) and in theory in
the writings of Locke. Locke even made a practical attempt to write constitutions for the two colonies of North and South Carolina, neither of which were
successful documents, being far too complex and also too old fashioned for
the colonists' taste. From then on, the idea of constitutionalism had surfaced
in the political philosophy of the eighteenth century, growing in importance
step by step, each time added to by the realities of the world in which the
philosophers found themselves.

Thus by the middle of the last generation of the eighteenth century Kant,
who was to become the founder of modern German philosophy, embodied
constitutionalism in his political philosophy. That was Kant's great success.
On the other hand, his failure was to fall into the trap of the Rousseauian
social contract and its devotion to absolute state sovereignty. The result was
that, while his constitutionalism was strong, his federalism did not recognize
the essential dimensions of federalism as a set of constitutional relationships
resting on the dynamics of federal relationships, not on the locus of political
sovereignty. In that respect, Leibnitz, his predecessor by a century, was the
greater *political* philosopher, better understanding the world of power and
how to organize it for human good, recognizing its realities rather than sounding realistic but being caught in the never-never land of political sovereignty.

The authors of *The Federalist*, in particular James Madison, contemporaries of Kant, also exceeded him in this respect. They assumed that civil society
was founded on a political compact because their national civil society and
the states' civil societies that constituted it had been, and most explicitly said
so in their founding documents. Thus their effort was spent on explicating the
best way to govern civil societies founded on those principles. A spirit of
realism pervades their work, even tragic realism, as they present a federal
system of civil government for a polity of men, not angels, with all the ambitions and weaknesses of men. As products of English and Scottish political
thought, they could take Hobbes and Locke for granted and did not need to
repeat the arguments of those great figures to their audience, many of whom

had also been raised on those very ideas. Not only that, but they also had a body of American political thought resting on the same ideas, derived from the same Reformed Protestant-biblical sources, often expressed earlier than the ideas of Hobbes and Locke, and sometimes in ways better suited for American purposes. Hence they could concentrate on the realia of governing a federal republican civil society, which they did superbly.

Kant had no such advantage. As a continental European living in the final days of the Holy Roman Empire and at the beginning of the practical opening of a new age on the European continent, with new forms of political expression, he could only philosophize and then only in certain ways.

Fichte: From Classic Contract to Romantic Nationalism

In continental thought and perhaps in classic philosophy altogether, Kant may be seen as the high point of contract theory, which he absorbed into his comprehensive system. Johann Gottlieb Fichte (1762–1840) took Kantian thought into the nineteenth century as the basis of a liberal romantic German nationalism. The first to systematically present dialectic philosophy, in his *Grundlage des Natureichts*, published in 1796, Fichte uses social contract theory to solve the contradiction between individual freedom and organized society.[39] But his emphasis on the will of the law already began to move beyond Rousseauian contractarianism toward Hegel, who was to move German philosophy away from any contractarian associations.

Three Approaches to Compact Theory

While the secular advocates of the political compact as the basis of the commonwealth did not differ as much on the fine points of their doctrine as did the covenant theologians, three major lines of division did appear among them. The first is whether or not they used the Bible as the source of their original political compact, and biblical history as the authoritative description of how men established their commonwealths. The second is whether or not compact for them was a historical compact or whether it is merely to be assumed through a process of rational analysis. The third is whether the original compact was between equal individuals or between rulers and ruled.

Hobbes, for example, does not rely on a biblical basis for the compact, holds the first compact to have been a historical fact, and views it as one between free individuals. Indeed, he denies the very existence of a secondary compact between rulers and ruled, holding that government flows from the first. Locke, on the other hand, begins with the biblical basis, at least formally; agrees with Hobbes that there really was a first compact and that it was between individuals; but also claims a subsidiary compact between rulers and ruled. Rousseau and Kant, on the other hand, do not begin with a biblical base and do not see the contract as historical. They view the idea of a social contract as a reasonable starting point for the philosophic discussion of the origins and nature of civil society, but differ in that Rousseau sees the original contract as having been among individuals while Kant sees it as between rulers and ruled. In other words, there is a dividing line between those who begin with the idea of political compact derived from covenantal thought and those who begin with the idea of a social contract, influenced far more by continental canons of political philosophy.

Notes

1. Harold Fisch, "Authority and Interpretation: Leviathan and the 'Covenantal Community,'" *Comparative Criticism* 15 (1993):103–23; Douglas J. Den Uyl, "Power, Politics, and Religion in Spinoza's Political Thought," *Jewish Political Studies Review* 7:1–2 (Spring 1995):77–106; Richard Sherlock, "The Theology of Toleration: A Reading of Locke's *The Reasonableness of Christianity,*" *Jewish Political Studies Review* (forthcoming); Eldon J. Eisenach, "Hobbes on Church, State and Religion," *History of Political Thought*, vol. 3, no. 2 (Summer 1982):215–43. Thomas Hobbes, *Leviathan* (Harmondsworth: Penguin, 1986).
2. Thomas Hobbes, *Leviathan*, Michael Oakeshott, ed. (New York: Macmillan, 1962), p. 106.
3. *Ibid.,* p. 108.
4. *Ibid.,* pp. 114–15.
5. *Ibid.,* p. 9, n. 24.
6. *Ibid.,* p. 134; italics in the original.
7. *Ibid.,* p. 165.
8. *Ibid.,* p. 132; italics in original except as noted.
9. *Ibid.,* p. 342.
10. *Ibid.,* p. 228.
11. *Ibid.,* p. 214.
12. Vincent Ostrom, *The Meaning of American Federalism: Constituting a Self-Governing Society* (San Francisco, Cal.: Institute for Contemporary Studies, 1991), p. 35.
13. Ostrom, *The Meaning of American Federalism.*
14. A.P. Martinich, *The Two Gods of Leviathan: Thomas Hobbes on Religion and Politics* (New York: Cambridge University Press, 1992).
15. *The Federalist, no. 1.* Hamilton refers to "reflection and choice" as the best or most correct means to establish a polity in contrast with force or "accident," the other ways which he emphasizes as having existed prior to the "new science of politics."
16. Douglas J. Den Uyl, "Power, Politics, and Religion in Spinoza's Political Thought."
17. Norman Snaith, *The Distinctive Ideas of the Old Testament* (New York: Schocken Books, 1964); Den Uyl, "Power, Politics, and Religion."
18. John Locke, *Two Treatises of Government* (New York: Hafner Publishing Co., 1956).
19. Aaron B. Wildavsky, *Assimilation vs. Separation: Joseph the Administrator and the Politics of Religion in Biblical Israel* (New Brunswick, N.J.: Transaction Publishers, 1993).

20. Robert Filmer, *Patriarcha, and Other Political Works of Sir Robert Filmer,* Peter Laslett, ed. (Oxford: B. Blackwell, 1949).
21. Locke, *Two Treatises,* p. 196.
22. *Ibid.,* pp. 196–97.
23. John Locke, *An Essay Concerning Human Understanding,* Peter H. Nidditch, ed. (Oxford: Clarendon, 1954); Richard Ithamar Aaron, *John Locke* (Oxford: Clarendon Press, 1955).
24. Wolfgang von Leyden, *Hobbes and Locke: The Politics of Freedom and Obligation* (New York: St. Martin's Press, 1982).
25. Garry Wills, *Inventing America: Jefferson's Declaration of Independence* (Garden City, N.Y.: Doubleday, 1978); Vincent Ostrom, *The Political Theory of a Compound Republic: Designing the American Experiment* (Lincoln: University of Nebraska Press, 1987); Daniel J. Elazar and John Kincaid, *The Declaration of Independence: The Founding Covenant of the American People* (Philadelphia: Temple University Center for the Study of Federalism Monograph, 1980).
26. Montesquieu, *The Spirit of the Laws* (New York: Hafner Publishing Co., 1949), p. 126.
27. Frederick M. Barnard, "Herder and Israel," *Jewish Social Studies,* vol. xxviii, no. 1 (January 1966); Robert T. Clark, Jr., *Herder: His Life and Thought* (Berkeley: University of California Press, 1955); Alexander Gillies, *Herder* (Oxford: Blackwell, 1945).
28. Barnard, *Ibid.*
29. Jacob Leib Talmon, *The Origins of Totalitarian Democracy* (London: Mercury, 1961); Douglass Adair, *A Grand Experiment: The Constitution at 200* (Wilmington, Del.: Scholarly Resources, 1987).
30. Catherine Zuckert, ed., *Understanding the Political Spirit* (New Haven, Conn.: Yale University Press, 1988).
31. Mortin Grodzins, *The American System: A New View of Government in the United States,* Daniel J. Elazar, ed. (Chicago: Rand McNally, 1966), pp. 2–10.
32. Patrick Riley, "Rousseau as a Theorist of National and International Federalism," *Publius,* vol. 3, no. 3 (Spring 1973).
33. Alfred Fabre-Luce, *Benjamin Constant* (Paris: Librairie Fayard, 1939).
34. Steven Holmes, *Benjamin Constant and the Making of Modern Liberalism* (New Haven, Conn.: Yale University Press, 1984); and Jerry Muller, "Four Cheers for Liberalism?," a review of Steven Holmes, *The Anatomy of Anti-Liberalism* (Cambridge, Mass.: Harvard University Press, 1993) in *The Public Interest*; Guy Howard Dodge, *Benjamin Constant's Philosophy of Liberalism* (Chapel Hill: University of North Carolina Press, 1980).
35. Benjamin Constant, *Principes du Politique Ouvre* (Paris: Gallimard, 1964), p. 1071.
36. *Ibid.*
37. *Ibid.,* p. 1154.
38. Ralph Nelson, "The Federal Idea in French Political Thought," in Daniel J. Elazar, ed., *Federalism as Grand Design* (Lanham, Md.: University Press of America and Center for the Study of Federalism, 1987), p. 126.
39. Johann Gottlieb Fichte, *Addresses to the German Nation,* George Armstrong Kelly, ed. (New York: Harper and Row, 1968).

3

Britain: From Whiggism to Liberalism

The Decline of Theological Federalism

Covenantalism was fast ebbing on the European continent after 1648. The Treaty of Westphalia meant the triumph of the conservatives, whether Catholic or Protestant, throughout the continent. Those little countries, Switzerland and the Netherlands, that avoided the worst of the conservatism of the time, did so by laying low and playing ball with the Great Powers. It would take a Napoleon to stir them up again, half an epoch later.

Both of those little countries were compensated in that they became, for them, rich, at least for a while. But they did so at the price of their ideals and their motivating visions, however much their political culture survived and continued to be expressed through their local governments. Indeed, the more authority and power their local governments retained, the more their political culture survived in practice. Fortunately, both Switzerland and the Netherlands had federal systems with strong constituent units, including provinces, republics, or cantons, and communes.

The decline of theological federalism or Puritanism in England came most strongly after the failure of the English revolution at the end of the seventeenth century's first generation. Theologically, English Puritan federalism was pulled in two directions, both distortive of the Puritan synthesis: antinomianism, on the one hand, with everything depending on a purely voluntary covenant, and legalism, on the other, that reduced covenantal religion to punctilious observance of that which the law required. The polarization between these two openly shattered the creative tension between both "pulls" that was required for the covenantal system to work both in theory and in practice.

Where and when the tension between the voluntary character of the covenant and its legalistic tendencies could be balanced within an appropriate federal system and structure, theologically as well as politically, then covenantalism could work as a dynamic if delicate synthesis and the covenantal tradition had a great impact on the shaping of civil society. This was true in the early seventeenth-century British Isles and throughout the century in British North America, or in sixteenth-century Switzerland and the Netherlands. But the balance needed for that dynamism to survive was—and is—difficult to preserve, people being what they are.

The beginning of the search in the mid-seventeenth century for a new direction for the emerging modern epoch was to be found in the emergence of the strong radical movements which had formed in connection with the English Revolution, and the strong body of radical thought that they generated. Those radicals failed, in the immediate sense unequivocally, but some of their ideas survived to lay the foundations for a post-Puritan Whiggism—more secular to fit the new age but not less covenantal for all that. Subsequent historians have tried to suggest that the radicals' ideas helped shape late seventeenth- and eighteenth- century Whiggery and that there is some correspondence between them. Some historians even find in mid-seventeenth-century radicalism the origins of radical, liberal, socialist, and feminist orientations of the twentieth century. That is more problematic.

In any case, the original radicalism represented an antinomian deviation from the covenantal tradition of the Reformation which, while it must be examined in order to obtain a proper understanding of modern covenantalism, also needs to be seen for what it was. While ostensibly relying on covenantal ideas, many theorists used those ideas just as a "hook" on which to hang their radical theories. These radicals would not have hesitated for more than a moment, if that, to sacrifice the covenantal tradition for the sake of advancing those ideas, just as in the twentieth century at the end of the modern epoch new groups of radicals were ready to sacrifice constitutional democracy in the hope of advancing their ideas. (Because the latter were more successful, millions, nay tens of millions of people, were killed and as many more displaced and exiled as part of the "breaking of eggs" to make a new omelette.)

Harrington's Oceana: The Next Step in the Transition

For others, the idea of covenant was the foundation stone and starting point for their programs, and they viewed covenant in a far more radical form as both authorizing and empowering individuals or the people according to their principles. In this respect they were the operational obverse of the English political philosophers who, very radically, shifted the basis of political philosophy from natural law to natural right by providing the same empowerment for individuals or the people in philosophical terms. This latter group of radicals found many of their ideas in the thought of James Harrington (1611–1677), who provided a program for reconstituting England along the lines of civil reform that appealed to republicans, libertarians, and egalitarians, in many ways akin to that of Althusius for Germany.

Harrington, who came from an aristocratic English family, was broadly educated, learning Hebrew, Greek, and Latin as well as modern languages. He studied at Oxford and travelled on the European continent during the Thirty

Years' War, becoming involved in the conflict in Germany. He also sojourned in the Netherlands during its golden age. All told, he spent five years on the continent before returning to England on the eve of the Civil War, well aroused politically and already firmly republican. He was a supporter of the parliamentary cause but also a personal friend of Charles I, and served as an intermediary between them. His friendship kept him from being a mere doctrinnaire republican.

While they had somewhat earlier antecedents in the seventeenth century, radical movements for the most part arose and flourished between 1646 and 1649, continuing until 1660; in other words, from the Civil War through the Cromwellian period to the restoration of Charles II. The Cromwellian military coup (for that is what it really was) in 1648–1649 stimulated the expansion of radical thought as practical activity among the radicals became increasingly hopeless. Cynics may say, as always, "if you can't do, talk."

In doing so, the radicals turned to the ideas of Harrington. Because he was a republican, most of whose influence was as a republican, Harrington is frequently included among the mid-century radicals as perhaps the greatest of them intellectually or philosophically. Historians may debate over just how radical Harrington was, but it is rather clear that he was republican from any perspective.

Harrington, like the Jewish statesman and political theorist Don Isaac Abravanel (1437–1508) and other republicans of his time, was much taken by the Venetian constitution. Biblical Israel and the contemporary Venetian republic were the two great influences on his thought. Thus, in his mind, he was not presenting a utopia but a practical plan. His followers organized the Rota Club to bring that plan to fruition and Harrington himself was involved in the club and in their other efforts, which ended upon the restoration of Charles II.

The Restoration ended Harrington's political career. His ideas lived on as the political counterpart to the Newtonian law of motion which became so important in early modern thought. Harrington carried the new science of politics one step further to tie it even more closely to developments in the natural sciences, even to the point of using scientific terminology and to making efforts at scientific measurement of matters political. While Harrington greatly admired Hobbes, he rejected Hobbes's effort to model political science on geometry, preferring instead anatomy, the study of complex living organisms. In this, he was inspired by the work of William Harvey (1578–1657), the founder of modern biology.

Harrington elaborated his ideas, presented in several works, the principal one of which was *The Commonwealth of Oceana* (published 1656), a thinly disguised fictitious account of an island like Britain that achieved political and social reform and established a model commonwealth based upon popular consent. It was based on a system of division of private landed property that would mitigate inequalities and promote the equality of its citizens, what Harrington referred to as the Agrarian: a system of parish, provincial, and commonwealth governments, the first two of which chose the representatives for the latter.

Oceana concentrated on the form of civil society and its government and with relatively little focus on its political dynamics. Those radicals who became Harringtonians attempted to supply that lack.[1]

The Levellers and James Harrington did the most to propose an alternative constitutional order, in an attempt to stabilize as well as advance the Puritan commonwealth. They, too, turned to what, for them, was the Old Testament for their models, seeing in the Mosaic polity the best regime for their England as well as for ancient Israel. The Levellers did so within the spirit of the old intellectual order. Harrington carried his thought a step further to cross the threshold into the modern age without abandoning the idea of the Mosaic commonwealth.

Twentieth-century analysts of Harrington's thought have claimed that he, like Hobbes and Locke, used the Bible and religious matters only out of expedience, because it was expected at the time, but was actually rather indifferent to religion and in any case did not need biblical or other religious sources as a grounding for his thought, which was derived from human prudence analyzed on scientific principles. Space does not permit a thorough examination of that question, but it can be stated that there is no way for the reader to approach Harrington's thought without doing so through the biblical prism that he presents.

The commonwealth he set out in detail in his *Oceana* was a more secularized form of the Mosaic polity, which he referred to as the "commonwealth of Israel," carried beyond the immediately political frame of government in an effort to transpose the Mosaic land divisions to his England to form the basis for the socioeconomic distribution of power in the commonwealth. Harrington's Agrarian was remarkably similar to the Mosaic distribution of land among the twelve tribes of Israel. In that sense Harrington better captured the spirit of the biblical polity than the many others who turned to it only for governmental arrangements, missing at least half the essence of the biblical ideal, namely, a carefully equitable distribution of property that was restored every fifty years in the jubilee year when every family regained its inheritance.

Harrington also saw Oceana as a single nation with federal divisions, functioning under a constitution (that he referred to as "orders") in a kind of English prevision of American federalism of over a century later.[2] Thus federalism and constitutionalism were combined by Harrington early on, derived from the original covenantal system. Indeed, the whole purpose of Harrington's effort was to introduce a proper constitution of government; that is why he spent so much time discussing and describing the proper institutions and less

discussing proper principles. In the last analysis Harrington and the Harringtonians proposed a realistic commonwealth that James Cotton called "suffused
with republican virtue and a political order little short of the city of God."[3]

Harrington's influence on the American founding should not be underesti-
mated. During the seventeenth century he exercised what Charles Blitzer referred to as "a profound influence" on the governments of Carolina, New
Jersey, and Pennsylvania, all three proprietary colonies whose proprieters
sought to build within them model commonwealths.[4]

At the time of the American Revolution Harrington's writings had a profound influence, especially on the revolutionary leaders from New England,
most especially James Otis and John Adams. Blitzer refers to Adams as "at
once the most ardent and the most distinguished American disciple of the
English theorist." Drawing heavily on Harrington for his ideas of checks and
balances, Adams's famous 1780 constitution of Massachusetts rested heavily
on the New Englander's interpretation of *Oceana*.

The Rise of Whiggism

Not surprisingly, Oceana and its Agrarian remained entirely in the realm
of ideas which, however, were influential in providing a vision within later
British politics. The radicals disappeared as a voice as well as a possible force
with the restoration of Charles II. Ultimately, the more realistic among them
who stayed in politics as well as those from the Puritan party who had transformed themselves became part of the new Whig party which emerged in
1688 as part of the Glorious Revolution. The name was from the term
"whiggamore," apparently of Scottish origin and referring to the Scottish
covenanters. The Whigs developed a civil version of covenant theory for mid-
seventeenth-century Britain that unfolding as the century progressed.[5]

Earlier efforts to establish a Whig party were led by the Earl of Shaftesbury
but were crushed by Charles II. The party achieved a permanent existence
only after the Revolution of 1688. It was already very much deradicalized, in
tune with the English establishment and its interests. The leaders of this new
Whig party, known as the Junto, were major actors in the settlement of 1689,
when the English constitution was reestablished. By 1695 the Junto had gained
control of William III's government.[6]

The main body of these new Whigs rapidly distanced themselves from
radicalism in the following years. The Whig party itself divided into two factions: the court Whigs who favored governing from London, supported a
strengthened king and parliament; and the country Whigs who sought a greater
measure of local control based outside of London. The mainstream Whigs
shifted so quickly that by the late 1690s John Toland, a proclaimed deist, took
the lead of a group of radical Whigs seeking to go back to what they saw as
original Whig principles. Their success was principally in the literary field.

Inter alia, they published or republished radically oriented works from the civil war years, including those of John Milton and Harrington's *Oceana*.

The radicals were republicans like their predecessors. Among the most prominent men in this group were survivors of the political debates of the 1640s and 1650s such as Major John Wildman, John Hampden, and the Reverend Samuel Johnson, whose work spanned a period of nearly fifty years. Wildman actually had been an associate of Harrington's in the 1650s and a member of the republican Rota club named after Harrington's plan in *Oceana*. Neville had been a leader of the commonwealth group at the time. He served as Harrington's right hand in the 1650s and remained active until his own death in 1694.

The Whigs were both Presbyterians and Puritans or ex-Puritans. Late in the nineteenth century, Lord Acton, looking back at them, was to observe that the Whigs were nothing more than moderate Roundheads, that is, they continued to carry Puritanism and Puritan covenantalism (of which, as a Catholic, he did not approve) with them. Indeed, Whig doctrine tends to confirm Acton's observation. The Whigs saw constitutions, especially the British constitution, as designed to teach people how to be citizens. Their theory of history held that history is designed to instruct later generations in that task (an idea that Acton himself embraced and added to it the task of judging as well as instructing).[7] Virtually all of them had their political and intellectual roots in the various covenantal traditions that competed at the time of the civil war, Presbyterian, Puritan, or Leveller. They and their network of masonic lodges, publishing houses, congregations and churches became known collectively as the Commonwealthmen. Goldie describes these Commonwealthmen as "the direct inheritors of civil war republicanism."[8]

This meant that they were truly out of spirit with the times, when the mainstream in both England and Scotland were tired of civil wars and preferred the tamed monarchy of the settlement of 1689 to continued struggles over the principles of monarchism versus republicanism. Here, indeed, was the nub of the situation. The Commonwealthmen represented an earlier epoch in human history; much of what they proposed and struggled for might have been laudable but it was based on the social integrity of an earlier age, redesigned to become the political vehicle for achieving a certain moral integrity that had emerged out of the last half of the previous epoch. All of these required more integrity or virtue than the majority of people, or at least the majority of those who mattered, sought in this new age.

In place of a commonwealth, the new generation sought a civil society with a proper constitution. They were willing to accept the mixed character of society and the imperfections of the polity, but were swayed by the new ideas of civil society, that is, of a substantial separation between public and private; and within the public sector, between governmental and nongovernmental, that would confirm the people in their liberties by right and substantially reduce those obligations which could be coerced from them. In the eyes of the new men, all of this mix needed to be ordered by a proper constitution that embodied the dimensions of covenant, popular consent, and morally based pledging, but that produced not an integrated commonwealth in which those who pledged, whether to God or on a mutual basis, would be bound on an integral basis; rather, a society in which, through a constitution, they would undertake, by their compacting and pledging, to consent to political arrangements more limited in scope and thus more clearly enforceable, mandated through specific measures incorporated into the constitution by design.

The Commonwealthmen opposed not only the monarchy but also the Anglican Church establishment, a stand which was quite consistent with their origins in Puritan congregationalism and the more radical offshoots of Puritanism. Once again, they failed in their efforts, but they did lay the foundations for the transformation of Puritanism into religious dissent, leading the way to the establishment of what became a permanent minority of religious dissenters in England and Wales for the next 300 years. They succeeded in carving out an increasingly protected minority position within an Anglican-dominated society without the constitutional protections provided to Scottish Presbyterianism north of the English border.

The nonconformists among the Commonwealthmen supported each pretender to the English, and later the British, throne who, in turn, served to keep nonconformism alive and hopeful and perhaps even contributed to its establishment as a minority but no more. The pretenders were simply seeking support for their pretensions and did not have the true interests of the nonconformists at heart.

Covenant and the Settlement of 1688–89

The choice of William of Orange and his Queen Mary in place of James II can be seen as a demonstration of the place of the covenant tradition in the compromise of 1688–1689. William was from the Netherlands, where he was stadholder, the chief executive of that federal republic. He was of the House of Orange, so closely associated with the rebellion of the Netherlands against Spain one hundred years earlier and grounded in Dutch Reformed Protestantism. This suggests some covenantal political culture, if not commitment, on the part of William or Mary. William in particular had been brought up within the tradition of Reformed Protestantism and with at least a cultural appreciation of the constitutional limits on the king that derived from that tradition.

This was to be enough, although it was not always smooth sailing. The real battles between monarch and parliament did not begin again until the next century when the House of Hanover was brought in as a result of the peculiarities of the royal succession in Britain and the cultural remains of covenantalism further reduced. Even then, the clashes did not become serious since many constitutional principles had been fully settled by that time.

Meanwhile, the ideational core of Whiggism took form around principles of political compact and mixed monarchy. The Revolution of 1688–89 brought the two together in a constitutional synthesis but there remained tensions between them, as in every founding or refounding. In every such situation, the fundamental principles are the principles that emerge in the founding, brought into a satisfactory synthesis. Nevertheless, these principles still remain in tension under certain conditions, so that within the synthesis those tensions establish both the basis for continuing political conflict and the outer boundaries of the synthesis. These tensions may be resolved for each generation, but reassert themselves around different issues in the next so long as the polity as constituted or reconstituted continues to exist as such.

The Commonwealthmen adapted their position to the new realities. They accepted the synthesis but threw their support to the compactual side with regard to the tension. They may have attracted John Locke as an ally in that Locke's theories identified him with the same side and he may well have had personal relationships with exponents of the commonwealth position as well. The exploration of this possibility might indeed reveal that Locke's understanding of civil society was part of the bridging between the old commonwealth position of the Puritans and the new constitutional position of the Whigs.

Nevertheless, the development of a coherent Whig position on the relationship between the political compact and the mixed monarchy and the inconsistencies it may have contained moved Whiggism from commonwealth to constitutionalism. The old Whig concern was the abandonment of the conservative view that the English constitution came from time immemorial and hence could not really be changed in any significant way. The Whigs espoused the view that the public could make constitutional changes so long as the method used involved popular consent, along with the traditionalist approach already built into the constitution, and expanded from that.

Algernon Sydney played a role in developing this view, leading to his execution by James II. Sydney also developed a political philosophy to systematically express his views. Unlike his currently more famous contemporaries, however, he did not cross over from a premodern understanding of natural law to embrace the new foundation of natural right.[9] In that sense his works spoke to those who might have found it difficult to reconcile themselves to the ideas of Hobbes and Locke. In his time, Sydney was very influential, obviously to the point of frightening James II and bringing the king to take the most extreme steps against him. Sydney's writings remained influential on both sides of the Atlantic a good century after his death.

Like his other seventeenth-century contemporaries, Sydney drew heavily on both biblical and classical sources, obviously relying more on classical sources than upon those of his contemporaries, who turned from natural law to natural right. For our purposes here it is important to note that Sydney drew not only upon the Bible but on the Jewish political tradition that flowed from it, using and citing the great Jewish Bible commentators and medieval political theorists available to him in translation, such as Rashi, Maimonides and Abravanel, as sources in which to anchor his thought.

By 1688, conservatives had concluded that James II was guilty of violating the ancient constitution and hence deserved to be expelled; while, for the advocates of change, James II had violated the principles of popular consent. Hence the views of both groups on the issue of the expulsion of the last Stuart king were in agreement, if for different reasons. That served as a starting point for reaching an acceptable synthesis and also for the tensions within it that persisted thereafter. The final foundations were anchored in the more radical position that the parliament that sat to accomplish the settlement actually had the powers of a popular constituent assembly. Parliament, therefore, could reconstruct the constitution as it saw fit.

This argument was advanced in four principal pamphlets by Commonwealth Whigs, of which that of Wildman, *Some Remarks upon Government, and Particularly the Establishment of the English Monarchy relating to this Present Juncture*, was Harringtonian in tone, as filtered through Neville.[10] It presented a radical theory of natural rights and placed great emphasis on the relationship between economics and politics, looking for radical constitutional change to cope with both. In that sense, it followed in the tradition of Wildman's pamphlet of thirty-five years earlier, *The Leveller*, adapting his earlier ideas to the different times.

In reference to the Parliament sitting as a constituent assembly, at least the Commonwealthmen used the term "covenant" in their discourses, not always distinguishing it from terms like "original contract." The conservatives, however, preferred to talk about ancient liberties. In the final bill of rights, reference to "original contract" was dropped in a serious defeat for the Commonwealthmen at the hands of the more conservative Whigs. Goldie argues that "the split between court and country Whigs, which has been said by some historians to have emerged in 1691 or 1692, is surely present at this moment."[11]

Nevertheless, the Commonwealthmen made one more attempt, through the coronation oath of the monarch, to make the coronation ceremony a formal compact between king and people. The effort to make explicit changes in that direction also failed and the oath remained at best ambiguous on the subject. The coronation oath issue was the occasion for a debate on the idea of political compact as the basis of the polity. Partisans of the monarchy defended, as we know, patriarchalism and the divine right of kings, while the Commonwealthmen and their supporters argued for a source of authority for the polity in a political compact. Those who were on their way to becoming the court Whigs were circumspect on this matter because their interests were much stronger than their principles. It was King William's recognition of those interests that led him to buy them off in 1690, thereby undercutting authentic Whiggism by exploiting the cleavage among the Whigs and further dividing them so that their power was lost both in the court and in the country.

The Commonwealthmen revived the old republican-royalist links that had been behind the Scottish Presbyterian alliance of the 1650s to join the Jacobites. In 1688–89 the Scottish as well as the English had revolted against James. The Scots did take that extra step and offered the kingship to William on the basis of a political compact. He refused and indeed succeeded in making his refusal stick. This led some of the Scottish and English to join the Covenant-ers and to reject the House of Orange in order to seek the return of the Stuarts.

By 1694 the Junto had risen to power in England and the Common-wealthmen had separated themselves from it. The "modern" Whigs had come into being and triumphed. Before that decade was out the older generation of Commonwealthmen died, ending the last direct influences of veterans of the mid-century civil war period, who were, at the very least, gone from politics. Modernity had triumphed in England. The ideas of covenant had faded into the background, surviving only in their more secularized form as political compact.

The Union of England and Scotland

One major political compact was still before the Whig-dominated govern-ment the Act of Union of England and Scotland, which would not take place until 1707, but which was a compact that unified the smaller covenanted pol-ity with the larger organic one. Essentially it was a compact to end all com-pacts, which it did in short order. While there would be periodic recrudescences of a kind in modern British history, the covenant idea and its tradition sur-vived elsewhere, if only because it could not survive in England.

In the end, the radicals wanted to be like Harrington but ended up like Hobbes. The consent and convenience of free individuals could be the foun-dation and goal of their thought, clearly secular even when couched in reli-gious terms, but to get there they could not strike the covenantal balance of Harrington's good commonwealth but could use the language of covenant to reach the unitary models of Hobbes. While they failed in an immediate sense in the seventeenth century, somehow they were able to establish radicalism as an integral part of modernity. It was to resurface in the modern epoch, first among the Jacobins, then among the Marxists, and then among the totalitar-ians of the left as well as of the right, to become the bitterest of modern enemies of the covenantal tradition.[12]

Hebraism in the Seventeenth Century and
Its Importance to Covenantalism

While the late medieval world was being overturned by the philosophers, scientists, and politicians of early modernity, members of all three of those groups pursued Hebraic studies well into the late seventeenth and early eighteenth centuries. Not only the exponents of Reformed theology and Puritanism or those who continued to base their political philosophy and politics on earlier doctrines, but playwrights like Ben Jonson and civil servants such as Samuel Pepys turned to the study of the Bible as "a sourcebook of history, law and anthropology" as well as religious circles.[13]

In this connection, we might first look at those modern forms of Protestantism that grew out of Puritanism or in confrontation with it. For example, George Fox, the founder of the Society of Friends or Quakers, as they became popularly known, took much of Friends' doctrine from his interpretation of the Bible (for him both the Old and the New Testaments), which he quoted in Hebrew. He makes many references to Hebrew sources and has left copies of his Hebrew exercises for us to see. Indeed, he attributed much of what became Quaker plainness to Hebrew origins.

It is true that John Locke and his supporters downplayed the study of Hebrew as part of their downplaying of the study of the classics in favor of the modern. John Locke, on the other hand, had a demonstrated interest in Hebrew and Jewish books, including an interest in Maimonides, even though he deprecated Hebrew learning for the next generation. It was not until the beginnings of romanticism in the 1750s that there was a renewed popular intellectual interest in Hebrew. Neither of those were tied to the covenant tradition, neither the turning away nor the turning back.

Earlier, John Milton, torn as he was between Puritan tradition and modern expectations, tried to be a bridge between both and included the study of Hebrew as part of that bridge. For seventeenth-century English intellectuals, like their predecessors, this was second nature; Harrington and Sydney both were rooted in this tradition.

If one wants to find a Western society from which Hebrew was almost totally absent, one should look at France, especially after the expulsion of the Huguenots. It is no wonder that France was first authoritarian and then Jacobin. Its mainstream had for so long rejected any part of the covenantal tradition; and the one group in French history that were of that persuasion remained a minority, obtaining some power only because of the historical circumstances that made Reformed Christianity useful to the aristocrats in their fight against both the populists and the absolute monarchy. Once the fight was won, they were eliminated.

On the other hand, the English, even if they did not know Hebrew well enough themselves, could find many Hebrew works translated into Latin and thus they could carry Hebraism and the ideas rooted in it into the English worldview even without the language itself. In politics senior civil servants like Pepys studied the works of Hugo Grotius. The Englishman John Selden, was not only a Hebraic but also a rabbinic scholar. Selden's explorations of international law and the law of the sea, derived so much from biblical sources, were just perfect for the English Admiralty of the late seventeenth century.[14]

Opponents of the English position, especially French ones, accused Selden of having no theory of his own, of merely copying from the rabbis' thinking based upon the seven Noahide principles.

In the last analysis, two figures stand out from the seventeenth-century scientific world who dominated the scene for the first half of the modern epoch: Sir Francis Bacon and Sir Isaac Newton. In the manner of their times they were natural philosophers, not like the humanistically illiterate scientists of a later age. Both knew Hebrew and thought it important for unlocking the secrets of the universe. Newton, indeed, had more than a nodding acquaintance with Kabbalah and considered himself something of a Kabbalist.

Bacon (1561–1626), like Althusius, was a child of an earlier age and died before the onset of modernity, but his works forshadowed modern ideas without necessarily abandoning those of the more integral world of his times. Indeed, Baconian natural science was to reassert itself in the early nineteenth century in a renewed effort to find a synthesis between science and society that would rest upon earlier conceptions of commonwealth, and Baconian science only disappeared as a force with the coming of Darwinism.

Newton (1642–1727) already was a modern, but an early modern who carried over into modernity the religious worldview of an earlier time. He could make the most far-reaching scientific discoveries with a spirit of piety that soon became lost to successor generations. Of the two, he was the most committed to a covenantal view of humanity and the universe.

We should not discount the influence of Hebraism on covenantal thought and the way the two informed the world in that century of transition from late medieval to early modern society, not only in the fields of politics and political science but throughout the scientific and indeed the intellectual world. This was especially true in the great English-speaking Atlantic commonwealths in Britain and North America, where the foundations were laid for a new constitutionalism grounded in the old even as it transformed the old, a constitutionalism that launched the world on the road to democracy.

The Eighteenth-Century Interlude

While politics in England for the first third of the eighteenth century was Whig politics, based on struggles between the court and country Whigs, covenantalism itself went into eclipse and federalism was nowhere on the horizon.[15] The union of England and Scotland in 1707 may be seen to have had federalist elements, but not in the minds of those who acheived it.

The Scottish Enlightenment picked up the slack and made its contribution at a critical moment in the history of the English-speaking world. It has been described as filtering Locke's compact through Pufendorf's continental natural law and original contract tradition. In essence, it began from that special Scottish view of covenantalism grounded in a mixture of civil and common law that had to find explicit theoretical ways in a Whig age by which to combine both. In doing so the leading figures of the Scottish enlightenment frequently lent themselves to non-covenantal interpretations, but underneath it all there remained a strong covenantal dimension, however secularized. This is even more apparent when their contribution to the political theory of the American Revolution is taken into account.

In a certain sense there were those active in the Scottish Enlightenment who directly continued the Scottish covenantal tradition. Andrew Fletcher, for example, not only tried to adapt the context of civic republicanism to the pursuit of wealth for the community so as to help Scotland escape from its collective poverty but he argued on behalf of a political solution to Scotland's difficulties by restoring its independent parliament and militia and then joining it in a federal union with England. This federal union with Great Britain would in turn become part of a general European system of federated states.

The better-known David Hume, despite his departures from Fletcher's thought, also projected this "idea of a perfect commonwealth" which was a federal republic, not dissimilar to that of his predecessor only more individualistic than the strict civic vision of the former that remained within the civic republican tradition.[16]

While Adam Smith moved beyond this civic tradition, he did so by absorbing parts of it within his own thought.[17] To cultivate virtue, Smith not only wanted empowerment but universal education.

The differences between Hume and Fletcher and then between Smith and Hume of course did not end with them. In the nineteenth century, Dugald Stewart shifted from his eighteenth-century predecessors. Stewart's conception of moral and civic virtue was no longer a concomitant one. Rather, he saw moral virtue as a precondition for political participation. Politics was to be for men of intellect as well as men of property,[18] thereby presenting an elitist perspective.

For our purposes here, what is important is the continuation of the combination in a Scottish yet nineteenth-century manner. In essence, what Stewart was proposing was that those who were entitled to be involved in public life had to have what the Germans called a *bildung*, that is to say, to be educated in the general culture of the mind. His students continued this line of thought. They, however, already were in the more formal mode of professional students of philosophy which emerged in the nineteenth century and was to become the trend of the century and even more so the next one, leading to the separation between academic philosophy and public affairs.

In the effort to precisely clarify the fundamental terms of philosophy, Stewart's student James MacIntosh, while moving in that direction, also found himself pulled to the religious considerations of the Reformed Protestant religion from whence he came and even toward the medievalist revival of the nineteenth century. In both cases he sought to demonstrate that those accepted views did not contradict the ones he put forward. This widespread and deep Scottish embrace of moral philosophy over the course of two centuries is in itself telling.

This situation did not change after the shift in British politics to a struggle between Whigs and Tories or, more accurately, Whig and Tory elites.

The opportunity of adopting a federalist position presented itself with regard to the British empire, with the development of Britain's North American colonies. From mid-century onward, if not earlier, the leaders of the thirteen American colonies in what is now the United States began to articulate a theory of imperial federalism whereby the British empire was deemed by them to be a federation of self-governing dominions headed by a common monarch. It was on this basis that the colonists rejected the authority of the British Parliament in matters not directly related to imperial defense, denied Parliament's power to levy taxes upon Britain's American dominions, and, after the American Revolution broke out, blamed the King, not Parliament, for allowing or stimulating the train of abuses listed in the American Declaration of Independence.[19] These ideas were explicitly rejected in England.

In a sense, these ideas were the application of British Whiggism to British territories overseas, an application that could not take root at home. Indeed, the American Revolution was seen by many at the time as the triumph of the Whig idea in British North America. It was no accident that loyalists to the Crown were called Tories, but even Whig supporters of the American cause in Britain did not accept the American theory of imperial federalism.

Hume and Burke: Is There or Isn't There a Political Compact?

Both noted eighteenth-century British philosophers were ambivalent about the idea of political compact. In the first place they were concerned with weaknesses in the covenantal approach, particularly in its secular derivatives, compacts, and contracts. In holding covenantal ideas up to the problems they found, whether intentionally or not they also sought ways to resolve those problems. This led them to useful sytheses of covenantal and other forms of political thought in an effort to find remedies for covenantal diseases.

David Hume (1711–1776), the Scottish philosopher and historian, in his skepticism not only rejects the origins of society in an original compact, but raises a greater logical question: namely, why are we bound to keep our promises? His answer, that the obligation to keep promises must be based on a preexisting law or simply on force, in a sense points out the weakness of secular compact theory, a weakness absent in covenantal thought. Hume does agree with Hobbes that promises must be kept if civil society is to exist. He developed a synthesis between common sense and faith to justify keeping them. Hume's critique then, must be seen as at least partly an implicit critique of secularism on the part of a non-religious Scot coming from a tradition with a strongly developed covenantal political theology and not as an attack on the covenant idea itself.

Edmund Burke (1729–1797), as a Whig, while making obeisance to the idea of a political compact, simultaneously reinterpreted it in a way that moved it in the direction of an expanded understanding that incorporated elements of an organic approach to the social order.

> Society is indeed a contract. Subordinate contracts for objects of mere occasional interest may be dissolved at pleasure—but the state ought not to be considered as nothing better than a partnership agreement in a trade of pepper and coffee, calico, or tobacco, or some other such low concern, to be taken up for a little temporary interest, and to be dissolved by the fancy of the parties. It is to be looked upon with other reverence; because it is not a partnership in things subservient only to the gross animal existence of a temporary and perishable nature. It is a partnership in all science; a partnership in all art; a partnership in every virtue, and in all perfection. As the ends of such a partnership cannot be obtained in many generations, it becomes a partnership not only between those who are living, but between those who are living, those who are dead, and those who are to be born. Each contract of each particular state is but a clause in the great primeval contract of eternal society, linking the lower with the higher natures, connecting the visible and invisible world, according to a fixed compact sanctioned by the inviolable oath which holds all physical and all moral natures, each in their appointed place.[20]

In that, perhaps the most oft-quoted paragraph of Burke's works, we have what is, in one sense, the fullest statement of secular compact theory, in its best English synthesis, one which, even as it diminishes mere contractarianism, brings it up to the level of covenantalism.

British Liberalism and the Federal Idea

Sometime in the generation after the fall of Napoleon, British Whiggism gave way to British liberalism. The end of Whiggism led to the partial demise and partial transformation of what remained of the covenantal tradition in Britain into a set of ideas and a political platform concerned with democratization, greater protection for individual rights, and capitalist economics based on free trade. The roots of all three might possibly be traced back to the older Whiggism and to the covenantal tradition but in their manifestations they usually took on very different dimensions.

By the nineteenth century what was left of the covenantal tradition was politically embodied in the Nonconformists who were particularly prominent in the ranks of the Whig, then the Liberal party. Religiously, there were four divisions among the Nonconformists: Congregational, Baptist, Presbyterian, and Methodist, the first three of which clearly grew out of the covenantal tradition. In 1896 congregations of these four groups came together to establish the National Council of Evangelical Free Churches and by 1901 there were 700 local Free Church councils.

By the end of the nineteenth century, Nonconformists had gained recognition with full rights in the realm although they failed in their effort to disestablish the Anglican Church. They also secured support for their own educational institutions. The great Liberal prime minister William Gladstone even stated that the Nonconformists were the backbone of British liberalism. The Nonconformists were also tied in with the British cooperative movement which, as in Scandinavia, attempted to rebuild society along humane federal principles in the economic and social realms. The Nonconformists also had a strong leaning toward imperial federalism as the way to transform the empire into a commonwealth of equals. Those who did not support imperial federalism saw liberalism and imperialism as contradictory and opposed the latter.

The Anglo-Boer War threw the Nonconformists into confusion. On one hand they were generally for peace and some sympathized with the rights of the Boers. Others, however pro-British, saw a war among Christians as outrageous. Still others saw the war as evil but a necessary evil. There were also some out and out imperialists, although they were a small group. Apparently, the Methodists were more supportive of the war than were the other three church unions, as reflected in the actions of their national council or their members. The Church of England, not surprisingly, continued to support government policy in South Africa throughout.

Just as Great Britain was overwhelmingly dominated in the nineteenth century by the idea of England and English ideas, so, too, was the attitude toward federalism in British thought essentially the English attitude. After their brief flirtation with covenantal thinking in the seventeenth century and their obeisance to the conventional ideas of political compact in the eighteenth (suitably redesigned, of course), English thinkers, under the influence of English traditions as much as nineteenth- century romanticism, turned back to their usual posture even denying the utility of political theory as such in designing political systems and governing them. This English conceit was dropped only on a functional basis; that is to say, in the latter half of the century there developed a group of imperial federalists, theorists who advocated transforming the British empire into a federal system in some way so as to preserve it in an increasingly democratic age. In their search for ways and means to do so they also explored the history and theory of federalism.

John Stuart Mill, the most noted British liberal political theorist of the nineteenth century, did write a chapter "Of Federal Representative Governments" in his *Considerations on Representative Government*,[21] and in his essay "On Liberty," but he was not a particular friend of federalism. He simply recognized it as a possible form of government, adopted out of necessity.

Far more important was Mill's equal in reputation, then and now, Lord Acton. He was a liberal, a Catholic, and a federalist, perhaps the most profound that England has produced. Unlike Mill, who accepted the conventional modern statist notion that the state and the nation must be coextensive with "national unity...the ideal of modern liberalism," Acton held that "the coexistence of several nations under the same state is...the best security of its freedom" and federation the "most efficacious and the most congenial of all the checks on centralized oppression of minorities."[22]

Neither Mill nor Acton went much beyond the practical political reasons for federalism. Nor did the British school of federalists, led by E.A. Freeman, whose *History of Federal Government in Greece and Italy* appeared in 1863.[23] Freeman intended to write a complete history of federal government, to be entitled "History of Federal Government, From the Foundation of the Achaean League to the Disruption of the United States," of which only this first part appeared before he died prematurely. Freeman also left his comments on the Constitution of the United States, which he saw as federalism's "perfect form," and a small discussion of Germany, plus references to Switzerland in the volumes that were published. His book remains a classic in the literature of federalism and he helped to establish federalism as a subject of academic study in Britain, but for all that he really did not get into the deeper intellectual roots behind federal arrangements.

Freeman influenced James Bryce, perhaps the most politically prominent of the Englishmen of the time interested in federalism, who visited the United States and wrote *The American Commonwealth*, an instant classic, much hailed but with many errors based on misleading information and improper observation. It, too, concentrated on what Bryce saw as the realities of federal government in the United States and not on the ideas behind it, which he missed almost entirely. Nevertheless, Bryce was sympathetic toward federalism.

Bryce's friends included Henry Sidgwick and A.V. Dicey; the first taught at Cambridge and the second at Oxford. Dicey explicitly rejected federalism on the grounds that any federal constitution had to rest upon a fundamental compact, which was incompatible with the English (organic) model and in any case would lead to problems of governing.[24]

Sidgwick, not quite as negative toward federalism as Dicey or his mentor John Stuart Mill, still was not a friend of federalism, though he wrote about it.

The fact that all of these British theorists wrote about "England" and not about Great Britain, essentially ignoring Scotland, Wales, and Ireland except insofar as they could not be ignored because of the problems they presented to England, tells us much about how they saw the United Kingdom. Indeed, their work brought English theories of the organic state into the nineteenth century and the modern epoch, specifically as well as generally. In general, the nineteenth-century English from Jeremy Bentham and John Austin through their neighbor, Mill, began with a very unitary view of sovereignty and were thus limited at the outset in any thinking they might have done about federalism, not to speak of covenants and compacts.

If liberal theorists had their doubts about federalism, liberal political leaders became partisans of the federal dimension in liberal thought when it came to writing constitutions for the British colonies, beginning with Canada in 1862. Indeed, they encouraged the development of a synthesis between Westminster parliamentary and federal government that would encompass both dimensions of liberal constitutional thought. Earl Grey had proposed federalism for Australia as early as 1846, although it was not until the 1890s that the idea took root there and led to the Australian Federation in 1900. The British liberals also sought federation for South Africa but, following the lead of the Afrikaner leaders of South Africa themselves, settled for parliamentary union on the United Kingdom model, ostensibly on the grounds of economy. Federalism was also proposed and even tried in New Zealand but abandoned, and for an Irish state within Great Britain which came close but which neither the English nor the Irish leadership really wanted.

In 1871 John Seeley, professor of modern history at Cambridge, in a series of lectures that were subsequently published, argued for European federal union and a federation of Britain and those of its self-governing colonies settled by British and other Europeans.[25] His writings inspired the Imperial Federation League that became attractive to many liberals, including Joseph Chamberlain and Alfred Milner.[26] Again, the purposes of federalism for those active in the League were tactical. All of these ideas remained in the realm of the structural and did not take into consideration cultural and political factors.

The reasons for the Imperial League's popularity in those circles that supported it and its inability to provoke interest beyond them lie in its adoption and internalization of the principles of federal constitutionalism. The idea of a written constitution linking separate polities on the basis of full equality was strange to English ears. Moreover, to the extent that the idea was designed to develop a means for imperial defense, that could be achieved without federation, when the dominions rallied to the cause of the mother country unstintingly. In truth, even many of the League's leaders were uncomfortable with the term federation, so un-English, and were continually explaining it away. In the end the League faltered on the combination of lack of interest on the part of the dominions that were rapidly moving toward their own self-definition and the English fear of federalism, what Michael Burgess, a great partisan of the federal idea in Great Britain today, describes as "a word which the British have traditionally loathed."[27]

The League did come up with its federal plan of 1892, which emphasized customs union and the sharing of the burden of imperial defense. Burgess describes it as a pyrrhic victory. By supporting a particular scheme, they opened themselves to rejection. In April 1893 Gladstone, then British prime minister, rejected their plan and their request for a conference. By the end of the year the League had collapsed.

The next generation of British federalists was led by Sir Ernest Barker, an Oxford graduate who later taught at his *alma mater* and ended up as professor of political science at Cambridge in 1928. He became a federalist, apparently as a result of the bankruptcy of European statism which he, like many others, came to recognize in World War I. Perhaps because he was less optimistic, he became a deeper student of federalism and to a certain degree was able to rediscover its covenantal roots. He and his school were influenced by Gierke's conceptions of pluralism, Acton, and the Proudhonians of France.

Harold Laski, who later became the intellectual leader of the British Labour party, was a student of Barker's and was much influenced by Barker's ideas prior to the Great Depression, when Laski shifted his ground. Laski, who also was shaped by a certain covenantal influence, even if submerged, from his Jewish background, pursued federal ideas in his *Studies in the Problem of Sovereignty, The Foundations of Sovereignty and Other Essays* and finally in his better known *A Grammar of Politics*.[28] However, as he became more of a Marxist he first deferred the possibilities of federalism until after the class struggle had been won and finally under the weight of the Great Depression came to the conclusion that federalism was obsolete.[29]

The breadth of Barker's thought, like that of Acton before him, was exceptional. However, even his star pupil Laski never passed beyond the conventional issues of federalism: governance and sovereignty. With Laski's defection, two generations of interest in federalism, even minority interest, ended. With the exception of Acton and Barker, none of the English federalists ever discovered the tradition from whence federalism came, seeing it only as a governmental technique or structure and at best lukewarm about that.

Meanwhile, more recent researchers into the history of the federal idea in Britain have concluded that "British federalism is an Irish invention."[30] While there is some measure of exaggeration in that, it seems that nineteenth-century British federal thought was stimulated by Irish recommendations for a federal Britain in the 1830s, formulated by Daniel O'Connell and William Sharman Crawford, the first a Catholic leader of Irish demands and the second a prominent Protestant landlord in Ireland. Nor were the Irish the only source of British federal thought. Federalist movements also appeared among the Welsh and the Scottish. Lloyd George himself flirted with federalism for Wales in the 1890s.

In the last gasp of liberal interest in federalism, Phillip Kerr, Lord Lothian, was in the vanguard of a new wave of those who sought federal arrangements to preserve world peace. Some measure of his understanding of federalism can be seen in the fact that he was also part of the British establishment that could not take Hitler seriously enough in the 1930s and supported the appeasement of the Nazi government to preserve peace. These externally oriented federalists had enough of an impact to bring Winston Churchill to offer federal union to France in June 1940 to prevent its falling into German hands, but it was precisely the superficial character of these federal ideas that became evident as people tried to form them into practical suggestions.

Notes

1. Published anonymously as: "or, a discourse wherein is presented to the view of the Magistrate, and all others which will peruse the same, a frame of government by way of a republique" (London: printed for live will, Chapman, 1659). Its thesis is based on the idea that the Harringtonian commonwealth can be implemented within six days, hence the process of implementation on a day by day basis, thoroughly reminiscent of biblical creation only with men as its architects rather than God and so embodied his constitutional proposals, saving and reforming the commonwealth rather than restoring the monarchy in England, a model of a democratic government of modest and "practical" work, but one that emphasized republicanism.
2. Samuel Hutchinson Beer, *To Make a Nation: The Rediscovery of American Federalism* (Cambridge, Mass.: The Belknap Press, 1993).
3. James Cotton, "The Harringtonian 'Party' (1659–1660) and Harrington's Political Thought," *History of Political Thought*, vol. 1, no. 1 (Spring 1980):51–67.
4. See Charles Blitzer, *Harrington: His Political Writings, Representative Selections* (Indianapolis, Ind.: Bobbs-Merrill, 1955), p. xi; chapter on Harrington in Samuel Beer, *To Make a Nation*.
5. James Rees Jones *The First Whigs: The Politics of the Exclusion Crisis, 1678–1683* (London: Oxford University Press, 1961); Kenneth H.D. Haley, *The First Earl of Shaftesbury* (London: Oxford University Press, 1968); J.R. Western, *Monarchy and Revolution: The English State in the 1680s* (Totowa, N.J.: Rowman and Littlefield, 1972); J.H. Plum, *The Growth of Political Stability in England, 1675–1725* (London: Macmillan, 1967); J.P. Kenyon, *Revolution Principles: The Politics of Parties, 1689–1720* (Cambridge: Cambridge University Press, 1977).
6. Mark Goldie, "The Roots of True Whiggism, 1688–94," *Political Thought*, vol. 1, no. 2 (Summer/June 1980).
7. Gertrude Himmelfarb: *Lord Acton: A Study in Conscience and Politics* (San Francisco, Cal.: ICS Press, 1993).
8. Goldie, "The Roots of True Whiggism," p. 206.
9. Algernon Sydney, *Discourses Concerning Government*, Thomas G. Wert, ed. (Indianapolis, Ind.: Liberty Classics, 1990).
10. Goldie, "The Roots of True Whiggism," pp. 212–13.
11. *Ibid.*, p. 220.
12. J.C. Davis, "Radicalism in a Traditional Society: The Evaluation of Radical Thought in the English Commonwealth, 1649–1660," *History of Political Thought*, vol. III, no. 2 (Summer 1982):193–213. This article is written from a contemporary radical perspective. I am indebted to it less for its conclusions than for the questions it raises.
13. Leon Roth, "Hebraists and Non-Hebraists of the Seventeenth Century," *Journal of Semitic Studies*, vol. VI (Autumn 1961):204–21.
14. Abraham Berkowitz, "John Selden and the Biblical Origins of the Modern International Political System," *Jewish Political Studies Review*, vol. 6, nos. 1–2.
15. Reed Browning, *Political and Constitutional Ideas of the Court Whigs* (Baton Rouge: Louisiana State University Press, 1982).
16. John Robertson, "Scottish Political Economy Beyond the Civic Tradition: Government and Economic Development in the Wealth of Nations," *History of Political Thought*, vol. IV, no. 3 (Winter 1983):451–82.
17. Nicholson Phillipson, "Adam Smith a Civic Moralist," in *Wealth and Virtue: J.R. Lindgren, the Social Philosophy of Adam Smith* (The Hague, 1973); J.G.A.

Pocock, "Virtue, Rights and Manners: A Model for Historians of Political Thought," *Political Theory* 9 (1981); J.G.A. Pocock, "Cambridge Paradigms and Scotch Philosophers," in *Wealth and Virtue: The Shaping of Political Economy in the Scottish Enlightenment,* Istvan Hont and Michael Ignatieff, eds. (Cambridge: Cambridge University Press, 1983).

18. Knud Haakonssen, "The Science of a Legislator in James MacKintosh's Moral Philosophy," *History of Political Thought,* vol. 5, no. 2 (Summer 1984):245–80.

19. Carl Becker, *The Declaration of Independence* (New York: Alfred A. Knopf, 1953).

20. Edmund Burke, *Reflections on the Revolution in France,* Thomas H.D. Mahoney, ed. (New York: The Liberal Arts Press, 1955), pp. xxiv–xxv.

21. John Stuart Mill, *On Liberty and Other Essays* (Oxford: Oxford University Press. 1991).

22. Lord Acton, *The History of Freedom and Other Essays* (London: Macmillan, 1907).

23. Edward A. Freeman, *History of Federal Government in Greece and Italy,* J. B. Bury, ed. (London and New York: Macmillan and Co., 1893).

24. Albert V. Dicey, *Introduction to the Study of the Law of the Constitution* (London: Macmillan, 1952).

25. John Seeley, "The United States of Europe," *Macmillan's Magazine,* vol. 23, March 1871.

26. Vladimir Halperin, *Lord Milner and the Empire: The Evolution of British Imperialism* (London: Odhams Press, Ltd., 1952); John Kendle, *The Round Table Movement and Imperial Union* (Toronto: University of Toronto Press, 1975); Michael M.L. Graham, *Britain and Joseph Chamberlain* (London: G. Allen and Unwin, 1985).

27. Michael Burgess, "The Federal Plan of the Imperial Federation League, 1892: Milestone or Tombstone" in *The Federal Idea: The History of Federalism from Enlightenment to 1945,* vol. I, Andrea Bosco, ed. (London: Lothian Foundation Press, 1991); Michael Burgess, "Empire, Ireland and Europe: A Century of British Federal Ideas," in *Federalism and Federation in Western Europe,* Michael Burgess, ed. (London: Croom Helm, 1986).

28. Harold Laski, *Studies in the Problem of Sovereignty* (London: G. Allen and Unwin, 1968); *The Foundation of Sovereignty and Other Essays* (New York: Harcourt Brace, 1924); *A Grammar of Politics* (London: George Allen and Unwin, 1967).

29. Harold Laski, "Is Federalism Obsolete?" *Cooperation and Conflict: Readings in American Federalism,* Daniel J. Elazar et al., eds. (Itasca, Ill.: F.E. Peacock Publishers, 1969).

30. George Boyce, "Federalism and the Irish Question," in Andrea Boscoe, *The Federal Idea,* p. 119.

4

From Tocqueville to Personalism: Covenant and its Displacement in Post-Revolutionary European Thought

By the time of Bentham and Hegel, theories of political compact had been replaced in political philosophy by theories of the organic state. What remained from the seventeenth-century revolution was the idea that human will or consent was the underlying principle of civil society or the state. That principle was to have its own historical development in the nineteenth century, becoming increasingly radical in its detachment of humankind from heaven. In the end, will without covenant was to open the door to the horrors of the twentieth century by giving those horrors a priori philosophic justification.

Still, theories, even if no longer in fashion, do not die. Throughout the nineteenth century there were those who were willing to keep the ideas of covenant, political compact, and social contract alive, even if only apologetically. Meanwhile, the organic theories of the state, which emphasized the triumph of will, gave rise first to racism in the late nineteenth century and then to twentieth-century totalitarianism. Both were rejected in the aftermath of the *Gotterdammerung* of World War II.

One exception during that period demonstrated the rule. Woodrow Wilson, who as a political scientist did so much to introduce the organic theory to replace the covenantal-compactual political thought of the American founding fathers,[1] went back to his Presbyterian roots when, as president of the United States, he proposed a new basis for international order, including a new kind of diplomacy of "open covenants, openly arrived at" and a new international organization, the League of Nations, to be established by covenant. The former principle was either ignored or laughed out of court by the Old World powers, while the latter, rejected by his own United States, was made a mockery in the interwar generation by the rest of the world.

Otherwise, theoretical concern with the covenantal tradition in the nineteenth century increasingly became confined to discussions of federalism and ever more narrow ones at that. The exceptions were the French, probably

81

because they were so far removed from federalism in practice that they could afford to stay with grand theoretical ideas.

Tocqueville Discovers America

The French, who did not come out of a covenantal tradition (the Huguenots had assimilated or been exiled by the late seventeenth century), actually came closer to drawing upon that tradition or some variant of it in the nineteenth century than ever before or since. The two major figures in question were Alexis de Tocqueville and Pierre-Joseph Proudhon. Of the two Tocqueville was the more profound and the more covenantal. Tocqueville increasingly is being recognized as one of the greatest political and social thinkers of the nineteenth century, the only one to produce a body of systematic thought that rivals that of Marx in depth and profundity, and far exceeds Marx in accuracy. Only in the last generation have scholars and thinkers, led by Tocquevillian "schools" in France and the United States, begun to probe the real depth and significance of Tocqueville's thought.

On his visit to the United States, Tocqueville discovered how much the American system of federal democratic republicanism rested on a covenantal base, and while in the end he concluded that it was in many respects uniquely American and could not see it applied *as such* to France, he treated it very admiringly in *Democracy in America*.[2] He then went on to treat the Swiss, another covenantal people, less admiringly but still, on the whole, positively. The covenantal part of his teaching often has been overlooked in the mid-twentieth-century rediscovery of Tocqueville's teaching and needs to be drawn out, since the influence of the covenantal tradition on his thought seems to have been more profound than most current commentators on Tocqueville have recognized.

Tocqueville's writing on federalism, particularly *Democracy in America*, is the principal vehicle through which to reach into his larger system of thought. That is not without significance. The fact that what Tocqueville himself defines as democracy in America is presented as federal democracy, with particular emphasis on the states and localities and the relations between them and their citizens, should be seen as a direction-finder of major significance. Moreover, Tocqueville's linking of "the spirit of religion and the spirit of liberty" in the United States at the very opening of his magnum opus, and his emphasis on the New England states as paradigmatic of America, should point us toward an understanding of his recognition of the covenantal roots of American federal democracy in Reformed Protestantism.

Keeping in mind the three models for the organization of the polity presented earlier, the structure of *Democracy in America* becomes especially revealing. Tocqueville sees that, unlike the hierarchical and organic models, the covenantal model rests on the principle of equality properly understood. In the very first sentence of his introduction, he indicates that *Democracy in America* is to be a book about the greatest society and polity known to him to have been founded on the covenantal model. Visualize how Tocqueville's opening and continuing emphasis on the role of equality in the United States would resound to his French readers, living in a country far removed from covenantal foundations. Indeed, in the sixth paragraph and for the next several pages he draws the contrast between the United States and France on this matter.

In an echo of *The Federalist*, intended or not, he describes the hierarchical France of the Middle Ages as founded and controlled by force, at first the only possible means of control. Tocqueville describes the subsequent development of France as an organic modification of a hierarchy imposed by force. Tocqueville tells the reader: "The gradual progress of equality is something fated" (p. 5), but that in the Old World it is through an evolutionary process periodically punctured by revolutionary steps, whereas in the New World it was present at the birth of a new society. Like the other moderns, Tocqueville makes it plain that God can be discovered through reason and not only through revelation, and that the New World needs a new political science.

Tocqueville concludes his introduction with a description of the discontents of the Old World civilization of his time:

Men of religion fight against freedom, and lovers of liberty attack religion; noble and generous spirits praise slavery, while low, servile minds preach independence; honest and enlightened citizens are the enemies of all progress, while men without patriotism or morals make themselves the apostles of civilization and enlightenment!"[3]

He then contrasts the hierarchical and organic Europe that he and his compatriots had inherited with the covenantal United States:

The emigrants who colonized America at the beginning of the seventeenth century in some way separated the principle of democracy from all those other principles against which they contended when living in the heart of the old European societies, and transplanted that principle only on the shores of the New World. It could there grow in freedom and, progressing in conformity with mores, develop peacefully within the law.[4]

Tocqueville uses his descriptive analysis of this new society and the land that has brought it forth to illustrate what he looks toward as the good commonwealth:

A society in which all men, regard the law as their common work, but love it and submit to it without difficulty; the authority of the government would be respected as necessary, not as sacred; the love felt toward the head of the state would not be a passion but a common rational feeling. Each man having some rights and being sure of the enjoyment of those rights, there would be established between all classes a manly confidence and a sort of reciprocal courtesy as far removed from pride as from servility.[5]

After giving us a brief tour of the physical geography of North America, which he views admiringly, and presenting his theory that societies, like individuals, are most shaped and influenced by their foundings, Tocqueville then takes us to look at what he considers the essence of the American experience, namely, New England.[6] Tocqueville indicates that he did not simply stumble onto New England by happenstance, but that after starting his contacts in the United States with federal officialdom, he chose to dwell on the development of democracy in America through the New England experience. We can see how he saw New England, in a manner consistent with his understanding of the matrix model, as the most complete and best articulated expression of that model.

In the 1830s, when it was visited by Tocqueville, New England still lived consciously within the basic elements of its covenantal history. Tocqueville explains and justifies his choice in book I, chapter 2, stating that "it was in the English colonies of North America, better known as the states of New England, that the two or three main principles now forming the basic theory of the United States were combined," (p. 29) and "It was from there that those principles spread throughout the United States."

Moreover, the foundation of New England was "something new in the world" (p. 29) because it was founded by people who were willing to face "the inevitable sufferings of exile" because "they hoped for the triumph of *an idea* [Tocqueville's emphasis]." Tocqueville describes the Puritans who founded New England and their idea: "Puritanism was not just a religious doctrine; in many respects it shared the most absolute democratic and republican theories" (p. 30).

To demonstrate his point, Tocqueville brings quotations from contemporary New England historians describing the founding of Massachusetts two centuries earlier. It is important to note that the quotations that he chooses are those that tie the New England founding and the Puritan experience to that of the ancient Israelites as demonstrated in the Bible, quoting liberally from Scripture, citing chapter and verse. Tocqueville no doubt purposely quotes from a historian who treats the early history of New England as sacred history.[7]

He is obviously touched by the fact that Plymouth Rock where the Pilgrims landed, is a place of veneration and that he has seen fragments of the rock

carefully preserved in several American cities.... Does not that clearly prove that man's power and greatness resides in entirely in his soul? A few poor souls trod for an instant on this rock and it has become famous; it is prized by a great nation; fragments are venerated, and tiny pieces distributed far and wide. What has become of the doorsteps of a thousand palaces? Who cares about them. (p. 31)

Tocqueville then quotes the Mayflower Compact, wherein the Pilgrims "in the presence of God and one another, covenant and combine ourselves

together into a civil body politic" (from the Plymouth Combination or Mayflower Compact, as it is now known). Tocqueville understood this to be what
the Pilgrims said it was; in a footnote he indicates that the founders of Rhode
Island, New Haven, Connecticut and Providence in the year 1631 to 1640 all
began with similar documents (which Tocqueville refers to in the familiar
French terminology as social contracts), which were "submitted for approval
to every person concerned." Tocqueville also notes that the Puritans were
essentially from the middle classes, which further strengthened their commitment to democracy based on equality and liberty.

Tocqueville describes how the New England settlers set themselves up
as independent for all intents and purposes from the beginning. "One continually finds them exercising rights of sovereignty; they appointed magistrates, made peace and war, promulgated police regulations and enacted
laws as if they were dependent on God alone" (p. 34). In illustration he
liberally cites from the Connecticut Code of Laws of 1650, which consisted
of two parts: one, a series of provisions which he describes as "taken word
for word from Deuteronomy, Exodus or Leviticus" (p. 35), and the second,
the constitution or civil compact entered into by the three founding towns
that established Connecticut (as a federation) in 1638–39. But Tocqueville
also describes the democracy, equality and liberty in civil and political affairs in Connecticut from that time. His whole tone is approving, even when
he seems a little incredulous, especially approving when he cites the provisions requiring each town to provide facilities of public education, the preamble of which he quotes in full, concluding: "In America it is religion
which leads to enlightenment and the observance of divine laws which leads
men to liberty" (p. 38).

If this were not sufficient to make his position clear, Tocqueville quotes
from Cotton Mather's *Magnalia Christi Americana* selections from John
Winthrop's speech contrasting federal and natural liberty, introducing it by
writing: "In that unconsidered democracy which had as yet produced neither generals, nor philosophers, nor great writers, a man could stand up in
front of a free people and gain universal applause for this fine definition of
freedom." Tocqueville's precise excerpt from Winthrop's speech is also
enlightening:

> Nor would I have you to mistake in the point of your own *liberty*. There is a
> *liberty* of corrupt nature, which is affected by *men* and *beasts* to do what they list;
> and this *liberty* is inconsistent with *authority*, impatient of all restraint; by this
> *liberty*, *sumus omnes deteriores*, 'tis the grand enemy of *truth* and *peace*, and all
> the ordinances of God are bent against it. But there is a civil, a moral, a federal
> *liberty*, which is the proper end and object of *authority*; it is a *liberty* for that only
> which is *just* and *good*; for this *liberty* you are to stand with the hazard of your
> very *lives*...this *liberty* is maintained in a way of *subjection* to *authority*; and the
> *authority* that over you will in all administrations for your good be quietly sub-
> mitted unto, by all but such as have a disposition to *shake off the yoke*, and lose
> their true *liberty*, by their murmuring at the honor and power of *authority*.

Tocqueville concludes this second part of the introduction of his theme as follows:

> I have already said enough to put Anglo-American civilization in its true light. It is the product (and one should continually bear in mind this point of departure) of two perfectly distinct elements which elsewhere have often been at war with one another but which in America it was somehow possible to incorporate into each other, forming a marvelous combination. I mean the *spirit of religion* and the *spirit of freedom*. The rest of democracy in America essentially plays out these themes and their successes, their failures, their weaknesses, their promises, and their threats.

Tocqueville emerges as a sober friend of modern democratic republicanism as long as it can be held to the federal principles of its conception regarding religion, liberty, and the organization of government as well as equality.

In the United States Tocqueville is usually read only in connection with his analysis of democracy in America. Tocqueville's place in political thought is much greater than that. Moreover, that place rests upon his argument on behalf of the covenantal tradition in politics as essential to the achievement of the highest political and social goals in the modern world and otherwise.

Tocqueville explicitly noted that Americans are not only animated by civic virtue but by interests that are balanced by the political system. As an observer, he recognized the effectiveness of this in the United States, albeit only to a degree. However, he did not recommend that system as an adequate substitute for civic virtue. He simply noted that in the unique physical conditions of the United States it worked. The boundlessness of the American continent offered opportunities for almost unlimited private aggrandizement that would give rise neither to mass jealousy nor mass deprivation. Other polities, less rich, required a larger measure of civic virtue to achieve that. More than that, Tocqueville, noting the natural tendencies toward centralization fully present among Americans as among others, argued that such civic virtue was necessary even in the United States for the preservation of provincial liberty which in turn was necessary for the preservation of the kind of politics and society to which Tocqueville aspired for humanity.

Tocqueville was a national federalist, that is, he believed that federalism was best when it was used to unite and govern single nations on the basis of consent and constitutionalized noncentralization or decentralization.[8] This can be understood by contrasting his writings on the United States and Switzerland; his great appreciation of the former, albeit soberly and with doubts about the future of American society, and his initial doubts about Switzerland as what he called "a league of independent states," and later greater appreciation after the Swiss reconstitution from confederation to federation in 1848. When we view his discussions of these two federal systems in light of his discussions of France, we can see that in the terms used in this book Tocqueville was interested in countries organized on the matrix model precisely because he came from a country so rooted in the hierarchical one, that his interest for humanity was to foster the matrix model; and, for France, to learn how to transform a hierarchical model polity and society into a covenantal one constituted and organized as a matrix.

Tocqueville was concerned not only with achieving that change but with what its consequences would be. In this and other respects he understood that France and most of the rest of Europe had to adapt properly to modernity, and that the United States was the quintessential modern civil society because of its covenantal-matrix character. That is why Tocqueville and Tocquevillean thought can and should be seen as the alternative to Marx and Marxism. It is also why he teaches about the limits of democracy, that democracy unrestrained by constitutional federalism will lead to governmental and administrative centralization and totalitarian despotism. Understanding people as he does, this leads him to no little pessimism about the future. Covenantally rooted systems and their derivatives suffer from the same problems in modernity that they suffered from in the past. They go against certain natural penchants of humans, whether in those systems' efforts to establish federal as against natural liberty or in their efforts to prevent the operation of the iron law of oligarchy. Both of those natural movements rest on human passions and both lead in the last analysis to centralization and despotism. Occasionally or periodically there are moments in history when humans take themselves in hand and invent, discover or rediscover ways and means to harness the unbridled expression of their passions through covenant and federalism, but, as Tocqueville notes, those moments pass. If their founding covenantal-federalistic movement was strong enough, its residue restrains polity and society for a greater number of subsequent generations.

Tocqueville saw centralization as the fate of France but he suggested a way in which centralization and despotism could be prevented by combining federalism, the separation of powers, the checking power of voluntary associations and institutions (including interest groups), and strong local government, but all four of those factors must be present and operating effectively.

Tocqueville was writing in the nineteenth century two hundred years after the basic covenantal-compactual theories of modernity had been established and two generations after the great revolutions of modernity. Therefore, he was concerned with what was needed to enhance and preserve the achievements of modernity and what were likely to be the forces operating against them. If Tocqueville was pessimistic about the outcome in the United States as well as in France, half an epoch later we can understand why.

Proudhon Emphasizes Equilibrium

The other great French federalist of the nineteenth century was Pierre-Joseph Proudhon, who sought to wed his particular vision of socialism to an equally particularistic vision of political federation. Proudhon's thought was based on his understanding of the Kantian idea of mutual respect and his (Proudhon's) own perception of society as based on contract or compact. Proudhon sees those contracts as occurring between groups rather than individuals and involving both economic and political relationships.[9]

Proudhon was concerned about the problems of exchange in capitalist society rather than production, and sought to build a system which would be based on reciprocity of service. Proudhon's theory of mutuality can be said to accept a bargaining society but one in "which all relationships between the constituent parts are arranged contractually."[10]

This mutuality and its economic basis contributed to the theory of cooperation that animated the cooperative movement (itself a product of the nineteenth century) the theory of guild socialism, and ultimately philosophic anarchism.

Proudhon started by advocating the abolition of the state but said later that he moved from pure anarchism to accepting the idea of political federation, though Nelson argues that he never really rejected his anarchist premises. All of this was based on an opposition to hierarchy which Proudhon rightly recognized that, however functional, would subordinate one person to another and make human equality impossible. Proudhon even criticized his contemporary, Saint-Simon, who looked favorably on the idea of a hierarchy of talent as the foundation for a proper political social system. Proudhon responded: "A hierarchy of talent is still a hierarchy."[11]

In familiar nineteenth-century fashion Proudhon saw politics as subordinate to economics, with the latter essential and the former only instrumental. Thus he saw federalism as a political arrangement that was advantageous because it could protect mutualist social practice with minimum exercise of governmental authority. In a federation, government would perform only those functions that would not impede social autonomies or the autonomy of what Proudhon referred to as natural groups. The key term for him was mutualism. Nelson emphasizes that Proudhon also used the dialectical method,[12] one that does not lead to synthesis in the Marxist sense but, rather, seeks an equilibrium that does not suppress the polarities from which it starts. In other words, it is a dialectic of equilibrium in which all the parts are maintained, instead of synthesis in which the previous contradictions disappear.

It is important to note that, at least inadvertently, Proudhon defines the relationship between the three models of the polity in ways very similar to those of this book. Thus, to him, monarchy and communism are natural political systems while democracy and self-government (or anarchy) are spiritual forms, that is, require artificial effort to achieve.[13]

Yves Simon, an authoritative interpreter of Proudhon, claims that Proudhon was clearly an anarchist in the original meaning of the term, which Simon gives as "a regime in which social order is established in the absence of all government."[14]

Yet Proudhon recognizes that there is no way to live without authority in some form. Federalism was his solution since it would establish a contractual equilibrium between authority and liberty, not only allowing for authority but limiting it.

Anarchy for Proudhon is the reduction of political functions to industrial ones so that they will lead to a social order based on transactions and exchanges.[15]

Contracts—real contracts, not the hypothetical one of Rousseau and Kant—can and should bring about equilibrium between opposite principles on the basis of equal relationships. As one would expect, Proudhon overall is critical of Rousseau and sees him as the source of the Jacobin idea of the unitary state. Proudhon is the enemy of the Jacobins and whatever form they want their state to take. He makes a special effort to separate his federative contract from the Rousseauean social contract. Proudhon, who did not have the advantage of coming from a civil society influenced by the covenantal tradition, came to the conclusion that morally based contracts (he used the word accepted in French thought since the time of Rousseau) were the bases of the world he wanted to design.

Personalism: A Twentieth Century Continuation

Federalism next reappeared in France after World War I, in many respects as a result of the disillusionment with that conflict on the part of so many people. It took the form of integral federalism or personalism, a philosophy developed primarily by Frenchmen of Jewish background and French-speaking Swiss operating within the French philosophic tradition. Ultimately its leaders were Robert Aron, Denis de Rougement, and Alexandre Marc.

At the beginning of the movement's history, it was also influenced by a group of ultra-conservative figures who emphasized the organic elements in integral federalism just as the others emphasized its federal elements. The latter became French Fascists in the 1930s and were among the founders of the Vichy regime after the French defeat at the hands of Nazi Germany in 1940. Henceforth, they abandoned whatever interest in federalism they had ever displayed and became its enemies.

Integral federalism was renamed personalism by the very anti-fascist federalists in the 1930s and its leaders became active in the French Resistance during World War II. Thus personalism was born in the 1930s as a result of the economic crises of the Great Depression, on the one hand, and the political crises of Fascism and Nazism on the other. In addition to the three aforementioned figures, Karl Barth, Jacques Maritain, and Martin Buber were identified with personalism from the 1930s onward. The founders of personalism traced their ideas back to Proudhon. They wished to escape what they believed was the Jacobin-inspired atomization of society which led on one hand to the absolutist state and on the other to an individualism of disintegration. Denis de Rougement formulated the idea as follows: "The cement of the totalitarian states is made of the dust of individuals."[16]

In essence, personalism was an attempt to reestablish commonwealth in place of civil society, albeit without the traditional religious basis. Modern civil society seemed to be unable to sustain itself and so, through a covenantal system, the personalists sought to rebuild the characteristics of earlier organic society in modern form in which people would be integrated with one another and with their environment on the moral basis of consent. Opposing and abjuring centralization and atomization both, they saw in federalism the possibility of doing so, especially a federalism of the Althusian variety.

The personalists argued that they believed in praxis rather than theory.[17] Not surprisingly, then, after World War II they became advocates of a United States of Europe and lobbyists for it, organizing the Centre International de Formation Europeanne (CIFE), founding its periodical *L'Europe en Formation*, and establishing a graduate educational program at the University of Nice to promote their ideas. CIFE established branches throughout Western Europe. While Alexandre Marc settled in Nice, where he was the founder of these instrumentalities, his partner Denis de Rougement returned to Geneva and established the Centre European pour Culture, an institute half political and half aesthetic in its orientation, dedicated to promoting the same ends. CIFE established a summer school for federalism in Aosta, in Italy, to bring university students to the federal idea, especially as it applied to Europe.

CIFE's demands were more than the Europeans of the 1950s could absorb and, moreover, they were outside of the European ideological mainstream, so even as Europe moved toward greater integration the Personalists were pushed aside. They continued in their advocacy role and added a research dimension, probing especially into the idea of federalism and the reconstitution of Europe as a "Europe of [substate] regions."[18] In the 1970s, they joined with the academic students of federalism led by this writer and the Center for the Study of Federalism at Temple University in Philadelphia, Pennsylvania, to establish the International Association of Centers for Federal Studies, today an international body embracing all of the extant centers for federalism studies throughout the world, with member institutes from every inhabited continent. Most of the institutes in IACFS are interested in the empirical workings of federalism and perhaps in the political idea of federalism rather than the political goals of CIFE, whose role is consequently limited. Meanwhile, Alexandre Marc, the only surviving founder, celebrated his 90th birthday in 1994, still as vigorously committed to his philosophy as ever, but the movement seems to have spent most of its energy. Marc refers to the federalism of civil society as polyvalent federalism which he considers an advanced form of federalism but not as advanced as integral federalism.[19]

Integral federalists claimed, like Marxists, to be "scientific" and, like other twentieth century systems of thought, to be futuristic as well. They, too, tried to be comprehensive. De Rougement made his reputation writing about love as well as about politics.[20]

It is also "truly socialistic," according to its adherents. Libertarian socialism is another term they have used, a theme particularly developed by Martin Buber in *Paths in Utopia*.[21] Marc's sucessor at CIFE, Ferdinand Kinsky describes Personalism as seeking "to reestablish the equilibrium between the four dialectical tensions of man confronted with the world, his neighbor, society and destiny."[22] It is the recognition of these dialectical tensions and the need to develop an equilibrium between them that leads Personalism to federalism as the means to do so without falling into an overly individualistic liberalism.

Personalism is deliberately antimaterialist and sees itself as rooted in the European religious tradition, a Catholic Christian formulation, which in turn is rooted in biblical monotheism. The most recent Personalist writings have emphasized the connection between Personalism and the Judeo-Christian vision. In the last analysis, this makes Martin Buber the greatest of the Personalist philosophers in the sense that he is the most comprehensive and articulated, this without denigrating the philosophic contributions of de Rougement and Marc.

Personalism, then, is an effort to avoid the extremes of individualism, or collectivism, by recognizing every person as an individual linked to a community and indeed obligated to be so linked. Although Personalists do not speak explicitly of the covenant or the covenantal tradition, they seem to have discovered the same obligational requisites that have animated the issues of individual, community, and polity in the covenantal tradition since biblical times. Martin Buber seems to have been the one person identified with the Personalist movement who made that linkage explicit.[23] Alexandre Marc was influenced by the Workshop in Covenant and Politics of the Center for the Study of Federalism while visiting there in the 1970s and subsequently added covenant to his philosophical vocabulary. Through him and his disciple, Ferdinand Kinsky, Proudhonian federalism was finally integrated with the covenantal tradition directly.

Since World War II, the French federalist tradition has been more pragmatic and less given to federal theorizing, no doubt because the possibilities of federalism have become more real since World War II and are embodied in real institutions, most especially the European Community, now European Union. The issues that drew activists and thinkers are practical issues of politics and governance rather than theoretical issues of covenant, compact, and contract. Like the United States after 1787, the theoretical discussions are being put behind the Western Europeans and federalism is becoming more a matter of the nuts and bolts of intergovernmental relations, whether in the covenantal tradition or not.

German Theories of Federalism

While French political thinkers were belatedly finding their way to the covenant idea, German thinkers were trying to reshape federalism on organic lines in line with the German romantic quest for restoring organic society on the basis of what to them were the even more real medieval foundations, complete with physiological or biological analogies, to describe, *inter alia*, their dreams of the "reunification" of the German body, politic and social. This was so even where they related to the covenantal traditions of the past, as Gierke did in his resurrection of Althusius. They looked for the organic motifs that could be discovered in those earlier German political philosophers.

In German, too, there is an extensive literature on federalism in the nineteenth century, replacing earlier discussions of confederal or political compact. It is ponderous, heavily legalistic, and preoccupied with the great federal question of modern German unification, namely, the difference between a *Bundestat* (a federal state) and a *Staatenbund* (a confederation). Only a few of the German thinkers who wrote on the subject rose above those ponderous and rigid issues, in particular, Otto von Gierke, George Simmel, and Ferdinand Toennies. Despite the differences between them, all displayed substantial nostalgia for the premodern organic community, which they saw as being a *gemeinshaft*. Gierke was most taken by what he saw as the richness of the Middle Ages, with all of its autonomous freely associating bodies that were destroyed by the modern state.[24]

Toennies was the one who drew the explicit distinction between *gemeinschaft* and *gesellschaft*, the presumably close and integrated communities of preindustrial society and the complex and alienating postindustrial societies.[25] Toennies was not interested in political arrangements, so if there is any federalism in his work it is as a social arrangement only. Another German social philosopher of this type was George Simmel. Simmel too was primarily a sociologist who looked at the differences in communally autonomous communities and modern societies.[26]

The German political discussion of federalism reached its apogee between 1830 and 1870 among the radical traditionalist Hegelians, who by that time had divided into philosophical camps, both of which came under the influence of historicism.[27]

Political federalism in Germany was held by these theorists to date back at least to the fourteenth century and was seen to be spiritually legitimized on the basis of the covenant between God and the emperor of the Holy Roman Empire. Needless to say, the political discussion revolved around the issue of sovereignty, the least helpful issue around which to discuss questions of federalism. Since that was where the Hegelians pushed it, the practical impact of these discussions was minimal. Count Otto von Bismarck, the architect of German unification, designed the post-1870 German federation based on his pragmatic and politically realistic assessments of the interests of Prussia in light of the situation in Germany. These theories had more of an effect on the designers of the contemporary German federation after 1945.

Gorner argues that preeminent among these nineteenth-century German federalists was Constantin Frantz, whose followers referred to him as the "teacher of federalism" and the founder of a "new age federalism."[28] He became a federalist through the political application of Hegel's theory of dialectics. Though educated in Saxony, Frantz sought to serve the Prussian establishment. His initial writings were also sociological, and indeed he wavered between the right and left Hegelians and criticized the Prussian regime which he sought to serve, an unheard of act. Bismarck recognized his talent and tried to win him over but Frantz responded by criticizing the "Iron Chancellor" as well. He was gradually dismissed from all his official positions and by 1862 had been removed from all of them. Overall he acquired the reputation of being politically unreliable, which influenced the acceptance or lack of acceptance of his federalist theories. Frantz's federalism was based on the German concept of nature which held organic societies to be "natural."

A Protestant, he supported the Austrian-led Catholic League for that region. He was also anti-Semitic because he believed that Jews could not be integrated into a Christian environment. More than that, he saw them as a threat to both Protestantism and Catholicism. What his attitude toward the Jews teaches us about his federal theory is that while he accepted the biblical idea of a covenant between God and the Jews, he argued that federation should be among equals in an organic society. All told, he, like most of his fellows, was an unmitigated German romantic who looked back fondly on the medieval German Reich (the so-called First Reich) as his inspiration.[29]

Frantz rejected the relationship between constitutionalism and federalism, dismissing constitutionalism as "politicism." In this he differed from most other German federalists by seeing federalism primarily as social while the others saw constitutionalism as critical. Frantz's idea of social federalism was supported by Karl Georg Winkelbach, whose ideas became prominent in post-World War II Germany.[30]

Rare among the German federalists of the time, Robert von Mohl began his studies of German federalism for Germany by studying the constitution of the United States. Those German federalists who did look at the United States concluded that the American system was one of fragmentary state power (*fragmentarische staatsgewalt*). Given their romantic orientation, this was not necessarily a compliment. It certainly was a sign that they ignored any kind of covenantal, compactual, or contractual basis, since they sought to restore the old German Reich which they saw as an organic polity. Indeed, Frantz used biological analogies even in his discussion of federalism.

For nineteenth-century Germans, constitutionalism was a liberal phenomenon, and federalists like Frantz who rejected liberalism used social federalism to oppose liberal constitutionalism. Thus the most prominent German federalist thinkers opposed constitutionalism as an artifact of despised liberalism and pursued their dreams of restoring the organic society through social federalism, that is to say, restoring medieval institutions whose strength lay in their rootedness in society and which together could provide a political-social order that could be called federal and thereby rebuild the fabric of Germany.

The fact that these theorists were Protestants and Catholics both demonstrated how powerful this system of thought, derived from Hegelianism, was in nineteenth-century Germany. Their one contribution to the theory of federalism was an emphasis on the need for people to internalize the principle of federalism if federalism is to have any meaning, to act in a federal manner. Only in this way would people develop the will to come together in order to establish something new, to undertake joint ventures without abandoning their own separate integrities. Thus, in the end, these social federalists were forced back into the essence of the covenantal tradition even in their effort to reject it.

This idea came close to the doctrine of subsidiarity as propagated by the Catholic Church in the late nineteenth century. It may turn out to have some meaning for the contemporary European Union in its search for a principle of noncentralization through the revival, in secularized form, of that old Catholic idea. Frantz, for example, rejected state citizenship as a goal for social federalism, seeing humans as communal citizens and, alternatively, world citizens in a formulation not far from that of today's advocates of strengthening the European Union by developing a Europe of regions outflanking the Europe of states, thereby combining community spirit with cosmopolitanism. Hence the rejection of liberalism, which many saw as promoting the state citizenship of individuals instead of world citizenship through communities. Unfortunately, several of these federalists, led by Frantz, were also opposed to individual freedom, which they believed would interfere with the life of the organic polity.

Despite these dubious features of social federalist thought, federalism did serve in Germany as a major intellectual means for resistance to Prussian centralism and later Nazi totalitarianism. Moreover, at least one of the German socialist federalist theorists, Julius Froebel, was an advocate of European federalism as early as 1866.

A major part of the problem in Germany subsequent to the Reformation was one of reconciling covenantal Reformed Protestant with hierarchical religion rooted in both Catholicism and Lutheranism. In the nineteenth century this issue took the form of a new struggle over church-state relations necessitated by the pressures for disestablishment, on one hand, and for maintaining state order, on the other.

Unlike the situation in Great Britain where there was one established church (technically one in each country, Anglicanism in England and Wales and

Presbyterianism in Scotland) as well as a somewhat limited freedom on the part of other religions and Nonconformist Christian denominations to organize outside of the established church, in Prussia there were at least three established churches, the Lutheran, the Reformed, and the French Reformed (Huguenots). All were under the Prussian Department of the Interior, and were officially parts of the state church. The three maintained very real regional, confessional, and ecclesiastical differences. For Prussia, all changes in church-state relations were designed for political purposes to foster the unification and centralization of Prussia and then Germany. Nevertheless, German realities, including the just-mentioned reality of three separate established churches, not to speak of the Jews who also were under government control but in a slightly different way, meant that things would not be so simple.

In both countries, two positions suggested themselves, the Erastian position, whereby a strong state-church connection would be based on the subordination of the churches to the general government for ecclesiastical authority, and the autonomous church tradition whereby the churches would be independent. In England, the relatively noncompetitive situation meant that a relaxed Erastianism persisted. The struggles of the Nonconforming churches for separation of church and state continued through the century and consistently failed, unlike Wales, where separation took place. Prussian Erastianism, however, was heavy-handed.

Moreover, the Reformed Protestants especially rejected the idea of vesting ecclesiastical authority in the state since they had a tradition of autonomous ecclesiastical authorities since their founding. Reformed Protestantism dominated Prussia's western provinces and there the churches were governed through synods and presbyteries. Moreover, the churches fought to retain those institutions and to prevent the great desire of the Prussian government, a union of Lutherans and Calvinists, that would either be confessional or constitutional. The Prussian government fought for twenty years and lost, with almost as much opposition among the Lutherans.

Both conservatives and liberals both opposed an Erastian solution in both countries. In the end, while a framework of older Erastian institutions remained, both governments lost and the churches remained substantially autonomous, more so among Prussian Reformed Protestants than among English Anglicans. This was not a struggle over disestablishment but over structure and control. In that sense it was not a repudiation of older Reformed traditions but a federal position in terms of both governance and ideology.

In the end, Germany itself was unified on ostensibly federal principles. Bismarck, for tactical reasons, endorsed federalism and established a centralized federation in which Prussia had the leading role not only politically and militarily but constitutionally as well. This Second Reich collapsed in World War I and the Weimar Republic that replaced it both opposed federalism for liberal reasons and included a weak federal structure in its constitutional order only out of political necessity. Of Hitler's attitude toward federalism nothing need be said, so it was left to the architects of the German Federal Republic in 1949 to make modern federalism the cornerstone of a revived and democratic German polity in the aftermath of World War II, at last properly linking federalism and democracy as the foundation of a federal, democratic, and free regime. The German federal system of 1949 is a constitutional federation with a proper federal structure, based on fostering appropriate political and social attitudes among the German people.

For the Swiss, the issue was just the opposite. The needs of the nineteenth century either led or forced the Swiss to consolidate their federalism, but they never contemplated doing so on other than federalist lines. Three times in the nineteenth century they had to reconstitute their federal system in practice and not only in theory. It is not surprising then that Swiss thinkers produced a certain amount of theoretical consideration of how best to do so.[31]

The leading Swiss federal theorist of the period, Johann Kaspar Bluntschli, was also the leading Swiss political theorist in the nineteenth century. Bluntschli's theory was very much in the Germanic tradition and like those of his German and Austrian colleagues has subsequently faded into obscurity to become of antiquarian interest only. The distinctiveness of the nineteenth-century Swiss lay in their paractice not in their theory. Only in the twentieth century did significant federal theory emerge in both French-speaking and German-speaking Switzerland.

The "Organic" Making of Italy and Its Federal Alternative

Elsewhere in nineteenth-century Europe, a school of Italian federalist thought developed as part of the Risorgimento and the unification of Italy as a single state. A not insignificant minority among those pursuing that goal sought unification on a federal basis.[30] They were opposed by and lost to those who accepted the conventional European statist model, but the debate they opened never precisely ended and today is more alive than ever in Italy.

No one of the contemporary European nation-states is more a matter of will than Italy. As late as 1820–21 and 1830 the uprisings that today are treated in Italian national historiography as the national beginning of the Italian Risorgimento were actually quite local, designed to secure constitutional guarantees within the existing regional states, not to replace them with a new Italian state. Mazzini, the father of modern Italy, understood that and denounced them as local uprisings that could only serve to sustain the regional states on the Italian peninsula and thus Austrian power over the peninsula. Indeed, as did his counterparts in Germany, he posed his liberalism as a counter to Italian regionalism and its federalist derivative.

Mazzini and the liberals faced a problem. They had to generate a sense of Italianness so that they could build an Italian liberal state. While they succeeded in doing so for the nineteenth century, in recent years we have seen how temporary their victory was for much of the population. Carlo Cattaneo opposed Mazzini because he opposed the idea of statism. His goal was to transform the Hapsburg empire into a democratic federal state along the American model as a first step toward a United States of Europe.

The question legitimately may be asked whether this was not simply nationalism and statism on a larger scale. While both Mazzini and Cattaneo sought to establish modern constitutional states, neither drew upon the covenantal tradition except in the most indirect manner through its expression as constitutionalism. It seems that they were not aware of the connection. That would only come in the 1990s as a strong federalist movement developed in northern Italy. Theoreticians of that movement drew heavily on the work of this writer and the Center for the Study of Federalism and in that way discovered the covenantal roots of federalism which strongly attracted some of them and led them to incorporate those ideas into their thoughts.

Nineteenth-Century European Federalist Thought

Nineteenth-century European federalism and federalist thought ran up against two insurmountable obstacles: the first, European nationalism and its identification with the nation-state; and the second, European philosophy with its striving for a consistency in the philosophic ideal rather than a reconciliation of the paradoxes, contradictions, and tensions in the world in less than an ideally consistent manner. It seems that federalism can live only where there is a mild dose of chaos, philosophically as well as empirically.

Both of the foregoing were accompanied by the consequences of the early modern collapse of covenantalism. Just as Puritanism was replaced by Victorianism, in which a system of tributes paid by vice to virtue replaced a flawed but very real moral striving, so, too, did a system of conventions replace the willingness of people to establish moral communities. The triumph of civil society led to its replacement by the idea of "society," which not only no longer denominated itself "civil" but in the respects that counted was not, even though social civility was fostered almost as never before. Perhaps social civility was designed to replace moral civility when the latter could no longer be sustained. In the end, the price of the former was too high and it, too, collapsed in the twentieth century.

It was only when nationalism turned to fascism that liberals began to identify in any way with federalism. Neither position drew upon covenantalism. The pull of federalism was the desire for European peace. One can see in the turn to federalism as part of the search for peace an effort to establsh a framework of covenants or at the very least compacts and constitutional arrangements through which disputes could be settled and interests adjusted, but one can also see the hope of imposing an overarching authoritative framework which could through its authority prevent war. The first would be in the spirit of covenantalism, the second would be in the very hierarchical spirit of imperialism.

In reality, both positions were flawed. Partisans of the former expected too much from the world in which they lived and partisans of the latter too little. The results were tragic, although with a clear disparity between the two groups. The former became appeasers and the latter Nazis and Fascists who took advantage of the appeasers. The end result was half a century of European civil war, generally known as World Wars I and II, that rapidly involved the rest of the world and led to the diminution of Europe in the world scheme of things.

Notes

1. Woodrow Wilson, *Congressional Government: A Study in American Politics* (New York: Meridian Books, 1956); *idem.*, "The Study of Administration," *Political Science Quarterly* 2 (June 1887), pp. 197–220; Vincent Ostrom, "Can Federalism Make a Difference?" *The Federal Polity*, Daniel J. Elazar, ed. (New Brunswick, N.J.: Transaction Publishers, 1974).

2. Alexis de Tocqueville, *Democracy in America*, 2 vols., translated by Henry Reeve, introduction by J.S. Mill (New York: Schocken Books, 1961). "Confederation" is the French term that Tocqueville uses to describe the United States both before and after 1787, but then he describes Switzerland as being a league of independent states, something less than a confederation.

3. *Ibid.*, p. 11.

4. *Ibid.*

5. *Ibid.*, p. 8.

6. *Ibid.*, pp. 1–11.

7. Tocqueville cites Nathanel Morton's *New England's Memorial* (Boston, 1826) and also mentions Hutchinson's *History*, vol. 2. Tocqueville makes it clear that he is not writing a panegyric (his term) of the United States. Nor does he think that there can be only one form of democracy. It is just that he finds the American form extraordinarily interesting and illustrative of where the modern world and its "great democratic revolution" are going. Tocqueville sees this modern democratic revolution as "irresistable" and wants to turn it from a situation in which it is "a fight against God himself" to one in which the spirit of religion and the spirit of liberty march hand in hand.

8. See, for example, John Koritansky, "Decentralization and Civic virtue in Tocqueville's 'New Science of Politics,'" *Publius*, vol. 5, no. 3 (Summer 1975), pp. 63–82.

9. Ralph Nelson, "The Federal Idea in French Political Thought," *Federalism as Grand Design: Political Philosophers and the Federal Principle*, Daniel J. Elazar, ed. (Lanham, Md.: University Press of America, 1987); Henri de Lubac, *The Unmarxian Socialist: A Study of Proudhon* (London: Sheed and Ward, 1948); and Alan Ritter, *The Political Thought of Pierre-Joseph Proudhon* (Princeton, N.J.: Princeton University Press, 1969).

10. Nelson, "The Federal Idea," p. 136.

11. Proudhon, *Dans la Justice, Dans la Revolution et Dans l'Eglise* (Paris: Riviere, 1930), vol. 2, p. 72.

12. Nelson, "The Federal Idea," p. 137.

13. Proudhon, *Du Principe Federatif*, translated and introduced by Richard Verno (Toronto: University of Toronto Press, 1979).
14. Yves Simon, "A Note on Proudhon's Federalism," trans. by Vucan Kuic in *Federalism as Grand Design*, p. 225.
15. *Ibid.*, p. 229.
16. As quoted in Ferdinand Kinsky, "Personalism and Federalism," in "Federalism as Grand Design," a special issue of *Publius*, vol. 9, no. 4 (1979), p. 133.
17. Alexandre Marc, "New and Old Federalism: Faithful to the Origins," in "Federalism as Grand Design," *Publius*, vol. 9, no. 4 (1979), p. 117.
18. *Ibid.*, p. 119.
19. *Ibid.*
20. See Denis de Rougement, Alexandre Marc, "Et landension de personnalisme," in *La Federalism*, Alexander Marc, ed. (Lausanne: Centre de Recherches Europeennes, 1974), pp. 51–69; also "Toward a New Definition of Federalism," *Atlantic Community Quarterly*, vol. 8, no. 2 (March 1970):224–33.
21. Martin Buber, *Pfade in Utopia* (Heidelberg: Lambert Schneider, 1985).
22. Kinsky, "Personalism and Federalism," p. 149.
23. Martin Buber, *Kingship of God* (London: G. Allen and Unwin, 1967); *Paths in Utopia*; and Bernard Susser, "The Anarcho-Federalism of Martin Buber," in *Federalism as Grand Design*.
24. Otto von Gierke, *Das Grundbegiffe des Staatsrecht und die Neuesten Staatsrechtstheorien* (Aalen: Scientia, 1973; *Political Theories of the Middle Ages,* trans. Frederic William Maitland (Cambridge: Cambridge University Press, 1927).
25. Ferdinand Toennies, *Community and Society* (East Lansing: Michigan State University Press, 1957).
26. Georg Simmel et al. *Essays on Sociology, Philosophy and Aesthetics*, edited and translated by Kurt H. Wolff (New York: Harper Torchbooks, 1965).
27. Rudiger Gorner, "Constantin Frantz and the German Federalist Tradition," in Andrea Boscoe, ed., *The Federal Idea, vol. 1, The History of Federalism from the Enlightenment to 1945* (London: Lothian Foundation Press, 1991), pp. 77–90.
28. Ernst Deuerlein, *Foederalismus* (Munich: P. List, 1972), p. 106.
29. Gustav Frantz, *Polen Preussen und Deutschland: ein Beitrachtungen uber dien Reorganization Europas Hans Elmar Onnau* (Siegburg: Schmitt, 1969).
30. Gorner, "Constantin Frantz," p. 83.
31. Johann Kaspar Bluntschli, *The Theory of the State* (Oxford: Clarendon Press, 1885).
32. Filippo Sabetti, "The Making of Italy as an Experiment in Constitutional Choice," *Publius*, vol. 12, no. 3 (Summer 1982).

5

Four Twentieth-Century Federalist Thinkers

The pressures of nineteenth-century nationalism in North America and the New World as well as Europe mitigated against great philosophers and grand designs in the covenant traditions. By the end of the century, however, the bloom was fading from the nationalist impulse, at least philosophically, and space reappeared for new grand designs, including two avowedly federalist ones.

William James (1842–1910) was a New England Yankee who was born, raised, and lived at the very heart of Yankeedom, first just across the street from the Harvard campus (his family home is today the Harvard University Faculty Club) and later as a member of the Harvard faculty. Martin Buber (1878–1965) was a Jew born and raised in Germany who spent the last half of his life in the Land and State of Israel, to which he was drawn as a Zionist from his earliest days and from which he continued to spread his universal message. Thus both imbibed the culture of covenantalism from their youth.

Both James and Buber drew their federalistic views from the nineteenth century. Reinhold Niebuhr and Mordecai M. Kaplan already had to come to grips with the twentieth century and with the modern epoch in its final moments. They, too, are part of the twentieth century bridge from the modern to the postmodern epochs.

Niebuhr (1892–1971) after service as a pastor in Detroit, became professor of applied Christianity at Union Theological Seminary where he emphasized a "realistic" liberalism rooted in Reformed Protestantism. Mordecai M. Kaplan (1881–1983), although born in Lithuania, was brought to the United States as a baby. He became a Conservative rabbi and spent his entire career at that movement's Jewish Theological Seminary in New York. There he developed an "optimistic" social democratic political theology, in a sense parallel to that of Niebuhr's. The religious and political roots of both were deep in the covenantal tradition, Protestant, Jewish, and American.

William James

William James is conventionally included among the school of American pragmatists along with Charles Peirce and John Dewey, two other New En-

101

glanders; but unlike his predecessor Peirce, the founder of pragmatism, who was all abstraction, or his younger contemporary Dewey, who could afford to be an instrumentalist who claimed that the only test for the good was whether it worked but who could implicitly lean on a New England moral tradition that served, at least subliminally, to define what "works" meant, James articulated his premises as well as his conclusions and how they related to the real world. In reading James's writings we are apt to look at his pragmatism without considering his deep religious commitment (he described himself in *Varieties of Religious Experience* as a religious fundamentalist) and as a pluralist without noting that he saw pluralism as both requiring and being rooted in a basic federalism. He himself described the universe as "federal by the hand of God."[1]

James's argument is that the world is "more like a federal republic than an empire or a kingdom." Whatever order, coherence or harmony that there is in the universe is, according to Henry S. Levinson, a foremost interpreter of James's thought, "constituted by the independent powers which inhabit it."[2]

Unlike his European counterparts, James built his philosophy according to the ways of the world as they are, not the way he might want them to be. This was already the thought of a later and more mature James, whose initial view of pluralism did not allow him to claim even that much order. The turning point for James may well have come in his essay on "American Religion" published in 1897, in which he construed the federal republican principle of "one out of many" as a principle of salvation, harmony and perfection.[3] Levinson argues that this claim was costly for James because "it meant giving up allegiance to the Western philosophical tradition." Levinson explores the processes through which James arrived at these conclusions in detail.

Levinson claims that William was following his father, Henry James, Sr., whose sole object, according to his biographer Giles Gunn, "was to fuse Christianity and democracy in what might be called a new religion of the kingly commons."[4] Levinson continues, "This meant articulating the Western cultural myth of 'mankind as co-worker with God continuously hovering over the primordial chaos, creating a universe' in federal republican ways." God was not an absolute monarch. "Salvation was neither a matter of beholding the sovereign monarch governing the universe, nor serving his liege in an unearthly kingdom. Salvation was the actualization of 'the principle of democracy', i.e., the assertion that 'the people are rightfully sovereign, and possess the exclusive claim to the governing function.'"[5]

No idea could be more covenantal, biblical, or Puritan. This covenantal view that God and man together would build order out of chaos James, Sr. understood to be part of the founding fathers' vision. He even spiritualized if not sanctified the very name of his country, stating that "The form of our polity bears on its very face, that is, in its name, an intimation of the spiritual change it represents. It is not America, but the United States of *America*, 'one out of many,' as its motto reads, to which the expiring states of Europe bow,

or do deepest homage, in sending over to these shores their starving populations to be nourished and clothed and otherwise nursed into citizenship, which
is a condition preliminary to their being socialized."[6] By socialized, Henry,
Sr. in effect meant saved.

James, Sr.'s emphasis on the social consequences of the religion of the
republic rather than the political ones is clear; not that he eliminates the political, only that, in the nineteenth-century manner, he sees the social as a
larger sphere with democracy and pluralism at least as much social as political, if not more so. In this he is fully a nineteenth-century man in the spirit of
the nineteenth century, although with a twist, in the spirit of nineteenth-century America, criticizing Old World forms of polity and spirituality to advocate an American religion.

While his son William did not simply reiterate his father's ideas, he was
his father's disciple. William's God becomes even more the presiding head,
the superhuman first among many active principles, than God was for Henry,
Sr., who still pictured God as the Supreme Agent in the universe. Both, however, saw religion basically as a quest for social salvation in a society where
coercion and restraint were replaced by persuasion and liberty. Both embraced
federal liberty, which they might have called cooperative liberty (they used
the term "cooperation" in that spirit), which meant not only recognizing the
expressions of all others but pursuing the obligation of seeking to achieve
harmony from what are initially many conflicting interests, desires, needs,
and ideals. William defined the American religion as "the faith that a man
requires no master to take care of him, and that common people can work out
their salvation well enough if left free to try."[7]

William wrote after the Civil War and the Gilded Age and no longer had
his father's simple distrust of the Old World. Rather, he saw the enemy as
coming from within, and that the American nation had to preserve its inner
quality, which he defined as consisting of two things: "trained and disciplined
good temper towards the opposite party when it fairly wins its innings," yet
"fierce and merciless resentment toward every man or set of men who break
the public peace."[8]

After an odyssey from religious monism and social pluralism to both religious and social pluralism, James rejected both "absolute monism and absolute pluralism" in favor of an interactive world that is one insofar as its parts
hang together by some definitive connection and many to the extent that they
do not."[9]

Here we find James's application of the federal principle to unify the two
elements. In the spirit of the nineteenth century, James liked to use the term
"cooperative" to define these connections. The world becomes "a social scheme
of cooperative work genuinely to be done."[10]

Here James comes close to the kabbalistic idea of the world as a shattered
vessel in which the task of humans is to repair the vessel. Were the world a

kingdom to be unified by the fiat of its sovereign, this would not be a human responsibility. But, according to James, in the real world only the world's agents who can do "cooperative work" have the power to repair the world's breaks and tears and "to transform collections of things into groups of interactive components."[11]

In place of the "absolute," James places the "ultimate." James published his hypothesis of the ultimate union in *A Pluralistic Universe* in 1908, clarifying in it just who were the agents of world reparation and how the world is constituted more like a federal republic. Levinson argues that in it James modified his long-standing position as "a common sense theist or crass supernaturalist" into a kind of pantheism of continuity, rejecting "the older monarchial theism" for something "more organic and intimate."[12]

Here James moves beyond the covenantal tradition, seeking organic connections where his father and those before him saw God and man linked in covenantal ones. By moving so far away from the religion of the American republic, James also moved farther from the political and from the covenantal tradition. What remains is the universe as God's federal republic, though James reserves the right of interpretation of each of those three words.

Martin Buber

Martin Buber published his first works while James was publishing his last, in a wholly different environment, amidst the philosophic idealists of pre-World War I Germany. Buber began with philosophic idealism but in the end was far more influenced by Hassidism and Zionism. Buber became a Zionist first, influenced by the Wandervogel youth movements of the Germany of his youth. Then he discovered the Hassidic segment of the world of Eastern European Jewry, which he reinterpreted in his own spirit, much moved by the Hassidic understanding of *hesed* (which may best be translated as loving covenant obligation), the root word of their own name.

Following his German philosophic education, Buber became a philosopher; following his Zionism he settled in Israel; and following his understanding of Hassidism he developed his system of thought. Buber attacked Hegelianism on the grounds that it fetters man by taking away a needed "messianism" which "sees in man himself, in this fragile and contradictory being, object of perplexity, an element capable of making as big a contribution to his redemption as of preventing it."[13]

Marxism, as the apotheosis of Hegelianism, therefore is unacceptable. We have already noted that Buber was identified with Personalism, an identification that he implicitly endorses in his writings, and hence that he has a broad view of federalism as the operative social, not only political, principle of the world. But his is an anarchistic federalism, federal mostly because he knows that anarchism alone will not work, given human nature.

Buber had high hopes for humanity, probably higher than humans can live up to, but even he recognized their limits and the need for political means to deal with those limits. What he tried to do was build an integral system around the kingdom of God whereby God's sovereignty is felt directly by individual humans and not mediated through rulers or ruling institutions. Buber began developing his thought in the still optimistic salad days before World War I, but he lived through World War I, the difficult interwar years, the rise of Nazism and the Holocaust. He could not accept the Jamesian belief (if he ever considered it) that eliminating the sovereignty of God would lead humans to social cooperation and a humanistic pluralism without the iron morality of God's sovereignty; but Buber was also an optimist; so he sought to have that sovereignty exercised directly on every human being, allowing humans the freedom that James sought but requiring that freedom to be exercised within Buber's conception of federal liberty.

Drawing on the Bible and its political tradition, Buber held that humans must achieve freedom within the context of the community, indeed a community striving to be holy. Here Buber's thought intersects with Personalism and integral federalism, yet steps beyond it in terms of the moral demands it places upon people. His ideas can be found throughout his works but particularly in three of them: *Kingship of God, The Prophetic Faith,* and *Moses.*[14]

Buber's ideal polity is best represented biblically in the Book of Judges, which describes a regime portrayed as between a federation and a confederation, that is to say, a polity for a single people with a common constitution and law, but almost without comprehensive national governing institutions, in which most functions of government were in the hands of tribal and local authorities. For Buber, this was just about the right amount of government.[15]

According to the biblical account, the Israelites ultimately were not content with this system and added human kingship to their federal system, something which Buber directly rejects. The Bible actually presents us with a dialogue between two possible good regimes: the Mosaic Polity described in Exodus through I Samuel and the Davidic Polity described from II Samuel onward. Buber unequivocally took his stand with the first. As Susser states:

> The philosophy of dialogue for which Buber is particularly celebrated, also feeds into his anarcho-federalist outlook. He understands dialogue as the politico-philosophical principle that bridges individuality and communality without thereby blurring the reality or responsibility of either. To engage in dialogue is to relate but yet withstand, to affirm my interlocutor without capitulating to his will. It means further to preserve the integrity of one's own life and identity while simultaneously accepting the reality of "otherness" as the larger meaning and context of personal existence. Understood as a political idea, dialogue is incompatible with either totalitarianism (even "totalitarian democracy") or with extreme individualism. It represents a tense mediate position that refuses to reify the collective or hypostatize the individual.[16]

One can see how Buber relies heavily on the work of Gierke, Simmel and Toennies. Buber's federalism is utopian. In Susser's words, it is "both a political and a metapolitical idea; the key to socio-political orderings, the foundation of personal integrity and responsibility, and, finally, bound up profoundly with the eschatological catagories of redemption and direct theocracy."[17]

Buber understood that his thought was utopian, finding little in the contemporary world that even came close to approximating what he envisioned. He stated firmly that "centralized socialism is not socialism. Socialism in which the relations of authority were changed to the benefit of the workers, without a change in relations between men is not socialism."[18]

Buber believed that the only way to attain this utopian federalism was to begin by building a society that would be constructed on the basis of reborn communes and structured federally as a community of communities. Here Buber explicitly referred to Althusius and his model, thus placing himself foursquare in the covenantal commonwealth tradition.

While he does not use these terms, Buber holds that civil society, whatever its virtues, cannot possibly provide the utopian polity and society of which he dreamed. He seeks a world anchored in matters of the spirit and regenerated by those matters. It is no wonder that he was disappointed in a world where the best that people can aspire to was decent civil society. He wanted not only commonwealth but a commonwealth of true communities, formed by covenant but transformed into organic entities.

It is not surprising, then, that Buber became world famous for the interpersonal relations dimensions of his theory of the life of the dialogue. In his heyday, Buber affected all of Western religious thought, but much of the effect was the effect of lip-service, even for matters interpersonal. Indeed, one might say that the federal parts of his theory did not even gain the respect of lip-service. They were simply beyond what people, even many of the most faithful Buberians, could conceptualize or tolerate.

Buber had to confine his hopes to the kibbutz in Israel, the only kind of commune that could possibly generate a social order acceptable to Buber.[19] In pre-state Israel it seemed for a while that the kibbutz could give birth to a community of communities. The Jews returning to their land shared more of a sense of community and common vision than any other modern population in the world, even with all of their schisms and differences of opinion.

But the struggle between Jews and Arabs for what the West called Palestine soon turned much of their Jewish communal energy to the problems of self-defense. Buber was heartbroken and sought to build a bridge between Jews and Arabs in the land, but the bi-national state he and his associates envisioned would have been by its very nature unable to achieve the kind of commonwealth of communities that Buber envisioned. Indeed, at this writing, with Israel reaching its fiftieth birthday it is not even clear that Jews and Arabs will together be able to have the kind of civil society that most people consider adequate today.

Thus, as the modern epoch came to a close we find that the covenant tradition in political thought has returned to the stage, most directly in the utopian form presented by Buber. Since the salad days of the kibbutz in the interwar years, no effort has been made to develop even the building blocks for it and only a relative few of those who pioneered the kibbutz saw that community in terms akin to those of Buber. Most were Marxists trying to build a new society on very different principles, which Buber himself abhored and was convinced—rightly—would never work. Others seeking a different utopia of equality turned to contractarianism to find the formula for achieving their particular utopian goals.

If neither the utopias of the life of the dialogue nor those of pure individualistic contractarianism offer us much, where then should the covenantal tradition go and what path should the covenantal tradition follow? Ideally, it would follow the path of commonwealth where people sharing the same understanding of federal liberty would seek to pursue it. Alternatively, there is a federal path to civil society in which federal liberty needs to be defined more broadly but still offers a kind of ordered liberty of equals where hierarchy will be kept to a minimum, equity and cooperation will be fostered, and the excesses of natural liberty abjured. We are still seeking along both paths.

The Survival of Covenant in Political Theology: Reinhold Niebuhr

The political-philosophical and political-theological heritage of covenant runs throughout the modern epoch in ways more direct or less. Speaking only of American philosophers and theologians in the twentieth century, John Dewey did not discuss covenant or political compacts, just as he does not discuss federalism. Yet his instrumentalist political thought is rooted in both just as his political program is rooted in the last. As Vincent Ostrom has described Dewey in connection with federalism, "so near and yet so far."[20] The same description can be used with regard to Dewey and the covenantal tradition. Mordecai Kaplan, a theologian with political concerns, who was strongly influenced by Dewey, was able to cross that bridge. He was covenantal in his theology and only somewhat less so in his political theory, influenced by his Jewish religious worldview.[21]

Perhaps the greatest of them all was Reinhold Niebuhr, probably the most profound American political thinker in the twentieth century among those who gained widespread public recognition. Niebuhr was a Reformed Protestant minister who came out of the covenantal tradition and who, while he did not dwell on covenant by name in his political works, remained within a Reformed Protestant understanding of that tradition. Niehbuhr had already begun to move in the direction of revived covenantal thinking in the interwar generation. Indeed, he revived that tradition by adapting it to the interwar and postwar periods. The League of Nations was the first concrete effort to implement the revived covenantal pursuit of peace brought to Europe by Woodrow

Wilson, of Presbyterian background, and in many respects the epitome of the late nineteenth-century Christian in politics. Its aspirations are reflected in its founders' use of the term covenant to describe its founding pact, and the failure of the League and that covenant did much to discredit the idealists who pinned such great hopes on their device.

One of the characteristics of Christian theological thought and for that matter popular Christianity in the twentieth century is its emphasis on love. There is good evidence to show that a proper tracing of the origins of this emphasis would bring us back to the concept of *hesed* through its Latin translation as *caritas*, but by ending up simply as the word love, the covenantal dimension of the concept effectively disappeared, leading it to be distorted in various ways. Love is now used as a generic term without the special sense of the original that it not only came with certain covenantal obligations attached but varied in relation to its object by virtue of the latter's relationship to those covenantal obligations, even if unconditional. (Unconditionality was the Christian gloss on the Jewish concept dating back to the beginnings of Christianity.)

The covenantal issue could not be avoided in the classic formulation. Not only that, but in the popular mind it was very difficult to separate sexual or sexually related and other forms of love. Christian preachers have tried to do so for generations and can be specific in their speech, but in the popular mind love is love and even if that is more than the expression of sexuality, it is not different from that expression. The New Testament Greek term *agape*, which in Latin was translated as *caritas* and in English, charity, did refer to a Divine or spiritual form of love and it was the term of choice of Christian thinkers, in contrast to *eros*, but it was a distinction that escaped too many people when both were translated simply as love.

Niebuhr was among those who weakened his covenantal message by emphasizing love as the law of life and the principal commandment. For Niebuhr, as for others, love was the prerequisite for justice. Love was for interpersonal relationships, justice was necessary for social relationships. Love is the moral ethic of society, justice is the political ethic. Justice is the manifestation of love in groups.

Niebuhr felt that Jesus' teachings were lacking in the spirit of justice and that the latter was the product of the left wing of the Reformation. Almost equal to justice in Niebuhr's political thought are order and freedom. When linked with justice the latter became equality. Reflecting his Reformed Protestant origins, Niebuhr saw even the best of people as at times sinners and saw the combination of the three as a means to make imperfect decisions in an imperfect world that could reduce the negative impact of sin. To accomplish all of this man is responsible for living in this world in such a way as to minimize sin and to maximize love, justice, equality, freedom, and order.

To avoid Calvinist views of predestination, Niebuhr rejected the idea that humans were by nature sinful, but held that sin is inevitable, if not original. It was those things that bring about sin—pride, covetousness, and sexuality—

that are of nature, as is the tendency to make vices of one's virtues by pursuing them in an exclusivist and overemphasized fashion.

Niebuhr was active in the period when discussions of covenant were most out of fashion. Hence he did not easily use the term. One has to discover his covenantalism. Attempting to combine kinship and consent, Niebuhr begins community from kinship but quietly slides over into covenantal issues of consent. Niebuhr considered himself to have a Hebraic view of history and that can only lead in one direction. In place of covenant he emphasized prophecy, but we all know what the prophets emphasized.

The Uses of Covenant in the Pursuit of Ethical Nationalism: Mordecai M. Kaplan

Reinhold Niebuhr was trained as a minister, served as a pastor for many years, and then became a seminarian, a professor of theology whose primary interests were in political and social thought. Mordecai Kaplan was Jewish, trained and ordained a rabbi. While he thought long and deeply about the synagogue and all those attached to it and even founded two synagogue movements that he hoped would translate his ideas into action, he remained a seminarian all his life, a professor at the Jewish Theological Seminary in New York, across the street from Niebuhr's own Union Theological Seminary.

Kaplan's priniciple orientation was to the Jewish and American communities both. He always was very interested in social and political issues stretching beyond. A religious naturalist, he had ceased believing in a living God, reconceptualizing the Deity as "the power that makes for salvation." If Kaplan had to redefine God, he remained extraordinarily faithful to the idea of covenant. Thus Kaplan took upon himself the formidable chore of translating God's covenant with the Jewish people into an entirely human affair. He did this by placing the Jewish people at the center of his covenantal thought although he abjured their role as a chosen people. He saw every people as potentially being covenanted, that is to say, embodying their vision of themselves and the world in which they sought to live in covenantal terms based entirely upon human reflection and choice. Not only that, he believed that it was both possible and necessary for Jews, Americans, and others to renew their covenants through actual ceremonies and commitments.

Kaplan was a follower of John Dewey, and like his teacher, he implicitly rested his covenantal theory on a heritage that had provided for Divine participation and sanction. Even after he rejected this Divine source in the traditional sense, it animated his thinking about Jews and the world. Kaplan may have rejected a living God but he saw religion as a sine qua non for human existence.

Kaplan was firmly convinced that everybody had some religion, either a real or an ersatz one. Religions, indeed, shaped peoples. Thus for him, "Judaism was the evolving religious civilization of the Jewish people." He was one of the first to openly recognize the existence of an American civil religion and at the outbreak of World War II tried to formulate a set of rituals and sacred texts for the American civil religion that all Americans would embrace.

Much concerned with social justice, Kaplan was a social democrat for much of his life since he believed that the social justice of socialism could be undertaken only within the democracy inherent in the American vision and its promise. He saw American democracy as pluralistic, as protecting individuals and groups as long as they subscribed to the rules of the democratic game. Still, he wanted more from them. One of his last books was entitled *The Religion of Ethical Nationhood*, a book that endorsed the sense of peoplehood or nationhood that was abroad in the world, as long as it was nationhood with an ethical vision and message.[22]

Perhaps because of his tradition, Kaplan was not afraid to explicitly use the word "covenant." Indeed, he was one of those who sought to maintain and even revive its use during those long years when organic images were so much more in vogue. While no one has yet written a systematic work analyzing Kaplan's political theory, especially not as it relates to the covenantal tradition, such a work would no doubt reveal that Kaplan saw the world as a network of covenants very much as his ancestors did with that one important exception regarding the nature of God. Indeed, he tried to use the term very explicitly in three ways: in relation to the reconstitution of the Jewish people worldwide as part of the Zionist enterprise, as part of the reanimation of the American vision in reaction to what he saw as rapacious capitalism, and in the development of a new world order which was needed in the wake of fascism and Nazism to bring peace, democracy and justice to the world.

Much of the effort of other Jewish theologians to revive the idea of covenant in the 1950s came from people who were much influenced by Kaplan's thinking whether they realized it or not. During his mature years Kaplan was the preeminent Jewish religious thinker in the United States. In the end, however, while he made what was perhaps a most valiant effort, his religious naturalism failed to provide the grounding necessary for moral commitment for more than a handful of people and thus left his covenantal system without adequate foundation.[23]

It was only in the postwar period that covenant became more fashionable again. The United States as the greatest of the covenantal nations, offered the most fertile field for the development of new covenantal ideas, although not necessarily using the term itself. Most of them were developed in a manner typical of American politics, emphasizing partnership in practical ways. Beyond those, first the civil rights revolution, then the Vietnam War, the Watergate scandal, and finally the U.S. bicentennial year provided great impetus for popular reconsideration of covenantal and compactual ideas, with the idea of reviving the covenant or renegotiating the social compact emerging from a number of quarters in the 1960s. Robert Bellah, William Johnson Everett,

Franklin Littell, Charles McCoy, Max Stackhouse and Douglas Sturm were among the most prominent voices.[24]

Some were students of Niebuhr, such as Littell, who followed him in his hardheadedness, who did not let their drive for justice lead them into sentimentality any more than it did him. Kaplan, in that sense, was less fortunate. Few if any of those who considered themselves his direct disciples continued in his covenantal vein, except perhaps pro forma because they were Jews and it was hard for any intelligent Jews not to see the covenantal foundations of Judaism. It may be said that at least one or two of those who had studied with Kaplan and had studied Kaplan's texts but who found themselves outside of the rabbinate pursuing other intellectual or academic careers, did follow his covenantal path, including this writer. However, it seemed that the dividing line came between those who followed in his rabbinical path and emphasized religious naturalism and those who followed in his political path and who may not have found religious naturalism either satisfying or appropriate but who followed in his covenantal path. Others who also followed similar paths included Rabbis Irving Greenberg and David Hartman, both students of Rabbi Joseph Soleveichik who was the foremost Orthodox Jewish theologian of our time to pursue covenantal ideas to understand the Jewish people; and Rabbis Eugene Borowitz, Emil Fackenheim, and Arnold Wolf of the Reform movement.[25]

The Late Twentieth Century Revival of Contractarianism

The first postwar generation of the twentieth century—which was also the first generation of the new postmodern epoch—having properly rejected the organic theories of the immediate past and their implications, needed a new theory upon which to build the new worldwide system of politically interdependent states and the new world order which linked them to a greater or lesser degree. The revival began more modestly with charters (as in the case of the United Nations) and treaties (as in the case of the European Union), rather than the by then more bombastic sounding and rather discredited term "covenant." The latter did survive in close to its original secularized form in connection with those United Nations-sponsored multistate agreements which involved moral rather than legal commitments and whose enforcement was left to the moral sense of each of the signatories rather than empowering any separate institutions. Thus, for example, the Universal Covenant of Human Rights remained in the realm of wishful thinking for most of its signatories, if that, for a long period until the end of the cold war made possible the first steps in its international enforcement—worldwide publicity regarding violation, negotiated efforts to make improvements, and international sanctions in a few cases where principle and interest coincided.[26]

By the latter half of the first postwar generation, new theories of contract and covenant began to emerge. In the 1950s, there was a revival of covenantal thinking among theologians, in part seeking to explain the need for and basis of God's justice in the world. Not surprisingly, the theologians most attracted to the covenant idea were the theologians from the Jewish and Protestant Reformed traditions. Beginning in the latter half of the 1950s, there was a major revival of covenantal thinking among Jewish theologians of all persuasions, so much so that, by the early 1960s, covenant again had become the dominant image in Jewish theological thinking, and by the early 1970s, in Jewish public thinking.

In 1971 the publication of John Rawls's book on justice revived Rousseauian contractarian theories.[27] Rawls's ideas were most timely. They were very much suited to the post-1968 spirit which emphasized the private and individual self-interest rather than moral obligation to the community. Contract was what they could afford, not covenant. Rawls's work swept the academic world because it offered a justification for the kind of radical egalitarianism and underdoggism which had become the prevailing ethos. Moreover, it had all the deficiencies of Rousseau's original ideas. The reaction to Rawls on the part of the emerging libertarian schools of thought was also based on narrow contractualism of the kind developed in the nineteenth century by laissez-faire theorists.[28]

In response, there emerged other, increasingly influential groups, individuals and schools, trying to develop a revived comunitarianism more faithful to earlier ideas of covenant. These included the aforementioned thinkers seriously concerned with the revival or further development of democratic theo-political ideas, more secularized covenantalists such as John Taylor and Aaron Wildavsky,[29] serious philosophers such as Lenn Goodman and Michael Walzer,[30] liberal communitarians like Amitai Etzioni and Michael Sandel,[31] and a number of political theorists such as Vincent Ostrom and Donald Lutz who went back to Hobbes and Locke and to Reformed and Puritan political thought for their sources.[32] As we move well into the second postwar generation, it may well be that this new epoch, like others before it, will at least initially lean on covenantal ideas for its intellectual foundations.

While these developments appealed to a significant and even prestigious group of adherents, they did not have the wide echoes that Rawls's contractarian thought did. Covenantalists could understand why. Like all covenantal thought, even when it seems to emphasize rights, it is based upon obligations, first and foremost, while contractarian thought, is based upon rights protections first and foremost, and appeals to people who are not looking to be obligated but seek liberties in spheres which are suited to their individual predelictions, whatever their social consequences. So contractarian thought became uppermost at the end of the first generation of the new epoch, but by the middle of the second, voices were being raised as to what this was doing to civil society. That is where matters stand.

Notes

1. William James, *A Pluralistic Universe* (Cambridge, Mass.: Harvard University Press, 1977), p. 145. James argued that the world is "more like a federal republic than an empire or a kingdom."
2. Henry S. Levinson, "William James and the Federal Republican Principle," in *Federalism as Grand Design*, p. 65.[FULL REF. NEEDED]
3. William James, "Robert Gould Shaw" in *Memories and Studies* (New York: Longmans, Green and Co., 1934), p. 43.
4. Giles Gunn, ed., *Henry James Sr.: A Collection of His Writings* (Chicago: American Library Association, 1974).
5. All quotations are from Gunn, p. 93.
6. Gunn, *Henry James Sr.*, p. 242.
7. James, *Memories and Studies*, p. 43.
8. *Ibid.*, p. 61.
9. William James, *William James' Pragmatism* (Cambridge, Mass.: Harvard University Press, 1975).
10. *Ibid.*, p. 139.
11. Levinson, "William James," p. 28.
12. James, *Pluralistic Universe*, p. 18.
13. Martin Buber, *Das Problem des Menschen*, fifth edition (Heidelberg: L. Schneider, 1982), p. 38.
14. Martin Buber, *Kingship of God* (London: G. Allen and Unwin, 1967); *The Prophetic Faith* (New York: Harper and Bros., 1960); *Moses* (Atlantic Highlands, N.J.: Humanities Press International, 1988).
15. Buber, *Kingship of God*; Bernard Susser, " The Anarcho-Federalism of Martin Buber," *Federalism as Grand Design*, pp. 103–15; Daniel J. Elazar, "The Book of Judges: The Israelite Tribal Federation and its Discontents," *Interpretation*, forthcoming.
16. Susser, p. 104.
17. *Ibid.*, p. 106.
18. Buber, "Warum muss der Aufbau Palastinas ein sozialisticher sein," *Der Jude und Sein Judentum* (Koln: Josef Melzer Verlag, 1963), p. 381.
19. Martin Buber, *Pfade in Utopia* (Heidelberg: L. Schneider, 1985).
20. Vincent Ostrom, "Dewey and Federalism: So Near and Yet So Far," *Federalism As Grand Design, Publius*, vol. 9, no. 4 (Fall 1979).
21. Mordecai M. Kaplan, *Judaism as a Civilization* (New York: Schocken Books, 1967).
22. Mordecai M. Kaplan, *The Religion of Ethical Nationhood: Judaism's Contribution to World Peace* (New York: Macmillan, 1970).
23. Charles S. Liebman, "Reconstructionism in American Jewish Life," *American Jewish Yearbook* (New York and Philadelphia: American Jewish Committee and Jewish Publication Society of America, 1970), pp. 3–99.
24. Robert Bellah, *The Broken Covenant: American Civil Religion in Time of Trial* (Chicago: University of Chicago Press, 1992); William Johnson Everett, *God's Federal Republic* (New York: Panlist Press, 1988); Franklin Littell, *From State Church to Pluralism: A Protestant Interpretation of Religion in American History* (Garden City, N.Y.: Doubleday, 1962); Douglas Sturm, *Community and Alienation* (Notre Dame, Ind.: University of Notre Dame Press, 1988); Max Stackhouse, *The Ethics of Necropolis* (Boston: Beacon Press, 1971); Charles McCoy, *When God's Change: Hope for Theology,* (Nashville, Abingdon, 1980);

and *the Greatness of America: People, Promise, Dream,* (Berkeley, CA: Glenn Berkeley Press, 1993).

25. Arnold Jacob Wolf, *Renewing the Covenant* (Philadelphia, Pa.: The Jewish Publication Society, 1991); Irving Greenberg, *Voluntary Covenant* (New York: Jewish National Resource Center, 1982); *idem.,* "Toward a Covenantal Ethic of Medicine," *Jewish Values in Bioethics,* Levi Meier, ed. (New York: Human Sciences Press, 1986), pp. 124–49; David Hartman, *A Living Covenant* (New York: The Free Press, 1985).

26. *Human Rights Sourcebook,* Albert P. Blaustein et al., eds. (New York: Paragon House Publishers, 1987).

27. John Rawls, *A Theory of Justice* (Cambridge, Mass.: Belknap Press, 1971).

28. See, for example, Robert Nozick, *Anarchy, State and Utopia* (New York: Basic Books, Inc., 1974).

29. John F.D. Taylor, *The Marks of Society* (New York: Appleton-Century-Crofts, 1966); Lenn Goodman, *On Justice.*

30. Michael Walzer, *Spheres of Justice: A Defense of Pluralism and Equality* (New York: Basic Books, 1983).

31. Amitai Etzioni, *New Communitarian Thinking: Persons, Virtues, Institutions, and Communities* (Charlottesville: University Press of Virginia, 1995); Michael Sandel, *Democracy's Discontent: America in Search of a Public Philosophy* (Cambridge, Mass.: Belknap Press of Harvard University Press, 1996).

32. Donald S. Lutz, *A Preface to American Political Theory,* (Lawrence, KA: University Press of Kansas, 1992); *Popular Consent and Popular Control: Whig Political Theory in the Early State Constitutions,* (Baton Rouge: Louisiana State University Press, 1980); *The Origins of American Constitutionalism,* (Baton Rouge: Louisiana State University Press, 1988). Vincent Ostrom, *The Meaning of American Federalism: Constituting a Self-Governing Society,* (San Francisco: ICS Press, 1991); *Rethinking Institutional Analysis and Development: Issues, Alternatives, and Choices,* (San Francisco: ICS Press, 1993); *The Meaning of Democracy and the Vulnerability of Democracies: A Response to Tocqueville's Challenge,* (Ann Arbor: University of Michigan Press, 1997); *The Intellectual Crisis in American Public Administration,* (Tuscaloosa: University of Alabama Press, 1989); *The Political Theory of a Compound Republic: Designing the American Experiment,* (Lincoln: University of Nebraska Press, 1987).

Part II

Covenant and the Age of State-Building

6

Europe: Modern Nationalism
and the Covenant Tradition

Federalism, Centralization, and State-Building in the Modern Epoch

In many ways, the history of modern nationalism starts from the modern revision and secularization of covenantal thinking. In the end, moderns influenced by the covenant tradition invented modern federalism as a synthesis that could link the covenantal tradition with that of the modern nation-state. In its truest sense, the federal principle stands in opposition to the centralized, reified nation-state which is the principal product of modern nationalism. In essence, modern federalism was invented to provide either an alternative to or a corrective for the classic nation-state model but one which would still be within the parameters of modern state-building.

The modern nation-state was born, or invented, in Europe in the century and a half between the revolt of the Netherlands against Spain (1567) and the Treaty of Utrecht (1714). Building upon the centralizing, hierarchical, statist principle of absolutism in combination with the new trend towards national identity on a territorial basis, modern nationalism led to the abandonment of the corporatism that characterized late feudal or postfeudal body politic. It was based on the notion of a single political entity commanding universal loyalty on the part of all subjects or citizens and possessing full authority, that is to say, sovereignty within its territorial limits.

The classic modern nation-state was based upon the principle that its sovereignty was indivisible, and indeed, that sovereignty had to be concentrated in a single center in order to be properly exercised. This idea was a natural outgrowth of the circumstances of its birth, which involved the bringing of very wide territories under the control of a single center, usually a single individual—a monarch—through conquest or dynastic merger. From the first, the nation-state either reflected or embraced hierarchical principles of formation, organization, governance, and justification. Hence it was a thorough rejection of covenantal principles in either religious or secular form. Indeed, its partisans put up doctrines justifying hierarchical models as the only legiti-

117

mate ones, rejecting medieval corporatism even more than modern federal pluralism.

France, the first European state, had developed even earlier. It was also the first of the modern nation-states; hence, it is not surprising that a Frenchman, Jean Bodin (1530–96), developed the theory upon which it rested, presented in full in his *Six Books of the Republic* (1566). The theory came along with the fact, if not after it, helping to shape people's minds so that they soon would come to see the world in terms of the nation-state and brook no other notion of political organization as fully legitimate. By the time Europe's age of revolutions began in 1789, the revolutionaries sought principally to seize the center of sovereignty and power in the name of the people, or if no such center existed, to establish one in their name. Absolutism gave way to Jacobinism; for moderns, a more popular way of reified state-building. This became the pattern for the next century and a half, until the epoch's end.

In the first stages of the development of the reified state, federalism stood in apposition, if not in opposition, to it. Modern federalism made its appearance in the same century and a half that saw the emergence of the sovereign state and its supporters. The federalists who challenged Bodin and his cohorts also recognized the necessity for constitutional change to adapt to the new age that was emerging, but they sought that change through adaptation of late medieval corporatism to the new territorialism, which was a principal feature of modern state-building, in such a way that at least the *exercise* of sovereignty would be dispersed among different territorial and corporate centers in order to preserve traditional liberties and prevent absolutism—a characteristic feature of the early modern state. While any number of now-neglected theorists articulated this view throughout the period under discussion, particularly in the Germanic world, and continued to do so well into the nineteenth century, the first, Johannes Althusius (1557–1638), who stressed the connection between the covenantal tradition and federalism, was its most articulate spokesman and systematic theorist.

The struggle between these two conceptions of the polity and their articulators was paralleled then superseded by the political struggle between rulers and peoples that set its stamp upon the epoch. Every nation in Europe that had the opportunity to achieve statehood and every state that emerged, at one point or another was forced to choose between the federalist and centralist models. Most chose the latter. Some made the choice they did before the invention of modern federalism and were faced with the option of choosing centralization or a system that would preserve their traditional liberties but which failed to provide them with sufficient security against the growing strength of other centralized states. Others were founded after the centralist ideology had become the European norm and chose accordingly.

From the mid-sixteenth through the mid-eighteenth centuries, France, Spain, England, and Prussia choose the path of the modern nation-state; Switzerland

and the Netherlands chose the path of traditional federalism or confederation; and the other German and Italian states tried to preserve their independence, usually through a modernized version of medieval personal rule. Russia and Austria were transformed into modernized empires with certain organizational characteristics of modern states but still multinational medieval autocracies in conception and character. They remained such until World War I.

While the first group waxed strong, the latter two ran into difficulties. The French Revolution and the Napoleonic Wars which followed threatened the regimes of both confederations, actually altering that of the Netherlands to bring it into line with the new statism, but failing to do so in Switzerland, succeeding only in bringing an end to its traditional federal form. The German and Italian states were also weakened and the stage was set for the transformation of their regimes in the nineteenth century. After 1784, Austria was plagued by nationalist revolutions. Only Russia was able to preserve its old order essentially intact until the twentieth century.

In the end, in the nineteenth and twentieth centuries, Switzerland, Germany and Austria chose federalism and stayed with it. Switzerland did so with a full heart because its political culture and situation combined to make federalism a universal desideratum. Germany begrudgingly adopted federal form because it was the only way that Prussia could secure that country's unification. Austria's transformation into a modern nation-state came almost at the end of the modern epoch under circumstances similar to those which elsewhere were to generate the postmodern federalist revolution. The transformed Russian empire also chose a nominal federal structure after its 1917 revolutions, as the only feasible means for reintegrating the old empire under Bolshevik rule. That structure did not become real until the collapse of the Bolshevik empire seventy years later.

While those changes were taking place in Europe, the newly independent American states were inventing modern federalism, which can be seen as an adaptation of the modern nation-state idea that would achieve some of the goals of traditional federalism, while actually reflecting a new set of federalist aspirations. Like other modern nations, the new American nation rejected medieval corporatism. Indeed, in British North America, there never was any such thing and the few efforts to introduce it remained insignificant at most. The American colonies were territorial republics from the first and, with some early and transient exceptions, citizenship went with the territory. At the same time, Americans were congenitally opposed to absolutism or the centralization of power in any form. Even so, having fought a revolution against a superpower, at least the American leadership had come to realize that the country's security needs alone required an appropriately strong and energetic general government.

In a brilliant invention, the American Founders came up with the answer to their problem. As republicans they had come the understand sovereignty as

120   Covenant and Civil Society

residing in the people rather than in any state, government, or ruler. A *res publica* (or thing of the people),as they understood it, was a commonwealth in which the sovereign people delegated certain powers to the agencies of government that they established to function on their behalf, rather than a reified state.

If the people could delegate powers to the agencies of one government, why could they not divide those delegated powers among several governments? Since no government had other than delegated powers, there was no possibility of having a single sovereign government in any case, and having a single center of power was dangerous, perhaps fatal, to liberty. At the same time, one could argue that, in accordance with modern political thought, sovereignty was not divided since it was vested in the people. What was most important, however, was that the whole sovereignty question was laid aside and transformed into a question of powers and their exercise—who has the power and authority to do what? Thus modern federalism was invented. The new federal government of the United States of America did not serve a set of transformed medieval corporations. It served a state, or, more accurately, it served a community of states, each of which had full powers in those spheres delegated to it by the people through its own written constitution.

Shortly after the Americans had invented modern federalism, the Dutch, under Napoleonic pressure, abandoned their traditional system for a centralized Jacobin republic, later to be reconstituted as a unitary, decentralized monarchy (in the words of the Dutch constitution). The Swiss, however, managed to recoup and learn from the American experience so that in 1848 they transformed their traditional federal system into a modern federation, borrowing heavily from the American model.

The German states went through a period of political change, each step of which came in the wake of a war. The Thirty Years' War (1618–48) effectively ended the traditional confederation of German states known as the Holy Roman Empire. Although its shell survived until 1806, the rise of Prussia and Austria as modern states destroyed the basis of its existence. The Napoleonic wars brought about regional leagues of princes and a general customs union (the *Zollverein*) which led to an all-German confederation established in 1815 by the Congress of Vienna. That body, always weak, was finally destroyed by the Austro-Prussian War of 1866.

In place of the confederation there arose a Prussian-dominated federation of kingdoms established by Bismarck in 1871. World War I destroyed that regime, which was replaced by the reluctantly federal Weimar Republic. Needless to say, Hitler abolished federalism along with all other German liberties, all of which were restored to West Germany in the aftermath of World War II with the constitution of the present German Federal Republic (1949) and its completion with the addition of the five *lander* of the former German Democratic Republic in 1990.

Elsewhere in Europe, the Scandinavian countries moved out of their medieval frameworks to become fully independent states, statist in form but emphasizing local home rule in fact. Despite a strong tradition of local liberties and noncentralization, Belgium was forced to adopt the reified state model, within which it effectively developed an internally decentralized quasi-federation of provinces. Spain and Portugal eliminated all but vestiges of the medieval *fueros* which had once kept those countries noncentralized. Indeed, both were among the earliest centralized states. In Spain, this could only be done at the price of repressing regionally based nationality groups, which contributed to the state of almost constant civil war which plagued that country in the nineteenth century. Italy was unified by force in the middle generation of the century, and opted for full centralization.

To the east of the German states, Ottoman imperial rule was reduced by force, allowing the rise of the nation-states of Greece, Bulgaria, Romania, and Serbia, each of which was based on a preexisting nationality group seeking its place in the sun. The transformation of the Russian and Austro-Hungarian empires came at the very end of the epoch. Austria lost its empire, which was replaced by a number of unitary states, some of which (e.g., Hungary) possessed a national integrity and others of which (e.g., Yugoslavia after World War I) tried—and failed—to impose a single artificial national identity on a multinational polity. Austria proper, although no longer a multinational state, became a federal republic, a reflection of the German leaning toward federalism. The new Bolshevik regime in Russia, desirous of preserving as much of the old empire as possible, reluctantly turned to a federal structure to accommodate the various nationalities seeking independence, but proceeded to minimize the reality of federalism by extending the dominant role of the highly centralized Communist party throughout the USSR.

The situation in the Americas, particularly North America, was the complete reverse. All three independent polities to emerge in North America were founded as federations, while the major polities of South America, especially Argentina, Brazil, and Venezuela, adopted federal structures for reasons which reflected the differences between the American and European situations. These deserve extensive treatment in their own right. Suffice it to say that in all but the case of the United States, there was a struggle between centralists and federalists, with the latter equating federalism with liberty, reflecting the clash between European and American theories of state and nation-building.

Similar struggles are still taking place in the twentieth century in Africa and Asia with the decolonization of the Third World. There, too, European and American theories of state-building are struggling with one another for control of the hearts and minds of people as reflected in the structure of their new polities.

This struggle and its results in each of the world's polities is a matter that should be of concern to students of federalism and comparative politics generally. Why did each nation or state make the choice that it did? What are the consequences of its choice? Where there was a struggle, what echoes remain of that struggle after its initial resolution?

This line of inquiry can be pursued profitably not only in connection with the states of Europe, but also in connection with the decisions taken in the New World and the Third World. For example, given the weak performance of federal systems in Latin America and their obvious incompatibility with the authoritarian regimes so prevalent in that region, why have federal forms been considered critically necessary in the major countries of the region? Why did only one country—Colombia—formally abandon federalism after fifteen years? Why have the boundaries of the constituent states remained essentially unchanged since they were established, generations, if not centuries, ago?

Or, to take a different case, both India and Pakistan opted for federalism when they became independent in 1947. Why has federalism—albeit in relatively centralized form—taken root in the former while remaining so much weaker in the latter until the 1990s? These questions of original constitutional choice are tied up with issues of culture and circumstances of external security and internal power alignments, all of which deserve serious consideration.

For example, a systematic and analytic tour of the Austro-Hungarian experience introduces us to the nature of the conflict. The Hapsburg Empire, from its medieval beginnings to its collapse during the First World War was at the fulcrum of the conflict.[1] Its ancient traditions were corporatist with a tendency toward the kind of structured pluralism which could have encouraged federalist expression in the Althusian mode while its political culture made it prone to absolutism. As a result, its history involved half-hearted efforts at federalist accommodation which were, in turn, unfulfilled because of stronger commitments to absolutism. Its struggle to achieve a modus vivendi was frustrated in the end because it embraced so many different nations, peoples, and ethnic groups, each seeking its own place in the political sun through modern statehood. Hence the pressures for dissolution of the empire in the name of national self-determination were constant from the time that the nation-state was born.

In the sixteenth century, the Hapsburgs inherited the Spanish throne and gained control of the Lowlands, whose northern provinces became the second league of polities to successfully revolt against Hapsburg domination (the first was the Swiss confederation three hundred years earlier). Both were in the territory that embraced what had been the borderlands between the limits of the Roman empire and the area settled by the Germanic tribes that lay beyond the empire's reach many centuries earlier. Later, after the time of Charlemagne in the ninth century, the same area from the North Sea to the Adriatic was the kingdom of Lothar, one of the three kingdoms into which Charlemagne divided his empire for each of his three heirs. This, the middle kingdom, embraced that borderlands region and, unlike the western and eastern kingdoms which developed into France and Germany respectively, remained the most faithful to its older traditions of local self-government and group, if not individual, freedom, particularly in its northern and southern reaches. Thus the Hapsburgs, the heartland of whose empire was more comfortable with authoritarian and hierarchical rule, inherited a hornet's nest.

The revolting provinces' dissatisfaction with Hapsburg rule was further intensified by the Protestant Reformation. True to their already established character, they embraced Reformed Protestantism, the most covenantal form. These provinces formed a traditional federal system, what we would style a confederacy today, known as the United Provinces of the Netherlands. They enjoyed a golden age during the seventeenth century, then dissipated their strength in contests with their great, powerful, and increasingly centralized neighbors, foolishly seeking to compete with them as an equal power on the international scene.

After 200 years, certainly a substantial length of time and one which prevents us from judging the Netherlands confederation a failure, the weight of its medieval institutions did indeed become too great to resist the popular demands for greater participation in the governance of the body politic. Having become overly oligarchic and not very effective, the regime was swept away in the tide of the French Revolution. Nevertheless, its principles retained sufficient support and the political culture which it both reflected and fostered was sufficiently entrenched among the Dutch that, after a brief experiment with a Jacobin-style republic and then a Napoleonic-style monarchy, the Dutch adopted a constitution establishing a regime that was both unitary and decentralized. The old provinces retained substantial powers and the communes, real local liberty.

In the nineteenth century, the pluralism that was characteristic of the Netherlands took a new turn, one that was not expressed through medieval corporations or through territorial jurisdictions, but through religious and ideological communities. The Dutch drew upon their own political cultural heritage to integrate this new pluralism into their regime through what a century later would be termed by the Dutch political scientist, Arend Lipjhardt, consociationalism, and which can be seen as a rebirth of federalism in the Netherlands on a nonterritorial basis.[2]

One of the last European states to be established and to adopt the ideology of modern nationalism was Italy, in 1860, considerably after the invention of modern federalism. Regionalism on the Italian peninsula became strongly entrenched after the fall of the Roman Empire, through various regional and city-states. Many of them were republics in the medieval style. Most of these developed their own political cultures which have remained distinct throughout the years.[3]

When Italy was unified, the struggle between centralists and federalists became open and explicit, with the centralists winning but never able to consolidate their victory.[4] Italy today is still engaged in trying to find a way to accommodate the regionalist impulses which gave rise to the federalist movement in the first place.

Ethnic and Covenantal Bases of Modern Nationalism

The European experience with statism and, for that matter, most experiences with statism on other continents that grew out of the European model, was reinforced by the emergence of modern nationalism. The identification of nationalism and statism gave the latter a powerful boost. While nationalism often presents itself as primordial, in many if not most cases it is based on a myth of its own, that is to say, nations often are no more than combinations of preexisting tribal and territorial groups within a particular territory that, for reasons just as artificial as any other form of conquest, were pressed together in a common mold or under common rule over many intervening centuries and so took on a patina of common primordial origins.[5] Since new nations are forming at this time, we can watch this process in operation and measure its similarities and differences from era to era.

In sum, nationalism often is the making of a moral virtue out of a spatial necessity. This is by no means an unimportant task since humans must live with their spatial necessities and try to become moral in response to them. On the other hand, recognizing this rather dilutes any primacy that nationalism might have. As always, the Bible accurately describes or reflects the process, indicating how new nations represent a splitting off from earlier groupings and combine to form new ones through both kinship and consent, organic and covenantal means. That is the way the Bible portrays the story of the origins of the Jewish people and the other peoples around them, particularly in the Book of Genesis.[6]

Nationalism has been pervasive and powerful in the modern and early postmodern worlds. The elements that form it can be traced back to the emergence of a sense of common descent, manifestations of a common culture, and the development of a consensus about the existence of the nation and the identification of its members with it; but the proportions of each are different, often extremely different, in each case. For example, in Eastern Europe nations such as the Poles, Hungarians, Slovaks, and Rumanians have a long consciousness of their similarity, common descent, and common culture, especially a primordial language, all of which combine to give them a fairly clear sense of national identity and enable advocates of nationalism to foster a sense of common political aspirations and common obligations to defend the nation and to express its culture.[7]

German-speakers, on the other hand, have been fractured into at least three separate national groupings—German, Austrian, and Swiss—over time, because of their spatial necessities. The Swiss, indeed, have become a nation without the usual commonalities of descent, language, and primordial culture. For them, the consensus that it is better to be Swiss than to be German, Austrian, French, or Italian has been a powerful force for nationalism, much reinforced by their spatial necessities.[8] For them covenantal consent was more potent than kinship.

The Italians, on the other hand, have only acquired a sense of nationalism within human memory, although they had a sense of a common culture prior to that. It was only with the unification of Italy in 1870 and the resultant pressure of the new Italian state and its educational system to foster a common sense of Italianness that Italian nationalism emerged, and it is constantly under challenge. Indeed, the vast majority of Italian immigrants to the United States did not discover that they were Italians rather than Sicilians or Lombardians or Tuscans or whatever only after they came to the United States, because Americans defined them as Italians.

American nationalism, which has rarely been discussed in those terms, is clearly a matter of choice and consent. With all but the tiniest handful of its population having removed themselves to the United States or its predecessor colonies by their own volition or, in the case of the Africans, by force, and detached from any earlier identities, the preservation of what Americans see as primordial identity is for Americans a matter of ethnicity or, as it was called in earlier years, nationality, not nationhood, and as suggested above, in the case of the Czech, German, and Italian immigrants, some of that is also an American invention.

Then there are the Jews, one of the very oldest of nations, with strong traditions of common descent and critical dimensions of common culture, especially in manifest ways, but with no common language in daily use for a thousand years, and without the ordinary forms of spatial concentration in their own land for nearly two thousand, except as a historical memory that in every century some among them tried to transform into current reality.[9] The Jews continued to form a nation; indeed, they defined themselves and were defined by their neighbors in the Old World as a nation in exile until, in the twentieth century, they developed a common project to return to their ancient homeland that served to unite virtually all Jews. The Jews are among that handful of nations who recognize that kinship is not enough, that they need covenant as well, to establish consent and some critical dimensions of consensus for nationhood. Having both, their national identity is doubly strong, which may be why it has survived for over 3,500 years, since the second millennium before the Common Era, and the fact that hundreds of those years have been spent in exile.

Here we must keep in mind the distinction between nations and states. Nations are ethnic phenomena that may strive for national statehood or may be content to find cultural expression within some other state framework. Exponents of modern nationalism have had as one of their goals the establishment of nation-states whereby the two are identical or they have been only partially successful in this. Reality has had an impact at least as strong. Fewer than 10 percent of all states are as homogeneous as they pretend to be, and in many situations the complexity of the population makes it impossible to satisfy the national demands of many groups. The modern epoch was devoted to that pursuit and the postmodern epoch must pick up the pieces from it and find other solutions.

That leads us to a second distinction, between peoples and publics. Peoples may have national consciousness and yet not form a public, that is to say, an intergenerational collectivity that seeks special political status. What often occurs when that happens is that the publics include more than one people or only part of a people. Spain is an example of the first. For many of its citizens, there is a strong sense of being Basques, Catalans, or Galicians, but most share a desire to be part of a common Spanish public provided that those peoples who want it can have a degree of autonomy or self-rule within the common Spanish shared rule framework. The Germans were examples of the second prior to the reunification of the two Germanies in 1990. During the forty-five years of their separation as publics as a result of the pressures of world politics, they never lost their sense of common Germanness.

Finally, we should recognize what has now become obvious, namely, the pervasiveness and power of nationalism despite apparent Western rejections of it for various ecumenical political ideologies—humanism, socialism, and communism, to mention the "best known" among them. Each of these ideologies was cosmopolitan in that it suggested that once humans were freed from atavistic commitments, religious, ethnic, national, they would all become far more identified with the world order that each proposed. Early on, it became clear that this would not be the case. Humanism and modern nationalism were born at approximately the same time and nationalism has certainly won. Socialism found out the power of nationalism at the outbreak of World War I in 1914 when socialists the world over expected the workers of the world to refuse their nations' calls to arms to fight against one another in what, even at its beginning, seemed to them to be an unnecessary war. Yet the workers of all the principals in the war responded to the call to arms without hesitation and continued to support their national governments throughout that horrible conflict.[10]

After the Bolshevik Revolution, the Communist party sought to learn from those earlier experiences by imposing Communism through the media of different ethnic and national cultures. In the end that, too, proved to be insufficient and nationalism contributed much to the downfall of Communism in various countries of the world outside of the Soviet Union and then in the Soviet Union itself at the end of the 1980s.

There are three bases to modern nationalism. One is the ethnic assumption, the second the territorial reality, and the third the covenantal synthesis.

All three are necessary; the first if nationalism is to exist, the second if it is to survive, and the third if it is to fulfill itself, even in its own terms, which, in the modern epoch, invariably make the claim that nationalism has a moral dimension.

With regard to the ethnic assumption, we have already commented on the nationalist idea and the ideal of organic peoplehood, that is to say, people bound by blood ties. It can be said that this is the ideal of modern nationalism and its central myth. Real peoples or nations are bound by culture far more than by kinship, although because of cultural sharing, kinship is likely to come in time, through endogamous marriage within the same culture and the rejection in some form of extensive exogamous marriage with people from other cultures.[11]

Shared culture almost inevitably triumphs over elements more primordial. The nationalist myth has it that cultures are inherited but we know that cultures can be formed. For example, the French ruling class formed French culture by imposing it on non-French or marginally French groups, outlawing their local languages, even as names for their children, and fostering a common French high culture through the state schools and made compulsory by state law as well as custom and sociological preference.[12]

The problematics of the nationalist assumption has to do with who is "in" and who is "out" and how do people get in or stay in and how do they get out or drop out. For the Jewish people, at least until very recently, outmarriage moved Jews out of the Jewish nation and the Jewish people. Not having a clear language or territorial base, Jews had to place great emphasis on endogamy, often even to the point of being reluctant or simply refusing to convert non-Jews who sought to come into the Jewish people or religion. In the postmodern epoch this at least two-thousand-year old system is collapsing. It remains to be seen whether the Jewish people will simply write off those who marry out or seek some other definition of how to be Jewish.

The greatest cement for Jewish nationalism over the years has been the Jewish religion, that is to say, the sense of being religiously obligated to live according to the Torah and its commandments as embodied in *halakhah*, Jewish law, which is either religious or religiously grounded. In the modern epoch this religious cement also began to dissolve. The efforts made to replace it by secular nationalism have been less than successful for the majority of Jews in the world.

Migration normally is one of the major ways in or out of a nation. Unless one resides on the nation's territory (whether it is an independent state or not), historically it is not likely that he or she will retain the national culture or identity. Indeed, for most peoples of the world, migration has been one of the great change agents in matters of national identification. The role of migration in separating one people from another has been known since biblical days. Large migrations that have brought settlers into already inhabited territories and who overwhelm the original inhabitants and bring them into a new nation are matters of historical record.

The American nation is one of the greatest examples of conscious national development through migration. The American national myth emphasizes the fact that all or virtually all Americans became Americans because they or their ancestors migrated to the territory now the United States and willingly joined the American nation or, even if coming unwillingly at first, did so subsequently, while retaining consciousness of that original migration. Indeed, in the late twentieth century, American blacks seeking to develop a proper American identity have sought to discover their African roots so that they can be like those Americans with European or Asian roots. Native Americans, who cannot make such claims, have had to adjust by claiming a special place because of their aboriginal status.

One of the cardinal tenets of American public policy is that every human being has a right to choose his or her nationality and can emigrate as freely as he or she desires, or at least should be able to. Some nationalisms, on the other hand, argue that one can never sever his or her national ties, even by emigration. Germany and France, for example, treat children of emigrants as nationals in the same way that the children of those who remain in the homeland are treated, (e.g., they are subject to compulsory military service) although, again, in recent years world pressure has modified the exercise of those claims, especially since the United States is not only the world's greatest power but also holds to a diametrically different principle because of its own historical experience. The acquisition of citizenship often is referred to as naturalization rather than nationalization since it may or may not confer nationality at the same time.

This leads to the issue of the territorial reality. Most nationalisms require a very strong territorial dimension to exist. At the very least, territories solve most of the problematics of who is in and who is out for most nations. Recently, the rise of large national diasporas in other countries in the form of *gastarbeiter*, foreign business establishments, or tenacious ethno-tribal groups, have challenged this rather simple convention. In Germany and Switzerland, for example, the Turks, North Africans, and various Yugoslav peoples who have come as *gastarbeiter* do not become settlers on a citizenship track. Even their children born on German or Swiss soil do not. The problematics of this arrangement are just beginning to be felt and have led to the revival and reconsideration of group rights.

This is a reversal of another statist assumption. Since territory is so obviously important in the definition of nationalism, it was not difficult at the beginning of the modern epoch in Europe for people to make assumptions that the territorial congeries of estates of the premodern epoch should be formed into nation-states, that is to say, their privileges as separate estates were abolished. Ethnic or religious minorites either were forced to conform and become parts of the dominant nation or they were to be repressed or expelled in some way from the territory. In these ways, the nationalists sought and thus brought about formally the complete or essentially complete convergence between nation and state.

In reality, this turned out to be impossible. The Germans and the French came closest, the Germans by expelling and murdering those who were different, even those different by "blood" who could not become Germans even if they wanted to, and the French through more humane means of forcing French culture upon all. In neither case were even they successful. There were just too many minorities in the world and they just kept springing up within these so-called nation-states. After achieving homogeneity through bloodshed in World War II, the Germans imported hundreds of thousands, even millions, of *gastarbeiter* from North Africa and the Balkans because their economies needed them as workers, to engender new problems of heterogeneity on German territory. The French had to do the same and have inherited problems of their own as a result.

Most other states never even came as close as the French and the Germans. Some did not even try. Even the ones who sought homogeneity, however, ultimately have had to move toward postmodern solutions whereby the nation-state ideal began to be transformed into the norm of the citizen-state, whereby all within a state's borders would have an equal opportunity to become citizens of the state. Minorities would be recognized, certainly as individuals, and sometimes even with group rights, and basic services were extended to all residents of a particular territory on an equal or very close to equal basis. All of this was pioneered in Western Europe by the European Community, now Union, for citizens of its member states. It did not have to be pioneered in the New World states because they, as countries of migration, had sought to develop new nations which would be perforce citizen-states and had, in general, succeeded. Even so, after the 1960s, many services were extended to "undocumented" (read illegal) immigrants to those countries.

At this writing, the United States is attempting to take a newly reformative view of those services. In Western Europe, however, the original repository of the whole statist and nation-state idea, a real adjustment has been made. It became the task of the European Community/Union to make that adjustment. While still not universal, the new idea based on the new reality or on recognition of old realities spread quickly around the world. Various experiments are now underway to find means to implement it.

Throughout the modern epoch, however, the territorial reality was assumed to be more influential than it could be. Even at that time there were problematics since most territorial states were states of conquest rather than organic entities. France, for example, seemingly the quintessential nation-state, actually represented a series of conquests over hundreds of years, spreading out from the original territory of the Comte de Paris to the Atlantic, the Pyrenees, the

Mediterranean, the Alps, and the German regions. The physical features stopped French expansion with relative ease. The Germans stopped French expansion only after centuries of warfare. Nevertheless, the territory of France was relatively fixed by the beginning of the modern epoch and the French state could impose its culture upon that territory throughout that epoch.

In Germany, the strongest German states conquered the weaker ones and imposed Germanness at relatively low cost since almost all the population was German and German-speaking. Still, as the history of the United States demonstrates, hundreds of thousands, even millions of Germans, either liberals or uninterested in becoming cannon-fodder for Prussian or other armies, emigrated (read "fled") from the country in the nineteenth century to the New World. Similar stories could be told about most of the other so-called nation-states in the world.

Nevertheless, the combination of territoriality and ethnicity have brought peoples closest to fulfilling their ideal of the nation-state. In this many of the most successful were aided by taking a leaf out of the covenant tradition to forge their nation-states through the addition of a dimension of consent and constitutionalism, what we might refer to as the modern covenantal synthesis in recognition of a shared national feeling. To gain or establish the requisite measure of consent, the nation would be conceived as having a moral purpose and as resting upon a consensus around that moral purpose. In most cases, that moral purpose was very narrowly defined in nationalist terms that rested on organic assumptions, namely that every nation had its own culture and that the world would be enriched if that nation could express its culture on the world scene. Some went further to argue that the national culture offered certain virtues that no other culture could provide or could provide equally well. Therefore it was morally imperative for the nation to develop its culture and make it available. It was not hard for this thinking to move a step further to cultural imperialism even while morally it could stay within the realm of cultural nationalism.

In the last analysis, however while most modern nationalism could rely on organic and territorial foundations, all required the consensus of those they touched that they were indeed a nation. That consensus required choice on the part of many people and that choice sooner or later had to be produced by some covenantal act, even if the very ideas of covenant and choice themselves were rejected. While rarely true covenants in the sense of being consciously covenantal, in every one of the nations at some point there is some act or set of acts usually given ideational expression in some document or set of documents that marks the proclamation of nationhood and its purposes. In the modern epoch, these were most often embodied in declarations of independence or constitutions. This is not to say that every declaration of independence or constitution was the product of consciously informed popular consent, but if the declarations or constitutions survived as documents with meaning, they ultimately reached out to maximize the degree to which they were accepted by the people or public to whom they were addressed.

In those national cultures fundamentally covenantal the process worked in reverse. The moral basis of those covenantal cultures was used to build a sense of nationalism. The Jewish people and the United States are the most prominent examples. As Saadia Gaon wrote in ninth-century Babylonia, the Jews are a nation by virtue of their Torah, that is, by virtue of their covenant-founded, morally grounded constitution and laws.[13] Though much has happened to change the Jewish people since then, that is still true.

Both the founding and the refounding of the United States at the time of the Civil War were strongly rooted in the definition of American moral purpose and the development of a consensus around that definition, set into words by Jefferson and others of the founding fathers at the time of the American Revolution. Lincoln's idea of a new nation conceived in liberty and dedicated to the proposition that all men are created equal represented a renewal and reinvigoration of that effort at the time of the Civil War. The same was true even before 1776 in the founding of many of the American colonies and it can be argued that the refounding of the United States on the basis of the extension of equality to previously excluded or subordinated groups in the 1960s and 1970s was dressed in the same language in an effort to make it the same kind of search.

Three Political Responses

The problematics of the covenantal synthesis involved the first two kinds of polities. The addition of a covenantal dimension to otherwise organic or hierarchical societies added architectonic but still limited purposes. In the first, an organic community of the Middle Ages was turned into a modern state. In the second, a conquered empire was turned into a modern state.

In the third, the covenanted polity was turned into the modern state. In covenantal societies, the tendency to move from covenant to pact as the covenantal message may have been useful only for mobilizing the generation effected by it, who often were likely to translate it into ideas that were viewed as traditional and conventional. Still, nationalisms without some covenantal synthesis have had a difficult time, even in the heyday of nationalism as an ideal in the nineteenth century.

In the organic communities-turned-states; estates, guilds, countries, peoples and communities in the same territory came together. These new states had aristocratic or oligarchic tendencies. Frequently they maintained established religions throughout the modern epoch and, even if subsequently disestablished, those religions retained a special place and status in the polity. Their power structure is based on the center-periphery model and they went through a major crossroads during the modern epoch in which some like England, chose the path of evolution and others, like Turkey, chose the path of revolution along the Jacobin model.

The second group of polities, based on empires established by conquerors, were, like France, built by conquest followed by national consolidation. They generally have autocratic tendencies and often maintain their state religion or a state political religion. Their power structure is usually hierarchical and in many cases they moved in the modern epoch from authoritarianism to totalitarianism.

The third model is the covenanted polity as state. Its founding was very important and the federal character established at that time very influential. These polities generally have republican and democratic tendencies, without any formally established religion but with a civil religion that is so widespread and socially accepted that it subtly guides the polity. The polity's power structure is federal and its major transformation to modernity was from union based on religious bonds to union based on civil ones.

We have seen that last form in the United States and, with modifications, in the other new societies. In Europe, however, those states in which statehood itself was important, the first two models predominated. They were influenced by the covenantal tradition, normally in secularized form, through their revolutions if at all. It is to those revolutions that we will now turn.

Between Nationalism and Revolution

Nationalism can be seen in the way late moderns saw it as a step toward democratization. As people were identified with their nation they also were identified as somehow fundamentally equal as nationals. From there, in the perspective of history, it was not a big step to move from being identified as a national to being identified as a citizen, especially if the nation had or was striving for its own state.

As nationality gave a person status, citizenship gave one rights. Both also bestowed obligations, not the least of which was compulsory military service in defense of the nation. This, too, can be seen in one sense as more of a step than an invention.

Communities of people always have had to defend themselves. In the premodern world that defense was provided by the obligation of every male above a certain age to bear arms in his appropriate community formation. If his community was a tribe, he fought as a member of the militia of that tribe. If it was a village or a valley, it, too, had its community and its militia. Each was composed of people whose full-time pursuits were in making a living, however it was done, but who had their responsibilities and knew them. Those tribal and village militias were not only democratic in their essence but were the sources of tribal or village democracy or republicanism, in the sense that arms-bearing, that is, participating in the militia, bought one certain privileges of participation in the life of the community on a more or less equal footing.

In feudal-style arrangements, that democratic dimension was replaced by hierarchy. It was still the community but it was a community of fealty to a feudal lord commander who had superior status, and superior wealth enabling him to be better equipped militarily and also to help equip those who owed him fealty. Kings and emperors who may have relied, in ordinary times, on professional soldiers, in extraordinary ones, however defined, relied on the mobilization of these feudal levies, but they mobilized them for their own personal, private interests, not for the public good or the common weal. Thus, where there was feudalism with lords, kings, or emperors, the basic democracy or republicanism guaranteed by the militias was lost and the polity became a vehicle for serving the private interests of its ruler or rulers. Young men had to go out to fight and die, not to defend themselves but for the private aggrandizement of rulers who claimed to speak in the names of the territories they ruled. As nationalism grew, those names often became the names of the states over which the monarch ruled and in which their subjects lived.

Here the differences in the character of the nationalism became important. Hierarchically based nationalism, in particular, generated tensions between rulers and the populations they ruled, leading in time to full blown revolutions in efforts to shift power from the former to the latter. Organically based nationalism could, in some cases, manage to limit the violence of revolutionary movements with similar goals. In both situations, however, the real revolution was the republican revolution, the transformation of the polity from being the private preserve of its ruler to the public domain.

Volume three of this work has treated the special expression of nationalism in the New World polities with roots in the covenantal tradition and its very special antistatist character. It is clear that the United States is foremost among these examples, a country that every objective observer will recognize as having developed a very strong national sense and a polity to match. Americans refer to their nationalism as patriotism, because of their covenantal roots. Nationalism in the United States, like every other human phenomenon, also has its less pleasant side, but if nationalism is in general a useful and productive phenomenon anywhere, it would have to be nationalism on the American model.

It is well to remember that the American model had its roots in the biblical model and that nationalism first appeared on the world scene 3,000 years ago, not only in ancient Israel but in the countries surrounding it that the Bible treats in connection with the history of Israel—Aram, Edom, Moab, Ammon—the four states east of the Jordan rift which, along with Israel, were the first nation-states shaped by nationalism.[14] According to the Bible, all were descended from related peoples. Four never developed beyond narrow nationalism in the way that Israel, did, to develop what Mordecai Kaplan in our times referred to as a religion of ethical nationalism.[15]

Indeed, one of the major aspects of the original covenantal tradition was to recognize that the world was (and was expected by God) to be divided legitimately into peoples or nations, but that all of these nations must be God-fearing if the world is to achieve biblical expectations. Hebrew biblical religion rejects the kind of ecumenical imperialism developed into a value elsewhere in the ancient world, given its highest political expression by Rome and then transferred to the Christian Church in its Roman Catholic form. The Bible, beginning with the story of the Tower of Babel (Genesis 11), recognizes the great dangers of such ecumenicism in fostering human hubris (to use a Greek word not found in the Bible). Therefore, the Bible tells us, God divided the world into *goyim* (nations) as part of His post-diluvian corrective to the errors (or lacunae) of creation.

Thus, from its earliest expression to the present day, nationalism in the covenantal tradition has meant something quite different from nationalism in the other two. For most Europeans, on the other hand, the politics of modern nationalism has been revolutionary, devoted to transforming the nations they produced into republics and democratic republics at that.

Several points must be noted in connection with this massive revolutionary movement. One, even Britain, usually cited as an example of a polity that managed the transition to modernity through evolution, went through the throes of a major revolution, the English Civil War, and its Scottish parallel, and of course the great conflict between England and Ireland that lasted throughout nearly the entire modern epoch. The centerpiece of that revolution was the English Civil War at the very beginning of the epoch. It has been treated at length in *Covenant and Commonwealth*, the second volume in this series. Its culmination in the Glorious Revolution has been treated in chapter 2 of this volume.

Two, some revolutions began as popular revolutions that had republican and democratic goals but were diverted in midstream. They were hijacked, as it were, by totalitarian forces that rested on their popular base but falsely represented themselves as representing a better form of democracy (the Russian Revolution and its Bolshevik hijacking) or as popular but rejecting democracy (the Fascist and Nazi revolutions).

Three, taken together, these and smaller revolutions all were part of the major revolution in the Old World, the republican revolution—the transformation of the polity from the private preserve of its rulers into a *res publica* (public thing), at least nominally the property of its people as a public, and were successful in devising ways to make this a reality.

Four, periodically and especially toward the end of the epoch, there were strong counterrevolutions in some countries, ranging from the Old Guard counterrevolutions in the post-Napoleonic years between 1815 and 1851 to the Spanish Civil War (1936–1939), where Francisco Franco, an old-fashioned Catholic authoritarian, took control of a Fascist movement, the Phalange, and bent it toward his will in a counterrevolution against a republican government soon seized by Communists.

All of the honestly republican and democratic revolutions among the above were to draw to some extent on the covenantal tradition for ideas of political compact and constitutionalism to give shape and form to their revolutions and the regimes they were to produce. Some of the other revolutions attempted to present themselves as drawing on those traditions of compact and constitutionalism, even if falsely. It is useful to look at how this was attempted, where it had at least some success, and where, why and when it failed.

Applying Compact Theory in an Age of Revolution

The key to the successful use of the covenantal tradition, to the extent that lay in the treatment of what moderns referred to as the issue of the locus of sovereignty. In the Bible and in the regnant ideas of medieval European Christendom derived from a synthesis of biblical and Greek sources, sovereignty, including political sovereignty, was vested in God. Nations or their rulers only exercised certain attributes and powers of sovereignty. The exercise of those attributes and powers was not good or necessary in and of itself; it was only good and/or necessary depending on conditions.

The conditions of modern nationalism are conventionally understood as demanding that sovereignty be vested in the state in order to preserve the nation. That was the approach which dominated Europe.

By the Revolutionary generation, the Americans as moderns could no longer rely upon the medieval theory of God's sovereignty, pure and simple. At the same time, they recognized the necessity of removing the imputation of sovereignty to individual human rulers as absolutely contrary to their understanding of republicanism. Nor did they want to reify the state. So they committed themselves to the idea that sovereignty rested with the whole people as a collectivity. While those willing to rest all on a secular view of the world found the people sufficient, most modern theorists of sovereignty and certainly most of the American people saw sovereignty as resting in the people under God (to use the American phrase). Thus no ruler could claim that the state was his private preserve, rather, a legitimate polity had to be republic. Nor could any state be reified as an entity apart from the people who comprised it.

Sovereignty, in this new view, was held by the people as a public, not simply as a congeries of individuals, that is to say, the people, who were expected to include many separate individual and group interests that both conflicted and cooperated still constituted a public with a common public interest and that public represented the people in their sovereign capacity.[16] The people as a sovereign public could and had to delegate the exercise of powers to their governments. Their task was to recognize that civil society was built upon many interests that could allow those interests play and expression and to build a governmental system worthy of a free people that could reach consensus or, at the very least, accomodation of the interests within it within the context of the virtues to which it aspired as a public. In the words of the *Federalist*:

> Ambition must be made to counteract ambition. The interest of the man must be connected with the constitutional rights of the place. It may be a reflection on human nature that such devices should be necessary to control the abuses of government. But what is government itself but the greatest of all reflections on human nature? If men were angels, no government would be necessary. In framing a government which is to be administered by men over men, the great difficulty lies in this: You must first enable the government to control the governed; and in the next place oblige it to control itself. A dependence on the people is, no doubt, the primary control on the government; but experience has taught mankind the necessity of auxiliary precautions.[17]

To make their republic work, it was best that they divide those sovereign powers and delegate them to different governments through the construction of a compound republic, of agencies (branches) of government in a system of checks and balances, so as to prevent the effective usurpation of their sovereignty by any single government or agency through a consolidation of powers in its hands.[18]

Hence the American emphasis on the separation of powers and on federalism, that is to say, not only separation by sphere of activity but also by arena or plane. The first could make certain that executive, legislative, and judicial powers would be sufficiently separate to keep them limited and to force them to harmonize their actions with one another which did require a real measure of cooperation. The second required the separation by size of arena so that appropriate responsibilities could be delegated by the people to governments of appropriate scale who would also have to harmonize their relationships with one another through intergovernmental cooperation.

Both kinds of harmonization could be achieved only through negotiation and bargaining which, to the extent that the polity was democratic, had to be open. Since there would be no single center of power other than the people, no government would be *central* and all holders of powers delegated by the people would be "governments" to the same degree, deriving their powers directly from the people through their constitutions rather than through any intermediary. That is the covenantal model translated into modern political and governmental terms, enshrined in constitutions designed to express the covenantal tradition in its modern form.

This was very different than the other modern models of republicanism, the Jacobin state or the Westminster parliamentary system, derived as they were from hierarchical or organic models of the polity. In the Jacobin state the people as a whole are presumed to have a general will which is embodied in a political center within a reified state. That is to say, rather than recognizing the existence of different interests as fundamental and the management of those interests the task of the polity, it is assumed that the general will exists over and above any special interests (which are essentially private) and that the tasks of government are to give it expression in the polity. Thus there can only be one central government with the power to express the general will. This has the effect of reifying the state. Sovereignty is seen to have been passed from premodern rulers to the reified modern republican state which was to be organized so that a leading cadre, speaking in the name of the people and their general will, dominate the state organization. Even if there was some separation of powers within it, the one central government remained the single center. All other bodies were no more than authorities, derivative from it.

The same was true of the Westminster parliamentary model, only the center was parliament which over time had acquired sovereignty from the king or, in the English formulation, which rested on an earlier form of separation of powers, sovereignty was located in the king-in-parliament. The Westminster parliamentary system allows the people to speak in various combinations without seeking to identify their general will, but authority still is concentrated in the sovereign-as-center and all other exercises of governmental power are merely delegated by that center. The one modification of this in Britain was that this theory was English, applicable to England and Wales only, whereas the Scots only partially accepted it through the Act of Union in 1707 in which they gave up their separate parliament but retained substantial original authority in the legal, economic, and religious spheres. All three recognized a single sovereign represented by the Crown, not the person of the monarch. That is, the realm became republican for all practical purposes but the incumbent monarch held the representation of sovereignty for it.

Thus modern republicanism took three forms, all of which claimed to be grounded in constitutionalism. In the United Kingdom, the originator of the Westminster model, that constitution took the form of a modernized continuation of Britain's ancient constitution. Other polities that adopted the Westminster system, with the exception of New Zealand, also embraced modern constitutionalism in the sense that they adopted written constitutions delineating that model and its application to the political systems.

The Jacobin model, at least in theory, rested on a fully modern constitutional base since it was grounded in the rejection of all premodern forms of government and power-sharing, emphasizing its foundation on right principles that had previously gone unrecognized. Those principles emphasized the general will and the necessity for a cadre that would formulate its expression for the people. In identifying and applying that will, Jacobin constitutionalism always was secondary to Jacobin theories of the state and its proper leadership.

Only in those polities following the covenantal model, however it was adapted to their situations, was modern constitutionalism fulfilled and able to embody older covenantal principles with modern form. Many became federal in the modern sense of the term. Since most covenantal polities grew out of an older covenantal political culture, they can be said to have been born covenantal. They simply had the special problems of founding that are attendant upon every polity. For those polities that had to modernize from hierarchical bases or to organically adapt to the new epoch, especially for the former, the modern epoch was a time of revolution whereby some combination of national and democratic aspirations led to violent upheaval to overthrow the ancien regime that inhibited the expression of one or the other and usually both. In the process, many of the revolutionaries turned to the covenant motif in one way or another for inspiration and application to their situation.

Notes

1. Robert Adolph Kann, *A History of the Habsburg Empire 1526–1918* (Berkeley: University of California Press, 1974).
2. Arend Lijphardt, "Consociational Democracy," World Politics, vol. 21, no. 10 (1969), pp. 207–25; *idem., Democracy in Plural Societies* (New Haven, Conn.: Yale University Press, 1977); *Publius*, vol. 15, no. 2 (Spring 1985), *Federalism and Consociationalism.*
3. Robert Putnam, Robert Leonardi, and Raffaella Nanetti, *Making Democracy Work: Civic Traditions in Modern Italy* (Princeton, N.J.: Princeton University Press, 1993).
4. *Ibid.*; Filippo Sabetti, *Political Authority in a Sicilian Village* (New Brunswick, N.J.: Rutgers University Press, 1984); Raphael Zariski, "The Establishment of the Kingdom of Italy as a Unitary State: A Case Study in Regime Formation," *Publius*, vol. 13, no. 4 (Fall 1983); Sabetti, "The Making of Italy as an Experiment in Constitutional Choice," *Publius*, vol. 12, no. 3, (Summer 1982).
5. Ernest Gellner, *Nations and Nationalism* (Oxford: Basil Blackwell, 1983). George Mosse, *Confronting the Nation: Jewish and Western Nationalism* (Hanover, N.H.: Brandeis University Press, 1993).
6. Harry Orlinsky, *Ancient Israel* (Ithaca, N.Y.: Cornell University Press, 1964); Thomas L. Thompson, *The Origin Tradition of Ancient Israel* (Sheffield: JSOT Press, 1987).
7. Gellner, *Nations and Nationalism.*
8. Denis de Rougemont and Charlotte Muret, *The Heart of Europe* (New York: Duell, Sloan and Pearce, 1941).
9. Jews did preserve Jewish languages that separated them from their neighbors but, except for the continuous elite use of Hebrew, these were different languages in different parts of the world, Yiddish in Eastern Europe, Judaismo (Ladino) in the Mediterranean world, Judeo-Arabic in the Arab world, and other lesser known languages where isolated pockets of Jews lived. So separate language remained a major element in Jewish culture but not to unite all Jews so much as to preserve the separateness of groups of them from their neighbors.
10. In only two countries did even the socialists themselves refuse to respond, Russia and the United States. In both cases they represented small minorities of the total working class population. Most of them were not working class. Even there, those who had political aspirations within the existing polity ended up reporting for duty, recognizing that the people would never forgive them if they did not. Communism, which rejected nationalism even in the first decades of the USSR, reemphasized it to generate patriotic sentiment in the Soviet Union during World War II and, recognizing nationalism as at the very least a necessary evil, pro-

moted it in the non-Russian republics of the USSR and in the eastern satellites after World War II in an effort to gain public loyalty. So whatever its origins, nationalism has proved to be extremely powerful in our time and must be recognized for its power.

11. In the United States, for example, the various ethnic-based groups that comprised American society until the present generation tended to remain endogamous for the first two or three generations on American soil and then became increasingly open to marriages with other Americans who were otherwise similar in background. Indeed, ethnic endogamy broke down much sooner than religious endogamy. Today, however, in the second generation of the postmodern epoch, even religious endogamy has become obsolescent, even for groups like the Jews who have been tenaciously endogamous for thousands of years. Americans are attracted to other Americans regardless of their primordial origins and more often than not marry them. (Thus American people is being forged by kinship after 200 years of relying heavily on consent alone.)

12. The French have been notably hostile to cultural pluralism in contradistinction to the Americans who are able to tolerate a great deal of it, albeit within limits. Thus, while France has accepted and at times even welcomed immigrants, pressures on those immigrants to conform to the French way of life have been very great. Only recently have their been signs that some immigrants and their descendants are prepared to argue the case for cultural pluralism, no doubt influenced by world trends and the freer movement of peoples generated by the European Union.

13. Saadia Gaon, *Book of Beliefs and Opinions*.

14. Orlinsky, *Ancient Israel*; Abraham Malamat, *Mari and the Early Israelite Experience* (Oxford: Oxford University Press, 1989); Donald Lutz, *The Origins of American Constitutionalism* (Baton Rouge: Louisiana State University Press, 1988); Andrew C. McLaughlin, *The Foundations of American Constitutionalism* (Greenwich, Conn.: Fawcett Publications, 1961).

15. Mordecai M. Kaplan, *A Religion of Ethical Nationalism: Judaism's Contribution to World Peace* (New York: Macmillan, 1970). Kaplan, perhaps the leading Jewish theologian in America ever and one of the leading American theologians of the twentieth century, presents an authentically modern Jewish understanding of authentic Jewish nationalism that deserves to be noted more widely than it has been.

16. Lutz, *Popular Consent*.

17. *The Federalist*, no. 51. Alexander Hamilton, James Madison and John Jay, *The Federalist Papers* (New York: New American Library, 1961), p. 322.

18. Ostrom, *The Political Theory of a Compound Republic.*(Lincoln and London: University of Nebraska Press, 1987).

7

The Covenant Motif in Modern Revolutions

By general reckoning, there have been four great modern revolutions: the English Revolution of the mid-seventeenth century, the American and French Revolutions of the late eighteenth, and the Russian Revolution during World War I and immediately thereafter. There have been many others as well, some of which, the Mexican Revolution for example, stand out as important but lesser episodes. All have been violent ones. In still other cases, especially in the twentieth century, major revolutions have come with a minimum of violence. This is the case with regard to the Fascist revolutions of the early twentieth century and the overthrow of the Communist empire in the late 1980s and early 1990s.

The first two of those great modern revolutions, the English and the American, discussed earlier, were violent revolutions within the covenantal tradition of politics, the English Puritan Revolution overtly and blatantly so and the American Revolution more a synthesis of fully covenantal ideas and secular derivations such as the idea of political compact. The French Revolution was far more secular and ultimately antithetical to those ideas and all that flowed from them. Although it began with an emphasis on a political compact and even more the idea of a social contract, even incorporating them into revolutionary ritual and practice in a manner reminiscent of earlier covenant-making ceremonies, it soon rejected all covenantly derived institutions or behavior. The Russian Revolution was the first to reject covenantal ideas entirely, although even it was perforce forced to return to the problem of political compacts and contracts because it wanted to pretend that it rested upon consent. This certainly was not the case in either of the Fascist revolutions, but by the late 1980s covenantal ideas in secularized form were creeping back into the ideological matrix of the revolutionary idea in the form of a renewed concern with civil society, a concept that in its original form was very much a product of Whig redefinitions of English Puritan covenantalism.

Covenant, Compact, and Contract in Revolutionary France

By and large, European theoretical speculations on the origins of society remained just that on a continent where society had so many incrustations

141

developed generation after generation over thousands of years. Except for a brief window in the modern epoch, it remained for the New World to try out the modern ideas of the Old. That window was the Age of Revolutions between 1789 and 1917, most particularly the beginning of that Age in the French Revolution and the revolutions generated by it. For a brief historical moment the revolutionaries attempted to reconstitute civil society through new political and social compacts, only to find that society was too stubborn. The stubbornness of what existed led them, impatient as they were, to even greater radicalism, which in turn generated opposition against them personally and ideologically, leading to their downfall and, in most cases, replacement by betrayers of the revolution, whether in the image of Napoleon, in the image of the Bourbons, or worse, in the image of the Bolsheviks.

Between 1789 and 1917, in country after country in continental Europe from France to Russia, revolutions took place designed to establish constitutional government on a popular basis in place of older autocracies. In almost every case the pattern was a violent revolution, followed by the convening of a constituent assembly or, in some cases, a constitutional convention elected by the people in some fashion and the drafting of a document intended to reflect the popular will and to advance the goals of liberty, equality, and fraternity. In most of the cases these efforts borrowed directly from the French model. Their theoretical underpinnings were to be found in Rousseau's *Social Contract*. Hence, they aspired to identify and embody the general will of the people or polity in question and to organize power in that spirit.

In almost every case, also following France, there was either a counter-revolution which attempted to restore the *ancien regime* which then led to a revolutionary cycle of civil conflict until matters were sorted out through some kind of synthesis of older patterns of socioeconomic power and newer distributions of political power. In other cases, following Russia, the liberal revolutions were merely interim and were replaced by subsequent revolutions that claimed the ideology of popular democracy to support authoritarian rulers.

France itself actually went through both stages. Almost immediately the original revolution, based insofar as possible on the American model, was aborted by the Jacobin seizure of power.[1] As part of their effort to achieve a Rousseauian society, the French revolutionaries went so far as to introduce an annual assembly of the citizenry to renew the social contract establishing their regime and to designate a fixed site for the ceremony, today the Champs du Mars in front of the national military academy in Paris. This recovenanting was designed to become a central ritual of the new civil religion of the Revolution which was to replace the Christianity of the old regime. Such ceremonies were actually held for several years but, of course, were limited by the fact that they were held only in Paris and could only involve those Parisians who turned up. This virtual representation was considered as sufficient (reflecting the long-standing French belief that, for all intents and purposes,

Paris is France) to establish the terms under which the revolutionary leadership could then make their own decisions in the name of the people and the general will.

What ensued was a struggle between the formal compactual structure of the refounded polity designed to impose a matrix model on France, and the indigenous hierarchical French political culture developed over some eight hundred years of monarchic government, whose twin pillars of conquest and centralization had succeeded in shaping political expectations and behavior in hierarchical ways, even if they could not change the rather anarchistic general culture of the French. Over the course of those centuries, the kings of France had progressively extended their domain through conquest until they reached externally imposed limits, whether geographic or military, and at the same time built up their courts as the center of power in France. What remained outside of Paris were limited local liberties that the kings did not view as worth trying to suppress or which could not have been suppressed except at too high a cost. Those local liberties, willy nilly, entrenched medieval, even feudal, patterns of governance and political and social organization.[2]

The revolutionaries, when they seized power, despite their desire to establish the new polity on a compactual basis, had an even greater desire to extirpate those remnants of social and political inequality which in their eyes had brought about the revolution in the first place. In order to do so they had to even further centralize power in their hands. Thus they used the powers conferred upon them ostensibly by the people through the social contract, in ways that actually strengthened the hierarchical character of French political life and institutions. The French situation was the paradigm for most European revolutionary efforts.

The process through which all of this unfolded is instructive, even paradigmatic. The French Revolution actually began with the breaking away of the Third Estate, the 600 commoners who were part of the States-General (in addition to 300 nobles and 300 clergy, the first two Estates) summoned to Versailles by the king on May 5, 1789. On June 17, 1789, they broke away and assumed the title of the Assemble Constituatente. They invited the other two Estates to join them and many of the clergy and some of the nobles did. On June 20 they all swore an oath not to separate until they had given France a constitution. Riqueti, Comte de Mirabeau, strongly influenced by the American experience, was the leading orator in the Assembly.

Amid rumors that the king was going to disperse the Assembly, the Bastille was stormed by the Paris mob on July 14. A provisional government was installed in the Paris city hall and the Marquis de Lafayette, who had been Washington's aide during the American Revolution and a great partisan of American-style democratic republicanism, was made commander of the newly established National Guard. On August 27 the Declaration of the Rights of Man and the Citizen, France's true revolutionary covenant, was adopted.[3]

The Constituent Assembly adopted France's first constitution on October 5–6, 1789, and the king accepted it on the first anniversary of the fall of the Bastille in 1790. At the same time, the old system of provincial government was abolished as were all formal vestiges of the nobility. France was reorganized into departments, districts, cantons, and communes (the only frameworks left intact from the old order), organized as a national federation with local assemblies in each department and district.

That constitution was the high water mark of covenantalism in France. It was changed a year later (October 1, 1791) after King Louis XVI tried to flee the country. As violence spread throughout France, the constitution was replaced by the Legislative Assembly already sharply divided into camps. The Mountain, including the Jacobins, was the most radical, at the far left, supported a united indivisible republic. The Girondists (so-called because its leading members were from the department of Gironde that included Bordeaux) advocated a federal republic. For some time Bordeaux had been among the liberal southwest Atlantic coast cities of France. Its leading elements were cosmopolitan merchants including many Jews—Marranos (that is to say descendents of converts to Catholicism who maintained their Judaism in secret) who had escaped from the Iberian Peninsula—and settled where they could become openly Jewish by the eighteenth century and played a leading role in the city's life.[4] As federalists, the Girondists were moderate progressives slightly to the left of center.

In August 1792, however, the Jacobins seized power and suspended the Assembly. Lafayette fled. The Girondists survived to enter the national convention, the new legislative body. There they were on the right since only republicans were entitled to be elected to it and the Jacobins were clearly in charge.

Shortly thereafter the Jacobin dictatorship began through the Committee of Public Safety appointed by the national convention. A second constitution was enacted by the convention and was sent to the people for ratification but it never came into force. Instead, the Reign of Terror led, inter alia, to the destruction of the Girondists and all democratic elements in the republic. New constitutions followed each other more frequently than ordinary laws could be amended, until Napoleon seized power.

When Jacobin rule became too bloody it was replaced by a series of experiments in what today would be called "guided democracy" culminating in Napoleon's seizure of power in the name of the revolution. Under Napoleon's leadership the fourth constitution adopted in 1799 by a national plebiscite (3,000,000 to 1,567) established a military monarchy in a republican guise. Among other things, it established prefectures to administer the departments and subprefectures within them, thereby establishing the centralized state administration that still prevails in France. The Code Napoleon was enacted to give it teeth.

Napoleon soon established an empire and proclaimed himself emperor in what was a prefiguration of subsequent authoritarian attempts to capture the revolutionary fervor. He introduced a new centralized uniform legal code, a set of territorial administrative divisions, and a meritocracy to administer the whole state and his army, thereby assaulting the very foundations of the old establishment. He did all of this to serve his authoritarian ends ostensibly by acting in the name of the ideology of the revolution.

Subsequent to Napoleon's downfall, the old Bourbon ruling family was restored but the revolution had done its work and they could not bring back what had been lost. France of the Restoration was polarized into three camps: radicals who sought the continuation of the revolution in the Jacobin tradition; liberals who wanted popularly based government with moderate social change; and monarchists who sought the restoration of the prerevolutionary regime. These three camps of the left, center, and right were to dominate French politics until the 1960s, with one, often two, of the three rejecting the legitimacy of the regime in power at any given time.

What all had in common was rejection of what they referred to as "Anglo-Saxon" models, not only in politics but equally in economics, which meant not only rejecting covenantal politics, but also its brother, free market economics, which included rejection of the dynamics of the covenantal tradition and its derivatives in every form. In fact, from the time of the Bourbon restoration until the adoption of the constitution of the Fifth Republic in 1956, France seesawed from regime to regime. The reactionary restoration gave way to liberal monarchy (1830) to republican revolutionary regime (1848) to Bonapartist imperialism (1851) to parliamentary republicanism (1871) to Fascism (1940) back to parliamentary republicanism (1945) and finally, since 1956, today's presidential system. While every regime was given its constitution in the spirit of the modern age, the gap between constitution and national consensus remained great until Charles de Gaulle effectively put an end to the French Revolution through the assembly of a wall-to-wall coalition of all three camps from communists to monarchists to write the constitution of the Fifth Republic.[5] De Gaulle's constitution also introduced a presidential system of government with a measure of separation of powers between its three branches, thereby weakening the center through the introduction of power-sharing among its components.

Only after 1962 and the settlement of the Algerian issue, could it be said that the French had at last come to terms with the forces unleashed in 1789 and that if no matrix was introduced, there was at least a softening of the pyramid in an otherwise highly hierarchical state. France's founding role and subsequent participation in the European Community/Union brought it into a major quasi-federal relationship. De Gaulle continued to soften the pyramid, while retaining its fundamental form, through his regional and local reforms in the late 1960s. Still the hierarchical character of French reality remained and was only challenged in the economic sphere in the 1990s as France's state-dominated economy found it difficulty to compete in world markets.

The French revolutionary impact on Germany had the immediate effect of leading Europe into a twenty-five-year war. In the long run, however, its impact was to strengthen the hierarchical as opposed to the covenantal aspects of German politics. Prussia, already much strengthened during the first half of the modern epoch, took a leading role in the European alliance against the French and further strengthened its position among the German states.[6] On the other hand, the smaller German states between Prussia and France, the repositories of such covenantal traditions and political culture as existed in Germany, quickly fell victim to Napoleon's aggression and had to be liberated by Prussia, making them more dependent upon that autocracy.[7]

Curiously enough, after the restoration at the end of the Napoleonic Wars, it looked, at first glance, like a restoration of the status quo ante. The Hapsburg empire emerged as the strongest power on the Continent with its strongest political figure, Prince Metternich, organizing the terms of the peace. Germany, including Austria and Prussia, joined in a common confederation to replace the Holy Roman Empire, abolished by Napoleon, with a more modern federal arrangement.[8] That confederation was to last for two generations, most of the nineteenth century, supplemented by the Zollverein, the German customs union, that gave it an added dimension of strength. The German states dominated the European heartland. The reaction that overtook Germany sent hundreds of thousands of liberals and just plain people who wanted greater opportunity to the New World in their search for freedom.

Metternich's effort to restore the old order as it were were successful for about half a generation. While absolutism triumphed in 1815, liberal nationalist efforts to revolt occurred in 1830 in France, Belgium, Germany, and Poland and more massively in 1848, the so-called "springtime of nations."

For a brief moment, the kind of consensual constitution-making that reflected modern liberal covenantalism was resurgent but the conservative forces quickly regained control. While these efforts were successfully repressed by the authorities, the wiser heads among the latter began to make some limited accommodation of the liberal demands. These mostly took the form of pseudo-constitutions more like charters handed down from rulers in the past and capable of being enforced only by those self-same rulers, that either had no liberal elements from the first or soon abandoned the limited ones included within them. Covenantal dimensions, even in the modern sense of political compacts, were notably absent in these efforts with even the liberals accepting the dominant continental European view that societies were basically organic and hierarchical rather than covenantal.[9]

Even the popular revolutionaries were much influenced by the organic theories that reemerged among political philosophers in the nineteenth century in opposition to the covenantally grounded ideas of political compact of the seventeenth and eighteenth centuries. So even they were moving away from the foundations of modernity. In a very real sense Weimar Germany, coming seventy years later, was the apotheosis of the liberal vision of the centralized organic state, inspiring many of the intellectuals who experienced it and its failures to turn elsewhere for their political ideas and yet others who remained unaware of how Weimar's failures prepared the way for the greatest disaster in German history to seek to introduce Weimar-style liberalism elsewhere, including Israel where so many of them and their children found refuge from Nazism.

Meanwhile the Prussian leadership became discontented with merely sharing the dominant role in the confederation and always looking over its shoulder at Austria, a fellow confederate and its only challenger for German leadership. In a series of swift wars, first with Denmark (1864), then with Austria (1867), and finally with France (1870–71), Prussia reduced both its immediate external and internal rivals and emerged as the sole dominant power in Germany. The German Confederation was reorganized as the North German Confederation, totally dominated by Prussia. Austria withdrew and simply remained the leading state in the Austro-Hungarian empire under the relatively "soft" absolutism of the government of the emperor, Franz Josef.

After the Franco-Prussian War, Prussia succeeded in unifying almost all of the German states outside of Austria within a Prussian-dominated German federation, essentially a federation of monarchs in which the Prussian government also served as the German government (1871). Prussian absolutism continued under this new arrangement only slightly modified by federalism, while the Prussian-German federal chancellor, Count Otto von Bismarck, introduced social reforms that effectively bought off working-class opposition to the new regime. All of this worked well under the new head of the German state, Kaiser Wilhelm I, but when his son Wilhelm II succeeded him on the throne he showed his impatience with Bismarck's conservative policies by removing his chancellor from power and introducing militarism along with absolutism as the other hallmark of the German regime. That militarism was ultimately to bring Wilhelm II to his downfall, but first it brought Europe World War I with all of its attendant destruction and the collapse of the German imperial Reich.[10]

Postwar restoration under the Weimar Republic ostensibly was more democratic and federal, but the Weimar republican leaders were more Jacobins than federalists. So while they eagerly abandoned autocracy, they still advocated the theory of the centralized organic state. Only the state they founded was an exceptionally weak one in a still very hierarchical society.[11]

As the troubles that plagued the Weimar regime in the 1920s grew worse, the older forces of absolutism that had survived the war, most particularly the Junker-dominated officer corps of the army, the great conservative industrialists, and the old aristocracy were swayed by a populist upstart who, in fact, was their antithesis and who was to rapidly reduce their powers upon attaining power on his own—Adolph Hitler. They supported him in his efforts to seize power while the Weimar regime opened the door for him through its weakness, grounded in a kind of false liberalism that, because it lacked the covenantal dimension, could not distinguish between federal and natural liberty. That meant that they could not distinguish between those who were parties to the covenant—that is, supported the constitution and the polity it framed—and those who were not. In the name of liberal democracy, they extended a kind of absolute liberty to all. That led first to the decadence of society, thereby alarming the middle class, and fostered the growth of anti-democratic elements who wooed the more solid citizens by promising to end the decadence, restore Germany's economy after the disastrous postwar inflation and then depression, and restore German pride after their loss of World War I.

Unable to act because of their reliance on false doctrines, the Weimar Republic leadership allowed Hitler to gain power through free elections (so free that Hitler's supporters could intimidate many voters unrestricted by those in power at the time, on ostensible democratic grounds). Once in power, Hitler moved quickly to end the Weimar Republic. In its place, he established a populistic dictatorship of the right with himself as the supreme ruler or fuehrer and proceed to rebuild the German state and its economy as a war machine accompanied by the worst racism.

He was aided in operationalizing his racism by the fact that racism had swept the Western world after 1870 as an extreme expression of the argument for the superiority of European whites (Aryans or Caucasians as they came to be known) over all others. This racism strengthened the hand of European colonialism then at its height, so it was widely accepted, not only in Germany but in the other European countries as well. Nazism added a populist dimension to that spirit but in the end carried both militarism and racism so far that the Nazis led Germany into a second war of self-destruction, a *Gotterdamerung* even worse than the first, that not only led to the murder of millions of innocents and ended up bringing the German people themselves great suffering and loss while nearly destroying the world, but whose bestial efforts at genocide placed a permanent stain on the German people and German history.

Like the French, the Germans seem to have achieved a reconciliation of their covenantal and hierarchical traditions after World War II. Fortuitously, they, too, had a great leader, Konrad Adenauer, and a great opportunity. The division of Germany between the Communist East and the democratic West allowed the Rhineland Germans, earlier the bearers of such covenantal traditions as existed in Germany, to dominate the newly established German Federal Republic built by Adenauer, a native of that region, on Christian Democratic principles, albeit with him playing a leadership role not out of keeping with the hierarchical strains of German political culture in order to do so.[12]

Adenauer succeeded in putting an end to the worst elements of the conflict between the two traditions and the political cultures each produced because of the fortuitous circumstance of not having to cope with Prussia. He was able to locate the capital of the new German Federal Republic at Bonn on the Rhine, traditionally a quiet Rhineland town whose citizens had represented the best of liberal Germany in the nineteenth century.

The constitution of the German Federal Republic not only was federal but was federal in a covenantal way, providing for the very serious participation of the federal states, the laender, in the national government through the house of the states, the Bundesrat, and providing for federal comity, called in German *bundestreu*, to guide federal-*land* and inter-*land* relations and to guide the federal constitutional court in interpreting those relations.

The sudden collapse of the Communist German Democratic Republic in 1989 led to German reunification on fully federal principles. As rapid reunification became possible, the GDR reestablished the five *lander* that had been formed in the immediate aftermath of World War II and which the Communists had abolished early in the 1950s. The GDR then ceded its authority to those five *lander* and they in turn applied to join the German Federal Republic. They and Berlin, which had been an associated state under Allied occupation since 1949, were admitted to the GFR as *lander*. To complete the process of reunification, the German Federal Republic established a government corporation, the Treuhandelstalt, to undertake to dismantle the state-owned economy of the former Communist East and to bring it into line with the market economy of West Germany.

The Low Countries: Between Territorial and Consociational Federalism

Two other continental European states were dramatically affected by the French Revolution but, because they were rooted in the covenantal tradition, came through it with an accelerated process of adjustment to the modern epoch without abjuring their political culture, institutions, or constitutional history.

The French Revolution brought an end to the confederal regime of the United Netherlands, the best example on the continent of a Reformation-induced covenantal commonwealth. When Napoleon's armies swept into the Netherlands they were received joyously by Dutch liberals who viewed their own *ancien regime* as a degenerate oligarchy. Napoleon put his brother, Louis, on the throne of a new Dutch regime in which the federal elements were abolished and a centralized Bonapartist state established. With the Restoration, Jacobins and conservatives reached a compromise of sorts, whereby the Netherlands were reconstituted as a unitary decentralized constitutionalized monarchy. More than most of the time, the Dutch Constitution and political system provided for real powers to remain with the provincial and local governments within the formally more consolidated state.[13]

Nevertheless, the ideological divisions of the nineteenth century brought in a new set of cleavages that made the old territorial ones insufficient for governing the Netherlands or even holding the Low Countries together as kingdom. What once had been an essentially homogeneous society, at least in political culture and ideology, soon became divided into three great camps: the older Calvinist camp, no longer automatically dominant in the Netherlands; a resurgent Catholic camp; and a new secular camp, originally liberal in the nineteenth-century manner and later to become socialist, consisting of people who rejected confessional politics.[14] The Netherlands, once one of the most prosperous countries in Europe, sank into poverty and diminished capacity. Its Catholic southern provinces seceded in 1830 to form the new kingdom of Belgium.

The great Dutch political leader Abraham Kuyper revived the Dutch polity in the latter half of the nineteenth century. Kuyper, a strongly religious Calvinist trained as a minister in the Netherlands Reformed Church, became the great leader of nineteenth-century Dutch politics. He developed a consociational system to encompass Dutch politics and the three grand divisions in Netherlands civil society.[15] His ideas grew, one might say, directly out of the covenantal tradition and were more directly covenantal than those of any other major political leader in nineteenth-century Europe, rooted as they were in his Calvinism and in his effort to accommodate that Calvinism to the modern epoch.

As a minister, Kuyper not only knew Scripture but based his thought on it. He found the grounding for his system of pillars in the Noahide covenant, of which he demonstrated a very good understanding. Kuyper was a good example of the old Calvinist adage: "Where the Reformed are, there will be the covenant." He stated that he derived his social theory from the "creation ordinances" of God as revealed in Scripture and history. He hoped through the system of pillars to achieve organic communities that would confine the state to a very limited role and would prevent atomism, on one side, and collectivism, on the other. The basis for this was his theory of "sphere sovereignty" whereby each functional, occupational, and geographic unit would be independent and the state would maintain order, provide for national defense, and address imbalances within and among the spheres.

Under Kuyper, the Dutch political leaders organized the three camps into three "pillars." Each governed itself internally while their leaders reached accommodation with each other in the name of their respective pillars through a negotiated "politics of accommodation" nationally and locally. The essence of that accommodation was what contemporary political scientist Arend Lijphart, himself of Dutch origin, borrowing a term from Althusius, was to label "consociationalism," in essence, nonterritorial federalism whereby each pillar received its share of all governmental programs—state, provincial and local—which it managed in the interests of its adherents. This was true of social benefits and sports clubs, positions in the civil service, and radio stations. This consociationalism rested on a quasi-federal division of powers among the state, the provinces, and the localities, but in essence trumped them on nonroutine matters with expressions that were truly covenantal.

Kuyper's consociationalism was truly within the covenantal tradition in every way. First, it was based upon a pact between the three pillars. Second,the way of implementation of that pact was spelled out within the Netherlands constitution, not so much by explicit statements but by the constitutional structure and accompanying processes that accommodated consociational arrangements. Third, all three pillars were grounded in a dominant conception of virtue that presumably lay at the base of their governmental activities and defined the ends of those activities. Finally, each pillar itself can be seen as formed by covenant or compact among its founders or members.

Indeed, it was the breakdown in the consensus of what constituted virtue and the passing of custodianship over it from territorial to ideological entities that legitimized consociationalism and made it necessary in the first place. Consociationalism was a modern accommodation of the covenantal tradition, that is to say, it was embodied in a modern constitution that attempted to grapple with the polity not only as a Calvinist commonwealth as in earlier times but as embracing a not-only-Calvinist civil society. In that connection it fully recognized different, even contradictory conceptions of virtue, and worked out civil accommodations among them. fifth, once the accommodation was reached and in place, governmental activities and citizens' behavior were judged on the basis of the new basis for federal liberty that it established.

The system of pillars was initially weakened by the German occupation which established a new basic cleavage, between collaborators and resisters, that cut across lines previously maintained by the pillars. Still, it took until the late 1960s before the political system established by Kuyper began to collapse. Among other things, the Dutch society became very tolerant, some would say permissive, of all kinds of deviant behavior associated with the "Aquarian" revolutions of the late 1960s.

They did so in a very Dutch way.[16] What they permitted or tolerated that deviated from mainstream Dutch society was also confined to special areas in Dutch cities, particularly Amsterdam. Thus substance abuse, while permitted more widely than in other Western countries, was confined to its own area just as prostitution had been confined to Amsterdam's red light district for so long. In other words, using the variation of territorial democracy that provided different spaces for different beliefs or practices rather than mixing differences within the same space, a very Reformed Protestant covenantal idea, the Dutch were able to combine the broad extension of freedom with the minimum amount of social damage.

This is not to say that the new definition of freedom was not more akin to that of natural rather than federal liberty, especially the traditional definitions of freedom and federal liberty that had prevailed in the Netherlands, but it was cushioned by a realism that included an implicit declaration of what were the community's moral standards and what were not. Nevertheless, even the Dutch distinguished between marijuana and hashish, on one hand, and heroin and cocaine, on the other, and when street crime mushroomed, the Dutch police were instructed to make every effort to put it down. This tolerance of substance abuse has brought other problems in its wake and there is growing skepticism about its viability in this case, but the police are content that at least they know where the abusers are.

One problem to emerge out of this is that of thousands of squatters who describe themselves as "the people who don't want to live the way everybody else lives."[17] The Netherlands governments have recognized their existence and actually provide them with support grants. The squatters are people who in many respects have never attained adulthood mentally. Nevertheless, one of the reasons that the Dutch system has worked at least to some extent is that the squatters, in the Dutch tradition, have themselves organized a government within a government with its own bureaucracy, radio and television stations, and controls over squatter apartments.[18]

Consociationalism as Kuyper developed it dominated Netherlands politics, government, and society for two generations, until the climax of the first generation of the postmodern epoch in the late 1960s when the three pillars that sustained it fell apart under the impact of postmodern changes that rendered all three ideologies and their conceptions of virtue obsolete for a majority of the Dutch. By then the Netherlands was well into other, more territorial, federal arrangements once again: greater administrative decentralization to the provinces, the expansion of the kingdom of the Netherlands to include not only the Netherlands proper but two associated states, the Netherlands Antilles and Curacao (which later seceded and was replaced by Aruba which had seceded from the Netherlands Antilles), the Benelux customs union which dated back to 1922, and active membership in the European Community. The Reformed Protestantism that had so stimulated Dutch covenantal political culture and its traditions no longer had the compelling power that had guided the Netherlands for four hundred years but the political culture that it had fostered appeared to be deeply rooted in the Dutch psyche and had found other ways to manifest itself.[19]

Meanwhile, in the late nineteenth and early twentieth centuries the idea of consociationalism had spread, especially to those polities that were heirs of the covenantal tradition and most especially to those that had a federal or quasi-federal territorial basis. Belgium seceded from the kingdom of the Netherlands in 1830 and, with the support of France, was recognized as an independent state the next year. One of the reasons for this secession was that Belgium was almost entirely Catholic. Nevertheless it was also one of the Low Countries prominently located in the boundary zone between Latin and Germanic Europe. Earlier cultural accommodations on the part of the two differently culturally endowed populations had led or contributed much to the emergence of a covenantal political tradition, if only as a means of survival.[20]

One of the ten southern provinces that seceded from the kingdom of the Netherlands became the independent Duchy of Luxembourg. The remaining nine formed the kingdom of Belgium on the basis of a quasi-covenantal political compact. The essence of that compact provided for the establishment of a common kingdom that would be constitutionally decentralized with each of the nine provinces preserving a full range of powers of internal government while the kingdom would act in matters of defense, foreign affairs, and such economic and social questions that were deemed of national significance.[21] The fact that Belgium was divided between French-speaking Walloons and Dutch-speaking Flemings was accommodated in this provincial decentralization and it continued to be as long as the Walloons were dominant. Since they were not even challenged until after World War I and did not lose their dominance until after World War II, that ethnic conflict remained off the political agenda for Belgium's formative century.

The new Belgium industrialized rapidly, especially in Wallonia, and the Francophone Walloons grew richer while Flemish Belgium grew poorer. In Belgium, too, a consociational system developed to harmonize ethnic, cultural and linguistic differences among the provinces, especially as the internal activities of the state government began to grow. As long as those demands remained relatively moderate, they could be accommodated in that manner. While Belgian consociationalism was less visible than Dutch, it was no less real. It, however, was based upon ethnic rather than ideological differences which ultimately made it less functional as ethnic conflict intensified.

Meanwhile, Belgium tried to preserve its neutrality in the great power rivalries of late nineteenth-century Europe. When that neutrality was violated by the Germans in World War I, the Belgians resisted and joined the Allies, holding on to a corner of their country throughout the war. After the war the economically poorer, politically weaker, and culturally ignored Flemings began to challenge the dominant Wallonians on ethnic grounds. World War II and the second German invasion of Belgium's neutrality provided the stimulus for intense postwar ethnic conflict which Belgium has tried to accommodate through constitutional changes in the spirit of the covenantal political tradition, shifting emphasis from provincial self-government to the self-governing ethnic communities, preserving the provinces but submerging them first in ethnically-based regions and then in a three-entity federation: a Flemish entity, a Walloon entity, and a mixed entity around Brussels.

On January 1, 1991, Belgium became a federation, the latest step in a series of federal acts going back to the formation of the Benelux customs union in 1922 and continuing through the establishment of the European Community of which Brussels became the seat of its principal governing institutions. Belgium ratified the Maastricht Treaty without difficulty in its usual spirit of federal accommodation. Even before that, its prime minister, Paul Maartens, had tried to carve out a middle ground between the strong European integrationism of Jacques Delors and the more statist position of Margaret Thatcher.[22] Thus Belgium entered the postmodern epoch foresquare within the covenantal tradition as modified by the realities of modernity and postmodernity.

Luxembourg, long a member of the Holy Roman Empire and then of the German Confederation even while maintaining its own internal self-rule, has followed in the spirit of the Germanic combination of hierarchical and covenantal traditions to seek to preserve its own independence through confederal linkages of one kind or another with the larger entities around it in one form or another. Initially part of the Holy Roman Empire, it later came under the Hapsburgs, Austrian and Spanish. There were times when its counts even ruled the empire. At the Congress of Vienna its independence as a Grand Duchy was affirmed but it was made part of the German Confederation in personal union with the Netherlands whose monarchs continued to rule the Duchy until 1890. In 1922 it joined the customs union with Belgium and, in 1947, the larger Benelux customs union. Then in the 1950s it was one of the founders of the European Community. Its policy seems to have been deliberately confederal in the sense that it has fought hard to preserve its own independence and integrity but always as a polity federally linked with others around it. That approach seems to have worked for it quite satisfactorily. In a sense, it was only fully independent between 1890 and 1922 when it was not constitutionally tied in any way to any of its neighbors.

Mediterranean Europe: Confusion Preempts Covenant

The situation along Europe's Mediterranean coast far to the south was vastly different. These countries had enjoyed a kind of decentralized feudalism as a result of local conditions (the Christian reconquest of the Iberian peninsula from the Muslims, the city-state tradition on the Italian peninsula and on the east coast of the Adriatic) in which oaths and pacts were prominent, but had not endowed them with a covenantal political culture.[23] Still, it took most of the first half of the modern epoch to impose hierarchical monarchic traditions on those countries and all of them suffered from civil wars in the nineteenth century in an attempt to either restore or eliminate elements of feudalism or to replace the regimes it had produced.

In all of the countries involved, however, the modern epoch ended up with hierarchy victorious, with the absolute minimum amount of decentralization possible, each with a constitution more a matter of window-dressing rather than a serious step toward democratic republicanism. Spain and Portugal remained autocratic Catholic states. In the brief moments that liberal republicans broke through, they were inevitably overthrown before too long and Spain's civil wars were between autocratic traditions of different dynasties or different communities seeking political power or national expression far more than efforts to achieve constitutional government. Both countries would be transformed only at the end of the first generation or the beginning of the second generation of the postmodern epoch.[24]

Spain's modern constitutional history begins with the constitution of Cadiz in 1811, its first effort to establish a constitutionalized, liberalized state in the wake of the defeat of Napoleon and the French occupiers. The framers of that constitution claimed that they drew upon the ancient constitutional traditions of Aragon and Castille. Those ancient traditions, especially those of Aragon, draw to a certain extent on oaths and pacts to protect rights, albeit in a medieval way. The Cadiz constitution came a century after the final monarchic dismantlement of the medieval system of *fueros* (feudal charters of rights) in Spain.

In Spain the only *fueros* to survive that general abolition were those of Navarre, a province in northern Spain that had remained an independent kingdom longer than any other part of the country. It had surrendered its independence only after assuring that its *fueros* would be preserved. In the first half of the nineteenth century Navarre allowed itself to be dragged into a series of bloody civil wars between branches of the royal family, for the Spanish succession in the name of the effort to preserve those *fueros*, at least part of whose substance was incorporated or guaranteed by other Spanish constitutions, even surviving the years of the Franco dictatorship (Navarre had been an early supporter of Franco for that same express purpose) and which still constitutes part of the constitutional arrangement between Navarre and Spain as a whole.

Initially Spain's liberals looked to their own political compact tradition as a source for their constitutional efforts and some even looked to federalism. Spanish conservatives held on to older medieval organic theories. Only later in the nineteenth century did liberals embrace modern organic theories of society that were more Jacobin in their orientation and began to seek state centralization. Still, some echo of the older tradition remained, emphasizing the legitimacy of the Basque and Catalan national communities, which gaine expression in the regionalization of the Spanish Republic in the 1930s and was only extinguished by Franco's victory in 1939. With the death of Franco and the fall of his regime, the successful introduction of democracy in Spain through its 1978 constitution restored regionalism and extended it to the whole country on an essentially federal basis. In four cases this was done through individual negotiations between Madrid and the regions involved to develop a modernized version of the old system of fueros.

Italy was not reunified until late in the nineteenth century following a struggle of the Italians against both their occupiers, primarily Austrian but partially French, and the papacy. Among the Italian nationalists were both federalists and unitarists. The federalists lost and, following the style of the times, the Italians established a unitary monarchy under Victor Emmanuel of Piedmont that lasted until it was replaced de facto by the even more centralized and autocratic regime of Mussolini and his Fascists that lasted until World War II. After the war, the monarchy was abolished. The Allies imposed constitutional decentralization upon Italy which did not take full effect until the end of the first postmodern generation.

Only then did modern Italian constitutionalism begin to fully take effect. The postwar Italian constitution provided for the division of the country into twenty regions, five either islands off the coast of the Italian peninsula or on Italy's peripheries with special status, and fifteen ordinary regions on the peninsula proper. The special status regions—Sicily, Sardinia, Valle d'Aosta, Trentino-Alto Adige, and Friuli-Venezia Giulia—were activated immediately to accommodate special ethnic and cultural differences, while the other fifteen were not activated until the 1970s. In none of them, except possibly for Sicily in a convoluted way, was the covenantal tradition of any significance.[25]

More recently, in the 1980s, a federalist movement reemerged in Italy whose primary interest is separation of prosperous northern Italy from the poverty-stricken south of the country which remained, in the eyes of northerners, a backward drain on northern resources and achievements. There is scientific evidence that the contractual culture of the civic republicanism of the medieval Italian city-states in the northern part of the country remains a subtle but powerful cultural influence on northern progress, as Robert Putnam has shown in his recent book.[26]

The Swiss: Resolutely Federal

Switzerland, resolutely federal as always, reorganized itself in the aftermath of Napoleon's defeat as a modern confederation, to which were joined the previously independent confederation of the Graubunden to the east and the French republics in the southwest in a much enlarged country relative to what it had been before. That confederation had its upheaval in 1847 and a Catholic-Protestant civil war was threatened. The Swiss political leadership on all sides came together, rewrote the Swiss constitution to make it a national federation rather than a confederation of separate republics, and so it has remained. Neutral ever since, as provided for at the Congress of Vienna, it maintains universal military service and is still stoutly prepared to defend itself at any time.[27]

After federation in 1848, the Swiss began to prosper, taking advantage of their beautiful mountainous terrain to capitalize on the new leisure available to the middle class and the tourism that it stimulated. They also capitalized on the water power of their mountains to build a new industrial base, driven by electrical energy and connected by a transportation system that became the envy of the world.

Since Swiss federalism was based upon deeply entrenched territorial divisions, they, too, had to confront their nonterritorial cultural and ideological divisions in a federal way in order to reenforce the system rather than undermine it. They also adopted a consociational system, not so much based upon an often oligarchical pillar system but on a system of recognized intergenerational groups, whether Protestant, Catholic, or, later when they were readmitted to Switzerland as a whole, Jewish, but also linguistic, political, and economic. As such, those groups perceived to be permanent, that is, intergenerational, were given a permanent seat at the Swiss negotiating table and were regularly consulted on all decisions deemed to require national consensus.

Significantly, even the term for citizen or member of the body politic in Switzerland is federal—Eidgenossen, roughly translatable as confederate or federal partner. Contrast this with the term for citizenship in the other continental European languages including English which has to do with being of a city, for example, citizen, burger or bourgeois.

Such Swiss constitutional devices as the plural executive (an executive council of seven instead of an executive president), the division of existing cantons into half-cantons, and the famous Swiss referendum system were all constitutional efforts to accommodate this consociational thrust. Swiss consociationalism is very quiet and has fit in easily to Swiss territorial federalism. As a result, strengthened by formal territorial federalism, Swiss consociationalism has continued to function well after other consociational regimes have disintegrated and has continued to provide the accommodations necessary to keep Switzerland unified yet noncentralized.[28]

Jacobin and Federalist Revolutions

Beginning with the French Revolution, the great revolutions of the modern epoch were all Jacobin in character, although it was an example of the tribute that vice often has to pay to virtue that they covered themselves with those symbols of the covenantal tradition that provided for regular popular consenting assemblies and the appropriate constitutional trappings. Jacobinism led, at its worst, to authoritarian regimes or, at its best, to liberal efforts to build a centralized state to carry out their programs. The difference between the two is great, but both shared a statist view of the world. These are the revolutions that we learn about in our history books because they are the ones that shaped the biggest European countries: France, Germany, Italy, and Spain. In every case, they were centralizing, both ideologically and in practice, rejecting traditional liberties and regional identities in an effort to build centralized states.

The tides of those revolutions rolled over the smaller European nations as well. All were affected by the Frence Revolution, especially in the Napoleonic phase which had centralizing consequences for them as well, in varying degrees. In the nineteenth century these smaller countries became centers of a different revolutionary direction introducing new federal ways to make covenantal ideas real. True, the first of those was not invented in Europe but across the Atlantic. The United States of America had a great revolution of its own, out of which came the invention of modern federalism, first of modern confederation and then of modern federation. Although huge in territory, the United States with its two and a half million people at the time was, in population terms, the equivalent of a small European country.

In Europe, it was not until the mid-nineteenth century that its federalist inventions were made. Because of the fact of the French Revolution and its continent-wide momentum, those inventions had to be made within the framework of the theory and practice of the Jacobin or organic state. In this chapter we have seen how one covenantal-federalist answer to that challenge was the invention of consociationalism by Abraham Kuyper in the Netherlands which spread down the Rhine valley to Belgium and then to Switzerland, which had remained federal and simply added another dimension to its territorial federalism. Later after the break-up of the Austrian-Hungarian empire, little Austria also adopted a federal consociational regime.

Consociationalism was a revolutionary invention in its own right; it was not a return to medieval organic society. Quite to the contrary, it was in those countries where the medievalist movement was strongest where consociationalism did not take hold. Rather, consociationalism was the invention of covenantal societies to provide them with a way to resist Jacobinism in their efforts to accomodate new heterogeneity in their polities. Indeed, a century later, when the covenantal elements in their societies were overwhelmed by ethnic revivals that put emphasis on the primordial, that is, organic ties, those consociational arrangements could no longer hold and most of them collapsed or were transformed.

Federation and consociationalism were two of the applications of covenantal principles invented in the modern epoch. The third, cooperation, was also designed to be used in the framework of the Jacobin state but less for political purposes than for economic and social ones. We will turn to it in the next chapter.

Notes

1. Simon Schama, *Citizens: A Chronicle of the French Revolution* (New York: Alfred A. Knopf, 1989).
2. Alexis de Tocqueville, *The Ancien Regime and the French Revolution*, trans. Stuart Gilbert (London: Collins, Fontana Classics, 1966); Pierre Goubert, *The Ancien Regime* (London: Weidenfeld and Nicolson, 1973).
3. Introduction to Tocqueville, *Democracy in America*.
4. Phyllis Cohen Albert, *The Modernization of French Jewry* (Hanover N.H.: Brandeis University Press, 1977).

5. Robert Goldwin, *Constitution-Makers and Constitution-Making* (Washington, D.C.: American Enterprise Institute, 1988).
6. William Carr, *A History of Germany, 1815–1945* (London: E. Arnold, 1984); Golo Mann, *The History of Germany Since 1789*, trans. Marian Jackson (Harmondsworth: Penguin books, 1974).
7. Mann, *ibid.*
8. Murray Forsyth, *Unions of States* (New York: Leicester University Press, 1981).
9. Ephraim Lipson, *Europe in the Nineteenth Century 1815–1914* (New York: Collier Books, 1962); William Langer, *The Revolutions of 1848* (New York: Harper and Row, 1971); Peter N. Stearns, *The Revolutions of 1848* (London: Weidenfeld and Nicolson, 1974).
10. Carr, *A History of Germany.*
11. Helmut Heiber, *The Weimar Republic* (Oxford: Blackwell, 1993).
12. Michael Balfour, *West Germany* (London: Benn, 1968); Hans Dollinger, *Die Bundesrepublik in der Ara Adenauier, 1949–1963* (Munich: Desch, 1966).
13. Ernst Heinrich Kossman, *The Low Countries, 1780–1940* (Oxford: Clarendon Press, 1978).
14. Lijphardt, *The Politics of Accomodation;* "Federalism and Consociationalism: A Symposium," *Publius*, vol. 15, no. 2 (Spring 1985).
15. James W. Skillen and Stanley W. Carlson-Thies, "Religion and Political Development in Nineteenth-Century Holland," *Publius*, vol. 12, no. 3 (Summer 1982).
16. Simon Schama, *The Embarrassment of Riches* (Lexington, Mass.: Fontana Press, 1988).
17. "Interview with Marcel, a 28-year-old Squatter," in Richard Reeves, "The Netherlands: Utopian Dreams are Being Interrupted by Reality," *International Herald Tribune* (23 October 1985).
18. *Ibid.*
19. Lijphardt, *The Politics of Accomodation.*
20. See the discussion in *Covenant and Commonwealth*, chapter 5.
21. Henri Pirenne, *Histoire de Belgique* (Bruxelles: H. Lamertin, 1909–1919), 4 vols.; John Gilissen, *Le Regime Representatif en Belgique Depuis 1790* (Brussels: La Renaissance du Livre, 1958).
22. Wilfried Martens, Speech at the International Conference on Federal-Type Solutions and European Integration, College of Europe, Bruges, Oct. 26, 1989.
23. Robert D. Putnam, *Making Democracy Work: Civic Traditions in Modern Italy* (Princeton, N.J.: Princeton University Press, 1993); Filipo Sabetti, *Political Authority in a Sicilian Village* (New Brunswick, N.J.: Rutgers University Press, 1983); Filipo Sabetti, Robert D. Putnam, and Rafaella Y. Nanetti, eds., *Italian Politics: A Review* (Wolfeboro, N.H.: Longwood Publishers, 1986).
24. Raymond Carr, *Spain, 1808–1975* (Oxford: Clarendon Press, 1983); Ricardo de la Cierva, *Historia Basica de la Espana Actual, 1800–1974* (Barcelona: Planeta, 1974); Manuel Ferrandis, *Historia Contemporanea de Espana y Portugal* (Barcelona: Labor, 1966); Harold Victor Livermore, *A New History of Porugal* (Cambridge: Cambridge University Press, 1976).
25. Sicily is another example of the covenantal tradition gone bad. It was brought to the island by its Norman conquerors in the Middle Ages through their oath culture, but since they were conquerors they used that oath culture for the division of spoils more than for the introduction of self-government. Over the next one thousand years that oath culture did become part of the island's heritage and was used for underground organization to resist foreign encroachment, but in

the end it became the basis for the Mafia because of the circumstances of Sicily's conquest by outsiders. Sabetti, *Political Authority in a Sicilian Village.*

26. Putnam, *Making Democracy Work.*
27. Wilhelm Oechsli, *History of Switzerland 1499–1914*, trans. Eden and Cedar Paul (Cambridge: Cambridge University Press, 1922); Peter Durrenmatt, *Schweizer Geschichte* (Zurich: Schweizer Verlaghaus, 1976).
28. Georges Andre Chevallaz, *Le Gouvernement des Swisses, on l'Histoire en Coutrepoint* (Lausanne: Editions de l'aire, 1989).

8

Revolutions: Cooperative, Collectivist, and Coercive

Scandinavian Cooperative Democracy

There remain the polities of Northern and Eastern Europe. The contrast between them is striking. The Scandinavian countries, having had their imperialistic aspirations literally beaten out of them in the medieval and early modern epochs, whereby each in turn lost in its effort to become a major European power, settled down and were among the earliest European countries to complete the transition to modern constitutionalism. More than that, the Scandinavian countries were among the world leaders in developing economic and social, in place of governmental, federalism, just as the Rhine Valley countries developed consociationalism as an ideologically based federalism to either replace or supplement territorial based federalism. This was done through the cooperative movement that arose in the nineteenth century in Scandinavia, Britain, and the American Northwest. Nowhere was it stronger and more important than in Scandinavia.

Centralized states ruled by monarchs emerged in the Scandinavian countries in opposition to self-governing local communities which the Danes, Norwegians, and Swedes had developed for themselves earlier. The monarchs were aided and abetted by the Roman Catholic church as part of the Christianization of Scandinavia. In the transitional period between the middle ages and the modern epoch those monarchies reached their apotheosis and unsuccessfully embarked on a series of adventures beyond their capabilities. By the beginning of the eighteenth century all had retreated to within the bounds of Scandinavia.

Despite all of this the spirit of local liberty remained strong. Although Scandinavia was less affected by the French Revolution and the Napoleonic wars than continental Europe, its countries also accepted the idea of the Jacobin or liberal reified state but, because of their prior traditions, they also accepted constitutionalism in a more willing and meaningful way. There was little or no discussion of federalism since each of the Scandinavian countries wanted to be independent and was afraid of too much entanglement with its more powerful neighbors. Each was also far too homogeneous to require consociationalism. What they did find suitable was a socioeconomic movement that could be both internal to each country and pan-Scandinavian in its character. The Scandinavian cooperative movement was a comprehensive one designed to promote local and popular empowerment through mutual action in a manner that may be deemed as covenantal.

From the first, Scandinavian efforts at establishing cooperatives were part of a movement whose economic goals were associated with a larger social effort to transform society into one of mutualism, cooperation, and continued human growth not simply to save money for consumers or to enable producers to realize a fairer share of profits earned. In this respect they were more fully covenantal in their pursuit of the virtues of cooperation and the human social and psychological improvement that organized and systematic cooperation was deemed to bring in its wake.

Cooperatives were formed through mutual association and pact on the basis of equality. Members of the cooperative movements were referred to in one way or another by terms equivalent to the English "cooperator," that is, a special term reflecting partnership. In the Scandinavian countries, the establishment of folkschools by and for the cooperative movement, which had as their goals raising the level of popular culture and education in general and preparing people for systematic cooperation in particular, added yet another dimension to the movement. While, like any other enterprises, cooperatives required some kind of anchoring in state law, basically, like most other nineteenth-century efforts, they prided themselves on being independent substitutes or alternatives to the state, fully voluntary in character.[1]

Thus we might suggest that one of the consequences of modernity for the covenantal tradition was its division into three channels: one, political and territorial through modern federalism a la the United States; the second political and nonterritorial through consociationalism a la the Netherlands; and the third, economic and social through cooperation a la Scandinavia. Each had its own brand of constitutional expression and all three leaned upon modern constitutional foundations designed to give citizens or the equivalent constituent groups, equal standing within the system established and an ultimately equal role in its governance.

Denmark may be the prime Scandinavian example of the cooperative democratic regime. It was part of the Viking heartland in medieval times where an oath society political culture predominated.[2] It, too, had a strong Teutonic background and inherited a hierarchical political culture as well. Taken together, the two created local oligarchies until Denmark was united.

Denmark's imperial age came earlier than the other Scandinavian countries, beginning in the tenth century when the Christianization of the country was completed. From then until 1523 it was always in union with one or more of the neighboring kingdoms. The combination of monarchy and Christianity introduced a long hierarchical period that was not transformed by the Reformation, which made Denmark Lutheran.

Denmark's embrace of both modern constitutionalism and popular reform in the nineteenth century transformed the country into a prosperous cooperative democracy emphasizing education and local self-government, both of which have been reinforced or adapted in each successive generation since then. It had the strongest and most extensive cooperative movement in Scandinavia, if not in the world, embracing economic, social, cultural, and educational activities.[3] As the cooperative movement either weakened or became strictly routinized after World War II, Denmark returned to the use of territorial democracy to maintain its internal decentralization, rewriting its constitution and laws to limit the role of the state government in internal affairs to one of setting grand policy and providing equitable financial arrangements while empowering Denmark's counties to actually organize and administer almost all domestic functions. The counties were to receive the lion's share of Denmark's revenues for that purpose. This system of decentralization became highly visible in Denmark with the counties in the forefront of governmental activities.

Norway lost its independence as a separate kingdom in 1397 when its crown was permanently united with Denmark's but it continued to exist as separate for internal purposes until its independence was restored in 1905. In 1814 Denmark ceded Norway to Sweden. Despite Norwegian resistance, it was forced to accept union with Sweden in 1815. In the intervening year Norway had written its own constitution (1814). It remained in force even under the union with the Swedish crown and is one of the oldest written constitutions in Europe, perhaps the oldest, to continuously remain in force.

Norway had been Lutheran since the Reformation but its Lutheranism was imposed upon an oath society that had been strongly nonhierarchical until it was Christianized in the ninth century. Since that oath society had a pagan rather than a Christian base, it could not be restored by appeal to Christian principles but its political culture could reassert itself under the modern principle of constitutionalism which relocated religion in the private rather than the public sphere, even though Lutheranism was the state church. Thus modern constitutionalism gave the Norwegians a chance to reassert their ancient tradition, which was at least parallel to the mainstream covenantal tradition.

From then on, Norway followed the modern constitutional path. While it never became a federal polity, it did emphasize local self-government and has provided both formally and informally for a great deal of local autonomy of the years, especially in recent ones.

Sweden had something of the same background but was far more hierarchical. Still, in its Viking period, it too had been a congeries of valley oath societies. Christianity and the Catholic Church were introduced in the ninth century and it strengthened the hierarchical political culture that the Swedes had inherited from their Germanic tribal ancestors. Nor did the Protestant Reformation change matters from a governmental perspective. Gustavus I, founder of the first independent Swedish dynasty, also established Lutheranism as the state church in order to strengthen his hierarchical rule.

Once it was united, Sweden became part of one royal union of Scandinavian countries after another until 1520 when it successfully revolted against its Danish rulers from within the Kalmar Union of Denmark, Norway, and Sweden and established itself as a kingdom in its own right. It then entered a period of European adventurism, at first successful, but ending in failure in the eighteenth century. Charles I established an absolute monarchy at the height of Swedish imperial success. It lasted until the time of Napoleon, when the last absolute monarch, Gustavus IV, was deposed by a liberal revolution.[4]

Since 1815 Sweden has remained neutral in all wars. While it rapidly advanced to the forefront of liberal and social democratic reform, Sweden always undertook those reforms in a basically hierarchical manner. The cooperative movement became widespread in Sweden in the nineteenth century as it did in the rest of Scandinavia. It was an internal populist answer to the problems of hierarchy in Swedish government and society, just as the mass emigration of Swedes, principally to North America was an external answer. The Swedish cooperative movement was a vehicle for promoting democratic self-government in a variety of fields. In time, however, those cooperatives combined into ever larger units to gain the advantages of scale, and by doing so they drew upon the hierarchical political culture for their methods. Then socialism became a powerful force on the Swedish scene, which reestablished the strong link between hierarchical government and social programs so that the cooperative movement became merely another link in a tightly structured, integrated public-private pyramid. While particularly attractive to outsiders in the twentieth century interwar period, when the worldwide Great Depression demanded economic reform and those democrats who resisted totalitarianism sought a middle way in the Swedish example, the Swedish way turned out to require a sufficiently Teutonic population to accept the kind of benign regimentation that it imposed.[5]

Finland remained a Russian grand duchy until World War I. It had been part of Sweden until 1809 when it was ceded to Russia in such a way as to preserve more of its internal autonomy than any other part of the Russian Empire. It had its own parliament and constitution and enjoyed semi-independence.[6] It, too, seized upon modern constitutionalism to break out of the hierarchical mold that both Christianity and Swedish political culture imposed on it after it was Christianized in the twelfth century, to restore something of the political culture of its oath society past, even though it remained tied to one of the most autocratic hierarchical regimes in all Europe until the twentieth century.

Other Holy Roman Empire Adaptations

Like Luxembourg, Liechtenstein was another fragment of the Holy Roman Empire that preserved its independence under its own prince because it was located between republican Switzerland and Hapsburg Austria. Not being a republic, it could not join the former. Not wanting to lose its independence, it would not join the latter. In due course it entered into a customs union with Switzerland and became something like an associated state and also a constitutional monarchy.[7]

Austria lived through all but the last generation of the modern epoch as the heart of the Hapsburg Empire, which was the least modernized politically and governmentally of all the European states west of Russia. The Hapsburgs successfully resisted Napoleon, crushed the internal Revolutions of 1848, and repressed all other disturbances to the status quo. Catholic to the core, the Austrians had very little, if any, covenantal tradition upon which to draw.[8]

The most divisive aspect of their empire was the multitude of ethnic groups within it. Ultimately that was to prove fatal, but only after various efforts were made within the empire at ethnic accommodation, including a limited amount of home rule. For example, the Hungarians gained nominally equal status in the Austro-Hungarian Empire, the reconstituted Hapsburg polity, even as they continued to repress other minorities around them and under their jurisdiction.

Nevertheless, a certain habit of federalism was born out of this necessity for ethnic accommodation throughout the empire and after it fell, the little Austria that remained became a national federation until it was absorbed by Hitler's Germany in the Anschluss of 1938. After World War II it restored its federal system and continues to preserve it through consociational arrangements, albeit as one of the most unlikely federations imaginable.[9]

Eastern Europe and Russia

The countries to the east of Germany and Austria began the modern epoch either as parts of empires or, in the case of Poland, soon lost its independence, and was divided between three empires. None could draw systematically on covenantal traditions although Bohemia and Moravia had some sources transmitted via their Reformed Protestantism. In Bohemia and especially Moravia a covenantal Reformed Protestantism had appeared during the Reformation and indeed even before. Jan Huss (1369?–1415) and the Hussite rebellion anticipated the Great Reformation by a century in Bohemia and Moravia, but they were defeated and the two lands submerged into the Hapsburg empire. Comenius carried on the intellectual tradition of the reformers in the seventeenth century.

The Czechs of Bohemia and Moravia sought national independence in the late nineteenth century. With the help of Czechs who had emigrated to the

United States and under the leadership of Tomas Masaryk (1850–1935), who was described by *The Economist* as "a philosopher, historian, literary critic, publicist, and moralist in the true nineteenth century tradition," they developed a nationalist movement with its operational base in Pittsburgh.[10]

Masaryk was very much in the Reformed Protestant tradition, urging Protestantism as a personal moral guide, believing firmly in the power of education to put things right and in the progressive agenda of his times. He was called "the Puritan" during his life and after his death.

World War I and the Versailles Treaty brought the Czechs success. The state Masaryk and his colleagues built was the most democratic in Central Europe between World Wars I and II, until sold out by Chamberlain at Munich in 1938, after which it was occupied by Nazi Germany. Liberated by Soviet troops, Czechoslovakia was seized by the Communists in 1948. After forty plus years of Communist rule punctured by one major rebellion (1968) it was restored as a democratic state. Its new president, Vaclav Havel, was the person perhaps most responsible for the revival of the idea of civil society in Eastern Europe and the West.

Nor was this the only influence of Protestants in Central and Eastern Europe in overthrowing Communism. The small Protestant churches, particularly those representing Reformed Protestantism, that had survived made major and active contributions wherever they were present in the Communist bloc. In East Germany, they gave the East German revolt its points of assembly and nonviolent direction. In Romania, the Protestants (of Hungarian background) began the general uprising in Timosoara in a protest against the announced removal of Pastor Lazlo Tokes of the Hungarian Reformed Church in a nearby village. Tokes, indeed, was not only outspoken but became a leader of the revolt. Protestant activity was directly drawn from the tradition of resistance of Reformation Protestantism and, one might add, likely from feelings of guilt that they had not resisted Hitler and local fascism sufficiently.[11]

In earlier times Poland had been a kind of aristocrats' federation in which every noble could exercise his veto in the Polish parliament at will, making the Polish political system so difficult to operate that the country could not sustain itself against its voracious neighbors.[12] Poland adopted its first modern constitution at the same time as France, although not in response to a social revolution but as part of its struggle for independence against its Russian, German, and Austrian neighbors. It included several features of modern constitutionalism, combined with vestiges from the medieval Polish regime.

The failure of the Polish struggle for independence in the late eighteenth and throughout the nineteenth centuries made that constitution and its successors prior to 1918 all dead letters. The reestablishment of Polish independence as part of the post-World War I settlement led to the formal adoption of a constitution not only guaranteeing individual rights but minority group rights as well. But the Polish government in the interwar period was at best authoritarian and toward the end had degenerated into fascism, making much of

Polish constitutionalism a dead letter. Communist domination after World War II meant that Poland did not even begin to have a chance to experience democratic republicanism in a serious way until the 1980s. What these countries did have was a growing ethnic nationalism calling for territorial self-determination when the territories involved were at best checkerboards of nationalities, usually overlapping.

In the end, the problems of modern nationalism grew out of the impossibility of combining territorially based self-determination on the exclusive nation-state model with the physical mix of ethnic groups characteristic of east central Europe. We still have not seen the end of the problems arising from trying to cope with that contradiction, as witness the wars of the south Slavs since the collapse of Communist Yugoslavia.

Of Russia little need be said. The closest the Russians came to ever having even a touch of a nonhierarchical tradition within their borders came in the years when Vikings from Sweden invaded the Russian lands to establish a trade route from the north to the Mediterranean. The northmen may have lived within an oath society but what they brought to Russia was a level of barbarism not out of place in that environment. There is no evidence that they left behind any remnants of their culture beyond the country's name; transients they were when they came and transients they were when they left.

Russia as a polity expanded by conquest and total conquest at that. The one thing that can be said about its rulers is that they were no better to their own people than they were to others. Then, in the nineteenth century, the Russian Empire was also stirred by the revolutionary winds of change that came into Russia via the officers of the imperial army who fought Napoleon in Western Europe and indirectly were influenced by American ideas.[13] These officers were moderate liberals but did not always know exactly what that meant. What they initiated was picked up by other Russians, particularly intellectuals from the aristocratic class, many of whom became much enamored of the United States.[14]

Russia, however, continued to be Russia. As its liberals and radicals talked about changes, its government became even more repressive and even completed the expansion of the Russian Empire by conquering the countries of the Caucasus and Central Asia. Liberalism was discredited, terrorism came in its place, but terrorists without anything more can only blow up people and possessions, they cannot provide a substitute. This left the door open to the socialists, ranging from social democrats to radical Bolsheviks. The former dominated the partially successful revolution of 1905 and the first stages of the 1917 revolution, from March when Alexander Kerensky and his government took power until October when they were overthrown by Lenin and the Bolsheviks. From then on, these most radical of the Russian revolutionaries, who also were able to combine radicalism with efficient action, were in control, although they had to fight a civil war to extend and consolidate that control.

From then on, politically everything went downhill. The Bolsheviks, by then simply the Communists, carefully kept the forms of constitutional democracy, but they robbed them of all content and imposed an increasingly harsh and bloody totalitarian dictatorship to uproot the old society as well as the old regime and to eliminate those of the new regime whom the rulers considered to be dangerous for whatever reason.

The Russian Revolution produced the concept of "peoples' democracy" adapted from Jacobinism with its vanguard cadres and elite class of bureaucrats who presumably ruled in the name of the people. The latter were given only the forms of political democracy but in reality, were permitted no effective voice in government. The federalist ideas of some of the Russian anarchists as well as the proto-federal program of "freely elected soviets" and free trade associations set forth in the Kronstadt revolt (1921), among others, were quickly crushed by the forces of Lenin and Stalin.[15]

Having gone through the motions, the Communists were able to consolidate their regime in the 1920s. After Lenin's death and a brief period of struggle for the leadership between Trotsky and Stalin, the latter emerged victorious and proceded to become perhaps the most heinous dictator of the twentieth century, at least quantitatively. Nevertheless, he succeeded in restoring Russia to a great power role as the Union of Soviet Socialist Republics.

After successfully fighting World War II, the USSR emerged as one of the world's two superpowers by combining totalitarian control through repression, concentration of national resources for military purposes, and to some degree bluffing the West. The USSR managed to survive until the 1980s when cracks appeared, first in its empire and then within the USSR itself. Mikhail Gorbachev tried to save the regime through judicious reform, but it was too late and it collapsed early in the 1990s.

The collapse of the USSR, was nothing less than another revolution which, to date, has gone through four steps: one, the transformation of the union republics into independent states; two, the linking of most of them to Russia and to each other through the Commonwealth of Independent States, a form of confederal arrangement somewhere between a league and a weak confederation; three, the sharpening of the autonomy of the internal units within Russia and several other of the newly independent states; four, the attempt of the new states to establish themselves and at the same time transform their economic, social, and political systems from top-down "command" systems to more open "market" ones, based not on orders passed down through a hierarchy but on exchanges among equals, in other words, a new system, drawing less on the covenantal tradition of politics than on the effort to introduce market economics.

Understanding this process can help us understand how constitutional, exchange, and market systems are derived fully or partly from covenantal roots. The newly independent states rapidly discovered that they lacked the most basic elements for the transition. They had no system of contractual relationships. Since everything had been by command, there was no law of contracts in any of them. There was no legal system capable of dealing with contracts and contract law. There were no lawyers, businessmen, or politicians who had worked in a contractual system even of the simplist kind. There were no banks or credit mechanisms of the kind common in societies based on contract rather than command.

Moreover, not only was there insufficient understanding of these vital mechanisms, but insufficient trust among the people to enable them to work. Here we reach down past the contractual to the covenantal. Contractual systems work, in the first and last analysis, because there is a sufficient dimension of trust built into the society which allows for the necessary faith in the system to enable agreements to be made because it is expected that they will be kept. That trust is derived from the moral underpinnings that must undergird even the most private and interest-oriented contractualism. That trust and its moral basis ultimately are derived from moraly informed pacts, of covenants.

What happened next in Russia and in its sister states was what had happened in Sicily and much of Italy under similar conditions centuries ago within the framework or shell of the state. A mafia arose, a network of agreements, rather primitive contracts, based upon mutual pledges enforced by the most extreme measures, up to and including murder of violators, yet at the same time requiring all those part of the mafia to maintain their promises as given or to be assured that they would suffer the consequences. Thus these mafias, like the Italian one, popularly noted for their use of criminal violence, actually are networks of mutual pledges that enable a society to organize itself and function when there is too little trust for legitimate public institutions to do so sufficiently and successfully.

A mafia provides the modicum of mutuality needed for society to work. It requires people to pledge to one another and maintains the enforcement of those pledges often in ways that are far from being nice. It then supplies credit, provides substitutes for banks, and introduces at least a simple system of contracts so that it can provide the services that it offers to those who are interested in availing themselves of those services or appreciate the necessity for doing so.

A mafia may be a temporary expedient, but a mafia alone cannot resolve the problems of Russia and its sister states. Other devices have to be found, devices that are sufficiently covenantal yet compatible with the political cultures in the area to succeed and at the same time sufficiently different to begin to modify those political cultures which, always dysfunctional, have become even more so in today's world.

From Revolution to Constitutionalism

In the last analysis, the second half of the modern epoch was not simply an age of revolutions although it was that, but also an age for the growth of constitutional government and the idea of constitutionalism. Every one of the countries of continental Europe underwent some kind of violent wrenching experiences during the modern epoch, beginning with the British Isles in the mid-seventeenth century and rolling eastward, northward, and southward until the end of the epoch. All of these violent wrenchings had as their avowed purpose at the very least the replacement of autocracy or absolute monarchy by republicanism or even democratic republicanism, although at the very end most were victims of counterrevolutions that brought equal or worse wrenching violence.

The twentieth century also produced the totalitarian phenomena of fascism and Nazism, while many of the newly independent nations found themselves ruled by civil and/or military dictatorships. Consequently, there was a strong thrust in late modernity toward polities which stood in sharp opposition to the ideas of either the covenanted commonwealth or modern civil society. This thrust involved an emphasis on centralized state institutions ruled by powerful leaders atop pyramidally structured bureaucratic command systems. Ironically, such systems were proposed and supported by many American foreign policymakers who, despite the development experience of their own country, have regarded newly modernizing or developing countries as being in need of authoritarian stability and centralized control of national peripheries. In this respect, many contemporary political systems have the character of conquest rather than covenant and show it.

At the same time, many such systems also emphasized forms of collectivism which are usually promoted in the names of equality, brotherhood, communitarianism, and national solidarity. This hierarchical rule was frequently cast in organic terms as in the blood ties of Nazism and ethnoreligious fascism, the "species consciousness" of Marxism, and the virtual bonding of the general will in Jacobinism. In turn, any elements of popular consent tend to give way to elite manipulation in such systems. Federal polities have experienced many of the same pressures, not only externally, but also internally as various circumstances and forces have combined to pressure for greater centralization of power and authority.

The modern revolutionary era generated two modern forms of covenantalism that were to become extraordinarily influential: modern constitutionalism and modern federalism. The first concentrated on developing practical ways of translating the principles of the covenantal tradition, or at least those acceptable to moderns, into forms of government while the second emphasized making those forms both self-governing and workable. Both rested on the idea of civil society with its private, public nongovernmental, and governmental spheres, as distinct from the older idea of the homogeneous commonwealth with no clear separation between public and private, governmental and nongovernmental. In time, both shifted their emphasis from forms of government to human rights.

In the newly settled parts of the world where new societies were founded, constitutionalism and often federalism were planted among the original seeds. In the Old World, however, polities, even states, already existed with deeply entrenched political, social, and cultural patterns, almost all of which were unfavorable to these new ideas. These had to be overcome if the new ideas and the practices that flowed from them were to be instituted. In most countries overcoming them even partially required violent revolution, often more than once, and even then it could require up to two centuries before significant change in the desired direction could be incorporated into the national consensus.

If we are to look at the impact of the modern revolutions in Europe according to the five dimensions of a political tradition: ideologies, cultures, institutions, processes, and behavior, we would find the following:

With regard to ideologies, modern revolutions brought great changes. They were in that sense the first nonreligious ideological revolutions, introducing secular political ideologies often in place of religious ones. Indeed the very idea of a secular ideology could only have come in modern times after religion was so substantially separated from society. All of the modern revolutions brought with them new ideologies and a substantial ideological change in the thinking of substantial groups of people. Some of those changes were more visibly consequential than others. Some were very consequential but their consequences were only partly visible as such and even less obvious as stemming from those ideologies. Some succeeded for short periods of time and then collapsed, leaving residues and remnants. Others have had enduring impact.

Marxism, for example, was an ideological revolution that led to several very violent political revolutions, foremost of which was that in the Russian empire in 1917. While Marxians confined themselves to the realm of ideology, deriving their "scientific" Marxism from the writings of Marx, Marxists overthrew societies, established new institutions, and, where successful, repressed and murdered millions of people in an effort to translate Marxist principles into realities on the ground. Marxism succeeded in the real world for more than two generations but ultimately collapsed under the weight of its own deficiencies (one is tempted to write "contradictions"). Marxian thought continues to be influential, often in negative ways.

The ideological elements of federal democracy, on the other hand, were not recognized as ideological for a long time and indeed were rarely articulated as such by their proponents or opponents. Nevertheless, they have had an extraordinary influence on shaping the modern and even more so the postmodern world, partly because their impact on the real world through the founding and development of the United States was so great. Only now, as the consequences of some of their basic premises are being questioned in some quarters, is the distinctiveness and strength of the American worldview being recognized for what it has been.

Fascism, on the other hand, with its variant, Nazism, flourished briefly and destructively in the real world. It lasted barely a generation but left behind a residue of destruction and transformation in the world and a remnant of committed Fascists and Nazis to carry on the ideas upon which it was built. It seems to be undergoing a bit of revival in the 1990s.

The French Revolution may have been the most successful other than the American. Its ideas, especially in their Jacobin form, certainly superseded American political thought for most of the world, for some 200 years, including most of the intellectuals in the world who stayed within the democratic fold. It also had somewhat more success in building long-lasting institutions where it took hold. It became the leading democratic rival to American federal democracy and indeed has been given far more recognition than the latter by scholars and intellectuals for most of the last two hundred years.

In sum, it is fair to say that modern revolutions were successful in bringing about ideological changes in human thought, not only those specific to particular revolutionary ideological movements but also in general in terms of modernism as a whole.

With regard to institutions, the modern revolutions also brought about major formal institutional changes. The complex of premodern institutions was replaced by a new complex involving major changes in specific institutions, the introduction of republicanism, the new emphasis on popular or at least nominally popular institutions as the basis for the polity, a new set of institutions to express the intended homogenization of nation-states and to replace the system of estates, guilds and communities of medieval times. These institutional changes took different forms in different polities but were everywhere real.

The case with regard to processes was distinctly mixed. The combination of ideological and institutional change did lead to some changes in processes, but more than was generally recognized, the processes continued relatively little affected by those changes, adapting themselves to new ideological expressions and institutional arrangements in every country. Thus, the difference between Napoleon and King Louis XIV had more to do with the sources of their legitimacy and the forms of organization that they applied but not with their processes of governance or control.

In time, the processes changed further as the postrevolutionary institutions that took root began to influence them. It took much time and one can still see in a Charles de Gaulle clear expressions of the French monarchic tradition. De Gaulle's success came from recognizing that his country's political system could no longer be anchored on the same foundations that were introduced by the revolution but had to be anchored on popular and constitutional foundations that suited the modern temper yet were in harmony with France's monarchic tradition. His success in doing that is what made him the greatest leader of twentieth-century France and the one who brought legitimacy to the

French postrevolutionary polity 170 years after the revolution itself took place. Elsewhere, the change in processes was also moderate to mixed throughout the rest of the modern epoch but accelerated in the postmodern years as processes began to catch up with institutional changes adopted much earlier.

If that was true of processes, it was even more so of culture and behavior. One might say that initially there was little to no real change in either, just some broadening of certain patterns for the same reasons that were true with regard to processes. In part, that is because culture changes so slowly.

Since the discovery of the importance of culture in the twentieth century and more specifically political culture since the 1950s, there has been a tendency in some quarters to confuse culture and style. In politics as in fashion, styles change, while culture is extraordinarily long-lasting. It is comparable to the difference between the length of hemlines and the fact that women in Western society wear dresses rather than pantaloons. While hemline lengths change frequently, women have been wearing dresses in the societies of Western civilization for thousands of years and only in our time have pants designed for women become an option in the West, just as dresses have become an option in societies where women wore pantaloons for thousands of years in the Far East. It is always necessary to keep in mind the difference between culture and style. Culture does change but since culture is both manifest and latent and functions on several levels, even manifest cultural changes come slowly and often mask persistent cultural latencies of critical importance.[16]

Modern revolutions brought considerable changes in style in relatively short order, although with the limits described above. Where they were successful in bringing about ideological and institutional change, in due course they began to influence cultural manifestations as well and may now be beginning to bring about more fundamental cultural change. But processes and behavior which depend so heavily upon culture have changed much more slowly than ideologies and institutions which, while also to some extent dependent upon culture, can be altered by revolutionary developments, political and otherwise.

Two Covenantal Variants

In the end, it is probably true that the commercial and industrial revolutions had as great or greater impact than the preceding or concomitant political revolutions, especially since successive industrial revolutions based upon newer technologies have continued that process far more intensively, either reinforcing earlier political revolutions, as in the case of the impact of the American Revolution, or altering them slowly, as in the case of the French Revolution, or more rapidly as in the case of the totalitarian revolutions of the twentieth century. As they have, the market economy they generated and reenforced has expanded and become ever more pervasive.

Three modern variants of constitutionalism and federalism were developed to assist in this task: federation, consociationalism, and cooperation through the cooperative movement. The latter two were indigenous to the European continent and reached their fullest flowering there. Consociationalism was in many respects a nonterritorial form of federalism whereby intergenerational ideologically based movements, religious or secular, sharing the same space, developed a constitutional means for sharing political power that enabled them to preserve their respective integrities, secure support for their adherents, and strive to achieve their goals on an equal or equitable basis compatible with modern ideas of republicanism, usually democratic republicanism at that. Just as territorial federalism was particularly prominent in the English- and German-speaking worlds, consociationalism was most prominent in the Low Countries and the Rhine Valley.

Cooperation developed as a form of economic and social but not political or governmental federalism, a means for people to band together within existing polities to pursue shared economic, social, educational, and cultural goals on an equal and democratic basis in the modern spirit through constitutionalized means that did not necessarily seek to capture the state. Cooperation was most prominent in the Scandinavian countries or wherever Scandinavians settled in the world. It was at the same time more private, less political, and more mutual than the other forms of federalism.

Both consociationalism and cooperation were designed to be used to advance constitutional democratic republicanism. On occasion both were used, usually by peoples coming out of similar covenantal traditions, to advance nondemocratic control of one group by another in hierarchical fashion. In the latter case almost every example was quickly recognized for what it was and rejected by the true heirs to the covenantal tradition.

Both consociationalism and cooperation, whether covenantal or pseudo-covenantal, disappeared or were drastically weakened early in the postmodern epoch. In every case there were specific reasons. They all added up to inability of either to sustain what they had promised for more than two generations either because of structural weaknesses (particularly in the case of the cooperative movement) or because of the loss of allegiance to the "pillars" on the part of their adherents (particularly in the case of consocationalism). They later began to pursue other more individualistic goals less amenable to the discipline necessary to maintain covenantal structures in general and nonterritorial ones in particular.

Given that territorial polities organized along covenantal-federal lines have been minority phenomena in world history, the future of the covenant principle as a historical reality is by no means certain. Those whose polities are organized around this idea will no doubt continue to debate the meaning of their covenants so long as they remain concerned with constitutional government and, in the long run, to quote Richard Niebuhr:

one may raise the question whether our common life could have been established, could have been maintained and whether it can endure without the presence of the conviction that we live in a world that has the moral structure of a covenant.[17]

Notes

1. Robert Lavergne, *La Revolution Cooperative* (Paris: Presses Universitaires de France, 1949).
2. Daniel J. Elazar, *Covenant and Commonwealth: The Covenantal Tradition from Christian Separation through the Protestant Reformation* (New Brunswick, N.J.: Transaction Publishers, 1995).
3. Clemens Pedersen, *The Danish Cooperative Movement* (Copenhagen: Danske Selskab, 1977); Petre Manniche, *Denmark a Social Laboratory* (Copenhagen: G.E.C. Gad, 1939).
4. Ingvar Andersson, *A History of Sweden* (London: Weidenfeld and Nicolson, 1956); Kurt Samuelsson, *From Great Power to Welfare State: 300 Years of Swedish Social Development* (London: G. Allen and Unwin, 1968); Franklin D. Scott, *Sweden, the Nation's History* (Minneapolis: University of Minnesota Press, 1977).
5. Marquis Childs, *Sweden, the Middle Way* (New York: Penguin, 1948).
6. John Henry Wuorinen, *A History of Finland* (New York: Columbia University Press, 1965).
7. Hubert de Havrincourt, *Liechtenstein* (Lausanne: Editions Rencontre, 1964); Walter Kranz, *The Principality of Liechtenstein* (Vaduz: Press and Information Ofiice of the Government of the Principality of Liechtenstein).
8. Edward Cranshaw, *The Fall of the House of Habsburg* (London: Sphere Books, 1970); Charles W. Ingrao, *The Habsburg Monarchy, 1618–1815* (Cambridge: Cambridge University Press, 1994).
9. Erich Zollner, *Geschichte Osterreichs* (Munich: R. Oldenbourg, 1970); Heinrich Siegler, *Osterreich: Chronik, 1945–1972* (Vienna: Siegler, 1973); Felix Kreissler, *La Prise de Conscience de la Nation Autrichienne* (Paris: Presses Universitaires de France, 1980).
10. *The Economist*, "Philosopher Kings," March 31, 1990.
11. Paul F.M. Zahl, "East Europe: The Protestant Factor," *Washington Post*, January 14, 1990.
12. W.F. Reddaway, ed., *The Cambridge History of Poland* (Cambridge: Cambridge University Press, 1950); Norman Davies, *A History of Poland: God's Playground* (Oxford: Clarendon Press, 1981), vol. 1 (origins to 1795).
13. Jesse Dunmore Clarkson, *A History of Russia From the Ninth Century* (London: Longmans, 1962); Basil Dmytryshyn, *A History of Russia* (Englewood Cliffs, N.J.: Prentice-Hall, 1977); Ronald Hingley, *The Tsars, 1533–1917* (New York: Macmillan, 1968); W. Bruce Lincoln, *The Romanovs* (New York: Dial Press, 1981).
14. David Hecht, *Russian Radicals Look to America, 1825–1894* (New York: Greenwood Press, 1968).
15. Martin McCauley, *Octobrists to Bolsheviks* (London: E. Arnold, 1984); Marc Ferro, *The Russian Revolution of February 1917*, J.L. Richards, trans. (London: Routledge and Kegan Paul, 1972).
16. I have written more extensively on this matter of cultural change in *The American Mosaic* (Boulder, Colo.: Westview Press, 1994).
17. Richard Niebuhr, "The Idea of Covenant and American Democracy," *Church History* 23 (June 1954), p. 134.

9

Swiss Exceptionalism:
Communal and Liberal Democracy

On August 1, 1991, as the second generation of the postmodern epoch reached its climax, Switzerland marked 700 years of national political life. It was on that date in 1291 that the representatives of three mountain republics—Uri, Schwyz, and Unterwalden—met on the Rutli field at the point where Lake Lucerne turns southward to become Lake Uri, to sign a pact of mutual assistance—a covenant—"to last, if God will, forever."[1] These three *Waldstatte* (forest states) became the nucleus of the Helvetic or Swiss Confederation. The original text of the pact or covenant of 1291 is preserved in the nearby town of Schwyz and August 1 is the national holiday of all Switzerland.[2]

The story (or legend) of William Tell and the Swiss revolt makes the point clearly. An honest huntsman, conducting his private and family affairs, uninterested in matters of public power and governance, is suddenly caught in a position where he must acknowledge serious inequality by bowing down to a regional governor's hat in the town square of Altdorf in Uri. He refuses and is punished in a particularly cruel way usually associated with conquerers or those who rule by force; namely, he is required to shoot an apple off of his son's head. Tell succeeds and is arrested following his success when he tells the local tyrant, Gensler, that had he failed, his next arrow would have been directed toward Gensler himself. Tell manages to escape but, by then, his private concerns, out of necessity, had given way to public ones. He organizes and leads the revolt against the local Hapsburg rulers, which is the beginning of Swiss political independence. Truth or legend, the story encompasses all of the ingredients of the covenantal tradition. (Compare it to the Jewish midrash—explication of the biblical text—about Abraham who gets his start when he refuses to bow down to the idols of Nimrod, the king.)

While the rest of Europe, even its covenantal or almost covenantal polities, was undergoing revolutionary change as the result of the coming of the modern epoch, Switzerland remained the one point of continuity. As a thoroughly covenantal country with a covenant-based polity, the Helvetic Confederation had already achieved a substantial share of the democratic, republican and federal tasks that represented the heart of modernization for

177

its continental neighbors. Hence, its adjustment was more one of fine-tuning
than of revolutionary change, although, as a small country bordering France
and Germany, Switzerland could not avoid being engulfed by the revolution.
Still, the Swiss and their political system came through it relatively intact and
could fine-tune it as they wished later in the nineteenth century.

The Swiss were the exceptions in Europe, recognized as such by Alexis De
Tocqueville no less than he recognized how the Americans were the exceptions in the world.[3] Made shortsighted by his commitment to modern nationalism and federalism within that context, Tocqueville was somewhat myopic
when it came to Switzerland, despite his overall recognition of Swiss
exceptionalism. Nevertheless, the fact of his recognition gives us reason to
look more closely at Switzerland as different from the rest of the European
experience.

Federal Independence

From the beginning, even before the pact at Rutli, the forest republics bordering on Lake Lucerne, which is known in German as the *Vierwaldstattersee*,
(Lake of the Four Forest States), had developed a rich form of communal
liberty in their Alpine valleys where each valley community provided for communal use of its forests, communal clearing of its pastures, and distribution of
the offspring of their herds and flocks. These communal obligations were
handled through constant meetings, discussions, and elections. Independent
for all intents and purposes, these mountain republics owed a symbolic allegiance to the emperor of the Holy Roman Empire who was formally sovereign over all of Helvetia. Imperial intervention was limited to maintaining the
route over St. Gotthard Pass which passed through Uri.

During the thirteenth century the ruling Hapsburgs from Austria began a
bureaucratic intervention that interfered with these local liberties, introducing a corps of officials interested in raising revenues from the locals for themselves and for the imperial treasury. It was against this externally imposed
administrative and judicial system that the three forest republics revolted,
initially without demonstrating any disloyalty toward the imperial crown, but
in the course of time moving to complete independence. In order to further
their cause, the three mountain republics came together in 1291 to establish
what was originally known by the medieval Latin term, *coniuratio* (those
bound by a shared oath) and the German term, *bundesbrief* (those bound by a
federal document).

The act of confederation, covenant and oath, signed and sworn on the field
of Rutli, became the foundation of the Helvetic Confederation which, over
the centuries, expanded into the twenty-six cantons and half-cantons of contemporary Switzerland. It was the people of these three mountain cantons
who, by resisting the Austrian efforts to subordinate them to imperial control

(as distinct from nominal suzerainty), brought about the 526-year war that led to the establishment of the territorial integrity and independence of modern Switzerland. After twenty-four years of skirmishing, the army of the three won a victory in 1315 over the Hapsburg troops at Morgarten, which secured their full liberation, at least de facto.

As in the case of many other countries, a mythic history developed much later around these founding events, but be that as it may, the Pact of Rutli, solemnly sworn by thirty-three representatives of the three original cantons, was a reality. The Swiss experience before and especially after the Pact at Rutli, based as it was on the functioning of small communities of equals who made collective decisions through deliberation and consensus, and who developed popular democratic institutions through which to do so, offered a form of liberty considerably different from the individualistic liberty taken for granted in the United States as the only real form of liberty.

Each of these mountain republics and their respective valley communes were governed through some system of direct yet collective democracy—for the republics, *landesgeminden*, that is to say, assemblies of all male citizens, as the final expression of popular sovereignty. Since individual citizens were part of the collective decision-making apparatus, they were expected to be bound by their decisions and, as long as they lived in the community, had limited individual choice. This made for considerable communal discipline but did not necessarily interfere with the individualism of the citizens in other respects, as anyone who knows the Swiss of today can see.

Covenantal or federal combinations were added on top of these communal democracies. Not only did those arrangements link them into larger units for common purposes, often defensive, but they also fostered a certain kind of territorially based pluralism whereby different communities could preserve their own ways of life within their respective territories, while at the same time confederating for larger common purposes. Thus, a pluralism of communal liberties was made possible through federal arrangements.

Antecedents: What Made the Swiss Special?

Feudalism was the mode of political and social organization of the Holy Roman Empire except in the alpine lands of Switzerland. There covenantal societies preserved or developed democratic-republicanism during the Middle Ages. Switzerland was at the heart of this territory which runs right along the old line of division between the Roman empire and the Germanic tribes encompassing that Romano-Germanic border region from Switzerland to Scotland. In that region four forces came together, each with making its own contribution to the forging of a covenantal political culture. The Helvetii who were Celts and the Allemani who became the South Germans combined liberty and community through sociopolitical arrangements secured by oath.

The Romans brought their law of contracts and the sociopolitical order it represented. The influence of the Hebrew Bible which provided a framework of ideological legitimation for that political culture became pronounced after the pagan tribes were Christianized.[4]

Expansion through Confederation

For many years, the three-republic Swiss confederation was the only substantial free territory on the continent. In 1332, forty-one years after the original pact at Rutli, the city-republic of Lucerne at the northern end of the lake joined the original three confederates; Zurich joined in 1351, Glarus and Zug in 1352, and Berne in 1353, so that two generations after the founding of the confederation, it had grown to eight cantons covering the country's alpine heartland and its urban fringe to the north. Together these cantons waged the battle for liberty for the next four generations, until five more cantons to the northwest and north of the eight joined between 1481 and 1513 to form what came to be regarded as the old confederacy. The cantons to the south, southwest, and east did not come into the confederation until the time of the Napoleonic wars between 1803 and 1815.

David Lasserre, in his book *Die Schicksalsstunden des Foederalismus* argues that the main importance of the covenant of 1291 was not so much a military but a legal one. To be sure the military aspect cannot be neglected but modern scholarship has quite convincingly established that the military part of the conjuratio goes back to another compact the physical evidence of which has been lost. Thus the innovative parts of the covenant of 1291 are the clauses dealing with the claim of the Swiss to having judges elected from among the people inhabiting their area and the ones that codify the criminal law of the time. It should be noted that similar codifications could be found throughout Europe at that time and reflected the desire of the people to put down on paper, in a time of turmoil and widespread insecurity, the principles of law hitherto handed down orally.[5]

This decision of the covenanters to resort to law rather than violence in the resolution of conflicts between them has its parallel in the arbitration clause. That clause provided that if there should be litigation between two or more parties those not involved should offer their services as arbiters. In case one of the parties did not implement the arbiters' ruling, all the other contracting partners were to support the harmed party. Clauses of this sort were included in all the subsequent covenants and, as Lasserre points out, frequently were put to use. As notable examples he cites the conflict between the city of Zug and its rural hinterland, the latter of which was supported by Schwyz. Another example is the war between the city of Zurich and Schwyz during which there were numerous attempts at arbitration. Besides these most notable examples, there is evidence of more than 100 cases in which the arbitration clauses were put to use.

Arbitration was not only used by the Swiss. What made their way of using it exceptional was that the arbiters were other partners to the covenant. By avoiding the then common custom of calling on a well-known aristocrat to resolve the dispute in question, the Swiss could secure a strong internal stability and keep outside influences at a minimum. Additionally, the very important notion of arriving at a compromise, or a majority solution for that matter, and the acceptance of the compromise or the solution by those whose position did not prevail became a part of Swiss political life from its very beginnings. It was to become rooted in Swiss political culture and to be of invaluable importance for the survival, despite occasional grave differences among the federal partners, of the original Confederation and of the present Swiss federal system.[6]

The Swiss invented or reinvented federalism in Europe and, indeed, represented the greatest expression of federalism in the world between the time of the Israelite tribal federation and the establishment of the United States of America. Until the Napoleonic wars, the constitutional design of Swiss federalism involved a series of overlapping bilateral and multilateral covenants which knit together the various territories comprising the confederation. Those covenants were renewed annually on the appropriate days so as to continue to rest on the consent of the governed. These multilateral and bilateral pacts were true covenants in the sense that they were more than international treaties since the people who made them saw themselves at least in some way bound as parts of a common proto-national whole. Indeed, the maintenance of these pacts relied far more heavily on moral commitment than on formal or informal uses of power, though the latter were not lacking.

The covenanting Helvetic states were themselves federations or confederations of independent communes, some of which remained separate republics for all but the most limited purposes until the Napoleonic wars. Gersau, for example, a village of a few hundred families on the *Vierwaldstattersee*, remained an independent republic until 1817. This constitutional scheme of covenantal networks was appropriate to the medieval constitutional outlook which did not seek single overarching frameworks but rather webs of allegiances.

The development of Swiss federalism is a classic case study in the use of covenants as devices to promote federal political integration. The importance of these documents lies in their role in the Swiss nation-building process. Nation-building in Switzerland preceded state-building; 700 years of nation-building passed before a full-fledged Swiss federation emerged.

Expanding the Confederation

The heyday of Swiss covenanting was the period from the founding covenant of the three *Waldstaten* (Schwyz, Unterwalden, and Uri) in 1291 until the beginning of the sixteenth century when the Reformation disrupted many of the formal relationships among the Swiss republics. During this period the early confederation of 13 was consolidated through three kinds of pacts: (1) those that dealt with the addition of other rural republics and cities to the original pact of 1291; (2) covenants which regularized or expanded inter-cantonal relations within the confederation; and (3) the *combourgeoisie* treaties that constituted the first step toward the expansion of the confederation by establishing what today we would call associated state arrangements with polities immediately adjacent to it. These covenants were used to adapt the terms of membership to the characteristics of each potential candidate, in-cluding its geopolitical position, its past and present diplomatic relations with the confederation, and its socioeconomic composition.[7]

The usual process for the expansion of the confederation was for the con-federates to first develop mutual *combourgeoisie* agreements with their neigh-bors and then to transform those agreements into confederal ones after a period of testing through the implementation of the original, more limited, ties. First the peripheral entities were made league partners and then after that worked, there was a recovenanting to make them confederates. As a result, each acces-sion was tailored to the particular situation. Zurich was leagued with the three original cantons by the agreement of 1315, but was not turned into a confed-erate until 1351. Lucerne was added in 1332 and Glarus in 1352, followed by Zug. Berne joined the confederation in 1353 by signing three different pacts with the members of the existing confederation in order to accommodate the terms of Berne's earlier treaty with Austria.

This confederation of eight continued until 1481, during which time other polities applied for membership but were obliged to wait. In 1481, two long-time allies of the confederation, the cities of Solothurn and Fribourg, were admitted as confederates over the opposition of the five rural members who were afraid of adding two more cities to give the three existing confederated cities parity in the confederal Diet. Since the cities had larger populations and were wealthier, a parity in the number of units would mean city dominance demographically. Again, a compromise was found in special covenants with each new member that kept both from full membership for a period while at the same time limiting their ability to undertake foreign policy initiatives that might adversely affect the rest of the confederation.

Only when Basel was admitted to full membership at the beginning of the sixteenth century were Solothurn and Fribourg given that status as well. With Basel, the confederation had no choice. It was the biggest city in Switzerland, attractive both for its wealth and for its geographic location. It, too, was ac-cepted through a special covenant. Schaffhausen and Appenzell were added in the early sixteenth century as well to make Switzerland a confederation of thirteen when the Reformation came.

All told, there were four principal covenants that formed the basis for the Helvetic Confederation between 1291 and 1647: the Priests' Charter, the Cov-enant of Sempach, the Covenant of Stans, and the Treaties of Defensional.

The Priests' Charter, signed in 1370, was the first covenant to try to reshape the internal arrangements of the confederation by harmonizing the laws of all the cantonal units. It was the first document to use the term *unser eydgnossenschaft* (our confederation) and brought that term into common use. It also provided for a common internal federal function, the protection of traffic along the major roads passing through the confederation.

Twenty-three years later in 1393, the Covenant of Sempach became the federation's first multilateral treaty, establishing a common code of conduct during war. Among other things, it was an attempt to standardize military instruction, regulate the distribution of pillage and war profits, and forbid private warfare initiatives. It was only partially successful.

The *Staner Verkommnis* (Covenant of Stans) was not signed until nearly a century later in 1481. It, too, was directed toward the safeguarding of internal order. Reconfirming the two former covenants, it included arrangements for governing occupied territories, the division of military gains, and increased coherence in the common foreign policy. Partners to the Covenant swore not to attack each other or to assist in the subversion of each other's internal regimes. This *Staner Verkommnis* became the basic constitution of the confederation. As such it included a provision for reaffirmation by public oath on the part of the members every fifty years, perhaps an echo of the biblical Jubilee.

These three great covenants were supplemented by the network of *combourgeoisies*, treaties that were somewhere between confederal pacts and international agreements. These were mutual defense pacts of indefinite duration principally between cities. Hence their name. They included provisions for mediation in case of potential conflict and economic arrangements. They were the first step toward the admission of new members to the confederation, provided for a trial period of mutual relations before the full marriage.

William E. Rappard, in his book *Du Renouvellement des Pactes Confederaux*, examines the habits of periodically renewing and repledging the old covenants. Introduced for the first time in 1351, the reasons and the procedure for this institution are outlined in the charter:

Afin que ce pacte soit toujours mieux connu de tous ceux, jeunes et vieux, qu'il concerne, il est aussi decide que tous les dix ans, vers le debut de mai, a la demande d'une des Villes ou d'un des Pays, il faudra, en vertu de nos serments, lire publiquement et renouveler ces engagements et l'alliance, avec les formules, les textes, les serments et tout ce qui s'y rapporte. Tout homme ou garcon age a ce moment d'au moins seize ans devra alors jurer d'observer eternellement ce pacte, avec toutes les clauses qui sont designees dans cette charte; sans aucune reserve. [In order that this pact will be always better known to all the ones, young and old, that it concerns, it is also decided that every ten years, about the beginning of May, at the request of one of the cities or of one of the cantons, it will be necessary, by virtue of our oaths, to read publicly and to renew these commitments and the alliance—with the formulas, the texts, the oaths—and all that which refers to it. Every man or boy aged at this time of at least sixteen years will have to then wear to observe eternally this pact, with all the clauses which are designed in this charter, without any reservation.][8]

This institution was not invented in 1351. Rappard lists, as one among many, the covenant between the cities of Bern and Fribourg (1243) which contained a like clause. But in 1351 it was used for the first time in one of the covenants that were slowly building up Switzerland. Additionally, it came to be an indispensable clause for the subsequent covenants.

Later, one particular weekend was designated during which all the members of the alliance would have renewal ceremonies in their respective seats of government and send envoys to all the other members in order to "receive the pledge." It seems that these ceremonies were held fairly regularly without adhering, however, to rigid intervals. There were some controversies as to where some of the smaller communes had to send delegates in order to fulfill their duties (this relates to the custom that the rural communes sent delegates to the cities as their representatives to participate in the ceremony) and as to the status of some members of the alliance, namely Fribourg, Solothurn, and Schaffhausen which, for a time, felt that they were treated as minor members.

Reformation, Recognition, and Revolution

The Reformation put an end to this institution. The year 1520 was the last time that all the members exchanged pledges. Five years later, the Catholic cantons refused to receive the delegates of, or send their own to the cities of Basel and Zurich, which, in the interim, had adopted the new Reformed faith. With the further spread of Reformed Protestantism, the wars that ensued between the members of the two religious camps further disrupted established procedures.

In Basel, for the sake of unity, a superficial acceptance of the new reality, particularly on the Catholic side, led to numerous attempts to reestablish the old custom. Elaborate compromises were offered by those cantons that were divided in their religious composition or put political considerations above religious differences. In the latter camp were the cantons that, because of their geographical location, were most vulnerable to external intervention and, therefore, most concerned about maintaining an undivided Switzerland.

All the attempts failed, however, because the Catholics insisted that the covenants had to be renewed according to the old formula in which "God and the saints" were mentioned. The Reformers, on the other hand, were not about to invoke the saints. Thus, the covenants remained unrenewed from 1520 until the eve of the French invasion of Switzerland in 1798, although the confederation remained intact and functioning. Then, significantly, they were ceremoniously renewed in a revival of the old way in an attempt to show unity in the Swiss effort to resist a potential invader. As it turned out, this attempt came too late.

In the interim, after four generations of religious wars and tension, two general covenants cut in the mid-seventeenth century reconstituted the confederation and gave it the formal framework that lasted until the Napoleonic conquest in 1798. The latter set in motion the processes which culminated in 1848 in the transformation of Switzerland into a federation. Meanwhile, in 1648, the Treaty of Westphalia recognized the independence of the confederates.

Upon conquering Switzerland in 1798, Napoleon tried to impose a unitary government on the Swiss which he named the Helvetic Republic, transforming the existing confederated republics into cantons, a term designed to show their subordination to the new national government. Because most of the cantons had fallen into the hands of patrician oligarchies in the late seventeenth and eighteenth centuries, eliminating the older medieval democracy in all but name, Napoleon's revolutionary effort was not entirely rejected by the Swiss, but they did reject his efforts to establish a unitary government. After five years, he was forced to partially restore the old confederation through the Act of Mediation (1803).

In 1815, with Napoleon's fall, the old confederation was substantially restored but on an enlarged and reconstituted basis. Graubunden, previously an independent confederation of communes loosely allied with the Helvetic Confederation, was incorporated into Switzerland as a single canton. Eight other cantons were added as well, including Vaud, Aargau, and Ticino, which had been ruled as subject territories, and Valais and Geneva which had been allied under the *combourgoisie* system. The Treaty of Paris guaranteed Switzerland's perpetual neutrality.

The 1815 restoration also restored much of the prerevolutionary patrician rule. It was not until the 1830s that the Radical parties (in the European sense of *bourgeoisie* liberalism) in most of the cantons were able to establish democratic governments. Because the Radical party was also secularist in its orientation, it aroused Catholic opposition which led to the Sonderbund War in 1847. The result was the transformation of Switzerland from a confederation into a federation through the constitution of 1848. That constitution combined American influences with Swiss traditions such as the plural executive. With it, Switzerland fully entered into the modern epoch.

A Covenantal Political Culture

On the eve of the modern epoch, Switzerland gave birth to the Protestant Reformation in its most covenantal form, drawing heavily on the Bible for political inspiration. Although it is dangerous to draw facile conclusions about that since the original republics of the Swiss confederation remained Catholic, and Reformed Protestantism was essentially an urban phenomenon, it may be that the Reformation strengthened covenantalism in the cities where its was most in danger of turning into something else. There is also the tradition of commitment to freedom and independence on the part of mountain people, which seems to be well-nigh worldwide. For example, the politics closest to republicanism found in South Asia before the twelfth century were the mountain polities in the foothills of the Himalayas, settled by people who fled oppressive rulers in India proper. In any case, the Swiss experience in the Middle Ages demonstrated the difference between real covenantal polities and the feudal synthesis of hierarchy and contract.

Swiss covenantalism is based on the twin pillars of a federal political culture and a strong religious tradition. In a sense, they represent what Alexis de Tocqueville was later to say about the United States, that felicitous combination of "the spirit of liberty and the spirit of religion" marching hand in hand. This is evident in every sphere, from the cantonal anthems, such as the "Ode to God" of Appenzell, that attribute that republic's liberties to its people's covenant with God, to wines such as the *Vin de la Republique* (wine of the republic) developed in honor of the adherence of the republic of Valais in 1798, to the Swiss confederation. This combination was forged in the Middle Ages and reforged during the Reformation and again in the seventeenth and nineteenth centuries at each reconstitution of the Swiss federal polity.

In 1991 Switzerland celebrated 700 years of Swiss confederation. The commemoration started at the beginning of the year in Ticino and ended in September in Basel. The actual anniversary day, August 1, was marked on the field at Rutli. In Ticino and Basel, the focal point of the commemoration was a tent of meeting (called by exactly that biblical name) designed by Switzerland's leading contemporary architect around thirteen arches representing the thirteen republics of the original confederation. It was designed to be portable, as was the biblical tent of meeting. In the Rutli area itself, the Swiss constructed a cantonal path covering thirty-five kilometers, with each canton allocated a section in proportion to its population (so many millimeters per individual inhabitant) which it became responsible for building and maintaining in the future.

Much emphasis was placed on *heimmat*, which means original home. Every citizen has a *heimmat*, an original home in one of Switzerland's 3,072 communes, to which, even if he or she was not born there, he/she is entitled to return and to be accepted. *Heimmat* is a living principle maintained in contemporary Switzerland as in the past—shades of the biblical idea of the permanent family and tribal allotments.

Today the Swiss are probably the most federal people in the world in terms of their political culture. Somehow they have internalized the proper combination of individual autonomy and commitment to group effort which is essential for successful federal arrangements and which is quite covenantal in its orientation. One can assume that the Swiss of today are perpetuating cultural patterns established centuries ago, since there was little in the modern world to encourage them to develop those patterns and much operating to undercut them.

Democracy and Federal Liberty

Switzerland is one of the fullest examples of communal democracy but, as post-World War II political anthropology has demonstrated, there are many other examples ranging from the tribal to postcolonial syntheses of tradition and modernity.[9] Our concentration here is on Western models.

In communal democracies, communal liberty stands in contrast to atomistic individualism as the highest good. Historically, the Swiss have emphasized individual liberty within the community, not apart from it. This approach differs from the radical individualism espoused by many in the contemporary Western world. Hence, those espousing the latter inevitably will accuse the Swiss of being undemocratic in this aspect of their politics. Here we have a confrontation between different understandings of what constitutes liberty and, by extension, democracy. Despite its claims, radical individualism is not the only starting point for defining democracy.

The Swiss Reformed Protestants in the sixteenth century, following the Bible, defined liberty as federal (from the Latin *foedus*, meaning covenant) liberty, that is, the liberty to live according to the terms of God's covenant with humanity as entered into, rather than as natural liberty. We are helped in our inquiry by examining this concept of federal liberty. Federal liberty can be interpreted as having to do primarily with religious commitment, as the Reformed Protestants did in the past, or it may be interpreted as having to do with the maintenance of constitutional liberties, as the U.S. Supreme Court has implicitly interpreted the Constitution with regard to racial and gender discrimination. In both cases, if we look behind their constitutional language, the judges have relied on what we can identify as the principle of federal liberty to modify what would otherwise be in their eyes, unbridled individual choice in matters constitutional.

Federal liberty in this sense stands in contrast to natural liberty (i.e., the right of every individual to do as he or she pleases, restrained only by nature). The latter is only possible outside of society. Otherwise it is both self-and socially destructive to the highest degree. Governments, including and especially democratic governments, are instituted to overcome the deficiencies of natural liberty that lead to anarchy and the war of all against all, whereby the strongest win at the expense of all others. So, if the Swiss political tradition stands in opposition to unbridled individualism, that is a sign that it is among the best friends of true liberty, which is based on restraining natural liberty through covenant for the good of all.[10]

The Emergence of Individualistic Democracy

For the last decade of the twentieth century it seems conventional wisdom to hold that the only real democracy is liberal or individualistic democracy as it emerged from the thought of the great seventeenth-century political philosophers, most particularly Hobbes, Locke, Spinoza, and Harrington; the English experience of the Civil War, and most particularly the Glorious Revolution, as it has evolved in theory and practice since then. Liberal democracy has its roots in methodological individualism, namely the view that every individual is actually or potentially sovereign by nature and only by leaving the state of nature through a political compact enters into society, or, more accurately, civil society. Civil society, in those terms is a sociopolitical order informed by an agreed-upon structure of government and authority but one in which the polity is not all-embracing but, rather, leaves substantial space for individual independence and public activity based upon voluntary association and cooperation. While recognizing the inevitable need for government and authority, the individual was conceived to be the measure of things, protected by his or her natural rights and a civil society organized to secure them.

Liberal democracy, then, can be defined by its theory, its form, its culture, and its practice. The theory of liberal democracy emphasizes methodological individualism or the individual standing naked in the world until he or she binds with other individuals to establish civil society and government. All institutions are subordinate to the individual or perhaps to the civil compact among individuals.

From here on, there are two theories. Under one, once established, the institutions of government constitute a state; the individual lives within the state, protected by his natural rights and the constitutional means established to protect them. Any institutions standing between the state and the individual are defined as mediating institutions, they are voluntary and their standing is subsidiary to both the individual and the state. As institutions they do not have rights, only such protections as derived from the natural right of individuals to freely associate with one another.

The second theory holds that all associations of individuals, public and private, are not only established by compact or contract but remain associations, differing only in their purposes and degree of comprehensiveness. Under this theory, the institutions of governance do not constitute a separate "state" but rather the largest and most authoritative set of institutions in civil society. While individuals may, by free compact allocate to the institutions of government powers of coercion—indeed they must in order to survive—this does not change the basic reality that all associations are freely created by combinations of individuals and may be altered by them through agreed upon procedures. Under this theory, not only is there no state to be reified but there are no collective institutions with rights of their own. As in the first theory, they are protected only to the extent that the natural right of free association of individuals extends them protection.

Liberal democracy takes several forms but invariably requires a basic covenant or compact translated into a constitution of government and a declaration or bill of rights (there is a difference between a "declaration" or a "bill" with the former more a statement of constitutional principles and the latter more a binding constitutional law), establishing a system of popular institutions of government whose members are chosen by free election (directly or in some cases indirectly). Those institutions will be charged with and capable of acting to protect and defend individual rights and will include checks and balances so as to provide effective limits on the exercise of political power.

The political culture of liberal democracy must include, *inter alia*, commitment to the individual as the main building block of civil society, a sense of mutual tolerance and respect among members of the political community, a commitment to the democratic processes delineated above, and self-restraint in pursuing one's political goals based on respect for the rights of others including minorities. All these must be reflected in political practice.

In the intervening centuries, liberal democracy has become even more individual-rights centered in detail and practice than those who originally conceived it may have anticipated. In Europe, the medieval structure of mediating institutions was eliminated or drastically weakened and transformed. The institutions that survived lost most of their original authority and power, either as a result of governmental action or changing modes of thought (e.g., the decline in the acceptance of religious authority). What remained were strong class and ethnic divisions, despite revolutionary efforts to eradicate them.

The United States—the model liberal democracy—was a modern, that is to say, post-medieval, civil society from its founding. There, new forms of voluntary institutions developed in the eighteenth, nineteenth, and twentieth centuries that became part of the warp and woof of American civil society. All Americans were expected to find a network of institutions and to be rooted within them. Classic American pluralist doctrine as it developed was based on a considerable amount of free individual choice, and people were not expected to be bound into communities or their institutions from birth. Migration and changing affiliation was an accepted part of the American experience, but at some point, individuals were expected to find their place and stay with it.

In the twentieth century, this voluntaristic "pluralism of associations" was challenged and, after the 1960s, replaced by a "pluralism of individuals" anchored in a new understanding, both ideological and constitutional (through Supreme Court decisions), of individual rights as precluding the long-term binding of individuals even by agreement past the time when the individuals so bound consent to be bound. To give an example of how far-reaching the change was, in premodern times marriage between a man and a woman was essentially a linkage of families as much as (or more than) a union of two individuals. For Catholic Christians, marriage was freely entered into but, once covenanted, was forever.

In the modern epoch, marriage became increasingly a matter of the individual choice of the two parties, but it was still expected that the parties would consider the families and communities of which they were a part to maintain religious, status, and certainly racial boundaries. Even in the liberal United States, marriages could be dissolved only for real cause (however defined) and with the risk of stigmatization. In the postmodern epoch, all of these barriers have fallen. Marriage is considered strictly an individual matter and if one of the couple tires of the other, divorce is an accepted and easily obtained step. From a covenant, marriage has become just another contract.

Communal Democracy: A Prior Form

This sea change has advanced so far in the name of democracy that many people in the contemporary Western world have forgotten that democracy in some countries and among some peoples developed along different lines. The Swiss developed their communal democracy centuries ago, whereby individuals were bound by custom and condition to communities but were full participants (originally just the men, of course) in guiding the life of the community and determining its governance. The Swiss did not have to go through a process of rejecting the bonds of community in order to achieve democratization. Quite to the contrary, they fought for democracy to preserve those bonds. Just as one can learn about individualistic democracy from the United States, one can learn about communal democracy from Switzerland.

Communal democracy begins from the theoretical premise that communities as well as individuals are by nature and that the individual finds his or her rights best protected within the framework of his community. To be democratic, that community, even if its origins are an organic outgrowth of its past, must at some point establish or reestablish its existence and the relationships among its members on the basis of a covenant or compact which either constitutes or leads to a constitution of government including means for protecting rights or liberties, both communal and individual. The theory of communal democracy gives the community a political status in its own right.

The form of communal democracy must include the fully republican elements of popular participation at all points in the process of governance, albeit with a greater emphasis on achieving consensus rather than winning by simple majority vote. The institutions of communal democracy are constructed accordingly since the maintenance of community is as important as the satisfaction of the individual. Indeed the two are presumed to be in no small measure inseparable.

The political culture of communal democracy is oriented toward the kind of self-restraint that comes from multiple and multigenerational interlocking ties needed to preserve community while also emphasizing a concern for the direction the community will take. Although it emphasizes consensus, it also allows for vigorous contests to define the consensus. The resolution of issues must ensure that everyone receives an appropriate piece of the communal pie.

The community is oriented more toward consultation than confrontation in decision making, although confrontational methods may be used to bring about consultation under appropriate circumstances. How this is done varies in practice in different communal democracies. In any case, it is expected that the individual will share with the community as part of maintaining his or her place within it. The community itself rests not only on shared history and fate, but on shared norms.

The system of liberal democracy that developed out of seventeenth century political thought and the modern political experience originally preserved elements of community. However, as radical individualism and liberal democracy became essentially identical, there was no place for a priori community. Indeed, the very idea of shared norms became difficult in the face of relativism, a doctrine that went hand in hand with radical individualism.

Nevertheless, the human need for community remained. To accommodate it in the twentieth century, the concept of liberal democracy was enlarged by the idea of group pluralism. In essence, the idea of pluralism was developed by those who, endorsing the individualistic and rights-centered understanding of liberal democracy, wanted to make some space for the preservation of voluntary group identities as well. Thus, group pluralism came to mean not only the right of every individual to choose his or her associations and commitments, but also the obligation to recognize the existence of groups without judging them within the body politic, provided that such groups existed on a strictly voluntary basis.

After World War II, pluralism was redefined to include not only group pluralism but also lifestyle pluralism. This has been a most pregnant redefinition whose consequences are a main element on today's public agenda. Now it must be said that liberal democracy today rests on the twin pillars of individual rights and pluralism which are in some quarters defined as the sum and substance of democracy.

Self-Government and Rights: Two Dimensions of Democracy

In the recent debates on the subject democracy seems to have been equated by the majority almost exclusively with individual rights and pluralism and with their most individualistic variety at that. That is only half the story. Even liberal democracy can be understood as having at least two dimensions: (1) self-government, that is to say, meaningful participation of individual citizens in the establishment of the polity in which they live and in its subsequent governance; (2) individual rights, that is to say, the right of every individual to develop for him or herself a way of life and a set of beliefs and opinions appropriate to it, consistent with agreed upon common norms, and to live accordingly, with minimum interference on the part of others, including and especially, on the part of government. Neither self-government nor individual rights are

absolute. Living in society requires the tempering of all in the face of the realities of the human condition but, for those who believe in them, they remain not
only basic aspirations but basic requirements for the good society.

The Swiss have followed the path of communal democracy when it comes
to democracy as self-government. There is no doubt about the republican
character of the classic Swiss polity. The particular character of Swiss republicanism had a communal tinge because of the prominent role it gave to collective decision making, whereby members of the commune had to share power
even in matters that liberal democracy would see as in the province of the
individual. Even when this led, at times, to the appearance of oligarchic rule,
in every case the regime remained republican, constituted by all of the people
and capable of being changed by the people.

This leads to the other dimension of Swiss republicanism, namely, that in
the traditional constitution the exercise of power always was divided between
the people, the magistrates, and the ministers of the gospel. The magistrates
were responsible for the day-to-day business of civil governance in the community while the ministers were responsible for communicating God's word to the
people and for being the link between the people and God. Although there have
been struggles for power among these forces and times in which one was stronger than the other, all three were always been actively present in the governance
of every Swiss polity from the local arena to the people as a whole.

The relationship between liberty and democracy has to be judged whole,
and it must be judged in the context of the Swiss polity as a communal democracy whose premodern origins antedate the development of liberal democracy. Thus, when it comes to the popular constitution of the polity, the
responsibility of the governors to the governed, and a proper separation and
distribution of powers among the governors—the three great criteria for democracy—the Swiss polity passes every test.

The Crisis of Modernity and the Swiss Polity

With the coming of modern individualism and liberal democracy, the classic Swiss political tradition was confronted by an unavoidable challenge.
Modern liberalism and individualism, by freeing individuals from the bonds
of the community, weakened the traditional Swiss constitution and forced the
Swiss to reconstitute their polity along new lines. The struggle to find an
appropriate balance between individual and communal liberty has been at the
heart of Swiss politics for the last 200 years. That struggle involves confrontation between the theories and practices of communal and liberal democracy
and the search for some synthesis of both forms.

Now that liberal democracy has triumphed in the West and in its triumph
has taken on more radical forms, its weaknesses as well as its greatness are
becoming exposed. By excessively atomizing society, it has achieved the un-

intended consequences of weakening the social bonds necessary for even liberal civil society to be a good society, not to speak of its inability to take cognizance of the very real existence of communities whose tenaciousness constantly surprises the partisans of undiluted liberal democracy. Thus, if the classic Swiss political tradition is no longer able to alone provide the answers that moderns and postmodern humans seek, the Swiss refusal to abandon either communal democracy or liberal democracy and the struggle of the Swiss as a people and a polity to find an appropriate synthesis should speak to contemporary humans.

The theories of consociational democracy developed by Lembruch, Lijphart, and others in the 1960s describe democratic practices in several different communal democracies.[11] The difference between the two forms of democracy was not noted as the reason for a different approach to democratic decision making that consociational democracy involves. A closer look, however, reveals the connection. Going beyond that to political anthropology, one can see how tribal communal democracies rely upon ostensibly informal but actually highly structured systems of reaching consensus. The scope of government activity in fields of religion and culture is also likely to be different in communal and liberal democracies and the relationship between them needs to be explored.

Notes

1. Daniel J. Elazar, *Covenant and Commonwealth: The Covenantal Tradition from Christian Separation through the Protestant Reformation* (New Brunswick, N.J.: Transaction Publishers, 1995).
2. For the history of Switzerland, see Jacques F. Aubert, *Petite Histoire Constitutionelle de la Suisse* [Short Constitutional History of Switzerland] (Bern: Francke Editions, 1974); Andre Siegfried, *Switzerland*, trans. Edward Fitzgerald (New York: Duell, Sloan and Pearce, 1950). Cf. also Benjamin Barber, *The Death of Communal Liberty: A History of Freedom in a Swiss Mountain Canton* (Princeton, N.J.: Princeton University Pres, 1974).
3. Tocqueville, *Democracy in America,* chapter 18, no. 3.
4. James Bryce, *The Holy Roman Empire* (New York: Schocken Books, 1961).
5. David Lasserre, *Die Schiksalsstunden des Foederalismus: Alliances Confederales, 1291–1815* [The Hours of Destiny of Federalism: Confederal Alliances, 1291–1815] (Zurich: Erlenbach-Zurich Editions, 1941).
6. On Swiss culture and political culture, see Denis de Rougemont, *La Suisse: Ou L'Histoire D'un Peuple Heureux* (The Swiss: Or the History of a Fortunate/Happy People) (Paris: Hachette, 1965); Siegfried, *Switzerland*; Barber, *The Death of Communal Liberty*; and Daniel J. Elazar, *Federal Systems of the World* (London: Longman, 1991); Richard Reich, "Notes on the Local and Cantonal Influence in the Swiss Federal Consultation Process," *Publius*, vol. 5, no. 2 (Spring 1975); Harold E. Glass, "Ethnic Diversity, Elite Accomodation and Federalism in Switzerland," *Publius*, vol. 7, no. 4 (Fall 1977). See also Daniel J. Elazar, ed., "Communal and Individual Liberty in Swiss Federalism," a special issue of *Publius*, vol. 23, no. 2 (1992).

7. On the *combourgeoisie* treaties and the Swiss method of federal expansion, see Aubert, *Petite Histoire Constitutionelle de la Suisse.*
8. William E. Rappard, *Du Renouvillement des Pactes Confederaux, 1351–1798* [Of the renewal of Confederal Pacts, 1351–1798] (Zurich: Gebruder Leeman, 1944).
9. Lucy Mair, *Primitive Democracy* (Baltimore, Md.: Penguin Books, 1962).
10. Daniel J. Elazar, "The Constitutional Protection of Rights: The Changing Meaning of the First Ten Amendments to the United States Constitution" (paper presented at the Liberty Fund Conference on the Bill of Rights, Philadelphia, November 1989). and Daniel J. Elazar, "The Multi-Faceted Covenant: The Biblical Approach to the Problem of Organizations, Constitutions, and Liberty as Reflected in the Thought of Johannes Althusius," *Constitutional Political Economy* 2 (Spring/Summer 1991):187–208.
11. Gerhard Lehmbruch, "Institutional Linkages and Policy Networks in the Federal System of West Germany," *Publius,* vol. 19, no. 4 (Fall 1989):221–35; Arend Lijphart, *Democracies; Patterns of Majoritarian and Consensus Government in Twenty-One Countries* (New Haven, Conn.: Yale University Press, 1984); Arend Lijphart, "Non-Majoritarian Democracy: A Comparison of Federal and Consociational Theories," *Publius,* vol. 15, no. 2 (Spring 1985):3–15; Arend Lijphart, "Consociation and Federation: Conceptual and Empirical Links," *Canadian Journal of Political Science* 12 (September 1979):499–515; and Daniel J. Elazar, "Federalism and Consociational Regimes," *Publius,* vol. 15, no. 2 (Spring 1985):17–34.

Part III

Covenant and Constitutionalism

10

Constitutionalism: The Modern Expression of the Covenantal Tradition

The key to the successful adaptation of covenantalism to modern conditions was intimately tied to modern constitutionalism.

Modern constitutionalism emerged in the colonies of British North America, later to become the United States. Constitutional design was improved, one might even say perfected, in British North America in the years between the beginning of the seventeenth century and the inauguration of the federal government of the United States of America toward the end of the eighteenth (1789). The latter year was the same that the French Revolution began. The ideas of modern constitutionalism and federalism crossed to continental Europe at that time, in many cases brought by European soldiers who had served in the American Revolution and were "infected" by its ideas; in particular, the Marquis de Lafayette in France and Thaddeaus Kosciusco in Poland.

Both France and Poland, then in revolt against Russian rule, adopted their first constitutions in 1791, the Polish first on May 3 and the French on September 3.[1]

Nor were France and Poland the only examples of American influence. In the years that followed, the whole world, from Russia and Norway to Latin America and Thailand (then Siam), was influenced by American constitutionalism, each country and region in its own way, not always in ways that could be recognized by the American pioneers. To understand how this was so, we must know more about the emergence of the idea and practice of constitutionalism, the processes whereby popular consent became an essential part of the constitutional process, and how all of this was given reality through new developments in constitutional design. Obviously it is not possible in the space of a single volume to explore this for every polity involved, but we can sum up the explorations which have been undertaken in order to generalize from them. Despite the lack of covenantal tradition in many of the countries involved, the reincarnation of that tradition into modern constitutionalism enabled it to spread to places where it had never been felt before.

In the true manner of the covenantal tradition we can identify four steps in the constitutional process that were transforming, where successful[2]:

- Constituting or reconstituting the people and their polity.
- Establishing the form of government, structure and functions, and division of powers.
- Consenting to and ratifying the foregoing.
- Changing the foregoing as necessary by interpretation and amendment.

Constituting (Reconstituting) the People or Polity

This task took on different forms in new and old societies. Whereas the problem in new societies was constituting the people and their polity on a covenantal or compactual basis, in the Old World the problem was reconstituting polities founded on hierarchical or organic bases according to covenantal principles. Earlier in this volume we described how in covenantal polities the founding covenant precedes the constitution, sometimes as a separate document, sometimes as the preamble or first part of the constitution itself. We have noted how this was true for ancient Israel, for medieval Switzerland, and for the modern United States. In the case of ancient Israel, the constituting document normally was referred to explicitly as a covenant. In the case of Switzerland it was referred to variously as a pact, a *coniuratio*, or by similar terms.[3]

The American Pilgrims referred to their founding document as a combination. The big transformation took place with the founding document of the United States, which took the form of the Declaration of Independence, a declaration of principles justifying the secession of the American colonies from Great Britain and declaring their independence.[4] While we have examples that approximate declarations of independence from earlier times going back to Exodus 12, the Americans really invented a new form of covenanting or quasi-covenanting to constitute or reconstitute their polity, suitable to the modern temper. In the French Revolution thirteen years later, the equivalent declaration was the revolutionary Declaration of the Rights of Man, and the Citizen, so very influential not only in France but in shaping the ideology of modern democratic republicanism in the Old World.

The first step in the constitutional process is the constitution of a new people or the reconstitution of an existing people into an organized public with clear political goals of self-government.[5] Donald Lutz has discussed this in connection with the founding of the American people and in the reconstitution of settlers from the British Isles as publics of their respective colonies even earlier. Whereas in the past, in most situations the key to polity-building lay in establishing rule or simply in building upon the realities shaped by organic development in a particular territory or some combination of those, one of the achievements of modernity was to introduce the idea that people could take such matters into their own hands and by political compact or covenant establish themselves as a separate people with their own institutions of self-government. The matter was stated concisely and precisely in *Federalist*, no. 1, the greatest guide to modern constitutionalism in the covenantal tradition.

> It has been frequently remarked, that it seems to have been reserved to the people of this country, by their conduct and example, to decide the important question, whether societies of men are really capable or not, of establishing good government from reflection and choice, or whether they are forever destined to depend, for their political constitutions on accident and force.[6]

Part of doing so was setting forth the principles upon which the people or polity was to be founded and pledging to maintain them as the basis of that people or polity of the new entity.

Where one state, country or polity was involved, a declaration of principles identifying or establishing a people or a new public was sufficient. Where polities were to be united in the new endeavor, then the declaration also specifically stated the basis upon which they would be so united. This process of covenanting, compacting or declaring has persisted down to the latest generation, most recently visible in the efforts of the republics of the former USSR to reconstitute themselves as the Commonwealth of Independent States and the individual republics to reconstitute themselves as independent states.[7]

Designing the Polity

The second step involves actually writing a constitution including designing the form of the polity, its structure and functions, the division of powers within it, and the ways and means by which the people whom it is to serve can participate and be represented in its governance. This was the part of the constitutional idea that spread most rapidly and that every polity adopted, but for many it took a long time to deal with two problems: one, distinguishing between an effective constitution and a fictive one instituted as "window-dressing" because the times appeared to call for it; and the second, designing a constitution that not only satisfied the ideals of the day but was workable in the context in which it was written. It was far easier to get the idea of having a constitution accepted and even easier to write one than to produce a workable one. Great skill is needed to find the right ways and means by which to harmonize constitutional ideals with political realities.

Not only that, but there are stages in constitutional development. Premodern constitutions either had emerged from organic polities and were like the English constitution—a set of ordinary laws enacted periodically to clarify accepted procedures once consensus was achieved—or charters handed down in a hierarchical manner by rulers in recognition of necessities for power-sharing or of certain privileges and liberties. As modern constitutionalism appeared on the scene, very few polities continued to pursue the organic route;

Great Britain is the only one of note to have anchored its modern constitution in that traditional system.

In some cases the charter system was preserved; that is to say, when popular demands for a modern constitution became too great in polities whose rulers were not willing to relinquish power, they would issue charters. At first those charters were the products of ruler responses to constituent demands and were mostly adversarial in character, designed to modify the impact of those adversarial demands and to bring them under control through partial satisfaction of them in such a way that the ruler preserved his sovereignty and freedom to act. In some cases, especially as time moved on, the charters themselves were negotiated before they were promulgated by rulers, who kept symbolic control of the process and maybe even more, but actually worked out the details with their constituents.

More attuned to modernity were constitutions drafted by representatives in the name of the constituents they were to serve, people or polities. Constitutions of this kind were foursquare within the covenantal tradition even if their initiators and authors did not recognize those origins. This was much less so when they were drafted by legislatures, more so when they were drafted by constitutional conventions especially chosen for the task.

As in so many other things related to constitutionalism, the American colonies-cum-states took the lead and exemplified the process. The first colonial constitutions were either charters promulgated from England or were written by colonial legislatures. In some cases the early state legislatures continued the practice of writing their states' constitutions but very quickly during the Revolutionary War the states adopted the specially designated and elected constitutional convention system which received its final and preeminant legitimacy for constitution-making by the calling of the federal constitutional convention of 1787. From then on (until recently, at least), with rare exceptions (for example, antebellum South Carolina), the American states have relied on constitutional conventions for comprehensive constitution-drafting, while legislatures are used only for drafting specific constitutional amendments to be submitted to the voters for approval.[8]

In Europe, constitutional conventions also came into vogue following the American example, but in time the European polities also began to rely upon constitutional commissions, appointed bodies presumably of people with expertise in constitution-drafting, who prepared documents for ratification by legislatures or by the people. The great revolutions of the latter half of the modern epoch were all marked by constitutional conventions in efforts to capture the spirit of the revolution and translate it into practical governmental terms.

Ratifying and Consenting

Modern constitutions, true to their covenantal origins, required ratification and popular consent to gain legitimacy. Processes for securing this consent varied from approval by popularly elected legislatures to approval by acclamation at popular assemblies, to approval by popular vote or approval by popularly elected ratifying conventions. The important task here was to gain the legitimacy conferred by popular consent, and ratification by popular means was the most clearcut way of doing so.

Changing the Constitution by Interpretation or Amendment

With the original religiously grounded covenants of the Bible, change could only come by further communications from God or through interpretation by the authoritative judges (interpreters) of each generation (as provided for in Deuteronomy), recognized for their piety. This was less of a limitation than it might have seemed. As long as prophecy existed in Israel, the prophets brought further communications from God that achieved constitutional change. Once prophecy disappeared in the fifth century BCE, interpretation by sages learned in the Torah and constituted into interpretive assemblies became the norm; indeed, so much so that those assemblies rejected ostensible communications from God, for example, voices from heaven, as being illegitimate, holding that the power had passed to the majority of sages sitting the assembly. Interpretation radically transformed the Torah, considered to be God's word, into a very different set of practices, albeit imbedded both structurally in and in the spirit of the original. At times this required doing apparent violence to texts, but not necessarily to the polity itself. As long as those who did the interpretation remained alive, activist, recognizably pious and cognizant of the needs of the times, change through interpretation was sufficient.

A more secularized variant of this was true in regard to legislative constitutional interpretation for the first half of the modern epoch. Legislation was in any case very limited, with parliaments for the most part claiming to interpret laws rather than to enact new ones. The shift from claims of interpretation to overt legislation came at about the same time that constitutionalism began to spread in the modern world. No doubt there was a mutual influence in that. If the people and their representatives could write and adopt new constitutions as fundamental law, they certainly could legislate within the framework of those constitutions without having to hang all legislative changes on some interpretive hook.

What about the constitutions themselves? If they were the agreed-upon fundamental law, any significant changes to them would have to be adopted by the same means, that is, through formal amendment of the constitution in a process specified in the document, involving the ratification and consent of the same publics that had installed the constitution in the first place. The new documents themselves made provision for their amendment, and no constitution was thought to be complete without such provision having been made. In some cases, the constitution could only be amended by calling a new convention. In others, legislatures could amend constitutions by following special procedures, and in still other there were combinations of legislative and popular action required. In every case, to be legitimate such amendment had to follow procedures akin to the adoption of the constitution in the first place.

At the same time, interpretation by a constitutional court (an institution whose members were presumed to have sufficient expertise in and piety toward the Constitution) also became a real option, as in the case of the U.S. Supreme Court. That method has gained in popularity and power over the years as formal amendment was demonstrated to be difficult and court interpretation easier. Not only did constitutional courts interpret that fundamental law directly, but even more important, they held ordinary legislation up to its standard. In Europe, constitutional courts have been a late development, really belonging to the postmodern epoch. The idea of a constitutional court was possible only where the idea that the constitution was a fundamental law and not merely a list of accepted practices had taken hold.

Constitution Making: The Preeminently Political Act

It may appear to be a truism to state that constitution-making is an eminently political act.[8] Indeed, part of its success in gaining such prominence and centrality in the modern epoch was the fact that it offered a political substitute which went beyond the daily politics-as-usual that often had a certain degree of grubbiness attached to it and gave politics a higher expression and purpose, enabling it to substitute for theology, which had provided secular benefit to people in premodern times.[10]

Constitution-making, properly considered, brings us back to the essence of the political. However much extrapolitical forces may influence particular constitution-making situations or constitutional acts, ultimately both involve directly political expressions, involvements and choices. In that sense, the dynamics of constitution-making have to do with questions of what Vincent Ostrom has termed constitutional choice.[11] That is precisely why constitutionalism is an outgrowth of the covenantal tradition rather than some other one. Not only does it involve choice, but choice by those presumed to be equals, at least for the task at hand. Proper understanding of modern constitutionalism, then, involves understanding not only what is chosen but who does the choosing, and how.

Constitutional choice is more art than science. There are scientific principles involved in the making of constitutions, as the fathers of the United States Constitution of 1787 demonstrated in their reliance on the "new science of politics," which had discovered such vital principles of republican regimes as the separation of powers, federalism, and the institution of the presidency.[12] But the combination of those elements and their adaptation to the constituency to be served is an art.

It is an even greater art to bring the constituency to endow the constitution with legitimacy. Constitutional legitimacy involves consent. It is certainly not a commitment which can be coerced—however much people can be coerced into obedience to a particular regime. Consensual legitimacy is utterly necessary for a constitution to have real meaning and to last. The very fact that while rule can be imposed by force, constitutions can only exist as meaningful instruments by consent, is another demonstration of how constitution making is the preeminent political act.

A constitution is also a political artifact.[13] That is why the making of constitutions combines science and art. The crafting of a constitution involves the identification of basic scientific principles of constitutional design and the technologies which are derived from them, which a proper constitutional artisan or group of artisans can then bring together to exercise the art and craft of constitution making. Classifying those models can enable a better understanding of the constitutions which result and the processes that go into making them. This is particularly necessary now that constitutions as a single written basic document have become the norm in contemporary government and constitutionalism has replaced theology as the sacred core of so many modern and postmodern regimes.

Five Constitutional Models

Proper classification of constitutions must rest upon the relationship between the contents of the constitutional document and the fundamental character of the form of the polity which it is designed to serve. Looking at that relationship in connection with modern constitutions and those extant in the world today, we can identify five basic models:

1. The constitution as frame of government;
2. The constitution as code;
3. The constitution as revolutionary manifesto;
4. The constitution as political ideal;
5. The constitution as a modern adaptation of an ancient traditional constitution.

The Constitution as Frame of Government

This constitutional model is characteristic of the United States, which possesses the oldest of the modern constitutions. As a frame of government, it delineates the basic structure, institutions, and procedures of the polity. It is not a code, hence it is not designed to be highly specific and is only explicit in connection to those elements which must be made explicit in order for the constitution to frame a government. American constitutions frame governments and not states because what is characteristic of the American system is the absence of any sense of the state as a preexisting phenomenon, a reified entity which continues to exist regardless of how it is constitutionalized (or not constitutionalized) at any particular moment.

Frame-of-government constitutions establish polities as often as they establish governments. Indeed, in many cases the two are inseparable. In fact, written constitutions of this model are often designed to be devices for organizing new societies founded in new territories, as in the cases of the United States (the Articles of Confederation), Canada (the British North America Act), Australia, and South Africa in 1910.

Reform in such situations really amounts to keeping the frame of government in tune with societal change, as in the recent case of the patriation Canadian constitution which involved transforming the BNA Act from an act of the British Parliament into a basic law adopted by the Canadian Parliament as its constitution to which was added a Charter of Rights and several other changes in the original. Australia is contemplating constitutional changes of its own as it approaches the centennial of the federation of its six states. South Africa has made a truly profound constitutional change, having abandoned the original constitution of the Union of South Africa because it was designed for a regime that segregated the white and subject black, colored, and Asian races in South Africa and replacing it with a document providing for a single polity held in common by all of its citizens on a federal basis.

Often, the frame can be tuned through mechanisms like Supreme Court decisions, as in the United States, which will not be formally written into the fundamental document if everybody accepts the fact that what the Supreme Court is doing is tuning. The tuning then becomes part of the constitutional tradition even if it is not written into the document itself. Only where reform requires changes in specific wording is formal amendment used.

In some cases, new constitutions may be adopted for that reason or when the mechanism of judicial tuning breaks down. In Switzerland and the American states the public has been brought more deeply into the constitutional process through devices such as the initiative and referendum whereby constitutional amendments either must be or normally are submitted to the voters for their approval. In both cases the difficulty in or undesirability of making major constitutional changes through court interpretation requires more reliance on formal amendment.

The Constitution as Code

The situation is quite different with regard to the Western European constitutional codes, which tend to be far more rigid and require precise and deliberate formal textual change to be tuned. The frame of government model works best in political systems where there exists basic consensus with regard to the character of the polity, while the constitution-as-code model reflects the reality of polities in which the character of the regime itself is sufficiently problematic for a large enough segment of the population for changes in its authority, powers, or functions to require explicit consent.

For most Western European states, the constitution is a state code designed to cope with an established order, with established preexisting constituencies, not to speak of a pre-existing state. As the word "code" signifies, it is long, detailed, highly specific and explicit, certainly by the standards of frame-of-government institutions. Major constitutional change in the case of such constitutions often reflects a change in regime but even relatively limited or minor changes require formal constitutional amendment to reflect the specifics of governmental powers for any particular regime, on the assumption that the state continues to exist a priori but that its regimes must be delineated and harnessed to whatever the specified ends of government are at a given time. The constitutions of Austria and the German Federal Republic are classic examples of that highly rigid model, but so for that matter is the 1978 Spanish constitution, introduced after Franco's death as the basis for the introduction of a more liberal regime in that country.

In a sense, this is a continuation of premodern thinking that is slowly being modified as time passes. For example, judicial review of constitutionality certainly is out of place in Communist regimes but was equally out of place in other regimes that were based on the idea that the king or the parliament was the supreme source of power, not the constitution, a carry-over from the struggle between parliaments and monarchs that led to the weakening of the latter and the empowering of the former. Only in the postmodern epoch, at least a century removed from that struggle, and with the separation-of-powers model becoming increasingly recognized as more democratic, has the constitution come to be viewed as a greater arbiter of power relationships and hence authoritative, requiring interpretation by a constitutional court.

The Constitution as Revolutionary Manifesto

The third model was common in the Socialist (Communist) states until they collapsed and in those that remain. It is designed for the comprehensive revolutionary reconstruction of an established state, based upon the achievement of a social revolution of the most fundamental kind, with all of its political manifestations and impact. This is a constitution designed to root out the old order and to reorder its elements in their entirety. Thus Communist constitutions tended to exclude certain groups or classes from participation in the body politic as much as to define the rights, roles, and responsibilities of those who were entitled to participate.

Moreover, the central feature of every Communist constitution is the location of power in the hands of an organized revolutionary cadre. Indeed, the constitution is not only used to establish the myth of the social revolution but as an instrument for fostering that myth and enhancing the power of the revolutionary cadres to make the revolution in the name of the myth. In the case of these regimes, however, the constitutions themselves are not sacred since there is an ideology and a "prophet" of that ideology (Marx, Lenin, Mao, Fidel Castro) who speaks with supreme authority in its name and they are the repositories of the sacred. The constitutions of such regimes, like the constitutions as codes, are merely instruments in the eyes of rulers and public and have no special status in and of themselves.

If there is such a thing as constitutional reform in such systems, it involves bridging the gap between the constitutional myth promoted by the ruling elite and regime reality. Such constitutions establish certain myths about the Communist state and its society which are far from the realities of political life under such regimes. At some point, the gap between the constitutional myth and the regime reality becomes too great and there has to be some attempt to reform. This was particularly true in Yugoslavia before it collapsed where the federal republican constitution was rewritten several times after the regime was instituted at the end of World War II to reflect changes in the distribution of power between the federal government and the republics and between the various classes and groups within Yugoslav society. Another such change was instituted in Czechoslovakia as a result of the 1968 revolt in the country. While the sociopolitical liberalization sought by the liberals was rejected by the ruling Communist party, a federal arrangement was introduced to accommodate the ethnic aspirations of Czechs and Slovaks which lasted until the country broke in two after the Velvet Revolution.

The USSR itself underwent the least constitutional change in this respect. A major effort was launched by Nikita Khrushchev when he was in power, principally to eliminate the federal structure which he, following Leninist doctrine, held was a temporary expedient to communize non-Russian nationalities and was no longer needed. After seventeen years of negotiations and long after Khruschev himself had passed from the scene, a new constitution was indeed adopted with the federal structure intact. Even the Communist leaders of the national states in the USSR had refused to accept the change.

Having no effective process of constitutional reform, the end result for these regimes was their collapse when the gap between expectation and reality grew too great. We have seen all of those such regimes with the exception of China, North Korea, Laos, Cuba, and Vietnam collapse since 1989. Indeed, the multinational polities among them actually have disintegrated into two or more states. All have rejected Communism and have adopted new constitutions that aspire to be democratic in form and content.

The Constitution as Political Ideal

This model is most closely identified with the third world. It was pioneered by the Latin American countries in the nineteenth century. This constitutional model combines an expression of what its citizens believe the regime should be with the basic structure of authority which will enable the current powerholders to rule with a measure of legitimacy. The former is presented without any serious expectation that the polity or regime will achieve that constitutional ideal, and the latter in anticipation of periodic change as rulers change, usually through revolution or coup. In other words, it pays lip service to the constitutional ideal but cannot do more than that. This model bears some superficial resemblance to the Communist model but it has a political rather than a social revolutionary intent. In essence, then, third world constitutions are designed to present an ideal picture of the institutional framework of the proper polity while simultaneously reflecting the character of existing power systems and the specifics of rule by the current powerholders.

Constitutional change in the third world involves balancing regime realities with constitutional aspirations. Hence, third world polities seem to be constantly changing their constitutions in their entirety. In fact, while each constitution is presented as new, usually there is a great continuity of basic articles from one document to the next, combined with changes in specifics to reflect each new regime.

The Latin American experience offers the best example of this fourth model since it is the oldest. An examination of Latin American constitutions over the past 150 years or more will reveal precisely this pattern; on the surface an apparently frequent change of documents but underneath substantial continuity in their contents. In each Latin American polity, there is a "classic" constitution, usually adopted some time during or at the close of the first generation of independence, after a period of civil wars in which the fundamental tensions of the founding were sufficiently reconciled to enable the new polity to take form. The authors of each subsequent constitution have accepted this original reconciliation and adapted it to reconcile proximate regime reality with long-term constitutional aspirations. In most cases, after a revolution or coup, when a constitution is changed, the new powerholders will explicitly make this point; that what they are doing is "temporary" or "interim," to make possible the achievement of larger constitutional aspirations. If this is so much rhetoric, as it usually is, it remains an important part of the Latin American political mythology.

The Constitution as a Modern Adaptation
of an Ancient Traditional Constitution

Polities utilizing this model have a deeply rooted commitment to what can only be characterized as an ancient and continuing constitutional tradition, rooted in their history or religion, or both. This commitment usually finds expression in what is conventionally referred to as an "unwritten constitution," which often encompasses a collection of documents of constitutional import, each of which marks (or purports to mark) an adaptation of the great tradition to changed circumstances.

The United Kingdom is the leading example of this model. The British Constitution is celebrated for being "unwritten," based on the ancient tradition of the Common Law. Essentially, its piecemeal constitutional development has been uninterrupted at least since the Norman Conquest and perhaps even before if William the Conqueror's claims to the throne are recognized. The Puritans tried, out of some desperation to disrupt that tradition as part of their effort to refound England in the seventeenth century. They failed to achieve their goals although they did succeed in introducing a certain number of their political ideas in the Whig modification into Britain's traditional constitution as manifested in the Glorious Revolution of 1688–1689, a generation after the English Civil War. It is instructive that the violent and comprehensive efforts of the English Civil War failed while the nonviolent political mobilization of the Glorious Revolution, which was more in keeping with English practice, succeeded.

The only time there has been constitution writing in the United Kingdom has been in connection with some strong necessity to clarify or adapt what are viewed as ancient principles, as in the case of Magna Carta (1215), the 1689 Bill of Rights connected with the Glorious Revolution, and the 1832 Reform Act; and/or establish new relationships among its constituent countries as in the case of the Act of Union between England and Scotland (1707) or the reconstitution of Ireland in the 1920s. Indeed, when this element has been lacking, efforts to change the British Constitution in so formal a way have generally failed. This was true most recently in the attempted devolution of powers to Scotland and Wales which was manipulated to fail by Margaret Thatcher's Conservative government but which succeeded in 1997 under a Labour government. At all times, constitutional change is achieved through ordinary legislative procedures which are endowed by convention with constitutional status.

Israel may be another example of this model. In Israel, the first Knesset was elected as a constituent assembly and spent the better part of a year debating whether or not to write a constitution. The body was deadlocked as the traditional religious parties opposed the idea of a constitution other than the Torah (Five Books of Moses-as-interpreted), which is the classic constitution of the Jewish people, while the left-wing socialists were equally opposed because they knew that the constitution which would emerge would not embrace their Marxian vision of what the new state should be.

In a classic speech, David Ben-Gurion, Israel's first prime minister, moved that the idea of writing a comprehensive constitution at one time be set aside in favor of a system of enacting basic laws piecemeal as consensus was achieved with regard to each subject, which would ultimately form a constitution. His argument offered good reasons for doing so (if not the real ones). He suggested that polities need written constitutions for one of two reasons— either to link constituent units in a federal system or to republicanize absolutism. Since Israel was not a federal state and the Jewish people has always been republican, Israel did not need a constitution written on the spot.[14]

The proposal for piecemeal writing of the constitution was accepted and, accordingly, every Knesset also is a constituent assembly when it wants to be, and can enact a basic law by a modest special majority, namely, half plus one of its total membership. Basic laws constitutionalizing its legislative, executive, and judicial organs, the presidency, state lands, civil-military relations, the status of Jerusalem and the Golan, and basic human rights have been enacted since the early 1950s. Part of Israel's Declaration of Independence (itself a model of a modern Declaration—Covenant) was given quasi-constitutional status early on by the courts and then by the Knesset in lieu of a formal bill of rights, since the Declaration specifies the basic principles of the regime. Unsettled issues such as local government and its status and powers vis-a-vis the state and controversial ones such as the relationship between religion and state, have been left in abeyance. The relationship between Israel and the Jewish people also has been constitutionalized through a covenant negotiated with the World Zionist Organization and the Jewish Agency, and enacted as legislation by the Knesset.

In the Israeli case, considerations rooted in the ancient Jewish constitution are rarely made explicit because of the ideological disagreements between those who seek a traditional religious grounding for the Jewish state and those who want the state to have a strictly secular grounding. Most Israelis view their state as a regime of secular rather than religious law but with a preference given to its Jewish character and a special status for Jewish laws in personal status matters. The Knesset has specified in law that the state's legal system should be based on traditional Jewish legal-constitutional principles to the extent possible. To the extent that the Torah, however understood and interpreted, is perceived to have constitutional import, at most it provides a larger theoretic constitutional grounding for the frame of government that is emerging out of the Israeli constitutional process. For the traditionally religious, since that Torah does not specific any particular regime, it is relatively easy for them to accept Israel's freedom in constitutional design on that level. At best, however, this model is only implicit to the Israel situation, since there are strong voices in Israel who would reject such an interpretation. Israel's Declaration of Independence, known in Hebrew as the "Scroll of Independence," serves as a bridge between this idea of an ancient traditional constitution still possessing a certain validity and a modern frame of government, as its language indicates.

One of the characteristics of this model is the inclusion of constitutional documents as basic laws which relate to ancient traditions. Almost all the documents of the British Constitution do just that, as do several of the basic laws of Israel, especially those relating to state lands, to Jerusalem, and to rights (which are to be interpreted and applied through a prism that is both

"Jewish and democratic," plus the Scroll of Independence itself and the covenant with the diaspora. Thus approximately of the fourteen constitutional texts of the contemporary Jewish state speak directly and explicitly to the issues of the ancient traditional constitution.

Are there other examples of this model? The matter bears investigation. One would be more likely to find such constitutions in connection with churches than with states, given the disruptions of modernity in the secular realm. It may be especially real in the Islamic world. Postrevolutionary Iran, for example, has adopted a constitution for an Islamic republic and in fact is the first Muslim state to have developed a modern constitution explicitly along those lines. Whatever the Western distaste for the Iranian fundamentalist regime, it bears examination from this perspective. Does Japan consider itself bound by some ancient traditional constitution even though its frame of government, imposed on it by the victorious Allies after World War II, is so deliberately modern?

In a sense this fifth model may be seen as an attempt to lessen the break between modern and premodern constitutionalism and to contain the transformation within a single continuous framework, united in a seamless web. In fact, in both the British and Israeli cases there have been substantial changes introduced separating modern and premodern constitutional developments, but unlike what is more true in other cases, the premodern has not been repudiated but only modified or transformed within a common context.

The five models are summarized in figure 10.1. Despite the tendency for each constitutional model to be prevalent in a particular geo-cultural area, the models should not be seen as strictly confined to a particular region. For example, India is an excellent example of a third world country that is closer to the Continental European pattern. The Indian constitution is not only more like a code than a frame of government, but it deliberately seeks to democratize the Indian political tradition through which the subcontinent has func-

---

FIGURE 10.1
Constitutional Models

---

1. Constitution as Frame of Government: e.g., English-speaking countries of the New World

2. Constitution as Code: e.g., Continental European democracies, India

3. Constitution as Revolutionary Manifesto: e.g., China, Yugoslavia, Cuba

4. Constitution as Political Ideal: e.g., Latin American and African states

5. Constitution as Application of Ancient Traditions: e.g., Israel, United Kingdom

tioned for millennia as a decentralized empire with a kind of relaxed system of governmental control that rarely penetrated beyond the elites.

The Significance of Federalism in Designing Constitutional Systems

Federalism has had multiple significances for designing and redesigning constitutional systems. In the first place, modern constitutionalism developed out of federal-covenantal principles as they developed through a synthesis of theological and political ideas during the Protestant Reformation and were transplanted to the New World of British North America in the seventeenth century. In the second place, there is the special character of federal constitutional systems which, in their most proper expression, combine two or at times three sets of constitutions—for federal, state, and at times local governments. These sets of constitutions must be basically complementary but also raise problems of conflicts between them that must be dealt with constitutionally. Third, federal systems have been especially important in contributing to the problems of modern constitutional design, especially popular participation in constitutional design. Finally, the spread of federalistic constitutional design for a variety of systems, especially in the interstate arena, has become a postmodern phenomenon worthy of special consideration because of its special characteristics and newness.

The Reformed Protestant leaders who studied the Bible at the time of the Reformation discovered in it the covenantal premises and expressions that assaulted the very foundations of the hierarchical order and denied hierarchy the Divine legitimacy which all of Christendom believed to be necessary for any political order. Moreover, as practical men, the Reformed Protestant leaders reconstructed the bodies politic which they inherited or established to reflect their understanding of the biblical covenantal system. Their constitutions of government were still rudimentary but their efforts at reconstitution or founding were rooted in pacts—covenants between rulers and ruled, magistrates and citizens—within the congregation of believers, thereby placing them all on an essentially equal footing.

It soon became apparent that covenants, while necessary for foundations of the new political order, were not sufficient. Constitutions of government were needed to translate those covenants into real institutions that would be both effective and be true to the principles of the covenants that underlay them. Those rules became the basis of modern constitutionalism.

In continental Europe modern constitutionalism emerged in those borderlands stretching from northern Italy to the North Sea, the area once embraced by the Middle Frankish kingdom established for Lothar, the oldest son of Charlemagne, at the end of the ninth century, a territory that embraced what later became both the heartland and most of the peripheries of Reformed Protestant ascendancy in the sixteenth and seventeenth centuries. Consitutionalism was even more powerful in its emergence in British North America, most particularly in New England in the seventeenth century. Indeed, the effective chain of modern constitutionalism can be traced back to the constitutional documents of the Plymouth Colony, the Massachusetts Bay Colony, Connecticut, and Rhode Island of the 1630s and 1640s, and from those early experiments on through the adoption of the Constitution of the United States of America in 1787–1789.

Developments proceeded along two fronts: First cam the elaboration and sophistication of systems of constitutional rules embodied in the documents and, then, the secularization of those constitutional documents. The first New England constitutions were either lists of principles without extensive procedures or elaborate codes, often included by adoption, from the Bible. Over time, these developed into better designed constitutional documents providing the institutional frameworks and increasingly the rights protections required in modern constitutions. Indeed, one can say that with the framing of the American state constitutions during the Revolutionary War, modern constitutionalism had arrived and reached its apotheosis in the Massachusetts Constitution of 1780 and the federal constitution of 1787.

This tradition was adopted with a few variants by the French and other revolutionaries after 1789 and from then became the standard for constitutional development in the modern world. The next great spate of constitution making was in Latin America in the early nineteenth century following the federal and constitutional forms of the United States. Latin Americans endowed their constitutions with a new meaning for federalism, seeing in federalism not simply an instrumental device for good government but also the embodiment of liberalism against the hierarchies established by the Spanish and Portuguese during the colonial period.

As modern constitutionalism spread, its overt covenantal basis disappeared. The covenants or their secular versions, political compacts, had been already entered into—to establish peoples and to form polities—and the constitutions were written to effectuate them in concrete situations. Once those constitutions were in place, there was no need to appeal beyond them in most cases. Constitutionalism came to replace direct covenantalism except under those conditions of foundings or refoundings where new covenants had to be made.

This replacement came to be so complete during the course of the nineteenth century that the covenantal foundations of constitutionalism were forgotten by all but a handful of scholars. Constitutionalism by itself became a hallowed as well as a practical means of establishing and maintaining democratic republicanism, but its federal/covenantal roots should not be forgotten in the process of seeking how to effectuate and to better constitutional systems.

Notes

1. Hubert Izdebski, "Constitutional Development in France and Poland Since 1791: A Comparative Analysis," in *Constitutionalism and Human Rights: America,*

Poland and France, Kenneth W. Thompson and Rett R. Ludwikowski, eds. (Lanham, Md.: University Press of America, 1991).

2. Donald Lutz, *The Origin of American Constitutionalism* (Baton Rouge: Louisiana State University Press, 1988).

3. Daniel J. Elazar, *Covenant and Polity in Biblical Israel* (New Brunswick, N.J.: Transaction Publishers, 1995); *Covenant and Commonwealth* (New Brunswick, N.J.: Transaction Publishers, 1996); and *Covenant and Constitutionalism* (New Brunswick, N.J.: Transaction Publishers, 1998).

4. Abraham Lincoln, "Address at Cooper Institute, New York City, Feb. 27, 1860," *The Portable Abraham Lincoln*, Andrew Delbanco, ed. (New York: Penguin Books, 1992); Daniel J. Elazar, "The Constitution, The Union, The Liberties," *The American Constitutional Tradition*, Daniel J. Elazar, ed. (Lincoln: University of Nebraska Press, 1988), ch. 10; Garry Wills, *Inventing America: Jefferson's Decalaration of Independence* (Garden City, N.Y.: Doubleday, 1978).

5. A public in this sense is a group of people linked over the generations who see themselves as sharing common political tasks and a common fate and who may or may not be as distinct and comprehensive as a nation or a people.

6. *The Federalist*, no. 1, Alexander Hamilton.

7. Timothy J. Colton and Robert Legvold, eds. *After the Soviet Union: From Empire to Nations* (New York: Norton, 1992); John B. Dunlop, *The Rise of Russia and the Fall of the Soviet Empire* (Princeton, N.J.: Princeton University Press, 1993); Sergei A. Karaganov, *Russia: The State of Reforms* (Guetersloh: Bertelsmann Foundation Publishers, 1993).

8. After a generation of withdrawal on the part of many political scientists from consideration of all that is labelled "constitutional" in the world of government and politics, on the grounds that such matters are merely "formal" and hence not "real," it is a truism that needs restating.

9. Since the mid-1970s, there has been a trend toward using appointed constitutional commissions in some states.

10. This use of constitutionalism as a kind of secular theology gave rise, in turn, to a concentration on its formal rather than its real dimension. A well-constructed document carefully reflecting the ideals of the time and place was more interesting than a document imbedded, one might even say mired, in its broader political context. So in time political scientists followed what had become conventional to confine themselves to the study of the formal dimensions of constitutions rather than their real ones.

11. Vincent Ostrom, "A Computational-Conceptual Logic for Federal Systems of Governance," *Constitutional Design and Power-Sharing*, Daniel J. Elazar, ed. (Lanham, Md.: University Press of America, 1991), pp. 3–21.

12. Alexander Hamilton, John Jay, and James Madison, *The Federalist*, no. 51.

13. Vincent Ostrom, "A Computational-Conceptual Logic."

14. David Ben-Gurion, "Laws or a Constitution," *Rebirth and Destiny of Israel*, Mordecai Nurock, ed. and trans. (New York: Philosophical Library, 1954), pp. 363–79.

11

The Three Dimensions of the Constitution

In the previous chapter, we focused on constitutions as frames of government. In the process, it has no doubt been noticeable that most are also "power maps," to use Ivo Duchacek's term;[1] that is to say, they reflect the socioeconomic realties of the distribution of political power in the polity served. They also reflect the moral principles underlying polities as regimes, explicitly or implicitly. These are, in fact, the three dimensions of constitutionalism, recognized as such by Aristotle and by clear-minded students of the subject ever since.[2] They can be visualized as being in a triangular relationship, as portrayed in Figure 11.1.

Every modern constitution must establish a frame of government. The various models more or less reflect the other two dimensions as well, the first perhaps less specifically, sometimes directly and sometimes by implication. A constitution which does not sufficiently reflect and accommodate socioeconomic power realities remains a dead letter. Revolutionary constitutions actually specify the new power arrangements being instituted by the revolutionary regime.

Even when the moral underpinnings of the constitution are confined to codewords or phrases in the preamble or declaration of rights, as in many cases, and are virtually unenforceable in legal terms, they have a reality and power of their own, nonetheless. Where the moral basis is enforceable, or is perceived to be, it is very serious indeed. Constitutionalism in the United States, for example, has gone from Whiggish statements of moral principles to a bill of rights with "teeth," with transformitory consequences for the entire polity and its vision. The moral dimension of the constitution serves to limit, undergird, and direct ordinary political behavior within constitutional systems. At the very least, it embraces the rules of the game; often it expresses far more. In every case, the moral basis of a constitution is an expression of the political culture of the body politic it serves and the covenants undergirding it.

It is very difficult to understand constitutions and constitution-making without exploring the relationship between them and these dynamic dimensions. Indeed, if there is one reason why the study of constitutions became arid two

FIGURE 11.1
The Three Dimensions of the Constitution

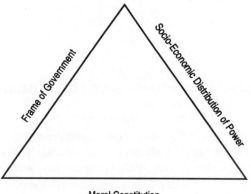

Moral Constitution

generations ago, it is because constitutional documents came to be taken in the abstract, divorced from the power systems of which they were a part and the political cultures from which they grew and to which they were responding. This, indeed, may be the best way to uncover the extent of the covenantal influences on constitutional expression at a time when an increasing number of constitutions have the same external appearance and the idea of the constitution as fundamental law based on consent and embodying democratic republican institutions and the separation of powers, has become ever more widespread in the world.

This means that the differences between constitutions are mostly differences in their implementation. These differences, in turn, to a great extent rest upon differences in political culture that shape political processes and behavior. Institutions and even ideologies may appear to be the same and externally may be, but it is the way in which they are implemented through processes, behavior, and culture that makes the difference.

For example, it is well known that constitution makers borrow from one another, not only within the frame of any particular constitutional tradition but across traditions as well—this despite a general recognition by political leaders and political scientists alike that institutions cannot be simply transplanted from one political system to another. At an earlier time in the modern epoch, such borrowings were commonplace under all circumstances and advocated by reformers as a matter of course. Through trial and error, constitutional designers have learned the limits of borrowing. Constitutional architects and designers can borrow a mechanism here or there but in the last analysis those mechanisms must be integrated in a manner that is true to the spirit and political culture of the polity and society for which the constitution is designed.

Take, for example, the Spanish Constitution of 1978. At first glance it may seem to have certain consociational features, reflecting the influence of the Belgian Constitution and its framers but Spain is not consociational because it does not give the nationalities within the country a guaranteed share in the national government as nationalities per se but through territorial organization. Similarly, there are many apparently federal features of the Spanish Constitution, in the sense that it applies decentralization on a territorial basis, but, at the same, it deliberately denies that it is federal nor does it give the autonomous territories a guaranteed role as such in the national government.

This remains a sticking point in Spanish constitutional affairs whose impact has been limited by virtue of the ability of the autonomous communities to gain some measure of territorial representation as communities in the national government through the arrangements for provincial representation that do exist, augmented by the fact that a significant minority of the autonomous communities are comprised of single provinces so they are actually represented as provinces. Even more important, the nationalities have carved out a share for themselves through ethno-regional political parties or regional branches of the national political parties whose electoral power is sufficient to secure them a real voice in national political councils.

The Spanish Constitution formally rejects the constitutional principle that the territories have ancient rights (*fueros* in Spanish) other than those provided in the constitution itself. Given Spain's own compactual heritage this is a matter of some contention in Spain's constitutional history. Nevertheless, not only was the method provided by the constitution through which the significantly separate nationality communities gained autonomous status a modern version of bilaterally negotiated fueros with Madrid but, in some cases, elements of the constitutional documents thus negotiated included those rights associated with the older fueros but not necessarily formally identified as such.

Today federalism and community autonomy can be discussed as such in Spain without rancor because the system has worked well for more than half a generation. As they can be discussed, the need for making formal changes to accommodate them seems to have been reduced.

Originally for their model, the authors of the Spanish constitution looked to the postwar Italian constitution with its system of regionalization, in which the regions are given certain autonomous powers of home rule without being involved *qua* regions in the general government. Indeed, the Italians borrowed their model from the pre-Civil War Spanish republican constitution and then Spain borrowed back some of the same ideas, very deliberately.[3] But Spain is not Italy and its nationalities do not see themselves as merely regional expressions of a common Spanish culture as is the case in the latter country, but as separate communities on the Iberian peninsula. Hence the reborrowing has involved a transformation as well, that has helped bring indigenous Iberian political cultural dimensions to the fore.

The Spanish Constitution of 1978 may have been the first step in the evolution of what I have elsewhere termed foralistic federalism, that is to say, a combination of self-rule and shared rule arrangements between the general government and the autonomous regional governments based upon bilateral negotiations between Madrid and each region, leading to special constitutional arrangements for each entity that desires them, within an established constitution minimum for all. This was the process completed for the first four regions (Basque Country, Catalonia, Galicia, Andalusia) and begun in all of them to define them as regions. After those four had reached bilateral agreements that defined them as regions, the others moved very slowly to complete the process and the Spanish Parliament finally moved it to completion by enacting a single law for all who had not negotiated bilateral agreements. That enabled Spain to get on with the business of federalization by eliminating the rather deliberate foot-dragging on the part of some regions. Still, foralistic federalism has become the basis of Spanish decentralization and offers the possibility of designing constitutional arrangements appropriate to the "personality" of each entity. Since each arrangement is then embodied in a constitutional document ratified bilaterally, the system is, in essence, a modern adaptation of the ancient system of *fueros* for a democratic state.[4]

Four Questions

Four other questions with regard to modern constitutions, constitution making, and constitutionalism also deserve to be explored. One has to do with constitutions as instruments of social control, consideration of which rests upon the character of the civil society which the constitution serves. The second relates to the role of consensus in constitution making, and the ability to achieve consensus which is the *sine qua non* for the acceptance of an constitution and its effective application.

Third is the issue of constitutional choice as a device of a self-government. Modern constitutional regimes are strongly committed to the idea—sometimes the myth—that they are designed to promote self-government. To the extent that they are, constitutional choice is a factor in constitution making, within the polity. Hence one question we can pose with regard to particular regimes is to what extent is constitutional choice a device for self-government and to what extent is there some myth of constitutional rights which may or may not be reflected in reality?

Finally, there is the question of reconstitution. Reconstitution, as distinct from founding, poses its own problems. Although they, too, fall within the framework of the models presented above, the tasks of reconstituting a polity are far more complex than those of founding it. In the latter case, the field is relatively open while in the former, there is the very nearly intractable problem of transforming an existing system.

The Constitution as a Mechanism

On another dimension, constitutions are mechanisms for achieving various goals. Take the case of two polities shaped or substantially influenced by the covenant tradition: South Africa and Great Britain. Until 1994, South Africa, although its white founders were direct products of a covenantal tradition, used constitution-making as a mechanism for maintaining racial segregation and apartheid. Since the abandonment of racism as the basis for the South African regime and the initiation of the present effort to establish a multiracial civil society with a new constitution appropriate to it, one of the major items on the agenda of the constitutional designers has been the issue of centralization versus decentralization.

The 1910 constitution, which brought into the Union of South Africa into being, was deliberately designed to centralize power in a single government uniting the two previously autonomous British provinces and the two previously independent Boer republics conquered by the British in the Anglo-Boer War. Throughout, the Afrikaners sought to reverse the results of the war by means of peaceful constitutional choice.[5] The constitutional convention which drafted that constitution deliberately rejected federalism as not being sufficiently centralized.

The Afrikaner drive for a full-fledged centralized state led to their abandonment of covenantal principles in government although they continued to be maintained in Afrikaner politics. Subsequent constitutional changes in 1960 and 1979 further centralized power in the RSA. Until the late 1980s, in a very real sense twentieth-century constitution making in South Africa was a mechanism for achieving even greater centralization of power in the hands of an Afrikaner-dominated state, by design. This, in turn, was a reversal of the nineteenth-century pattern of Afrikaner constitutional design in the Boer republics, which emphasized noncentralization, indeed, very loose political bands and weak institutions of general governance. That system, while in harmony with the covenantal political culture, had perpetuated Boer weakness and allowed the British to use their superior power to conquer them, by settlement and military force. The Afrikaner leadership which emerged from the war learned that lesson and applied it through the mechanisms of constitution making.

Then in a great reversal, the Afrikaner rulers of South Africa reversed their apartheid policy and determined to establish a system of constitutionalized power sharing involving all white and nonwhite groups, including blacks, in the hope of bringing peace and stability to their country. The African National Congress, the leading black-led political movement, was legalized. It and other black groups were empowered to enter into negotiations with the South African government for a new constitution and a new constitutional future for South Africa.

At that point, the Afrikaner-dominated government shifted in the direction of territorial decentralization coupled with consociational features that would protect the white minority, while the ANC wanted to establish a centralized unitary state which they could dominate without complications. After two years of negotiations in which early on it became apparent that a measure of constitutionalized regional decentralization would be inevitable if all of the significant groups that had to be reconciled to the new regime were to be brought in, the ANC agreed first to a quasi-federal and then substantially federal constitution, embodying territorial federalism and a measure of consociationalism in the interim constitution with provision for more, especially of the latter.

The ANC was influenced to accept this at least partly through the efforts of their ruling groups who had been otherwise influenced by the covenantal tradition. This constitutional settlement, completed late in 1993, went into effect at the beginning of January 1994. It was amended early in March 1994 to provide for even more federalistic power-sharing anchored in the constitution in an effort to conciliate the Zulu-dominated Inkatha Freedom Party. The final document took the hierarchical pseudo-consociationalism of the apartheid regime and turned it into an arrangement somewhere between that of the Netherlands and Switzerland, through constitutional mechanisms.[6]

The situation with regard to the United Kingdom of Great Britain and Northern Ireland is more complex. On one level, most of the key constitutional mechanisms in the United Kingdom have as their aim the strengthening of the common center. On another, most also include an effort to broaden the base of power sharing in that center. Examine such classic documents as Magna Carta, the 1689 Bill of Rights, and the 1707 Act of Union between England and Scotland and one will see that both of these dimensions shine through clearly. Thus the British constitution reflects the character of the British polity as inheriting the primarily organic character of England, its most populous country, redirected or nudged in one direction or another by the periodic introduction of documents of constitutional status which even as they reaffirm the general model of the organic polity, namely, the existence of a single center which draws upon its peripheries as well as governs them, reveal their covenantal base.

Several of the constitutions discussed here, particularly those of Belgium and Spain, are mechanisms of decentralization. They are designed to accommodate existing divisions in those civil societies by constitutionalizing them in such a way as to legitimize their efforts maintain their respective integrities within the framework of a common polity. In the Belgian case, this involves a two-dimensional process; the reduction of the power of the provinces and the state government, and the increase in the power of the linguistic regions and the cultural communities.

The Belgian case suggests some of the problems of constitutional reform. Taking too long to implement a constitutional reform, for example, as in Belgium, encourages the generation of new problems faster than they can be resolved.[7] In other words, if constitutional reform is to be used as a means to curb or channel revolutionary momentum it must come quickly enough. Spain and the Republic of South Africa acted quickly to face similar problems with seemingly better results.

It is notable that Italy could wait nearly thirty years to implement the provisions in its post-World War II constitution for devolution of powers to ordinary regional governments without suffering untoward pressures and another twenty before the emergence of a full-fledged federalist movement. It is possible that, given the generally low expectations of government as a problem-solver in Italy, there are minimal pressures on the part of the Italian public for any governmental change until a real crisis is reached. This is in contrast to the case of the five special regions, whose governmental institutions were inaugurated shortly after the adoption of the Italian constitution. In those cases there were regional ethno-linguistic or communal pressures for constitutionalizing their respective identities that could not be ignored. For those reasons, Italy quickly implemented the constitutional status granted them under the Italian constitution but then tried to deny them as much autonomy as it could through the normal processes of government.

Federal Constitutional Systems

As modern constitutionalism spread, distinctions between federal and unitary states and systems also became more pronounced in the constitutional as well as in other spheres. Unitary systems required only one constitution for the whole and all of its parts and it usually was able to reflect earlier hierarchical or organic cultures. Indeed, in many cases only the government of the whole was officially denominated a government, the other units of political organization within the unitary state were designed "authorities," provinces, or "countries" (land, *pays*) in the cultural rather than the political sense.

In federal systems, on the other hand, the idea was a greater or lesser measure of equality among governments within the political system, certainly federal and state, and at times local as well. Each of them was to have its own constitution, reflecting the will of the people who constituted that particular government and had to live according to its rules. Thus federal systems rest upon multiple constitutional documents, each drafted by, for, or on behalf of the particular public it is designed to serve. All such constitutions must be considered as interrelated in order to fully understand the constitutional framework and system of federal polities.[8]

While each of these constitutions may be independent, the federal constitution and the constitutions of the constituent units must share certain common principles and premises, a common spirit if you will, in order to fit into a common mosaic. Thus, for example, the federal and state constitutions of the United States are all based upon tripartite separation of powers systems,

although that is not required, while the federal and provincial or state constitutions of Canada and Australia are all based upon the combination of federal
and Westminster parliamentary systems. Indeed, to the best of this writer's
knowledge, no responsible political leaders even seriously raised the possibility of following a different course in a serious manner. Even more important is the harmonization of shared values among the polities within each
system. Indeed, we have seen the consequences of the demise of shared values in the former Yugoslavia. At times, the intensification of those shared
values lead to conflict rather than cooperation, even if the constitutional expectations and systems of the polities remain much the same.

It is true that some federal systems have only one federal constitution that
includes within it constitutional provisions for state and local government as
well as multilevel intergovernmental collaboration. Nigeria is an example of
this. In almost every case they represent very hierarchical federal systems
that barely meet the definition of federalism if, indeed, they do. Again, Nigeria is a good example.[9]

Even in those federal systems where separate constitutions for the major
constituent units are not required, to the extent that the systems have been
properly federal, matters have evolved in that direction. Canada may be the
outstanding example of this. The Canadian provinces, following the English
model, did not need to adopt provincial constitutions, but over time basic
laws have developed that have become de facto constitutional documents,
although not entrenched in the normal constitutional manner. They have gained
increasing respect from the provincial parliamentary and other governing
authorities.[10]

Often, local constitutional documents are denominated "charters" or the
equivalent, indicating that they are not coequal with the federal and state
constitutions but are derivative from the powers of one or the other. The
semantic distinction is an important one, as the rulings of constitutional
courts dealing with those charters reveal. The struggle between state constitutions and local charters may seem to be exactly like the struggle within
unitary systems but the addition of a federal government is a complicating
factor since it allows localities to develop a more independent constitutional
tradition by appealing in both directions. The United States, which probably started with less and has gone further than any other federal system,
may be the best example of this.

In the original American constitutional system no provision was made for
separate local constitutional standing. First of all, the matter was left to the
states and, with some important exceptions, principally in New England, the
states usually followed the English example of close subordination of local
authorities to the state government. Over time, however, the very existence of
federalism led to the development of greater local autonomy through general
laws empowering localities, without the need for individual municipalites to

have recourse to the state legislature for every constitutional matter, and through home rule provisions enabled the local governments to adopt their own constitutions, even if for only limited purposes.[11]

The existence of multiple constitutions within a single constitutional system increases the importance of intergovernmental relations on a partnership basis, including intergovernmental constitutional relations, an especially important dimension of federalism. All polities have intergovernmental relations, but there is a major difference in the character and quality of intergovernmental relations in federal and nonfederal systems. So, too, there are qualitative differences between hierarchical, organic, and covenantal (federal) systems. In the latter, intergovernmental relations must be truly intergovernmental, although constitutionalism, perhaps because of its covenantal roots, has introduced a measure of potential autonomy into intergovernmental relations in all constitutional systems that is worthy of further investigation in each specific case. For example, the changes that have taken place in highly centralized and unitary France in the past three decades deserve to be noted and examined.[12]

Federal Dimensions of Constitutional Design

Just as federal systems are among the major pioneers of modern constitutions, so, too, have they been pioneers in the development of patterns of continuing constitutional design. One of the foremost inventions of modern constitutionalism was the possibility for constitutional revision within the constitutional system. In earlier times, most constitutional change had to be achieved through some kind of revolution since the system itself did not make adequate provision for change except perhaps through authoritative interpretation. Changes of the latter normally were limited since it was not easy to justify them. It took a very daring group of interpreters to make major changes through constitutional interpretation alone. It was not impossible, but it was rare, even very rare. Moreover, the authoritative interpreters were almost always the people in power, which meant that their willingness to make changes was often limited since the needed changes often went against their immediate personal interests.

One of the great achievements of modern constitutionalism, part of its republican and democratic character, was the introduction of provisions for constitutional revision within the constitutional document itself. These took two forms: either a formal procedure for constitutional amendment through the institutions established by the constitution or formal provisions for calling a special constitutional convention which would look at the whole document or any part of it for that purpose. Both devices were developed at about the same time.

The United States and the individual American states were pioneers of both devices at the time of the American Revolution or immediately thereafter. Both have served federal polities well. Amendment through the formal institutions has been the most widespread device in the federal arena while both that kind of amendment and periodic constitutional conventions have been useful devices in the state arenas.

Subsequently, a third device was developed, the constitutional referendum. Switzerland pioneered in this form of constitutional change and it soon spread to other federal systems, particularly the American states, though it has not been used with regard to the U.S. constitution. The Swiss have developed the constitutional referendum to a fine art and in some respects an exact science. All three arenas of government in Switzerland use constitutional referenda and their use in connection with the federal constitution involves a combination of federal and state arrangements since majorities have to be secured by canton and not only through a federal majority. Referenda are in such demand that a calendar has been established scheduling them so that not too many will occur in any one election.[13]

The use of the referendum as a constitutional design device has spread to some three-fifths of the American states where often it is used more freely than in Switzerland. California, in particular, with its very large and politically activist population, has developed an exaggerated use of the constitutional referendum. California's people expect to be involved in state and local constitutional design. The various interests within the states are able to organize to take advantage of the opportunities offered.

The popular referendum has become a weapon in the state's normal process of political conflict. A few years ago when the matter of state regulation of automobile insurance came before the voters, six different and often contradictory amendments were on the ballot in the same election, the purpose of several of which was mostly to confuse the voters rather than to secure any kind of reasonable change.

California has not adapted the Swiss system of setting a referendum timetable so that no more than a limited number of referenda can be on the ballot in any particular election, nor may there be contradictory or confusing referenda on the same issue. Whatever passes the post in terms of the signatures on the appropriate petitions is placed on the ballot at the very next statewide election. This has lead to very long and complex ballots with more propositions than even especially attuned voters can assimilate and, as indicated above, often contradictory ones designed to obfuscate rather than elucidate.[14]

California is the extreme case. Most other states have been able to keep the referendum system within balance even without special legislation. In the United States and Switzerland it is no doubt the most widespread form of popular involvement in constitutional design.

In contrast, efforts to call constitutional conventions on federal matters in the United States have consistently failed because people are afraid to open up the Pandora's box of an unrestricted constitutional convention which may attempt to tamper with constitutional provisions deemed sacred by the country as a whole or by particular groups within it. Thus, interpretation by the U.S. Supreme Court has become the most prevalent mode of federal constitutional redesign used in the United States, a form which excludes popular participation except at the very margins and which may go against the spirit of modern constitutionalism as it was originally formulated.

Germany and the German-speaking countries have, for this reason, attempted to utilize constitutional courts but to restrict the scope of their activity by requiring the other institutions of government or the public at large to participate in any processes of constitutional change. Nevertheless, constitutional court interpretation is spreading as a form of constitutional change in those countries as well as in many, if not most, others and the American experience is looked upon admiringly and increasingly applied, especially in the field of human and civil rights where more popular bodies are less likely to expand the rights of individuals in the way the constitutional courts will.[15]

The Impact of Constitutions on Governance

What of the impact of constitutions and constitutional interpretation on governance and politics? The revolutionary change that constitutionalism brought to the covenantal tradition was the concretization of that tradition by giving it an even more extensive and operative practical dimension than in earlier times. It is not surprising, nay even necessary, since constitutions were to be used for governing and governing involves the translation of principles into practical applications.

Translation invariably means interpretation and every interpretation brings with it its own consequences. The Jewish people discovered that at the very beginning. The Bible itself describes the concretization of the Israelites' original covenants with God through *Sefer HaBrit* (the Book of the Covenant), the original code of Jewish law included in Exodus and Leviticus and presented to the Jewish people as such. By the beginning of the Second Jewish Commonwealth in the fifth century BCE, the constitutionalization of the biblical covenant chain already had reached the point where there were fewer references back to the covenants themselves and then only when it was necessary to turn to what *The Federalist* refers to as "a reliance on first principles." Instead there was regular referral to the Torah, already the term used to designate the comprehensive constitution of the Jewish people. In the period of the Second Commonwealth not only was the Torah and the rest of the Hebrew Bible canonized by the sages of the Jewish people but its law began to be codified as *halakhah* (the way), further removing it from direct reference to the original covenants. The Jewish political tradition has never abandoned that constitutional path.[16]

Similar developments took place in the modern world. The shift in the United States from higher to constitutional law after the adoption of the United States Constitution of 1787 has already been mentioned. That generally has been the pattern in the modern world except that moderns have been more self-consciously willing to introduce constitutional change since their constitutions, however they may be placed "under God," are not seen as of Divine origin. Hence the process of constitutional change more than ever becomes an integral part of the constitutional and hence the covenantal process, transforming that process from a one-time event or act to a continuing one, in this way addressing the problem of consent in its larger sense.

This leads us to pose several questions. In those polities where judicial review is an accepted constitutional procedure, does a constitutional court decision of constitutional import which is accepted as a proper interpretation of the constitution on one level become a major factor in governance and politics on another? Sometimes yes; sometimes no. What happens when a legislature sits as a permanent constituent assembly as in Israel, enacting or amending basic laws from time to time in such a way that they can be manipulated for immediate political ends as was the case in 1981 when the Knesset, suddenly and without warning, adopted a basic law on Jerusalem, formally constitutionalizing its status as an undivided city and the capital of the state. On one hand, the provision was a "motherhood" provision, that is to say, no one could oppose it on substantive grounds; on the other, it was a vehicle for Prime Minister Begin and the Likud government to make political capital at home and a political point abroad.

Constitutional Design and the Form of the Polity

Let us return to the three ways by which polities are founded: (1) polities founded by conquest which generate power pyramids in which political organization is hierarchical; (2) polities which evolve organically out of more limited forms of human organization and which over time concentrate power centers with their peripheries; (3) polities founded by design through covenant or compact in which power is shared through a matrix of centers framed by the government of the whole, on the basis of federal principles broadly understood.[17] The implications of these three models for constitutional design are portrayed in figure 11.4.

In hierarchical polities, constitution-making is essentially a process of handing down a constitution from the top, the ways medieval kings granted charters. Indeed, the principal constitutional mechanism in hierarchical systems is the charter. The basic means of consenting to such a constitution is through pledges of fealty up and down the hierarchy. Constitutions are changed only when there is a necessity to do so to restore fealty ties or to alter the lines of fealty.

FIGURE 11.4
Form of Polity and Constitutional Design

Form	Process	Mechanism	Means Consenting
Hierarchical	Handed down from top	Charter	Fealty
Organic	Ordinary acts through existing institutions	Legislative Acts	Informal agreement
Covenantal	Convention of partners	Comprehensive Constitution	Formal consent

Constitutions established by contemporary authoritarian and dictatorial regimes are of this kind, whatever trappings the regime's rulers or ruler may give them to make them seem as if they are something else. When Byelorussian commissars or Pakistani generals, or Iranian ayatollahs dictate constitutions, this is what comes out. This is probably the most prevalent form of constitution making in Africa south of the Sahara today. In the Communist world, while a patina of symbolic acts to establish consensus covered the constitution-making process, it essentially followed this pattern.

In organic polities, the process of constitution making is also an organic one, consisting of a series of organic acts negotiated among the established bodies that share in the governance of the polity, whether medieval estates, territorially based groupings, "clubs" of elites or certain other mediating social and political institutions, which speak for the various segments of society represented in the center, reflect their interests, and can negotiate among themselves to resolve constitutional questions as they arise. Formal constitutional change in such polities is relatively infrequent since it only occurs when custom and tacit understandings are no longer sufficient to determine the rules of the game. Ordinary processes of lawmaking often serve as the mechanisms for establishing such constitutional acts but those processes are involved only after consensus has been reached through negotiation.

The means of consenting to such constitutions is informal or at best quasi-formal. In organic polities, whole constitutions are rarely written and are even more rarely replaced. Rather, constitution making and constitutional change come in bits and pieces. The United Kingdom is perhaps the prime example of an organic polity with an organic constitution. Each step in the constitution-making process at least from Magna Carta to the present, follows this pattern.

In polities founded by covenant or compact, or seeking reconstitution through modern constitutionalism, the process of constitution making involves a convention of the partners to the pact, or their representatives. Constitutional changes are instituted through similar conventions or through referral of the issue to all partners to the polity, that is to say, all citizens, in a referendum. The reasons for this are obvious. As a pact among equals, or the political expression of such a pact, the constitution can only be changed through the consent of either all of the partners or a majority thereof if it has been so agreed. The result produced by such polities is what we commonly refer to as a written constitution, that is to say, a comprehensive document designed to serve as a frame of government (or more, depending on the model) deliberately given the status of fundamental law by the public it is designed to serve, written, adopted, and preserved through extraordinary rather than ordinary legislative procedures.

The means of consenting to such constitutions, the way in which consent is given, and the kind of consent involved, are all formal. There has to be a formal consenting among the partners, whether individuals or polities. Constitutions as covenants or compacts or extensions thereof, can either be changed in their entirety or can involve frequent amendment, because issues of constitutional choice become part of the coin of the realm, as it were, and publics constituted as partnerships see themselves as empowered to participate in constitutional design in a relatively direct way.

The American state and Swiss federal and cantonal models are perhaps the best examples of the constitution as covenant and the extension of covenant. In Switzerland and in the American states, the constitutional process has become an important way of building consensus and hence citizen participation in determining the basic policies and procedures of government, and in providing a popular check on representative institutions. Consequently, many of the issues that are dealt with on the level of constitutional choice, that is to say, through referenda, would not be considered major constitutional issues by an outside observer but are dealt with in a way that reaffirms the process itself. This, in turn, has become a political virtue in those polities. That is to say, a constitutional initiative or referendum reaffirms the power of citizens to shape the fundamental or organic laws of their polities.

Modern revolutions have tended to emphasize the reconstitution of the polity on the basis of a popular compact to replace either a hierarchical or an organic founding associated with the ancien regime. The extent to which such revolutions have succeeded is, in itself, a question. In most cases it seems that at best they have been able to temper the earlier model through the substitution of this third form of constitution making. Under such circumstances, constitutions may be extensions of revolutionary compacts but they do not become as fundamental in shaping the body politic as in cases where the polity itself is founded by compact.

France, whose revolution is the accepted model for the revolutionary overthrowing of old orders, is an excellent example of this phenomenon. Despite its great revolutionary upheavals, France has continued to exist no matter what, having come into existence through a particular combination of conquest and organic development, which is its historical heritage. French constitutions have been changed with relative frequency since 1789 because even comprehensive constitutional change in France really reflects regime change and does not address the existence of the body politic itself.

The Spanish situation is somewhat similar. Although, in fact, the Spain we know today is a product of the combination of conquest and pact; the Spanish state is probably perceived as organic on the part of most of its population, except for those groups who see themselves as forming their own organic communities with prior rights and that in the recent past would like to have seceded from Spain to form organic states of their own. Recognizing this, in 1978, Spain reconstituted itself on a new and democratic basis by balancing the conception of Spain as an organic state with the realities of the Spanish polity as a pact between the various nationalities and regions which constitute "the Spains." The Spanish constitution of 1978 essentially renegotiates the fundamental character of the Spanish state after some 500 years, which is what makes it so bold an effort.

There is a dimension of this in the Canadian situation as well. Canada's Anglophone population traditionally viewed the Canadian constitution as a product of the British constitutional tradition calling a constitutional convention of the representatives of the provinces in 1862 with action by the British parliament in 1867. On the other hand, the Francophone population has emphasized the constitution as a compact between Canada's two original peoples.[17] Struggle between these two theories goes back to the mid-nineteenth-century antecedents of the BNA Act and has continued through the recent struggle over constitutional reform. No doubt both theories will continue to be raised as the courts and legislatures of Canada attempt to interpret the country's revised and patriated constitution. This mixture of theories is part of the founding tension that is basic to Canada as a united polity. From another angle, Canadians understood that the original Confederation constitution was written at a constitutional convention, a reflection of a polity established by pact. From Britain's perspective, however, it was enacted as the British North America Act, through the ordinary processes of Parliamentary legislation, although with the understanding that the act was a constitutional document and hence had to be treated with greater respect and changed with greater caution.

In polities which are constituted through covenant or compact, the constitutions themselves often become the touchstones of their very existence as bodies politic. This was evident in the United States at the time of Watergate in the way that President Nixon's actions were perceived to have shaken the very fundaments of the American polity, far more so than even the Vietnam War. One could sense a palpable—this writer witnessed an audible—sigh of relief when the presidency was successfully transferred from Nixon to Gerald Ford. The new president's inaugural address and subsequent actions clearly were designed to take appropriate steps to reestablish the national consensus, thereby reassuring everyone that the republic was intact.[18]

Interstate and Global Constitutional Arrangements

When modern federalism was first developed in the United States in the eighteenth century, Europe was moving rapidly away from federalism in any form toward the unitary centralized state, usually defined as a nation-state, provided for in the international system established by the Treaty of Westphalia (1648) at the very beginning of the modern epoch. The Westphalia system provided for the principle of indivisible state sovereignty and all that flowed from it, whereas federalism required what in statist terms was called "divided sovereignty." In federalist terms this meant popular sovereignty with governments not being sovereign but rather being the products of powers delegated to them by the people, who could delegate whatever powers they wanted to as many different governments as they wanted and still remain entirely within the legitimate theoretical framework of federalism.

Indeed, the first American effort at modern federalism, the modern confederation embodied in the Articles of Confederation, failed in part because the way it attempted to divide sovereignty among governments went against the spirit of the times.[19] In its place the Americans substituted modern federation whereby the United States appeared as a single nation to the outside world while internally its people delegated powers to the federal and state governments and through the state governments to local governments as well. This "compromise" satisfied the demands (in certain respects these were aesthetic, rather than substantive) of the larger world and enabled the United States to develop as a single nation with a noncentralized political system over the next 200 years.[20]

The American model of modern federation was frequently copied in the nineteenth century and in some cases succeeded. In any case, the federation model was so successful that it totally eclipsed any other forms of federalism so that federalism and federation became, for all intents and purposes, synonymous. Nevertheless, the necessities of other situations required the application of federal principles in other ways in the twentieth century.[21] Principal among them were internal regionalization that became more than regional decentralization as in Belgium, Italy, and Spain, and the development of associated state relations between larger powers and smaller, usually offshore, entities that demanded autonomy but did not seek or could not sustain full independence, as in the case of the Netherlands and its Caribbean territories or the United States and Puerto Rico.

Reinvented Confederal Arrangements and Globalization

These new forms of federalism spread rapidly after World War II when they were joined by revived and reinvented confederal arrangements, confederations in a new style. Pioneering in this regard was the European Community, now the European Union. After the federationist idea of the United States of Europe fell by the wayside in the late 1940s because of the strong separate identities of the individual states, Western Europe was united through a congeries of functional authorities of limited scope that developed into confederal devices. These were strengthened over the subsequent forty years until the E.C. more or less formally became a confederation as the E.U.

Other confederations and confederal arrangements emerged at the same time or immediately thereafter. Figure 11.5 provides a list of the various forms of federal arrangements today and identifies each of them and in most cases the polities within them. We may describe this as a movement from federation to federal arrangements. Moreover, federalism, which in the modern epoch increasingly became a form of political organization for the very largest countries, at least nominally, began to spread to the smaller ones as well as individuals and groups sought greater control over their immediate political environment while at the same time needing to combine for security and economic purposes into larger entities.

Each of the new federal arrangements have required new forms and styles of constitutional design, following but adapting old principles and models. All were begun with a political compact or equivalent that was then followed by a constitution (or constitutions, in some cases) embodying the rules, structures, functions, and powers of the new federal arrangement. In most cases, constitutional referenda by one or both parties to the arrangements were required.

At first the revival of federal arrangements was a matter for individual states or nations and it was still possible to distinguish between federal and unitary states or political systems. Beginning with the European Community, initially a linkage of politically sovereign states through what was formally a network of treaties, that distinction began to diminish. From the first what was different about these treaties was that they were enforceable through common institutions and subject to the rulings of a common constitutional court.

These new "transnational" federal arrangements had ripple effects even within the member states. France, perhaps the most unitary state of all, became part of the new Western European confederation and was even forced to offer a degree of constitutional autonomy to Corsica, not to speak of those of its overseas territories that did not want or could not sustain independence. Moreover, when Charles de Gaulle in one fell swoop abandoned France's African colonies, he did so in such a manner that left them tied to their former mother country through control of their currency and economic systems in an arrangement that was not designated federal or even viewed as such by the participants and which was confined to the economic and military sphere but which had at least quasi-federal elements within it. Thirty years later, in the early 1990s, the French used it to try to force greater democratization on community members in Francophone Africa through refoundings via national

FIGURE 11.5
Forms of Federal Arrangements
(Political, Economic, and Religious Parallels)

Political	Economic	Religious	Principal Characteristics
1. Union	Multi-Division Corporation	Episcopal Church Polity	Clearly bounded territorial consti-tuent units retain "municipal" powers only while sharing power concen-trated in the common government.
2. Consociation	Guild Systems	Ethnic Communiities in Centralized or Hierarchical Church	Non-territorial constituent units share power concentrated in common overarching government.
3. Federation	1. Economic Community	Presbyterian Church	Strong self-governing constituent units linked within
	2. Conglomerate, if the constituent units are represented in the overall man-agement structure.	Polity	strong but limited overarching government.
4. Federacy	Customs Union	Autocephalic Church Linked to Polity of Larger Hierarchical Church	Asymmetrical permanent linkage between two self-governing units with the larger having specific powers within the small in exchange for guaranteeing the latter specific privileges.
5. Condominium	Joint Stock Company		Joint rule or control by two units over a third or over some common territory or enterprise.
6. Confederation	Common market	Congregational Union or Federation	Strong self-governing constituent units permanently linked by loose, limited purpose common government.
7. League	Free Trade Area	Congregational Convention	Loose but permanent linkage for limited purposes without common government but with some joint body or secretariat.
8. Inter-Jurisdictional Functional Authorities	Joint Enterprises	Joint Missions	Joint or common functional entities organized by the constituting units to undertake special tasks.

conventions in each.[22] In those conventions all the relevant parties in a particular country were assembled to establish the basis for the polity and to prepare the way for a new constitution that would reflect the national consensus through an act that can only be described as being within the secular parameters of the covenantal tradition.

By the early 1990s, it was hard to find any state in the world that did not have interstate ties that were more than simply treaty arrangements but which were constitutionally entangling. Most of these arrangements remained nominally open to unilateral dissolution but in practice few, if any, could be dissolved without such great cost that none of their members would think of dissolving them. This was particularly true in the economic sphere.

Prime among these was the General Agreement on Tariffs and Trade (GATT). GATT was formally no more than an international treaty but, as the nations of the world came to realize during the recently completed Uruguay round, not only was there no way for any single country to leave GATT without paying a huge price but even regional blocs had to learn how to accommodate one another within an improved and extended agreement. Thus, on one hand, the worldwide GATT system had to be divided into regional groupings and, on the other hand, the regional groupings learned how to compromise with one another to maintain, renew, and extend the GATT agreement. Indeed, at the conclusion of the long and exhausting Uruguay round, the final document provided for the replacement of GATT with a World Trade Organization (WTO) whose name already signified how far the constitutionalizing process had gone beyond simply an international treaty to being a kind of formal constitutional arrangement, however limited.[23]

Thus another arena of constitutionized federal arrangements is emerging, the international arena, that goes beyond individual states, even large states. While there is little or no talk of international federations, except among radical ideologues, and these international relations have not reached the intricacy of confederal arrangements, they are being constitutionalized, an extremely important step that is causing every state in the international arena to constitutionally recognize that exclusive state sovereignty is a thing of the past, that the Westphalia system has collapsed, and that what was initially achieved, de facto, as a result of the invention of nuclear weapons and the movement toward greater economic interdependence is now acquiring a de jure dimension as well so as to give it some regularization, stability, and to give the members of the international community, as polities, as groups, and as individuals, some measure of protection. This, too, is leading to new forms of constitutionalism and constitutional design.

How far this will go and how it will get there cannot be foreseen at this moment. There are too many imponderables and too many opportunities for directions to shift, but what seems to be happening is that mechanisms are emerging that have blurred the earlier distinctions between unitary and federal states and their constituent units and citizens and to bring all together in some increasingly, if only moderately, constitutionalized framework.

Conclusion

If this chapter, and indeed this volume, have anything to suggest, it is that constitutions, constitution-making, and constitutional choice are the modern and contemporary continuations of the covenant tradition in politics and should be understood and examined in that spirit, utilizing appropriate models that recognize the importance of institutions in the lives of humans, the significance of history and culture in shaping those institutions and rendering particular institutions effective or ineffective, and identifying the empirical and behavioral dimensions of the constitutional process in each case.

In the final analysis, modern constitutionalism is covenantal because for every constitution to be effective it must have a moral consensus behind it. This is true even though we properly emphasize the degree to which constitutions must be realistic to be effective. They must be appropriate to the people they serve and must take into consideration those people's strengths and weaknesses both.

Still, even the most realistic constitution that does not have the consent of the people it serves will have only a limited effect if at all. That is why publics or peoples not ready for constitutional government, even with the most elegant constitutional design, cannot achieve it. The moral basis of a constitution is, as we have seen, an integral part of every constitution in the larger sense. In the most operative meaning of the term it is the agreement of those who are bound by the constitution to be so bound, an agreement that can only be compelled up to a certain point. Beyond that, it is the trust necessary to make a constitutional government work.

Authoritarian polities have been dressed up with constitutional window-dressing, but it is the overwhelmingly compelling force of the rulers and their minions that hold those polities together, not the window-dressing. Constitutions are effective as constitutions only when they rest on sufficient moral consensus among those that they serve. This is hardly a new observation, although it has been lost at times in the modern political scientific search for realpolitik understandings.

Significantly, this knowledge has not only been the discovery of political philosophers or political scientists but also of some whose lives are devoted to realpolitik or, even more, the application of military force. When U.S. General John J. Pershing commanded the American punitive expedition into Mexico in 1916 in the wake of Mexican revolutionist Pancho Villa's attacks on American border towns that year, he asked one of his aides, Captain Hugh Johnson, then considered the U.S. Army's resident intellectual, to take advantage of the expedition's stalemate and undertake a study of why Mexico, which had a formal constitution closely modeled after that of the United States, was constantly in turmoil and never had experienced effective democratic government while the United States had succeeded in doing so. Johnson undertook what we would call today a comparative study of political systems and he came to the conclusion that the missing ingredient was trust, that in matters governmental at least, the Mexicans distrusted one another and particularly distrusted those holding political power. As a result, its constitutions, however beautiful on paper, remained unworkable. The American people, on the other hand, had very substantial trust, especially between governors and governed, so their constitutions worked and worked very well.

The story does not end there. A few months later, Johnson was called to Washington, to the War Department, to help develop plans in preparation for the by then anticipated American entry into World War I. The first problem he encountered was planning for large-scale conscription. Those assigned that task in the War Department had drawn up plans based upon the very bad American experience during the Civil War when there were draft riots all over the country and conscription produced very few people and was considered extremely inequitable. The plan they submitted to then-Secretary of War Newton D. Baker, in Johnson's words, was "bristling with bayonets" since it was based on the assumption that it would be necessary to send substantial contingents of U.S. regular army troops to the various parts of the country in order to enforce conscription.

Baker, who had been the Progressive mayor of Cleveland, Ohio, prior to entering the Wilson government, was horrified and told his people to go back to the drawing board. He then assigned Johnson to work with them. Recalling the lessons he had drawn from the Mexican experience, Johnson decided that the United States government could draw upon the trust of its citizenry if those citizens were trusted in turn. Thus was born the plan for selective service, for local draft boards under the aegis of state draft boards that were assigned quotas from Washington within a general framework and were responsible for selecting and mobilizing young men in light of those quotas. Under this plan, while registration for the draft would be nationwide, "little groups of friends and neighbors" in each county would actually do the calling up and would be able to grant waivers, exemptions, and deferments according to need as well as to select those who fit the requisite profile for military service.

Baker immediately took to this plan and it was adopted. There then proceeded to take place two extraordinary demonstrations of what trust meant in connection with the plan's implementation. By that time it was a few months before the U.S. declaration of war and it was becoming apparent to all those involved in war plans that the U.S. would be involved in the war very soon. More than that, it was apparent to the military leadership that unless U.S. military support could be given the Allies in relatively short order, the Germans and the Central Powers would win. That meant getting the selective service system into place immediately upon its authorization by Congress.

The War Department decided to arrange to print all the forms needed for registration of some ten million men even before there was any authorization of conscription by a likely-to-be-reluctant U.S. Congress. Baker took the Superintendent of Documents, the head of the Government Printing Office, into his confidence and made informal arrangements with him to have the GPO begin printing the forms, which they did. There soon came to be a serious problem of storage as the millions of forms accumulated. The Superintendent called together a few of his closest colleagues, who, like him, were members of the Cosmos Club, the most prestigious club of the Washington executive branch and scientific establishment. They met at the club to find some way to overcome the problem.

The postmaster of Washington, D.C., was among those so assembled and he promised to furnish a sufficient quantity of mailbags. He furnished what he could and called in other mailbags from around the country and still the paper kept coming. There was no place to store the papers nor were there sufficient mailbags to do so. The group met again at the Cosmos Club. There they decided on a bold step. They would write to the sheriffs of every county in the United States, over three thousand of them, tell them of their problem and ask whether the GPO could mail the forms needed for each county to them to keep until the U.S. entered the war and conscription became law. They proceeded to do that and every sheriff did what he was asked without a single leak. The forms were kept in secret until war was declared on April 6 and the selective service law enacted on April 19. The next day the forms were available and registration moved along at breathtaking speed, made possible by the trust that Americans had in their governments and in one another.[24]

Realism in constitutional design is absolutely necessary but it is not sufficient. Consent and trust must be added to make even the most realistic design work.

Notes

1. Ivo Duchacek, *Power Maps: Comparative Politics of Constitutions* (Santa Barbara, Cal.: ABC-Clio, 1973).
2. Cf. Norton Long, *The Polity* (Chicago: Rand McNally, 1962).
3. Antonio la Pergola, *Constitucion del Estado y Normas Internacionales* (Mexico: Universidad Nacional Autonoma de Mexico, 1985).
4. Cf. Cesar Enrique Diaz Lopez, "The State of the Autonomic Process in Spain," *Publius*, vol. 11, nos. 3–4 (Summer 1981):193–218.
5. Daniel Wilhelmus Kruger, *The Making of a Nation: A History of the Union of South Africa, 1910–1961* (London: Macmillan, 1969); Margaret Ballinger, *From Union to Apartheid: A Trek to Isolation* (New York: Praeger, 1969).
6. Bertus de Villiers, ed., *Birth of a Constitution* (Capetown: Juta and Co., 1994).
7. Arend Lijphart, ed., *Politics in Europe* (Englewood Cliffs, NJ: Prentice-Hall,

1969); Jacques Brassine, *Les Institutions de la Flandre, de la Communaute Francaise, de la Region Wallon* (Bruxelles: Crisp, 1981); Andre Molitor, *l'Administration de la Belgique* (Bruxelles: Institut Belge de Science Politique et Centre de Recherche et d'Information Socio-Politiques, 1974).

8. Vincent Ostrom, "A Computational-Conceptual Logic," in *Constitutional Design and Power Sharing*, Daniel J. Elazar, ed. (Lanham, Md.: University Press of America, 1991), pp. 3–21; Daniel J. Elazar, *The American Constitutional Tradition* (Lincoln: University of Nebraska Press, 1988); Duchacek, *Power Maps*.

9. Daniel J. Elazar, "Federalism in Theory and Practice: Some French, American and Nigerian Examples," *Publius*, vol. 3, no. 1 (Spring 1973); Ladipo Adamoleku, "Federalism in Nigeria: Toward Federal Democracy," *Publius*, vol. 21, no. 4 (Fall 1991); J. Isawa Elaigwu, "Nigerian Federalism Under Civilian and Military Regimes," *Publius*, vol. 18, no. 1 (Winter 1988).

10. Donald V. Smiley, "Federal-Provincial Conflict in Canada," *Publius*, vol. 4, no. 3 (Summer 1974); Ronald L. Watt, "Canadian Federalism in the 1990s," *Publius*, vol. 21, no. 3 (Summer 1991).

11. Elazar, *American Constitutional Tradition*.

12. Mark Kesselman, *The Ambiguous Consensus: A Study of Local Government in France* (New York: Alfred A. Knopf, 1967); *idem* and Donald Rosenthal, *Local Power and Comparative Politics* (Beverly Hills, Cal.: Sage Publications, 1974); Terry N. Clark, *Community Power and Policy Outputs* (Beverly Hills, Cal.: Sage Publications, 1973).

13. Andre Eschet-Schwartz, "The Role of Semi-Direct Democracy in Shaping Swiss Federalism: The Behavior of Cantons Regarding Revision of the Constitution, 1866–1981" *Publius*, vol. 19, no. 1 (Winter 1989); Leonhard Neidhart, *Plebeszit und Plurlitaere Demokratie* (Bern: Francke, 1970).

14. Austin Ranney, ed., *The Referendum Device* (Washington D.C.: American Enterprise Institute, 1981); David B. Magleby, *Direct Legislation: Voting on Ballot Propositions in the U.S.* (Baltimore, Md.: Johns Hopkins University Press, 1984).

15. Igor I. Kavass, ed., *Supranational and Constitutional Courts in Europe: Functions and Sources* (Buffalo, N.Y.: W. Hein, 1992); Donald P. Kommers, *The Constitutional Jurisprudence of the Federal Republic of Germany* (Durham, N.C.: Duke University Press, 1989).

16. Cf. Daniel J. Elazar, "The Political Theory of Covenant: Biblical Origins and Modern Developments," *Publius*, vol. 10, no. (Fall 1980):3–30.

17. Filipo Sabetti, *Covenant Language in Canada: Continuity and Change in Political Discourse* (Philadelphia, Pa.: Workshop on Covenant and Politics, Center for the Study of Federalism, 1980).

18. This writer was in the offices of the U.S. Commission for the Bicentennial of American Independence on the day that Nixon's resignation went into effect. As the hour of 12 noon approached, people came out of the offices surrounding the central reception area and gathered in front of a portable television set placed there by one of the Commission employees. As twelve o'clock struck Gerald Ford arose to take the oath of office. When he completed the swearing in, I heard an audible sigh of relief in the room as if to signify that the Constitution was intact and the republic was saved.

19. Murray Forsyth, *Union of States: The Theory and Practice of Confederation* (New York: Leicester University Press, 1981); Daniel J. Elazar, *Modern Confederation*, forthcoming.

20. Samuel Beer, *To Make a Nation* (Cambridge, Mass.: The Belknap Press, 1993); Daniel J. Elazar, *American Constitutional Tradition*.

238 Covenant and Civil Society

21. Daniel J. Elazar, ed., *Federal Systems of the World,* 2nd ed. (London: Longmans, 1994); *idem, Federalism and Political Integration* (Ramat Gan: Turtledove Publishing, 1979).
22. Kirk Preuss, *The National Conference in Francophone Africa- Grassroots Recovenanting or Paristroika?* Unpublished paper prepared for the Jerusalem Center for Public Affairs.
23. *International Herald Tribune,* July 10, 1994.
24. This story is documented in at least two memoirs of the period: Louis Brownlow, *A Passion for Anonymity* (Chicago: University of Chicago Press, 1958), pp. 56–62 and Hugh S. Johnson, *The Blue Eagle From Egg to Earth* (Garden City, N.Y.: Doubleday, Doran and Company, 1935), ch. 9, pp. 73–87.

12

The Covenant Tradition and Rights

Constitutional Expectations

The spread of constitutionalism throughout the modern world between the mid-eighteenth and mid-twentieth centuries transformed people's expectations with regard to government and their own position in the polity. Before modern epoch, only a few people in the world expected the kind of government of equals by equals under the rule of law on the basis of combining self-rule and shared rule, that now has become at least the stated aspiration of all, excepting only those few who seek to rule by force or who continue to claim their hereditary privileges. Such widely shared aspirations, however, did not reflect an equally widely shared commitment to, or capability of, establishing and maintaining polities of that character. Many of those newly converted to those aspirations had neither the cultural nor other capabilities to translate aspirations into reality. The result was the gap between aspiration and achievement, expectation and reality, found in an increasing number of polities.

Not only that, but even where the aspirations took root, often it took generations for there to be sufficient political cultural change to make it possible to begin to realize them according to expectations. Thus there slowly came to be three groups of polities that could be identified according to their constitutional base. First there were those that came out of the covenantal political tradition in times past that not only adapted to modern constitutionalism but indeed were its pioneers. Then there were those polities whose origins were rooted in the hierarchical and organic sources of the polity and their traditions of force and accident, that successfully adopted the forms of constitutionalism even though they moved more slowly in adopting the political culture inherent in those forms and needed to make them work as intended. Finally there were those polities that attempted to conform to modern fashion by adopting constitutions but had neither the wherewithal nor the abilities to move them beyond windowdressing.

In this way the moralistic political culture of covenantalism became the ideal, leading its bearers and the bearers of other cultures to recognize the gap between ideal and reality that perforce existed in varying degrees in one polity or another and that led to various reactions to the failure to overcome it. In those polities of the first group, that gap was intolerable and, when exposed, led to very sharp reaction. As the instruments for exposing it, that is, the mass media, grew more comprehensive and powerful, they extended the sphere of what was considered legitimate for exposure. Originally that sphere was confined to clearly public behavior or behavior with direct impact on public policy and public affairs. That remained the modern resolution of the issue, but as the postmodern epoch advanced, the distinction between public and private began to collapse. In this, as in most other cases, public people were subject to relentless and all-encompassing scrutiny. This had the manifest consequences of raising public norms and the standards to which public people had to adhere, but since no humans are able to adhere to those new norms exactly and all humans who live and act run afoul of them in some way, it also had the latent function of diminishing the trust needed to maintain constitutional government, engendering an almost impossible dilemma.

Those polities that were in the forefront of modernization during the modern epoch but were not covenantal offered a different set of problems. While norms were also raised among them, since their culturally rooted expectations were different, those expectations did not rise so fast. It was among these polities that the modern populistic counterattack against democracy in the form of Fascism and Nazism was most powerful and most successful. Hence, they had a different set of troubles which, while dissipating during the first generation of the postmodern epoch, remained a threat to the constitutional order, periodically raising its head in one or another of those polities.[1]

In the third group, those that began to modernize late, the problems associated with introducing constitutional government were so strong that these issues hardly could surface in any serious way. Instead, the people in those polities were confronted with an almost constant struggle to introduce or maintain even a semblance of constitutional government in many cases against internal authoritarian pressures. The effort to cope with these problems was not always grounded in modern ideas of natural right but was received already translated into the idea of constitutional, individual and human rights.

For all three groups, however, the seventeenth-century argument that individual humans were born with certain fundamental rights by nature was slowly translated into an extensive system of rights and rights protection that became an integral part of modern constitutionalism.

Prior to 1789 the prevailing belief was that the Whiggish one that proper structural and procedural protections embodied in modern constitutions would provide sufficient protection for rights. While, at least in the constitutions of the English-speaking countries, lists ("Bills" or "Declarations") of rights were incorporated into the constitutional documents, they were more exhortative than binding, a list of popular expectations from government rather than enforceable per se.[2] The sea change came in 1789, first in the United States and then, two years later, in France, and subsequently through one or the other, throughout the world.

In the United States, the state constitutions of the Revolutionary era incorporated the Whig view of exhortative declarations of rights in their documents, establishing a tradition in state constitutional design that survived long after the federal constitution had projected another way. The struggle over the ratification of the Constitution of the United States brought the matter to a head. The Philadelphia constitutional convention, following the older tradition, designed that document to establish institutions and procedures that would, in themselves, provide the necessary rights protections. Many of the state ratifying conventions, however, worried about the possible encroachment of the federal government on their citizens as well as on the states themselves, sought to make limitations on such federal encroachments explicit. Hence they demanded that a bill of rights be added to the new constitution that would prevent the federal government, especially Congress, from violating accepted rights in spheres in which the states used very different methods to secure those rights, in order to secure its gratification.

The Federalists agreed to immediately sponsor a series of amendments to the new document that would provide that kind of specification. They did as promised, drafting and submitting to the states twelve proposed amendments over the summer of 1789, ten of which were adopted and became the U.S. Bill of Rights, now considered by many to be the heart of the U.S. Constitution. In keeping with the spirit of the new bill, most of the individual articles were framed in the negative, that is, "Congress shall make no law...," thereby reaffirming the accepted thesis that rights were inherent in people and were best protected by the state governments.[3] Under that theory, all that had to be done was to ensure that Congress could not encroach on either the rights themselves or the state protections. This was the first enforceable bill of rights of modern times.[4]

In the meantime, the French Revolution had begun and the revolutionaries were imbued with ideas of the rights of man derived from the same modern philosophic sources, only with a continental European twist. This led them to draft the Declaration of the Rights of Man and Citizen, also adopted in 1791, that radically broadened the idea of rights to include certain social as well as political rights and to give the revolutionary government a more active role in fostering natural rights against the residue of the ancien regime.[5] Since most of the countries of the world had to be transformed through modernization, they followed the French lead more than the American. The influence of the American Bill of Rights was further limited by the fact that most of the world's new societies developed under British aegis and hence followed Westminster parliamentary models that had not accepted the new idea of the constitutional protection of rights but, rather, relied upon parliamentary protections, at most adding Whiggish exhortations to instruct parliaments regarding rights.

In this way the modern career of rights protection began. It was to develop to a point where in some polities, especially the United States, it would come to overshadow all other dimensions of the constitution by the late twentieth century. To better understand this shift, we need to understand the development of the idea of rights in connection with the covenantal tradition in politics.

One of the most pronounced and prominent features of the revolutionary generation in the eighteenth century, was the introduction of the idea of individual rights as a basis for political organization, and the protection of those rights as a major task of government. This idea, which now is uncritically accepted by conventional opinion, in itself represents only one conception of rights and must be understood as such. Moreover, it, too, has evolved since the time of its introduction in the seventeenth century as modern natural right until today both in theory and practice.[6]

Every conception of rights is shaped by a particular view of the nature of man, a particular understanding of the sources of rights, and a particular direction for the expression of rights.

Here we will concentrate on views prevailing among those who were or are deemed to reflect enlightened or prevailing opinion in a particular civil society. Their conceptions usually come to be embodied in the prevailing legal doctrine. The term "enlightened opinion" is used to reflect the self-perception of the opinion-molders in any particular polity. In hierarchical and organic societies, enlightened opinion is concentrated in a distinctly separable elite that can be identified as the ruling class. In covenantal societies, it is less possible to distinguish such a ruling class. Nevertheless, it is possible to identify those whose prevailing views that are considered to be enlightened within broad outlines.

Prior to the American Revolution, the rights of individuals, in practice, had been associated with particular traditions. For example, people could talk about the rights of Englishmen because the English constitutional tradition as it had developed made provision for same. As Mozart's librettist had one of his characters put it at the end of the second act of *The Abduction from the Seraglio*: "Ich bin ein Englander en freiheit gebornen" (I am English, born in freedom). Every audience in Europe could understand that claim.

Even that idea of rights was rare. For the most part, citizenship or its equivalent and the protections it afforded were associated with *obligations and liberties*. These obligations and liberties could be enforced by the polity's political institutions in tandem with its religious authorities, but provided no explicit protections for individual liberties with rare exceptions, such as the provision for writs of habeus corpus in England to prevent improper incarceration of individuals. This was true even in those polities viewed as having a high regard for the individual. What is most significantly different about modern human rights is that they constitute entitlements for individuals simply because they are humans.

The premodern systems most successful in protecting what we today call individual rights were, in all likelihood, those based on biblical covenantalism. In essence, the biblical covenantal approach was the only one to be developed before the modern epoch to provide a basis for obliging the protection of liberties and rights by making the obligation to do so the obligation of covenanted human beings as part of their covenant with the Deity. Thus the Bible presents us with an elaborate set of commandments to do justice to the poor, to widows and orphans, to resident aliens as well as to fellow-Israelites. These are mandated for the moral well-being of Israel. Most important, that approach provided for a legal-constitutional system specifying the obligations and what specifically was involved in fulfilling them, on a case-by-case basis if necessary.

The Bible never uses the term "rights." Rather it talks in terms of human obligations to God via covenant to act justly and "do justice." Not only is the body politic as a collectivity (*Adat Bnei Yisrael*—the congregation of Israel) obligated to provide protections for individuals so as to do justice, but the status of individuals is defined by their being obligated as part of a people to follow God's commandments (in Hebrew—*mitzvot*). In the covenantal tradition, the Bible makes it clear that people are free to choose whether or not to live up to that obligation. They do not obey God but hearken to Him, freely taking on the commanded obligations. The obligations define them nonetheless. If they do not live up to these obligations, they face the consequences—both in human law and Divine. Indeed, the very idea of obligations and liberties or rights is, at its base, covenantal.[7]

Sinai, the climactic Biblical covenant, makes clear what has been the critical primal element of covenantal partnerships from the first, namely that covenants establish justice through mutual obligation, indeed, systems of mutual obligations, from whence are derived (in modern terms) the partners' rights. Under the covenantal system there are no rights that are not derived from obligations. The primary covenantal obligations are those of being holy and being just. Hence they are excellent sources of what moderns define as rights, but covenant also keeps rights conditional on one's maintaining one's covenant with God which establishes basic morality, justice and law, at the very least transforming natural justice into just law.

Just as covenants establish different degrees of obligation based on the covenants one has entered into, so, too, they make possible differentiation in rights among those who are partners to different covenants or covenants of different scope. As in the case of the biblical view of covenant obligation, this is not designed to invidiously discriminate among humans but to allow humans greater scope for deciding for themselves by which covenants they wish to be bound, which obligations they take upon themselves, and hence, what rights are available to them. In the biblical worldview, all humans, without exception, are expected to be bound by the Noahide covenant which obligates them and also endows them with all the basic human liberties, at least by inference, that is, by not restricting them.

What follows is that those who refuse to be bound by God's basic covenantal restictions and requirements by accepting the obligations of the Noahide covenant are thereby not entitled to those basic human rights because they have proclaimed themselves outlaws. But it is their choice. Although, as humans, they can be punished for violating the terms of the covenant, as humans they cannot be outlawed by others except perhaps for the most blatant causes (what in contemporary times would describe as acting in "inhuman" ways).

Extrapolating from the Biblical worldview, it can be claimed that all human beings can also accept the covenant of Abraham, that is to say, join one of the monotheistic faiths and accept its more extensive obligations and gain more specific rights thereby. They may also accept the Sinai Covenant and become Jews, thereby taking on even greater obligations and winning the right to be numbered among God's singular people (*am segula*), that is to say, to have the full *brit* (covenant) and not merely benefit from Abraham's *brit* and *brakhah* (blessing). These are all matters of human choice.

In sum, the Bible sets forth a comprehensive covenantal system, establishing a framework for both justice and rights in this world, one that offers the civil and social protections of contemporary rights theory without succumbing to the excesses of that theory. It does so by providing constitutional means for guaranteeing rights while controlling the demand for rights by tieing them to obligations.

Subsequently, in European civilization, alongside the concept of obligations there developed the idea of *liberties*, that is to say, protected freedom within the group and its obligational matrix. Liberties could be collective or individual and are reflected in the development of medieval republicanism. The Swiss experience is paradigmatic. Swiss federal republicanism was built on the struggle to protect and operationalize a complex web of local and individual liberties woven together over time.[8]

The Puritans understood the implications of covenant on issues of obligations and liberties because covenant was the primary basis for moral principles in the Puritan worldview. According to the Puritans, God had set forth what constituted justice and embodied it in His covenant with humanity. While each person was free to choose whether or not to adhere to that covenant, choosing not to would bring Divine punishment. The choice was made through covenant, leading to the establishment of federal rather than natural liberty, or the liberty to do right and people were obligated to live and act according to the terms of God's covenant.

This, too, is the view of the Hebrew Bible, but since the Hebrew Bible stands alone in its plain text and Jews did not record extrabiblical commentators until much later, this step was a very practical one since the Puritans like others of the covenantal persuasion believed that "adherence to covenants and agreements [was] essential to maintain social cohesion and harmony."[3]

They also saw this view as more just, since it set humans on the right path, giving them freedom of choice in a world in which choices had consequences which needed to be understood in advance as well as felt after the fact. Hence they reaffirmed obligations as central to liberties (rights). In a sense theirs was a halfway position between the old notions of obligation as group and class-based and the new idea of rights as individual, equal, and universal.

Through covenant, obligation could also be appropriately equal and universal, yet still make the necessary distinctions that society required to allow humans freedom without giving every human who wanted to be free to do whatever he or she wished (i.e., natural liberty) the rights that adhered to other human beings who were willing to accept their obligations as humans. In essence, they revived ancient biblical ideas that were to help shape the first rights-oriented civil societies of modernity, even after those civil societies otherwise had broken with Puritanism. While Puritan thought did serve as the precursor of modern secular thought, it was not merely the precursor. It articulated a doctrine of its own which differed from modern secular thought in its foundations (and, indeed, would not have been happy with what replaced it) because it was theopolitical in character—the "theo" was as important as the political.

For most Europeans, the "obligations and liberties" formula reflects the more corporatist model of the political and social order of premodern times, whether with hierarchical, organic, or covenantal roots. Individuals functioned within intergenerational groups, whether peoples, corporations, or associations, and gained their status, obligations and liberties from their position in their group. What is characteristic of premodern republican systems of obligations and liberties was that what moderns came to understand as protected rights, adhering to the individual, in premodern time were derived from obligations to do justice that adhered to certain collectivities as collectivities. They are not presented as rights inherent either in individuals or the protected populations. It is relatively easy and appropriate to translate and understand those collective obligations as individual rights, but the starting point is the collective obligation to strive for moral well-being, not in individual rights as an entitlements.

Modern Natural Right

A principal characteristic of modernity is the shattering of that framework and its replacement by the concept of individualism, including *individual rights*. This concept was introduced into political philosophy at the very beginning of the modern epoch in the middle of the seventeenth century by Thomas Hobbes, John Locke, and their peers. In their break with classical philosophy, they replaced the concept of natural law, which reinforced the corporatist model, with one of natural right which opened the door to the idea of individual rights.

By the mid-eighteenth century, the idea of natural right had been supplemented in the political realm by the idea of natural rights. The polity, to be properly constituted had to be rights-based. This idea reached its apogee in the Virginia Declaration of Rights, the Declaration of Independence of the United States of America, the Northwest Ordinance of 1787, and the first ten amendments to the United States Constitution.

While proponents of modern conceptions of rights dropped the term "obligations" from their lexicon, they did introduce another term in its place—"responsibilities." For them, this removed the possibility that obligations could be imposed from outside the rights system, but instead reinforced the centrality of the individual by providing that individuals qua individuals had assumed responsibilities that went along with their rights.

According to that theory, individual rights derive from and are vested in the natural order to which natural law speaks. Humans must assume obligations in order to survive—so goes the theory—but in linking them to rights, the latter are given precedence. That is to say, every individual human being by nature has rights, but because those rights must be protected in civil society, humans take on obligations as a practical part of rights protection.

Moreover, while there is a continuing scholarly debate over the extent of religious belief among the seventeenth-century philosophers who articulated the new natural rights philosophy, among the public, including enlightened opinion, there was a general consensus that God was in His heaven, or at the very least that there was a transcendent Author of Nature who required the acceptance of obligations as well as being the author of rights. This was the view that more or less prevailed throughout the rest of the modern epoch in Western civil society.[10]

The postmodern understanding of rights as human rights shares the modern understanding that humans have rights simply by virtue of being alive. But in the postmodern view rights by biology stand entirely independent of obligations other than the obligation of reciprocity, that is to say, that each human has to recognize that other humans have the same rights. "Life" itself becomes the measure of all things—indeed the highest possible measure. This transformation reflects the decline of covenantal thinking, even in its secularized form of political compact and its replacement by other ideas of social contract.

Looking back at those developments, it seems as if the transition was clearcut and decisive. Philosophically it may have been, but on the political scene matters were more complex. Moreover, since the apogee of the natural rights doctrine, the idea of individual rights underwent further changes, both in terms of the understanding of how "rights" protect the individual against all corporate entities, not only government or the state, and with regard to what constitutes rights. The changes that have taken place may have made late twentieth-century civil society as different in its conception of rights from the generations of early modernity as the latter was from the late medieval expressions of obligations and liberties. In this, the American case is the most advanced and its model the most influential.

In one very real sense, the American tradition of rights goes back to the first colonial foundings.[11] From the beginning, those who came to American shores sought to protect their individuality and their liberties. One of the ways they chose to do so was to put those liberties in writing, embody them in constitutional documents, and proclaim them publicly. While they did not believe that governing bodies could be formally bound by those constitutional documents in specific ways, they did believe that their governors were bound to make every effort to preserve and protect those liberties and that the people should select or reject them on the basis of their willingness and ability to do so.

During the colonial period what we today refer to as the protection of rights was principally the acknowledgement and protection of liberties, which in the United States goes back at least as far back as the Puritan settlement of New England in the 1630s. The issue was sharpened in the Glorious Revolution in England in 1689 and the Whig tradition that emerged from it. The Whigs, influenced by Locke, changed the terms of the debate from liberties to rights. This is reflected in the terminology used. In 1641, the Massachusetts General Court adopted the "Body of Liberties" which defined what we would today refer to as the rights of the citizens and residents of the Commonwealth of Massachusetts. The English Bill of Rights of 1688 (old calendar—1689 current calendar) was entitled "An Act for Declaring the Rights and Liberties of the Subject and Settling the Succession of the Crown."

The Whigs changed the terminology but not the means of enforcement. Indeed, as Donald Lutz has demonstrated, the first American state constitutions, written during the Revolution, adopted declarations of rights in the Whig style, that is to say, they used the term rights instead of liberties, but they were declarations of eternal principles rather than specifically binding constitutional law. At first the United Colonies, later the United States, followed the same pattern, beginning with the Declaration of Rights of the Stamp Act Congress in 1765. The Bill of Rights added to the U.S. Constitution of 1787 marked a new departure. No longer content with declarations of eternal principles, from the first it was considered to be binding constitutional law.

The original state bills or declarations of rights of the Revolutionary period reflected the hidden or open assumption that every individual was part of a community and as such was bound by certain communitarian obligations. Separately, the community was obligated to secure that individual's life, liberty, property, and the rights that flowed from them. They reflected the sense that natural law and rights both meant a natural order. Whatever sense of rights as including obligations that has survived in the United States has sur-

vived within the states. In the nineteenth century this view still had considerable power and was even recognized by the United States Supreme Court in
the license cases which enabled the states to build up their police powers vis-
a-vis the federal commerce power, primarily for the purpose of maintaining
community and a common moral order.

By 1791, then, two great transitions had taken place with regard to rights
in American history: the first substantive, from the late medieval conception
of liberties to a modern conception of rights; and the second procedural, from
the idea that rights can at best be protected through hortatory declarations to
the idea that they can be protected through binding constitutional law.

After 1791, the United States entered a period when the idea of *natural
rights* gave way to that of *constitutional rights* with the task of the institutions
of government to protect the latter. Only those who doubted that American
institutions could do so, appealed beyond the Constitution to eternal rights,
natural or divine. This had two consequences of interest to us. On the one
hand, this represented the practical conclusion of the movement from an organic to a covenantal basis for civil society, a ceasing to look elsewhere to
God or Nature for fundamental law and to look instead to a fundamental law
established by the people by mutual consent. At the same time, it also meant
a further secularization of the law, a further detachment of law from any sense
of transcendental origins. Thus, if the covenantal tradition scored a major
advance, it did so in a minimally covenantal way. Here we encounter the roots
of the nineteenth- and twentieth-century struggle between federal and natural
liberty. When Abraham Lincoln declared in the Lincoln-Douglas debates that
there is no right to do wrong, he was arguing from a federal liberty perspective which seems to have been the basis of his position on the subject throughout his life.[12] He may have been said to have added the dimension of prudence
to the formula, that is to say, he recognized that there are many things that
should be prohibited or limited in terms of federal liberty viewed absolutely,
but that prudence prevents government from undertaking to limit or prohibit
because of the degree of coercion required, if at all possible to achieve even
through coercion.

Federal liberty bridges between the premodern and modern conceptions of
rights and recognizes the relationship between obligation and right. In its
original form, it grew out of the premodern notion of obligations that make
liberties possible. In its modern form it is an effort to balance rights and obligations. It has yet to acquire a postmodern form, although elements for defining a postmodern form of federal liberty can be discerned in current debates
on the subject.

Protecting Rights through Proper Institutions

Part and parcel of the conception of the protection of rights in the writing
of the U.S. Constitution was the principle embodied in the Constitution as

originally written before the Bill of Rights was added, namely that the best way to protect rights was through proper institutions. While the Bill of Rights went beyond that principle and even changed the terms of the debate, from the adoption of the Constitution to the Civil War the view that individual rights were constitutional rights, to be protected through proper employment of proper institutions, dominated American rights thinking, whether in terms of Acts of Congress as reflected in the Judiciary Act of 1789, U.S. Supreme Court decisions, or in the efforts of the Northern states to interpose state law to nullify the application of the federal fugitive slave laws within their boundaries on the eve of the Civil War.

In this respect, Hamilton and Madison's argument in *The Federalist* against a federal bill of rights had a life long beyond its rejection in the debate over the ratification of the 1787 constitution. Like most Federalist ideas, it was rapidly diffused among the states, especially, but not exclusively, the new ones. Ironically, from the Federalists' perspective, the states became the principal arena for the use of the executive and legislative institutions of government to secure rights.

Through legal and eleemosynary reforms, the law as an institution was reformulated to allow the free incorporation of private associations including private corporations and labor unions, transforming what was formerly considered a privilege into a right. This represented a radical change from common law and colonial practice where every significant association had to receive a special charter from the legislature in essence the granting of a liberty. Under the older view, all corporations were quasi-public and labor unions were considered combinations in restraint of liberty. Eleemosynary reforms, such as reforms in the care of the insane, the poor, and the aged, were also designed to secure rights in a positive way.

Legislatures, primarily in the states, did more for the protection of rights than courts. By midcentury, reformers were active in their states to achieve these reforms through legislation and even before that to expand the franchise to give all white males access to lawmaking and legislation to protect the helpless when voting was not enough. Later this protection of rights was embodied in antimonopoly legislation. Monopoly was defined not as total control of a market but as holding back resources from development. It was considered to be a violation of rights, as in the Charles River Bridge case, as attacked by both legislatures and courts, and was embodied in the antimonopoly provisions of early American state constitutions which were the first expressions of substantive due process in the United States. Federal involvement was principally confined to certain regulatory matters affecting interstate commerce.[13]

This period culminated in the adoption of the Thirteenth, Fourteenth, and Fifteenth Amendments to the U.S. Constitution which further clarified and concretized the constitutional basis of individual rights, what constituted individual rights within the body politic, and provided means for the enforcement of those rights.

Property as the Principal Right

It was then that *private property* was raised in status to become the principal institution for maintaining rights in the minds of many. In a sense this can be understood as the reification of property rights. "Property" should be understood as a bundle of powers and opportunities. The ability to own and control the use of property was always considered very important, at least as an auxiliary means or precaution, and was so recognized throughout the colonial and early national periods of American history. After the end of the Civil War generation, property rights were elevated to centrality in the definition of what were the primary individual rights, a position they were to hold almost indisputedly for a generation and then, although strongly disputed, were to remain the basis for constitutional law doctrines for yet another.[14]

Here, too, there were two dimensions. Property rights were defined to be the most important of all constitutional rights and the protection of those rights was defined as the principal means of protecting all individual rights. In many respects this was a product of the needs of an advancing capitalist system, made possible by the elimination of slavery from the property rights argument. In other words, the Southerners had raised the property rights argument in defense of slavery prior to the Civil War but, because so many Northerners opposed slavery, unrestricted support of property rights was unpalatable for them. After the war period, they could look at property rights without that burden.

The other point of emphasis was that of due process.[15] The subject of due process has a long history in the English-speaking world, at least back to Chief Justice Coke. As developed in the late nineteenth century United States, it was based on the idea of "taking"—the improper removal of the bundle of powers and opportunities that constituted property from some individual. Thus taxation, when duly enacted, could be considered constitutional, but if it was considered to be a "taking" it was subject to further tests. In those tests was some idea of productive use, although less than had been early nineteenth-century doctrine.

Substantive due process continues to survive today, in relation to property, equal protection, and privacy. With regard to property, the older form of substantive due process, it survives particularly in the states. With regard to equal protection, the United States Supreme Court has applied substantive due process to the criminal law to establish nationwide standards. Substantive due process in the field of privacy is connected with the postmodern conception of rights. Privacy is one of the new triad. It falls foursquare within the framework of substantive due process. In other words, privacy in certain matters cannot be abridged no matter how nominally proper the procedures used to abridge it might be. This is the argument of the pro-choice forces on the abortion issue.

Going hand in hand with the special status of property rights was the elevation of the right of contract to the same status, a further step away from the spirit of covenant in favor of a narrow self-interest-based contractual spirit in civil society.[16] The U.S. Supreme Court invoked the Fourteenth Amendment to extend "right of contract" protections into whole new areas. This shift had tremendous consequences for the American society and polity as a whole including, and in some respects especially, its covenantal dimension by pressing the covenantal idea into a contractual mold in an apparently official manner. It became necessary for Americans who wanted a different result, if they could not find a satisfactory way to express their pursuit of change through covenantal ideas, to turn to other ones, which they did, both intellectually and practically. Intellectually, they began to pursue the idea of the "Great Society," that is to say, utopian solutions that were both organic and hierarchical, that is, relied upon the organization of societies into "efficient" hierarchies to pursue goals that were considered integral or organic to humanity.

In essence, they were captured by a new "faith" that appeared, the faith in what came to be called "scientific management." This was a uniquely American faith and appeared among utopian reformers in the United States, among a people who had known only covenantal ways but who, after 200 years of experience with them had found them, like every other set of human institutions, less than perfect. So they sought perfection in an exactly opposite approach, assuming that hierarchy would be a better system; democratic hierarchy of course, not realizing that together the two were an oxymoron, a contradiction in terms.[17]

What Americans referred to as scientific management is old hat in the major European states, particularly Germany and France where hierarchical organization had predominated from the earliest times and from the seventeenth century onward had developed into modern bureaucratic systems based upon a civil service selected and promoted on the merit principle, and the effective concentration of the expanding state in their hands. For continental Europeans, the bureaucratic state was not a utopian movement of promise, but an expansion of already existing routines accepted by governors and governed alike because they were so in harmony with the root concept of their regimes.

The simultaneous transformation of American society from a simpler society of farms, villages and towns into one of large urban centers designed to support the new industrialization encouraged hierarchical thinking. The dominant covenantal model, which had been given expression in secular form, had suffered a further blow when Southern secessionists had drawn upon it in its expression as political compact to justify the legitimacy of their claims for secession. They did so on the grounds that the cstates were the truly organic societies in the United States and hence any state, as a more authentic organic society, could choose to sever the compactual relationship if its people felt the necessity to do so. Southern ideas had never been entirely persuasive to the North and were discredited by the Civil War.

Thus, the way was open for an entirely new form of self-definition for the American people. It was provided by the avant garde of the American intellectual classes. They were influenced by new ideas of management or by Marxism or simply by old fashioned European organic thought, especially if their other cherished goals seemed to be no longer advanced or at least not advanced well by the covenantal tradition.

At the time of the American Civil War, Abraham Lincoln understood the challenge being posed by the Southern effort to preempt the covenantal tradition. He launched a counterattack of his own and did indeed provide an alternative by returning to earlier ideas of covenant and associating them through the Declaration of Independence with the American people as a whole, not only with the states. He defined the Union as "a regular marriage" in the most covenantal illustration of all, emphasizing the American people as "an almost Chosen People" and a "nation under God," dedicated to "the Constitution, the Union, and the liberties of the people," and used his revival of covenantal theory for the ultimate institutional expression in the protection of human rights, the emancipation of the slaves.[18]

The Lincoln tradition remained alive in certain circles for at least a generation after the war,[19] and served as the basis for municipal reformers, "muckrakers" and progressives at the turn of the century, but its covenantal essence, while accepted, was lost. Its exponents saw that essence as connected with the effort to preserve an earlier America at a time when American society was changing rapidly in just about every respect, from its economic organization to its acceptance of millions of new immigrants most of whom knew nothing of the covenantal tradition and who in their search for an equal place in the American sun were to make their demands based upon other ideas of rights a generation later.

At the same time, when in the years before World Wars I and II, the post-Civil War redefinition of individual rights as property rights was challenged it was because of the social problems the application of that doctrine left in its wake for workers and farmers, for the urban middle classes and the poor, and for blacks. To meet their needs a new sense of individual rights as civil rights began to develop, drawing on the Civil War amendments.

A leader in this change was the United States Supreme Court. It began to limit state interference with the civil rights of blacks under the terms of the Civil War amendments and government interference with what are now known as First Amendment freedoms. By the end of that generation, the principle of civil rights was well established in jurisprudence and in the public mind, with strong organizations promoting and lobbying for specific civil rights measures.[20]

The Triumph of Civil Rights and the Shift to Human Rights

The idea of *individual rights as civil rights* triumphed in the 1950s and 1960s. Civil rights increasingly came to mean individual rights in the starkest sense, that is to say, the right of every individual to be free of most external constraints, certainly from all group constraints as distinct from governmental ones deemed absolutely necessary for the maintenance of law and order. Governments were forced to redefine and restrict their definition of what restraints were necessary to maintain law and order. The older idea that the fabric of society had to be kept intact, even if necessary, at the expense of individual liberties,virtually disappeared. After 1948 or thereabouts, maintaining the social fabric became distinctly secondary if not incidental in the face of individual rights challenges. Thus, as the idea of civil rights was winning its greatest victories, conceptually it was being replaced by a new idea gaining currency in the world, that of *human rights*.

The idea of human rights also had two dimensions. One was the elimination of external constraints on individual behavior in the spirit of natural liberty (whether intended to be or not) to the maximum possible extent, and second, to obligate governmental and public institutions to provide for the individual welfare to the maximum possible extent. In a sense this brought matters full circle. The question of rights was settled in favor of the individual human being without regard to race, gender, ideology, creed, and, increasingly, sexual orientation. On the other hand, the idea of obligations and liberties was revived but applied to governmental and public institutions which were defined as existing by virtue of their obligations to the individual and were occasionally granted liberties to protect themselves and society. That is where matters stand today.

Rights in Europe and the Old World[21]

The United States was the only civil society to be founded either without an earlier organic basis or on the basis of a more corporate covenantalism. Hence the American idea of rights remained in some respects unique throughout the modern epoch. All the other new societies acquired the British Whig rights tradition, English and Scottish; they continued to place their reliance on the kind of Whig conception that had prevailed in the American colonies-cum-states until the Civil War, relying on the institutions of government, most particularly legislatures, to protect rights on a collective basis rather than pursue individuals' rights protection through bills of rights and their interpretation by constitutional courts.

Few of the English-speaking countries even adopted bills of rights, continuing to rely upon legislatures for rights protections until the postmodern epoch when the American model began to interest them in connection with rights as in other respects. Canada and South Africa, for example, adopted bills of rights (in the case of the former, denominated a "Charter of Rights") only in the 1980s and 1990s, respectively. They introduced American-style enforcement of rights through judicial interpretation along with addition of the "new" rights of postmodernity.[22] In South Africa, a bill of rights including both actionable rights and rights that are more visionary in character was considered by the African National Congress an absolutely essential part of the post-apartheid regime and one was included in the new constitution in that spirit.[23]

On the European continent and those countries influenced by continental European modes, rights protection took a somewhat different turn. On one hand, the idea of individual rights protection had to be introduced into the political theory and practice of existing states that had to undergo the republican revolution and the elimination or at least the great reduction of old forms of privilege. In those states the gap between the governors and the governed was great, unlike the United States where the governed were also the governors almost from the first.

Inherent in the continental European conception of statehood was the idea that what were coming to be called inherent rights were essentially granted and not merely protected by states, an idea entirely foreign to modern rights theory which saw those rights as inherent in every individual. This meant that the modern epoch was given over to establishing the idea of individual rights as realities that were at least coequal with the reality of the state if not precedent to them in those continental European polities. Moreover, because of the demographic complexities of their populations at almost no time could those states entirely ignore the issue of group rights, a complication in its own right and one clearly out of style in the pursuit of rights during the modern epoch. Even the celebrated French Declaration of the Rights of Man became more exhortative than enforceable. Thus, in the last analysis, it was left to the United States of America to be the cutting edge in the development of the idea of enforceable inherent rights and individual rights along the lines of modern doctrine.

What could be said about the modern rights movement was that it was inevitably associated with modern constitutionalism. That is to say, where government, if not civil society as a whole, was redefined as the product of a political compact among citizens or between governors and governed, the idea of rights and their protection almost invariably came into play to enforce or reinforce the terms of the compact. The more this took place within the covenantal tradition, the more attention was paid to rights protection.[24]

If, however, the polities and societies in question followed the organic or hierarchical models, the results were not so clear. In the case of organic models, political compacts had to be grafted onto them without necessarily changing underlying conceptions of the organic state, conceptions whose strengthening was often pursued at the same time they were being (at least ostensibly) constitutionalized. Hence the new democratic republican dimensions derived from the covenantal tradition constantly found themselves struggling against very strong manifest or latent organic theories of society and limited thereby.

The matter was even worse where hierarchical models reigned. In them the tendency was for rights to be understood as "handed down" by the sovereign or the state rather than being recognized as inhering in individuals or even in the people in a more collective sense. Not surprisingly, with such an underlying view, the sovereign or the state usually took precedence in matters of rights enforcement, that is to say, raison d'etat—the needs and necessities of the state—could "trump," in Ronald Dworkin's language, individual rights in most if not all cases, hardly providing a sense of security to any form of rights protection.

The sum total of this was that in the modern epoch rights protection went hand in hand with the covenantal political tradition as translated into modern constitutionalism and existed as a living and contributing element of political life only to the extent that a covenantally derived constitutionalism existed. The connections between all of these elements were in some cases closer and more apparent and in some cases farther apart and less apparent, but the were always there.

The Postmodern Conception of Rights[30]

The postmodern conception of rights can be defined as two dimensional, including liberties and entitlements. People, simply by virtue of being living persons, are at liberty to do what they will, provided that what they do does not seriously infringe upon the rights of others to do the same. I emphasize "seriously." To take a relatively simple issue, in most Western countries divorce, which was once no more than tolerated out of necessity, if that, has now become a right. Everyone is now free to divorce as easily as is possible. Yet it cannot be said that divorce does not infringe upon the rights of others. It can be argued that the rights of children to be raised in a family environment are clearly damaged by divorce, but this is not deemed to be a serious enough infringement to limit the right of divorce.

The second dimension is that of entitlements. While individuals are free to do almost anything, civil society, usually through its institutions of government, is expected to guarantee them their basic needs and more, which have in essence become entitlements. The so-called "new rights," including the right to employment and to certain social benefits, are of this nature.

Accompanying this shift is the loss of the general consensus that there is an Author of Nature. Even though belief in God is still the predominant popular belief in the world, reaching extraordinary proportions in certain countries like the United States, the new image of God is one of a benign crutch who makes almost no demands other than a demand that we love one another. Since this God is no longer seen as the bestower or definer of rights and obligations or even as the Author of Nature from whose moral order rights and obligations flow, matters are much more fluid and the new understanding of rights as liberties and entitlement is easily fostered.

One good example of this is the shift from freedom of speech to freedom of expression as a right. Freedom of speech was developed as a political norm to help realize a free and just society. That is to say, it was concluded that in order for a free and just society to develop, individuals had to be free to express their opinions on public matters; ergo, freedom of speech became a norm. Freedom of expression, on the other hand, is a social norm that has no overt political dimensions. It is simply assumed that every individual has a right to express him or herself in any way that he or she deems fit (not only through speech). There are few restrictions and no public purposes required or necessarily involved.

To further sharpen and clarify the contrast between modern and postmodern conceptions of rights, it has been suggested that the principal modern rights—*life, liberty, property, and the pursuit of happiness*—were Aristotelian in nature, that is to say, they had some view of civil society as a comprehensive whole. The triad of postmodern rights—*welfare, expression,* and *privacy* as liberties and entitlements—are Epicurean in nature; they have to do with the individual, not with civil society. There is no social dimension necessarily involved in them. Indeed, the isolated individual takes precedence over any social dimension that might be introduced.

Individual and Group Rights[31]

On the other side of the coin there is an emergent balancing of individual and group rights. This is a result of the resurgence of what are often referred to as primordial groups in the postmodern world. The modern epoch was devoted almost singlemindedly to replacing primordial or premodern group ties with associational ties, or transforming the former into the latter; that is, eliminating *gemeinschaft* and replacing it with *gesellschaft*, in the words of Ferdinand Toennies.

Being associated with *gemeinschaft*, the primordial group was deemed by the cosmopolitans of society, those who formed the enlightened opinion that set its tone, to be hopelessly reactionary and primitive, to be rejected by all who saw them as selves enlightened. Suddenly, in the postmodern world, primordial groups have reasserted themselves and many people, led by many intellectuals, apparently feeling alienated and cut loose as individuals, have sought the comfort of such links (as long as they are not too demanding, of course, and do not interfere with the triad of postmodern liberties and entitlements). Thus both the United Nations Declaration of Rights and the even more avant-garde European Declaration of Rights simultaneously emphasize the new individual rights of welfare, expression, and privacy, and then try to balance them with some provision for group rights as well.

Once again, the United States is in the forefront of these new developments in rights definition and enforcement, but it has been joined by two new forces.[32] One is the United Nations which, because of the limitations on its authority, can hardly venture beyond the exhortative, but is slowly moving to try and do so. The first United Nations treaties on rights were covenants in the modern and postmodern sense, that is to say, moral pronouncements which states pledged to live up to but that had no "teeth" beyond that. The list of rights measures initiated by the U.N. or under its umbrella looks impressive, beginning with the Universal Declaration of Human Rights, but does there exist anyone in the world today that does not know the limits of those "covenants," "declarations," or what have you. Nevertheless, they offer the basis for partisans of rights to make their case and in some cases have served as a launching platform for further efforts such as the Conference on Security and Cooperation in Europe (CSCE) which, while in appearance similarly involve no more than an international treaty of primarily exhortative character, represent a major next step in the process of providing for universal rights enforcement. Indeed, the CSCE became a vehicle for bringing down the Communist bloc by backing the human rights claims for those inside as well as outside the bloc who opposed its totalitarian governments.[33]

The CSCE did so in no small measure because of the third leader in postmodern rights development, the European Community/Union. The European Community, now Union, was, like the United States, not merely an effort to re-form preexisting states but to establish a new governmental framework by compact (referred to as a network of treaties), one in which rights rapidly became inherent in the manner of modern constitutionalism but with a postmodern twist. The empowerment of the European Constitutional Court to exercise jurisdiction over rights matters in those spheres entrusted to the EC/EU and the pledge of all member states to accept its jurisdiction opened a new era in rights enforcement in Europe, one whose immediate impact was on the member countries but which extended to other European countries as well, in no small measure through the CSCE. The EC/EU Constitutional Court has, indeed, broken new ground in developing a postmodern doctrine of rights for the European situation with its complex of groups, preexisting states, and individual rights demands.[34]

Conclusion

In a sense, every conception of human rights must rest on the idea of a common humanity. Even as the idea of human rights differs from individual rights in that human rights steps outside of the law, it emphasizes the common humanity of humans in doing so. No doubt that is a contributing factor to the rise of international human rights concerns as a balance to economic globalization as the world economy becomes increasingly globalized, led by the great banking and financial interests and devoted to pusuing private profits. Economic freedom brings great benefits, but at times at great cost. The need for some countervailing power to the effects of economic globalization has been felt increasingly. In the same way that Tocqueville saw the spirit of religion walking hand in hand with the spirit of liberty in covenantal societies to moderate the deleterious or uncontrollable effects of liberty alone, so human rights is becoming a kind of "religious" parallel to accompany the global free market offering a moral stance to serve both as a moral compass and as a moral restraint. The fact that the human rights emphasis must be grounded in a moral base and must rely to a great extent on moral suasion both adds to and weakens its effectiveness. It certainly raises questions as to whether or not it is a continuation of the covenantal tradition on the global plane. Perhaps that is something we will only come to know better as we progress further into the era of globalization.

To recapitulate, the prevailing premodern conception was one of obligations and liberties. The modern conception began with individual rights in natural law, with nature the basis of universal order. Natural order in this sense includes obligations, but either does not link them with rights or gives rights precedence. The modern view was that natural rights were self-evident, but had to be discovered if they were to be transformed into political realities. Once discovered, they could then be extended by interpretation. In that system God was present as the justification. Distinction was made between human and other forms of life.

One of the characteristics of postmodern conceptions of rights is that all life is held sacred, indeed, we are moving to the point where for some all life is held to be equally sacred—the right to life of the snail darter is as important as the right to life of the starving Ethiopian child or an unemployed Appalachian family.

The moderns discovered that natural law alone is not enough. Rights that are universal by natural law serve nobody since they are unenforceable. Therefore they transformed the principles of natural right into positive law to overcome the difficulties of agreement as to their sources. Different people understood rights as derived from different sources. Some still sought a Divine source, others a source in nature with Divine sanction, and still others a source in a self-propelled nature.

Regardless of the differences of opinion as to source, it was possible in the real world to obtain agreement about what was desired in the way of rights in specific contexts or situations. Through consent, these agreements were embodied in positive law. Hence, consent became the critical dimension in transforming natural rights into enforceable measures. In a sense, the minimum consent necessary was consent to the Hobbesian covenants of peace which Hobbes proposed almost precisely in that spirit as the minimum around which all humans could rally as necessary for their survival.

It is important to note the relationship between rights and consent. Rights may be authoritative, but in practice they only have authority when accepted by the consent of the governed. Thus, consent is the bridge between abstract rights and concrete behavior in civil society.

Modern natural rights had three dimensions: rights as justice, rights as liberties, and rights as exceptions. The first has to do with the social order as a whole, how it becomes a just order and how individuals are treated justly within it; the second has more to do with individuals and what they are free or not free to do in civil society; while the third represents civil society's release of individuals from obligations. The postmodern idea of rights has added the idea of rights as entitlements as its contribution.

Contemporary theories of rights are results oriented. They are justified by the way they justify the cases they like. In other words, the theorists first pick the result that they want, then they find a theory that will justify those results. It is like shooting first and then drawing the target around the spot where the bullet hit. Among other things this has led to the revival of property rights in the form of entitlements, which represent a new property. The thrust of court cases in the United States and the European Community/Union is to secure entitlements from arbitrary withdrawal, recently including such items as driver's licenses which had previously been considered either a privilege granted or an objective measure of a skill.

The new doctrine of rights treats the moral autonomy of the individual as an absolute. Ronald Dworkin, a leading postmodern theorist of rights, puts it this way, that individual rights are trumps over the public good. This is the total reversal of the earlier understanding of rights as growing out of civil society as well as nature. Under such circumstances, civil society has very little standing.

The matter is carried further in that the effort to find the moral truth or the correct moral theory is replaced by relativism. Whatever the moral beliefs of the people happen to be will determine what rights the people have. Under such circumstances, constitutionalism itself is challenged. Under the original theory, constitutions, while they could be interpreted often with great liberality and flexibility, still had a veto over actions that went beyond a certain point, that is, that were unconstitutional. That, indeed, is the whole purpose of a constitution. Under the relativistic conditions of the postmodern understanding of rights, the most that a constitution will have is a vote. This eliminates the whole purpose of constitutionalism and opens up unlimited possibilities for a relativistic system of rights and actions.

If we were to summarize the relation between rights, constitutionalism, and the covenantal tradition, we would say that at first, at the beginning of the modern epoch, rights became the modern constitutional replacement for obligations and liberties and as such reinforced modern constitutionalism. Then, at the beginning of the twentieth century, rights embodied in constitutions began to replace other constitutional provisions in the hierarchy of importance. In our generation, rights have come to undermine those other sections in opposition to the covenantal dimension of constitutionalism which sees political communities and societies as a whole and relations between their parts as requiring balance so that the fundamental covenantal principles of federal obligation and liberty are maintained. That is where we stand today.

Notes

1. Jacob Leib Talmon, *The Origins of Totalitarian Democracy* (New York: Norton Publishers, 1970); Sigmund Neumann, *Permanent Revolution: Totalitarianism in the Age of International Civil War*, Second Edition, (London: Pall Mall Publishers, 1965); Hannah Arendt, *The Origins of Totalitarianism* (Cleveland, Ohio: World Publishing Co., 1964).
2. Donald Lutz, *The Origins of American Constitutionalism* (Baton Rouge: Louisiana State University Press, 1988) and *Popular Consent and Popular Control: Whig Political Theory in the Early State Constitutions* (Baton Rouge: Louisiana State University Press, 1980).
3. Robert Goldwin, *Why Blacks, Women and Jews are not Mentioned in the Constitution, and Other Unorthox Views*, (Washington, D.C.: AEI Press, 1990).
4. Robert A. Goldwin, *From Parchment to Power: How James Madison Used the Bill of Rights to Save the Constitution* (Washington, D.C.: AEI Press, 1997).
5. Simon Schama, *Citizens: A Chronicle of the French Revolution* (London: Penguin, 1989).
6. Leo Strauss, *Natural Right and History* (Chicago: University of Chicago Press, 1953); Thomas Pangle, *The Spirit of Modern Republicanism: The Moral Vision of the American Founders and the Philosophy of Locke* (Chicago: University of Chicago Press, 1988).
7. Daniel J. Elazar. *Covenant and Polity in Biblical Israel: Biblical Foundations and Jewish Expressions* (New Brunswick, N.J.: Transaction Publishers, 1995); Haim Cohen, *Human Rights in Jewish Law* (New York: KTAV, 1984).
8. John H. Hallowell, *Main Currents in Modern Political Thought* (New York: Holt, Rinehart and Winston, 1965); H. O. Taylor, *The Mediaeval Mind* (New York: Macmillan, 1925), R. W. and A. J. Carlyle, *A History of Mediaeval Political Theory in the West* (London: W. Blackwood and Sons, 1950).
9. John Witte, "The Essential Rights and Liberties of Religion in the American Constitutional Experiment," *Notre Dame Law Review*, vol. 71, no. 3 (1996), p. 46; John Witte, "Blest Be the Ties that Bind: Covenant and Community in Puritan Thought," *Emory Law Journal*, vol. 36, (1987): 579–601.
10. Edward Samuel Corwin, *The "Higher Law" Background of American Constitutional Law* (Ithaca, N.Y.: Cornell University Press, 1971); Carl Becker, *The Declaration of Independence: A Study in the History of Political Ideas* (New York: Alfred A. Knopf, 1953).
11. Daniel J. Elazar, ed., *Rights in America's Constitutional Traditions*, special issue of *Publius*, vol. 22, no. 2; Robert Licht, ed., *The Framers and Fundamental Rights* (Washington, D.C.: American Enterprise Institute Press, 1991).

12. J. David Greenstone, "Lincoln's Political Humanitarianism: Moral Reform and the Covenant Tradition in American Politcal Culture," in *Covenant in the Nineteenth Century*, Daniel J. Elazar, ed. (Lanham, Md.: Rowman and Littlefield, 1994), pp. 151–52.

13. Stanley Kutler, *Privilege and Creative Destruction: The Charles River Bridge Case* (Philadelphia, Pa.: Lippincott, 1971).

14. Bruce Ackerman, *Private Property and the Constitution*, (New Haven, Conn.: Yale University Press, 1977); Edward Corwin, *Liberty Against Government*, (Baton Rouge: Louisiana State University Press, 1948); Richard A. Epstein, *Takings: Private Property and the Power of Eminent Domain* (Cambridge, Mass.: Harvard University Press, 1985).

15. Raoul Berger, *Government by Judiciary: The Transformation of the Fourteenth Amendment*, (Cambridge, Mass.: Harvard University Press, 1977); Raoul Berger, *The Fourteenth Amendment and the Bill of Rights* (Norman: University of Oklahoma Press, 1989); Lawrence M. Friedman, *History of American Law* (New York: Simon and Schuster, 1973).

16. Samuel Krislov, "Property as a Constitutional Right in the Nineteenth Century: Or What Have We Learned Since Corwin?" *Publius*, vol. 22, no. 2, pp. 47–67; Edwin Corwin, *Liberty Agains Government*; Charles W. McCurdy, "Justice Field and the Jurisprudence of Government-Business Relations: Some Parameters of Laissez-Faire Constitutionalism, 1863–1897, *Journal of American History*, 61, (March 1975); Willard Hurst, *Law and Economic Growth* (Madison: University of Wisconsin Press, 1984).

17. Vincent Ostrom, *The Intellectual Crisis in American Public Administration*, second edition (Tuscaloosa: University of Alabama Press, 1989).

18. Garry Wills, *Certain Trumpets: The Call of Leaders* (New York: Simon and Schuster, 1994).

19. Greenstone, "Lincoln's Political Humanitarianism," pp. 159–60.

20. G. Alan Tarr, "Constitutional Theories and Constitutional Rights: Federalist Considerations," *Publius*, vol. 22, no. 2, pp. 93–108; Laurence Tribe, *American Constitutional Law*, second edition (Mineola, NY: Foundation Press, 1988); Ronald Dworkin, *A Matter of Principle* (Cambridge, Mass.: Harvard University Press, 1985); Ronald Dworkin, *Law's Empire* (Cambridge, Mass.: Belknap Press, 1986); Ronald Dworkin, *Taking Rights Seriously* (Cambridge, Mass.: Harvard University Press, 1977).

21. Albert Blaustein, "Human Rights in the World's Constitutions" in *Progress in the Spirit of Human Rights*, Felix Ermacora, ed. (Arlington, Va.: Engel, 1988); Albert Blaustein, Roger S. Clark, and Jay A. Sigler, *Human Rights Sourcebook* (New York: Paragon House, 1987).

22. Irwin Cotler, "Can The Center Hold?: Federalism and Rights in Canada," in *Federalism and Rights*, Ellis Katz and G. Alan Tarr, eds. (Lanham, Md.: Rowman and Littlefield Publishers, 1996); Tarnopolsky and Beaudoin, eds., *The Canadian Charter of Rights and Freedoms: Commentary, 1989. PUBLISHER????*

23. Robert Licht, ed., *South Africa's Crisis of Constitutional Demcracy: Can the U.S. Constitution Help?* (Washington, D.C.: AEI Press, 1994).

24. John Witte, "The Essential Rights and Liberties of Religion in the American Constitutional Experiment."

25. G. Alan Tarr, "Constitutional Theories and Constitutional Rights: Federalist Considerations," *Publius*, vol. 22, no. 2, pp. 93–108.

26. Albert Blaustein, *Civil Rights and the Black American: A Documentary History* (New York: Simon and Schuster, 1970); Ian Shapiro and Will Kymlicka, eds.,

Ethnicity and Group Rights (New York: New York University Press, 1997); Natan Lerner, "From Protection of Minorities to Group Rights," *Israel Yearbook on Human Rights*, vol. 18, 1988, pp. 101–20; Natan Lerner, *Group Rights and Discrimination in International Law* (Boston: M. Nijhoff, 1991); Louis Henkin, *The Age of Rights* (New York: Columbia University Press, 1990); Louis Henkin, *The Rights of Man Today* (New York: Center for the Study of Human Rights, Columbia University, 1988).

27. The primary declarations and covenants of human rights for the United Nations are: The Universal Declaration of Human Rights, International Covenant on Civil and Political Rights, International Convention of the Elimination of All Forms of Racial Discrimination, Convention Against Torture and Other Cruel, Inhuman or Degrading Treatment or Punishment.

28. Clive Archer, *International Organizations*, second edition (London: Routledge, 1992); Peter Wallersteen, "Representing the World: A Security Council for the 21st Century," in *The Politics of Global Governance: International Organizations in an Interdependent World*, Paul F. Diehl, ed. (Boulder, Colo.: Lynne Rienner Publishers, 1997), pp. 103–15; Marshall Russell, "Comprehensive Security" in *International Conflict Resolution*, Ramesh Thakur, ed. (Boulder, Colo.: Westview, 1988).

29. Ellis Katz and G. Alan Tarr, eds., *Federalism and Rights*.

Part IV

Present and Future

13

The Decline and Possible Revival
of Covenant in Our Times

Students of the covenant idea and its manifestations are confronted with a great modern paradox, one which has become even more pronounced in the postmodern epoch which began after World War II. As constitutionalism has spread, covenantalism seems to have retreated. This is not merely a matter of substituting concrete points of reference for more abstract ones. It is a matter of the transformation of the worldview that informs humanity, or at least its dominant expressions. The spread of constitutionalism involved not only the adoption of the idea and its forms and practice but the way in which constitutions were designed, the seriousness with which they were treated by governors and governed alike, and the involvement of the latter in the processes of constitutional design. In all of these ways the modern spread of constitutionalism was notable and continues into the postmodern epoch.

Throughout these four volumes we have looked at covenant as a theo-political idea, covenant as the foundation of society, covenant as a method of political and cultural organization, and covenant as a mechanism for shaping institutions and behavior. While we have not always distinguished between the five in specific usage, the distinction should have been apparent to the reader. However in attempting to assess the state of the covenant tradition today, it is useful to be more explicit.

Covenant is most fully expressed as a theo-political idea, resting on a belief in God and in a firm moral order derived from that belief. The human covenants with God not only establish that moral order, but provide for human liberty in the form of federal liberty, that is, the liberty to live up to the terms of the covenant. In this framework, all of the better part of life is organized through covenants subsidiary to the great covenant with God and life within this framework stimulates the development of a covenantal culture, both general and political, and the behavior appropriate to it.

Where covenant lacks the full theo-political dimension but serves as the foundation of society, society is organized through a covenant or covenants which, while lacking an intense belief in God, are often derivative from covenant as a theo-political idea once removed. By organizing society through covenant they too rest on federal liberty and lead to a covenantal culture and behavior. Covenant may not be the formal foundation of society, but it may be used as a method of politcal and social organization. In other words, life can be organized through covenants, as a methodology rather than a belief system with the resulting covenantal culture and behavior. In the case of both two and three, while overt expression of covenant as a theo-poitical idea is absent, both implicitly rely upon a moral base which provides the grounding necessary for maintaining the covenant and covenantal relationships and legitimates the trust required to enable covenantal relationships to exist. Finally, covenant can be used as a mechanism detached from its ideas and obligations. When covenantal arrangements have been reduced to mechanisms they offer much less to the people who use them. Often they degenerate to window dressing. Covenant as a mechanism involves the organization of institutions through derivatives of covenant several times removed, in vogue at the time. In late modern and early-postmodern times, derivatives of covenant often have been used as mechanisms for the formal organization of political and other institutions. In many cases, constitutionalism has been transformed from being a covenantally linked foundational idea of society to being a mechanism quite separated from its earlier covenantal linkage. The connection may be traceable historicaally but is not normally in the minds of those who use the mechanism.

All of this may be traced back to the covenantal roots of modern constitutionalism but the impact of those roots themselves has undergone and continues to undergo great changes. For one thing, fewer people take seriously their religious roots and certainly the belief in a transcendent divinity that gives those religious roots meaning. As these religious roots diminished, the moral foundations of covenantalism were also undermined. Many believe that there is a direct connection between the two, but even if we only note the correlation, it is important to ponder.

The traditional morality long associated with the covenant tradition has been under direct and major assault throughout the twentieth century and in some respects even earlier. Part of that assault was an assault on the very idea that there is truth in an absolute and not simply in a relative sense and that it is at least partially knowable by dint of human effort. Nothing is more devastating than the relativistic assault on the very existence of truth that has been a major feature of the twentieth century. If truth is only in the eyes of the beholder, then "anything goes" as long as someone sees it as "true." Moreover, everyone's concept of truth has to be equally respected because "who is to judge" what is true and what is not.

Under those circumstances, all we have are those conventions agreed upon by the majority that are valid only because they are agreed-upon conventions. Here, however, is a "catch." Those agreed-upon conventions, however they are seen as relative, are also seen as embodying a relativism that is itself absolute. In other words, there are no absolutes except relativism and there are no truths except the one that sees truth only in the eye of the beholder, and that, consequently, no one's behavior or ideas can effectively be challenged. Thus paradoxically we get back to a kind of absolute that, however humanistic it may be in the short term, can only be destructive in the long run. This is the exact reverse of covenantalism, although it lends itself to strengthening the rights of constitutionalism in a certain way, thus bringing about a growing separation between the two.

A question that must be posed in any inquiry into the covenant idea as a seminal idea in politics is how was it lost to view in the interval between the completion of the American Revolution and our time. The answer to that lies in the Western world's intellectual pacesetters' abandonment of covenantal and its secularized compactual thinking in the mid-nineteenth century followed by their shift to by organic and biological theories and analogies derived first from romantic and then from Darwinian ideas. That transformation was worldwide but the American experience in that respect is particularly important since it was in the United States that covenant ideas reigned most powerfully in the first half of the modern epoch.

In its most overt and direct sense, the covenant idea reached the point of its greatest influence in the first two or three generations of English, Dutch, Scottish, and French Huguenot settlement in British North America a century after it had peaked in sixteenth century Reformation Europe. The covenantal tradition had already passed its peak by the end of the historical seventeenth century (roughly 1713).[1] After that, it was challenged and partially replaced by theories of political compact closely related to it, as part of the process of secularization and "enlightenment" then occurring in the modern world, including the American colonies.[2] Nevertheless, throughout the eighteenth century the two ideas of covenant and compact lived side by side, were often closely intertwined, and both permeated the mindsets of the leading figures of that century. Together they were unchallenged as the intellectual sources of the American Revolution and the federal and state constitutions.[3]

In continental Europe, in the meantime, the eighteenth-entury Enlightenment dealt a devastating blow to covenant theory by attacking the Bible as the source of authority or even a source of right information. Those who led that attack were primarily French, champions of the Enlightenment who sought greater secularization in any case. But there were echoes of the same attack in the British Isles and even in British North America.

It would be too easy to label the attack as merely a product of the new liberalism since for the previous two centuries those arguing for more republicanism and less hierarchy in political society for the most part rested their arguments on Scripture (albeit with disputed degrees of sincerity). But the more secular compact theorists of the seventeenth century opened the door for more secular arguments on behalf of the complex of ideas and attitudes

and modes of behavior that became modernism. While in politics scriptural
justification could remain on the side of republicanism, in the social and to
some extent in the scientific realm new, very unreligious demands were put
forward. The latter won adherents, especially intellectual adherents, who, in
turn, constructed a more or less comprehensive worldview resting on a renun-
ciation if not denunciation of the Bible. By the latter part of the eighteenth
century, in the age of revolutions, they at least had coequal status with more
traditional forces and by the end of the century or early in the nineteenth they
became the dominant ones.

Needless to say, covenantal ideas were among the casualties of this assault
on Scripture. Although at first the adherents of the enlightenment were content with a philosophy of political compact as what might be called a halfway
station, subsequently, they moved toward the idea of the social contract which
went even further in the direction of secularization. Then, early in the next
century, they jettisoned the entire covenantal-compactual structure.

The Jacobin Challenge and Its Successors

As the eighteenth century turned into the nineteenth and the nineteenth
century progressed, covenant ideas, even, or perhaps especially, in their federalist form, were challenged by a series of utterly opposed ideologies. The
first was Jacobinism. The French Revolution began in 1789, in the same year
as the United States government was inaugurated under the federal Constitution. Its emphasis on the general will, while leading to Jacobin and subsequent tyrannies in France culminating in Bonapartism, did not keep Jacobin
democracy from becoming the darling idea of European intellectuals. Moreover, it was a very useful idea for both established and new European elites
seeking to hold onto or consolidate their power through the—now ostensibly
liberal democratic—state. Even many Americans were attracted to the French
Revolution and its ideas in the 1790s, including Thomas Jefferson. In a sense,
their responses were a prevision of what happened a century and more later,
in the 1920s and the 1930s, after the Russian Revolution, when even people
who were not Communists sympathized with what they then accepted at face
value as a progressive step in the unfolding history of liberty.

The harsh conservative reaction to Jacobinism also did little to strengthen
covenantal thinking. In the United States, the Federalist Party became increasingly an upper-class sectional party in response to their fear of Jacobin
ideas penetrating the new Democratic-Republic Party. The remaining Federalists moved as close to becoming Tories as was possible in postrevolutionary
America, and as a result, became extinct on the very anti-Tory American political scene. In Europe, the conservative parties were invariably supporters of
the ancien regime and sought its restoration. For most of the nineteenth century, only in Great Britain did this mean a conservatism that could be progres-

sive on specific issues (later Bismarck's Germany under the leadership of the Iron Chancellor developed a similar stance), so there was no expectation of finding covenantal ideas among them. What the conservatives did do was to develop their own synthesis of organic and hierarchical models designed to serve their ideologies and interests.

The slavery controversy generated another brand of conservative reaction which challenged the fundamental assumptions of American covenantalism, mainly that all men were created equal, replacing them with racist doctrines. David Greenstone has examined the beginnings of that challenge. In the Adams-Jefferson correspondence, the two men offer us a picture of turn-of-the-century thought on the subject.[4] Thomas Jefferson, representing the secularized compact ideology of the Enlightenment, exchanged ideas with John Adams, the eighteenth-century Unitarian heir of the Puritan covenantal tradition. Jefferson undermines the idea of covenant in his thinking by failing to respond to it while Adams develops a new "modern" synthesis which is manifested in his response to the slavery question.

Beyond that, the intellectual defenders of slavery also were influenced by the new nineteenth-century ideas of the organic state. Hence their argument, which was best articulated by John C. Calhoun, that the true polities of the United States were the states, which represented organic societies, rather than the United States, which was merely an artifact, the product of a compact among those organic states. This theory served them in two ways. In the first place, it explained the differences between whites and blacks, plantation owners, white free men, and slaves as the result of organic development, hence, natural and right, and it justified the Southern states in their growing willingness to secede from the Union on the grounds that the original federal compact had been violated.[5]

Radical antislavery forces responded by viewing the Constitution as what William Lloyd Garrison termed a "covenant with hell" because it allowed slavery to continue.[6] Still, many abolitionists rested their case on the covenantal character of the American people and the polity. Abraham Lincoln was to apply the force of arms to impose his understanding of the American union based on political covenant as against the Southern compact theory.[7]

The Civil War discredited the Southern compact theory even though its proponents argued, as did Alexander Stevens, former vice president of the Confederacy, that force of arms may have decided the issue in the field but could not change the validity of the idea. Meanwhile in the postwar generation, the idea of contract as the central principle of social order was shifted from the public to the private sphere.

Abraham Lincoln was the last great exponent of American covenantalism in the nineteenth century, presenting the Declaration of Independence as a covenant precisely in order to counteract the Southern compact theory *and* the Northern abolitionist view that the Constitution was, in effect, a pact with the devil. After the Civil War, however, Lincoln's views ceased to be intellectually modish. They continued to exist and to influence a postwar generation of reformers, but more as a call for activism than as an intellectual system.

While the direct consequences of sympathies for the French Revolution on American federal democracy were minimal—Jefferson, after all remained both a federalist and a republican (his words), faithful to the U.S. Constitution and the theory behind it—Jacobinism had strong repercussions in Eurasia, including Eastern Europe and the Russian Empire, and in Latin America at the time, especially in areas of revolutionary state building. They were to have later repercussions in American society after the European revolutions of 1848 led to an influx of continental European intellectuals into the United States and into positions of influence in American letters and institutions of higher education. Those intellectuals, including the first professor of political science in the United States, Francis Lieber, a distinguished German refugee, had been educated on organic theories of the state which fit in well with Darwinism, a theory that burst upon the world scene a decade later.

Lieber, appointed the first professor of political economy at Columbia University, soon became the center of a group of New York intellectuals and the guiding influence on the *Nation*, the journal founded by that group in 1865 in the closing months of the Civil War, to articulate a new philosophy and ideology of union. He was a Hegelian by training and a Jacobin by political instinct, synthesizing both in a theory of the organic state which became the guiding intellectual light for many American intellectuals. He and his associates challenged the ideas of the political compact and the checks and balances of American constitutionalism on both philosophic and ideological grounds.[8]

The Civil War opened people in the North to the ideas of Leiber and his group. A generation later, their students came to dominate American intellectual life. In the end, it was Woodrow Wilson, a southern Presbyterian and son of a Presbyterian minister, who lived through the war as a child in Virginia, who, as a political scientist educated according to the new doctrines, did more to undermine the principles of federal democracy than any other single person in the United States, even though he continued to use covenantal terminology in his public political rhetoric.[9]

Meanwhile in the Western world in those years between the American Civil War and World War I, Darwin's ideas were transformed into Social Darwinism, the idea that survival of the fittest was nature's way and that the human race progressed best by allowing nature to take its course. Connected with that harsh social theory were new theories of racial superiority and inferiority which soon became simple, even vulgar racism according to which the Northwest Europeans of Anglo-Saxon and Germanic-Teutonic stock were racially superior to all others by virtue of their evolution or whatever.

The combination of Social Darwinism, an ideology which had its roots in a vulgar application of Darwin's theories, Anglophilism, admiration for German order and bureaucracy, and the growing racism of Northwestern Europeans, including those who had settled in the United States, left very little, if any, room for covenantal systems.[10] Indeed, it may be to the great credit of the covenant idea that it could not survive as a dominant one in a racist society looking for justifications for the maintenance of white rule.

Under the new conservatism, the United States as a whole was increasingly understood by many to be an organic society. Hence the emerging class and caste structure was natural and right in their eyes and was not to be artificially tampered with by government action. Moreover, that structure was to be preserved through a new and far-reaching interpretation of the freedom of contract and substantive due process which were presented as growing out of the original constitutional principles of the United States but were used as what can fairly be termed as class weapons wherever possible. This was reflected in the behavior of the U.S. Supreme Court in the late nineteenth century. The justices elevated contracts to a level of near sanctity and replaced the covenantal principles of cooperation and shared sovereignty with the theory of dual federalism involving separate and distinct state and federal sovereignties.[11]

It is a credit to the deep rootedness and enduring persistence of federal principles that despite the apparent triumph of these new doctrines, in fact, covenantal ideas retained continued popular support, and, through the Populist and Progressive movements managed to have very substantial influence in shaping public policy even in those years. Thus Lincoln Steffens and Ida Tarbell sought to reform American cities, not to transfer their powers elsewhere. John Peter Altgeld served as governor of Illinois in the same spirit, opposing federal intervention which he saw as serving plutocratic interests and mobilizing the power of his state on behalf of the people. Jane Addams built Hull House in an effort to reestablish neighborhood community.

Progressivism, at least in its western wing, actually was an attempt to revive covenantal thinking as a tool for reform. While most eastern Progressives were intent on developing a new nationalism based upon organic models, the midwestern and western Progressives were harking back to Puritan models of the covenanted community and covenanted commonwealth.[12] This is not the place to go into a full-blown exposition of their thinking and why they did not succeed. The direction of their thought has been presented in chapter 10 of *Covenant and Constitutionalism*.[13] Their failure in part has to do with not being at the cutting edge of American civil society, as reflected in their continued allegiance to a Republican Party growing more conservative all the time and their detachment, by virtue of both culture and location, from the urban frontier and its strong ethnic base, out of which the new issues of the twentieth century were emerging and who were providing the support needed for the Democratic Party to confront those issues in a way congenial to the urban ethnics.[14] Another reason was the crisis over Jim Crow segregation in the South which split Southern Populism and Progressivism on the race issue.[15]

The twentieth century brought a further weakening of covenantalism as the world seemed to move toward hierarchy more generally, inspired by a feeling among those considered progressive that the only way to overcome the problems of an advanced industrial age was to mobilize large public institutions, organized hierarchically, to curb the appetites of large private ones. The state or, in covenantal polities, government, was primary among those public institutions in the eyes of these people. Those expanded public bodies were constructed as large bureaucracies dedicated to scientific management of problems of all kinds.

These ideas also overlapped into the religious sphere. In the United States, for example, as ecumenicism began to spread, many of its leaders came from among the Reformed Protestant denominations who saw the old congregational spirit of Reformed Protestantism as a barrier toward ecumenical religious unity. Mergers among churches brought about the establishment of new forms of hierarchy where none or only weak ones had existed earlier. Efforts on the part of more conservative members of these churches to fight back usually ended in failure. Often the congregational ideal was upheld but the hierarchical institutions were allowed or favored in the spirit of modern business organization.[16]

It was not until many years later that these hierarchical and managerial directions were challenged. After the national traumas of the 1960s and early 1970s, Americans turned, at first reluctantly and then with greater enthusiasm, to bicentennial celebrations, first of their national covenant, the Declaration of Independence, and then of its great product, the Constitution of 1787. In some quarters, at least, Lincoln's understanding of the covenantal character of the Declaration of Independence resurfaced and, where covenant itself was not explicitly highlighted, the compactual character of federal democracy was.

The rise of more activist and interventionist government in Europe stimulated hierarchical organization and thinking there, even more than in the United States because so much of Europe was already oriented in that direction. These tendencies were further exacerbated by the rise of twentieth-century totalitarianism. Fascism, Nazism, and Bolshevism all shared a strongly hierarchical and anticovenantal outlook and were far more overt in making it into an ideology and a set of right principles actively opposing noncentralized and nonhierarchical elements.

In Europe the latter came under increasing assault. In country after country as the cooperative movement matured, it either collapsed or was bureaucratized and managerialized so that it became indistinguishable from other institutions. At the same time, new social fluidity within countries disrupted traditional social and political relationships, making consociationalism difficult to maintain in the public sphere and increasingly less relevant to the people involved. Federalism was engaged in a continuing struggle against pyramidization in the face of these hierarchical trends and was accepted where it was as a necessity rather than a desideratum. More often than not, federalism was rejected in the face of statism and transformed into management-oriented intergovernmental relations to the extent possible.

The Fracturing of Covenant Morality

As manifest covenantalism declined or was jettisoned for other systems of thought, covenantal morality persisted in the United States and in other countries bearing the covenant tradition throughout the nineteenth century. The coming of the twentieth century brought with it such massive technological change that it began to subvert that morality as well. For example, as long as people lived in face-to-face communities, social sanctions served to uphold at least the public commitment to certain moral standards and often much private behavior as well since there was literally little room for secret violations of public standards. As cities began to grow in size and more people began to migrate frequently from place to place, the anonymity in their lives increased along with greater separation from friends, family, and neighbors, so that it became easier to find private space where people could pursue their appetites without punishment unless they were caught. Morality began to separate into what was necessarily tolerated private behavior and what were public standards through which the older morality was maintained.

In the twentieth century matters moved along another step. The coming of the automobile increased mobility and the ability to secure privacy for certain activities—sexual, for example—that previously had been more problematic. These brought about further subversion of accepted social mores and, while they did not have a direct political impact, to the extent that they undermined the social underpinnings of civil society, they had indirect political influence.

More important was the emergence of easily spread mass culture. Such devices as the phonograph, motion pictures, and radio served to spread mass culture in ways undreamed of before the twentieth century. Moreover, the first two were strictly commercial ventures (the last was commercial in the United States and in some other countries but was governmental in a majority). Hence they were governed by the rules of commerce, that is, they were privately owned and profit oriented. The subsequent addition of television followed by the cybernetic revolution, the development of the personal computer, and the spread of the Internet worldwide introduced an additional logarithmic expansion of media impacts.

Thus the mass media from the first were dedicated primarily to making money for their owners which meant that the larger the audience, the more money they could make. This, in turn, meant the lower their standard, the greater the sensation, and the more vulgar the display, the larger the audience.

This is a rule of thumb that does not derive from mass culture nor even from the famed "Gresham's Law," but goes back to the earliest days of the human race. It has been proved over and over again in this century, compounded as new media have been developed to spread and profit from mass culture and more money has become available to even wider circles, that mass media are less discriminating, less subject to social influences, and less responsive to public or private consequences, than any previously known influence, especially among the young at their most vulnerable, in their teenage years.

By the end of the century, the old order had been turned on its head. Parents followed the lead of their children rather than vice versa, youth rather than age became the valued norm, daring rather than experience the more respected, and relativism replaced the idea that there even was such a thing as truth. "Who is to judge?" became the only "truth" that attained widespread acceptance. Needless to say, all of this undermined the very underpinnings of every covenantal system.

Manifestly, then, there has been a decline in at least the moral dimension of covenant in the postmodern epoch. That is to say, the sense of political and social solidarity in entire countries, political communities, or civil societies derived from the sense of common agreement about fundamentals has been fractured. The search for the fundaments of a common way of life and consent to common arrangements that are more than arrangements of convenience to preserve life but are arrangements for preserving a certain kind of better life, seem to have diminished throughout the world, most particularly in the West and most particularly in those political communities once deemed to be covenantal or the most covenantal. It is in those communities that the decline is not only accelerated but is also most felt since it was in those communities that the moral and political expectations derived from covenant were most visible and pronounced. It seems as if the methods and processes of the covenantal tradition, that is to say, individual choice and collective action only by agreement, have been retained while the ideas that those methods and processes were to foster and which, reciprocally, hold matters in check, have been jettisoned.

In place of agreement to a common way of life has come a sense of "anything goes" as long as it is perceived not to harm others too much. The result is a kind of atomistic individualism, not like the individualism of modernity which was grounded on a common base and where neighborliness was a part of the political-social order and served as a restraining force on excessive individualism in most cases. The new individualism is an individualism of strangers without neighbors so that there can be no neighborliness. Instead, there are pseudo-neighbors held together by common attending to the same mass media and mass culture that, at their best, do give people a feeling of being part of a common community but a community that in fact has no characteristics of communality beyond shared sensations.

Whether watching a presidential funeral, a Super Bowl, or a catastrophe in some part of the world, the spectators may feel bound together by the sensations of watching the experience, but those sensations are totally detached from the pleasure or pain to being part of the experience, the obligation to help in its resolution, or to suffer its consequences. At the same time, those potential experiences close to home—around the corner, as it were—that can be comprehensive and in which individuals can be influential but are not covered by the mass media or incorporated into mass culture become less well known than these massive sensations that may be thousands of miles away but are so covered. Intimacy becomes pseudo-intimacy; one feels that one is there but one has no commitment to the consequences of that feeling.

It is not surprising, then, that more immediate interpersonal relations acquire many of the same characteristics. Sexual relations, once tied to covenantal acts of various kinds, whether the marriage covenant between the sexual partners or other kinds of covenants between the families to which the partners belonged become in the words of one best-selling author advocating the new arrangements, "zipless," that is to say, entirely impersonal, in which nobody has to bear any consequences.

Political campaigns become matters evoking other sensations, sports contests of a kind in which the parties to them score points and the only perceived consequences are not for the spectators, although in fact the latter suffer from the results of such elections, but affect the players who are doubly penalized for every perceived misstep or every act so defined, that is, displaying emotions that are "hot" and not "cool" or taking matters too seriously or violating some norm of perfection that is in itself an inhuman demand. Moreover, those who go into the arena must expect to lose all privacy on the ostensibly "good reason" that everything they do tells us something about their character while the real reason is that they become celebrities and therefore the media can capitalize on everything that they do, especially if it has a salacious or seemingly corrupt dimension.

Life becomes a series of "shows," one day sports, one day political, one day cultural, each in its "pop" form. What was once covenantal egalitarianism becomes the equal opportunity of "everybody" to fifteen minutes of celebrity if they play their cards right. All of this appears enjoyable to the spectators and offers the promise of being lucrative to the "celebrities," which makes them willing to go through the pain of such exposure. Moreover, both groups feel that they are free, unbound by earlier conventions or the limiting ties of obligation and community. But this is not federal liberty, it is natural liberty in its most raw form, a natural liberty that works if you can get away with it but which punishes by death if you cannot, as those celebrities who have embraced its most extreme expression, substance abuse, particularly taking drugs, have more often than not found out in terrible ways. While much of this is social and not primarily political, its consequences shape political life no less.

While this new sensationalism may satisfy the vast majority of the world's population, those deviants who do not have the psychological capacity to restrain themselves from truly violent behavior against their fellows, essentially have been released from prior moral, social, and cultural restraints on their engaging in violent behavior. Even if they remain a tiny percentage of the total population, in a world with over five billion people, they constitute a very large absolute number. As living human beings, their rights are protected to the nth degree. As members of this generation they have not been socialized into proper restraints. Having neither internal or external restraints, they are prone to commit the most violent acts that randomly affect those who accidentally cross their paths, thus leading to massive crime waves and radical diminution of safety and security, especially in those societies that are considered and consider themselves the "freest."

So, just as in the seventeenth century it was understood that humans originated in a state of nature and, recognizing the failure of living by natural liberty, covenanted together to introduce civil society and federal liberty, today, at the end of the twentieth, we have seen how the implicit redefinition of liberty as natural liberty and the rejection of federal liberty leads humans back into the state of nature with all the consequences thereof in terms of random violence (the biblical *hamas*—for the Bible, the source of human catastrophe) and the Hobbesian war of all against all. As Hobbes so well understood, when humans abandon their covenants of civilization, they return to the jungle where life is "nasty, brutish...and short."

The postmodern breakdown of the political-social structure of modernity has led to a new crisis in politics in at least three ways: One, in the relations between governors and governed; two, in the relationship among the parts of established political systems; and three, in the relationship among states in the international arena. Each of these brought its own danger. The crisis of governors and governed has brought with it the great danger of alienation as, on one hand, people are becoming better educated, acquiring a wider range of experiences, both personal and vicarious, and are extensively and quickly informed of developments in the world around them, even if in a distorted way. This led to a great decline in the confidence of the governed in those who governed them, aggravated by the fact that, increasingly, the governed elected the governors and so could be additionally disappointed by the failure of the latter to fulfill their promises.

In the case of the second, internal racial, ethnic, and gender challenges to the polities established in the eighteenth and nineteenth centuries changed the grounding of politics and often have led to political, structural, and constitutional changes as well. In the third, in an era of nuclear weapons, the modern system of independent, politically sovereign states contesting with each other in the international arena and surviving by means of balances of power became increasingly obsolete from a security point of view and at the same time increasingly irrelevent from an economic and social point of view as the world turned into one vast market.

Politically, these new challenges to democracy can be summarized under two headings: the conflict between territorially based and nonterritorial communities and the conflict between constitutional barriers and the mass media. The political hallmark of the modern epoch was the struggle to establish constitutional democracy and individual freedom through the erection of constitutional barriers to excessive exercise of power by "the state" or by one government or another. This was true whether we speak of the right of a public to be self-governing or the rights of an individual to be free to make his or her life choices and to live by them.

The modern solution to these challenges was through the establishment of territorially based polities of citizens, in which the citizens of a particular territory could combine to establish a self-governing constitutional order that suited their norms and needs. Such polities assumed a certain degree of homogeneity within them in order to function. In recent years homogeneity has been challenged by racial, ethnic, gender, or other groups that see themselves as parts of disadvantaged larger or smaller non-territorial communities. Territorial-based government was threatened, even if it happened to be territorial democracy.

Under these conditions, coupled with the social changes of the early postmodern epoch, the political solutions devised for the modern epoch no longer proved adequate by themselves. For example, modern federation was invented, inter alia, to provide a means for the people to make political decisions in both smaller and larger arenas as appropriate, utilizing representative democracy, except, perhaps, in few small arenas where direct democracy could exist. It was based on the assumption that the distance between citizens and their representatives would not be too great, at least in the smaller and intermediate arenas, and that the tasks entrusted to the larger arenas would be sufficiently limited so that if there was greater distance, it would have less effect on democratic republican government.

While no formula was actually applied, these relationships between democratic government and size essentially followed patterns already identified by Plato and Aristotle. In *The Republic*, Plato called for face-to-face governance in communities of approximately 4,000 citizens, where every citizen could know every other one and judge his abilities, capacities, and weaknesses. Aristotle moved beyond that to suggest that republicanism could work even in communities where every citizen might not know every other one, but was no more than one person removed from his peers; that is to say, if x was not personally acquainted with y, both x and y were acquainted with z so that all could communicate with one another regarding the abilities, capacities, and weaknesses of each. Communities in this latter catagory could be as large as 120,000 people under normal circumstances and even 250,000 if there were exceptional homogeneity. In the early modern epoch, towns and villages rarely reached the upper limits of the Platonic model and only the largest cities of Europe reached the upper limits of the Aristotelian model. The latter were considered ungovernable by many observers.

As populations soared, local civil communities increasingly reached and began to pass those two limits and another limit came into play. These were polities in which citizens could not know everyone or even be one person removed, but those citizens who wanted to, could with a minimum of effort come to know everyone or nearly everyone significantly involved in governance. In the United States, this was quite doable in states of up to six million in population size with increasing difficulty after the four million mark had been crossed, and could even be done in some cases in states up to ten million in population. In polities with more elitist political cultures where there was an acceptable separation between elites and masses, this number could be expanded, based principally upon who constituted the elite and how big it was. By the mid-nineteenth century many politically independent states were much larger than that. Thus, federalism became all the more necessary for democratic republicanism. But even for the largest arena, the combination of attentiveness to the mass media, then essentially the print media, plus available personal experience, allowed some measure of thoughtful connection between governors and governed, at least in the voting both, on a small number of issues. Even so, the rulers of Europe were able to plunge their nations into the disastrous First World War essentially by deciding on that course of action and then engineering the agreement of their people to accept what any rational calculus would have rejected.

As the mass media increasingly became dominated by the electronic media and the amount of detailed information was, perforce, expanded, the problem of conveying information became acute. The print media were being replaced as the major source of information by radio and television which, by their very nature, provided information that moved much faster but came in even smaller bites, hardly conveying more than the headlines in the print media.

Meanwhile, the print media themselves deteriorated. We can see just how much by contrasting the news section with the sports section in almost every Western country. The news is presented in usually superficial, often vague, and frequently biased terms, and few among the readers are sufficiently sophisticated to call the news writers to account. On the sports page, on the other hand, matters are presented in great detail, even down to masses of statistics, and the level of accuracy demanded by the readership is extraordinarily high. A mistake made, even in the smallest statistic, is rapidly challenged and must be corrected. There is clear separation between news and opinion since the audience is literate on such matters. As long as the print media were the dominant purveyors of mass information to the public, one could have a realizable utopian dream, namely that the news sections become like the sports sections.

Moreover, the mass media, beginning in the days of the penny press, attracted readers through their "stories," that is to say, they had to communicate dramatically and sensationally, whether or not in doing so they adhered to truth, not to speak of nuance. This need for exciting stories was further exacerbated by the shift to the electronic media. Once television came in, pictures, which gave the sense of reality, could be used to distort reality as well, based on a need for sensationalism and the biases of those reporting.

Already in the days of the print media, large numbers of the public had come to the conclusion that the news was biased by the newspaper owners and hence did not trust the political recommendations of those owners. In the United States, for example, first on national issues, then, when the states grew too large for independent verification, on state issues; and finally when, as the localities passed their size limits, on local issues as well. The problem became even more acute as the electronic media became more dominant and people moved from being poorly informed and distrustful to being uninformed and unconcerned. Many no longer read newspapers or watched television news unless some disaster or other sensation could be viewed "live." In short, they had become politically alienated.

This was further aggrivated by the fact that late modern centralization of power transferred decision-making in an ever greater number of fields to the highest level or the farthest removed arena of the polity, so that there was even less chance than there would have otherwise been that the governed would know and be able to evaluate the acts of their governors. As long as those acts seemed only to the benefit of the former, the voices raised against them were few and far between. But as costs rose and issues became more complicated so that more interests were affected by any change, both dissatisfaction and alienation grew.

This expressed itself in all three basic forms of government. Hierarchical government, dominated by administration, could avoid some of the group conflicts but only at the expense of favoring those whom the top of the hierarchy determined to favor. In the last analysis, administrators could no longer cope with these postmodern problems.

Parliamentary government was in the same fix. While parliaments were introduced to control governments, the rise of the political party system soon meant that governments, in power only so long as they could maintain a parliamentary majority, soon began to control parliaments by exercising the party control that brought them to power, to keep them in power. Parliamentary party members were concerned about the rewards or punishments that a sitting government could tender. Even when they objected to government policies, they normally objected to going before the voters sooner than necessary even more, so they went along. Parties promised programs to get elected, but when they came into power found that they had, almost of necessity, overpromised and could not deliver, lending to more alienation.

Even separation of powers systems that could avoid the first two problems found themselves in trouble in the postmodern epoch. While their legislatures could check overweening executives and vice versa, the ostensible stalemates that resulted led to greater judicial intervention into politics through constitutional courts. Once modest bodies that served as defenders of the constitution while avoiding many issues as political ones, that is to say, properly in the province of legislatures and executives; judiciaries, especially constitutional courts, fell into the hands of those who wanted to respond to the issues per se and were concerned that stalemates in the elected bodies or organs of government prevented those responses. So, too, if elected organs of government, reflecting large majorities, were not interested in providing sufficient protection to minorities in these judges' eyes, their courts would act. So they began to expand their decision making into fields previously held to be political and now have come to hold extraordinary power in their hands. At first this seemed to bring about more responsive government, but soon it, too, was overwhelmed by the new scale and complexity of the issues, contributing to greater public alienation.

All of this is exacerbated by the emergence of a new class system in place of the old one which was substantially reduced by democratic government intervention into matters economic and social in the late nineteenth and first half of the twentieth centuries and then rendered obsolete by technological change. It was not hierarchical in character but rather also followed a matrix model.

The new class system is framed by a new governing class, not particularly drawn from old elites but more from a meritocracy that was self-selected and allowing for cooptation of the meritorious, self-perpetuating. This governing class consists of the people who dominate the institutions of government, the economy, and the other institutions of society that have critical political, economic, cultural, and social decision-making power. While they may inform the frame of the civil society, they often see themselves as the top of the pyramid. To reach the governing class and to succeed in it one has to be ambitious, energetic, and driven, so that in the end its members work harder and more efficiently than most others they know. Moreover, they are increasingly isolated from others not of their class except as they choose not to be, so they become insular and see themselves as specially raised up or set aside by their talents.

Intertwined with them is the talking class, those people whose business is communication and who are opinion-molders by virtue of that business. This class includes intellectuals, academics, journalists, and teachers. Like the governing class, they, too, are self-selected but far more than the former, they are to be found in all arenas of civil society. The leading ones among them serve the largest arena, where they are intertwined with the governing classes, since most of what they talk about is what is manufactured either by themselves or by the governing class. Indeed, for a few, membership in the two classes overlaps, with people going from governing class to talking class or vice versa as their situation or the occasion demands. Moreover, since the talking class is diffused throughout all of the arenas, they serve, whether deliberately or not, as a means for spreading the ideas they share with the governing class.

The communicators of mass culture can be included in this class. Even if what they do is not the traditional work of the talking class, that is to say, talking or writing. They may communicate through film or through music, the new electronic forms of talking, but they are just as much members of that class.

Third is the middle class. In many respects this is a remnant of the old class system, though it does include some of the people who work with the governing and talking classes. Both the individuals within it and the class as a whole are increasingly confused. Many share what have long been seen as middle-class values, but as we have been told countless times, those middle class values have been eroding at least since the end of World War I and very heavily since the end of World War II, whether in connection with family, work ethic, sexual behavior, pursuit of pleasure, or leisure.

Most of the present middle class is trying to adapt its traditional or conventional values to new situations, that is, to still think of the family in the way that they used to except to add to it the idea of "blended families," or to still respect the institution of marriage but accept much longer and sexually active periods of courtship prior to marriage. In part, this may be working, but in part, the changes may be too drastic for society to bear.

A main feature of traditional middle-class values was the commitment to working and finding one's identity through one's work. This remains a strong anchor for the middle class, but the work itself is not only changing, but the possibilities of staying with one's work for a full career are diminishing. Hence, the confusion of many people in the middle class who accepted certain expectations and now find that they cannot be fulfilled.

Fourth is the working class. It has all of the same problems as the middle class, coupled with a large diminution in their economic status because of the changing work situation, even less job stability, with greater departures from the values and habits that sustained the fabric of civilization in their parents' and grandparents' day. Since the pillars of the working class often were essentially lower middle class in their values and habits, the erosion of those pillars causes confusion and havoc far beyond that easily recognizable. To take but one example, unwanted pregnancies in the middle class are likely to lead to abortions, while in the working class not only more abortions are likely but more illegitimate births as well. Those have their own consequences since the economic disadvantages that they bring with them push working-class mothers of illegitimate children down into the underclass, thereby starting their children on an even greater downward spiral.

Work, for the working class, not only has become less remunerative, but less stable and more fraught with risks with which the working class is not able to easily cope. The shift from manufacturing to service industries in the more developed world means the decline of manufacturing jobs and their replacement, if they are replaced at all, by far less remunerative service jobs. Service jobs for the working class generally carry lower status as well, which means that working-class children can no longer look forward to better lives for themselves and their families than were available to their parents, but can expect less from an economic point of view. In many countries, structural unemployment in the working class is growing by leaps and bounds, and the direction of the economy suggests that almost all new jobs will require brains, not brawn. Even the middle class is threatened by the level of the brainpower required and the fact that clerks as well as factory workers can be replaced by computers and robots.

At the bottom of everything is a growing underclass. The underclass has always been a problem in established societies. The American founders commented on the problem of the underclass in the great European cities of their time and how the United States was blessed by not having such a group, at least not of any proportions. But as time passed the underclass grew and not only became self-perpetuating but actually able to feed upon itself to grow larger.

For whatever reasons, there are now whole populations who are born into the underclass and who never escape it, which is not only a matter of "living off welfare," but of not having a value structure capable of sustaining civil society and democratic republican citizenship. Not only that, but because the members of the underclass devotes a major share of their income to leisure pursuits in an effort to overcome the pain and deprivation of their ordinary lives, they fill up the sports stadiums for the football games, stay glued to the television, consume harmful substances in greater quantity, and otherwise engage in activities that either are antisocial or rapidly become antisocial. Under the best of circumstances governments use the "bread and circuses" method to keep them quiescent, but, in reality, relatively little is done to change their situation, although there is always much talk about it from the talking classes and a lot of expenditure on the part of the governing classes, which usually ends up supporting members of the governing class more than in assisting the underclass or the working class. Now that the welfare state has, at least for the moment, reached its limits for economic reasons—countries no longer can sustain its costs—the safety net for the working class and underclass that was developed, particularly in Western Europe, is not being maintained at previous levels, thereby exacerbating the problems of un- and underemployment and lack of appropriate norms that are endemic to the underclass and are a constant threat to parts of the working class.

Finally, there is a small leisure class of people who are sufficiently wealthy to spend their lives outside any of these working frameworks, neither governing nor talking for a living, nor working in conventional ways. In some respects this is the most visible class of all since among them are celebrities who cultivate their image as members of the leisure class, sometimes when they are not really fully of it, since it seems to offer a utopian way of life, all pleasure and no pain. This leisure class really exists even though it is known mostly through the mythology of cinema and television.

Each of these classes can be located in relation to the matrix of civil society and world society. The governing class is the most isolated, either being part of the framing institutions of the matrix or the framing institutions of each arena. The talking class is diffused throughout the arenas, as is the middle class. The working and underclasses are confined to the smaller arenas while the leisure class in a very real sense floats above all the arenas, escaping control of the matrix for most purposes. What is critical, however, is the fact that the new class system is not based on a single pyramid with the ruling class at its apex followed by a small upper class and larger middle class and finally a really large lower class, piled one on top of the other in hierarchical fashion. Today's model is more like a ring of hills with modest hierarchies in each class but the classes themselves are spread out over a more or less even plane. All are considered roughly equally empowered for many purposes. This is almost unquestionably a reflection of the spread of such modern expressions of covenant as constitutionalism, citizenship, and equality.

Unlike earlier class systems, this is one with very fluid lines, as befits a democratic age. People may move back and forth from class to class with relative ease. To the extent that it is controlled, that control is in the hands of the governing classes with a share in the hands of the talking classes who often present themselves as the greatest critics of the governing classes but actually are in alliance with them.

This new class system is rapidly becoming common to all modernized societies as they enter the postmodern world. The older elite-led societies have had some greater breathing space than the new societies produced by the great frontier, but the older elite societies as such are dying or being reborn as something else entirely. One need only examine the history of Western Europe since World War II to note how this is so.

It is in this setting that the covenant tradition must function in our times. This has led to certain ironies. In the world arena, the anarchy or quasi-anarchy that existed under the old statist system is giving way to a new system that is slowly being constitutionalized into a new international system.

The Reemergence of Covenant?

As the covenants of modernity have disintegrated, new postmodern covenants and covenantal arrangements have begun to emerge in the world political arena. They are manifestations of the transformation of the state system, what might be called a paradigm shift from statism to federalism. While there is no significant diminution of the demand for political sovereignty on the part of publics who see themselves as entitled to a state, the states themselves, especially in the case of the more advanced among them, increasingly have become neutral vehicles for service delivery. Increasingly, the more advanced states are prevented from making demands on their citizens beyond such elemental ones as requiring them to observe the law and pay taxes. Even military service has been thrown into some doubt, though where universal military service has been traditional, it generally continues to be. At times these states cannot even maintain law and order sufficiently or provide expected governmental services either because of restrictions placed on law enforcement officials in the performance of their duties, as in the United States, or because of the collapse of governmental power on all fronts, as in the states of the former USSR.

This new system requires considerable moral commitment to accompany self-interest as its driving force. Hence in order to survive, it has to rest on a covenantalized base as the world's states and peoples find it to their advantage and, even more than that, a matter of necessity to combine self-interest and moral commitment to a new world order. In doing so they not only confront the problems of constitutional design inherent in building a democratic world system but they must do in the context of the moral and social erosions of postmodern society and to face up to the dark side of mass society.

Thus, the somewhat hopeful possibility of constitutionalizing globalization is paralleled in the smaller national and subnational arenas by this growing anarchy which the establishments of civil society cannot or will not control. In those situations, only voluntary or quasi-voluntary covenants, whereby individuals, families, and groups are prepared to make moral commitments, also, in no small measure, based on the recognition of their self-interest, can possibly help people carve out any patches of order. Such covenantal patches are emerging here and there, in a society increasingly anarchic from a social point of view, yet, simultaneously, increasingly overgoverned politically. Thus the covenantal tradition continues to be functionally, as well as theoretically and morally, relevant in those arenas as well.

In the modern triad of governmental, public nongovernmental, and private institutions that enable civil societies to form themselves and function, only the private remained unequivocally legitimate and for the most part functioning (although the weakening of law and order has its effect on the diminution of the ability of the private sphere to function as well). The governmental sphere, having lost its moral underpinnings, also lost legitimacy and hence some of its power to compel. With all the discussion of the fact that government is unique because it has a monopoly on coercive powers, it began to be discovered that government was successful in functioning not simply by virtue of its coercive powers but by virtue of its legitimacy, that is, of the trust that those subject to its authority and powers had in the polity and its regime. When and where that trust diminished below a tolerable level, there was not enough coercive power that could be effectively mobilized to maintain public order, the minimum requirement to maintain the legitimacy of any government.

Even prior to the crisis in contemporary government, public nongovernmental institutions had been under siege as a result of the expansion of governmental powers over the past century and more. As government entered many more fields than those in which it had been involved in the past, it replaced voluntary nongovernmental institutions, especially those with public purposes and the latter inevitably were weakened. At best, they came to be considered "mediating institutions," either of a corporate model as in totalitarian systems, whereby they provided a framework that better enabled the government to control its public, or in a more limited role in more democratic systems, where they became vehicles for interests to express themselves and fight over governmental rewards and services.

Sometime in the 1970s, there began to be a rediscovery of the importance of these public but nongovernmental institutions in the West, still as "mediating institutions," but by the 1990s there was a growing recognition of their power as institutions for the re-forming of civil society. Use of such institutions for purposes of rebuilding civil society from the inside was not new. Indeed it had acquired a certain burst of interest and attention in the 1960s when, as a subtheme of Lyndon B. Johnson's Great Society in the United States, efforts were made to establish civic associations of various kinds to enable the poor to assist themselves in raising themselves up. These associations were indeed public compacts, requiring more than mere contractual ties for them to succeed. In the 1970s civic associations of this kind spread to the middle class. So, for example, efforts were made to bring racial peace to American cities via pacts explicitly designed covenants that bound the various groups to have due regard for each other.

With the rise of religious fundamentalism in the United States, religious fundamentalists, drawing from the covenantal tradition, began to utilize this device to achieve moral as well as social goals. During this period Christian fundamentalists organized schools formally called "private" but, in fact, public non-governmental associations. At the same time they organized nationwide political coalitions to represent their ideas and interests in the political arena. Needless to say, their churches and church organizations continued to grow. Then in the 1990s pacts among teenagers began to appear stimulated by believing Christians, calling upon their signers to accept conventional Christian moral teachings including their restrictions with regard to personal behavior in connection with sexual matters and substance abuse.

High school students in Texas have begun a movement of voluntarily gathering around flagpoles at their schools to pray and sing to recovenant themselves to a synthesis of American patriotism and Christianity. The quan-

titatively most successful of all of these efforts is "Promise Keepers," founded
by Bill McCartney, former University of Colorado football coach. In an adaptation of an older American revivalistic style, McCartney has mobilized
over two million American men to commit themselves to standards of personal behavior and family life in the Christian tradition. By 1997, the group
had packed sports stadiums throughout the United States and had close to a
million men in a Washington march/prayer vigil at the beginning of October.
While all of these are devoted to private redemption rather than public transformation, they are clearly attempting to be foundational for American civil
society as a whole.

As predicted, what began as a series of voluntary and private efforts have
now gone into the public and legislative spheres. In 1997 the Louisiana State
Legislature enacted legislation establishing what the law defines as "covenant marriage," a marital state that, if people voluntarily wish to enter it, is
more binding than regular marriage and more difficult to end. Twenty other
state legislatures are in the process of enacting similar legislation.

In addition, there are those efforts to extend full recognition to other covenantal religions on the part of Christians who have had a long and not very
pleasant record of intolerance, especially anti-Semitism. For the most part
these have not taken the form of actual covenants but of public recognition
that both Christians and Jews are in covenant with God from ancient times.
The first formal moves in this direction actually came from the Roman Catholic
Church from the time of Pope John XXIII, the great reforming pope of the
1960s. The Church has since deepened its teachings on this subject, almost
always referring to God's covenants with both Jews and Christians ("elder
brother" and "younger brother"). A number of Protestant denominations joined
in that movement in subsequent years. Southern Presbyterians, for example,
in the early 1990s affirmed the acknowledgement by Christians that Jews are
in a covenant relationship with God and that not only relations among Christians and Jews but what this means for Christian evangelism must be considered by Christians.

Not only Jews have received attention through the perspective of the covenantal tradition. Nonwhites have received attention in recognizing their equality with whites in the same covenantal spirit. In the years since World War II
no doubt this was much influenced by the new world abhorrance of racism as
a result of the consequences of the Holocaust.

Still other religious groups coming from the covenantal tradition have tried
to use their Judaism or Christianity to address issues and what Richard John
Neuhaus refers to as the "public square" from a covenantal perspective. These
groups have been both liberal and conservative, but have been most visible in
the English-speaking world among both Jews and Christians, reflecting the
melding of those two covenantal traditions within English-speaking covenantal
or quasi-covenantal civil societies.[17]

In a much less religious and far more secularized Europe it was much less likely that any resurgence of covenantalism per se would occur. What did occur, however, particularly in those countries with a covenantal dimension within their political cultures, was the idea of a new social contract or civic charter to regularize relationships between labor, business, industry, and the government for the sake of economic and social stability. Such social contracts and civic charters usually were proclaimed with fanfare and occasionally had more than a brief impact, but for the most part they were like other contracts, based upon perceived interests of the parties without the deep moral commitment necessary to move them beyond that, even though the whole idea was to raise those interests beyond the contractual and anchor them in a framework of moral commitment for the improvement of civil society.

Nevertheless, some of these social contracts or civic charters are fairly elaborate, for example, the civil charter presented by John Major in Great Britain in July 1991. It was essentially directed toward improving public service bodies and was to be backed up by a series of subsidiary charters for parents, taxpayers, and customers or clients of different public service agencies. Incidentally, as in the case of classic charters, it was promulgated from the top, unlike social contracts which are deliberately products of open negotiation.[18]

Similar renewals of contractualism, if not covenantalism directly, also appeared in the secular world. Some universities restructured their learning programs to provide for agreed-upon contracts between teachers and students regarding material to be taught and student assumption of responsibility for mastering that material. Similar contracts were established with regard to work experience and what was to be learned from it.

Overall, more and more activities originally organized in a hierarchical manner in the late nineteenth century, as they became matters of public rather than private responsibility, were transformed into contractual arrangements whereby the parties involved made their commitments to one another and to the tasks at hand explicit so that they could be measured by mutually agreed upon performance standards. In short, the formal public structures which in the immediate past been hierarchical, at first were being supplemented and then slowly replaced by contractual arrangements of a covenantal character because they required trust and moral commitment more than commands and coercive enforcement in order to succeed.

All this became very public with the emergence of the "civil society" movement in Eastern Europe led by Vaclav Havel in Czechoslovakia, as part of the liberal revolt against Communist rule by explicitly attaching to it the name originally forged for those same phenomena in the West in the seventeenth century, and applying it in the late twentieth.

This was given fullest expression in the German Democratic Republic (GDR) in 1988–89. The Federation of Evangelical Churches (BEK) had succeeded in remaining one of the few bodies within the GDR that had retained a degree of freedom of movement under the Communist regime, the Communists recognizing that too much pressure upon the churches would be counterproductive. As the regime began to lose support, the churches became more active in developing the countervailing power in opposition to it. Even before 1989, activist groups had been developed in them. In 1988 and 1989, what was called the Conciliar Process for Justice, Peace, and the Preservation of the Creation was launched through a series of resolutions which were referred to as "covenants," adopted at church assemblies in the GDR.

These led to the demonstrations in the cities of the GDR in the fall of 1989, the establishment of roundtables to extend and coordinate activities, and in 1990 the rapid unification with the Federal Republic. The church then continued its struggle to change its own structure and to develop a genuine constitution for the new Germany. All told, the church was in the forefront of the collapse of the Communist regime through an explicitly covenantal process that its members developed for that purpose.[19]

The Conciliar Process was the most covenantal of these steps. It was accompanied by a commitment to political federalism and a federal governmental order which became dominant in the reunification process.

Thus the conceptual worldview that had first emerged in the modern epoch to provide the basis for the constitutional design of that epoch reappeared early in the postmodern epoch, prepared to serve that same purpose once again. In both cases it grew out of impulses derived more or less directly from the covenant idea. While it is too soon to tell how this model of constitutional design will work, it does strengthen one thesis of this project, that it is precisely at times of the greatest crises in human self-government that the covenant idea resurfaces as a force.

In this respect the covenant idea and the worldview embodied within it seems to resemble what the ancient Kabbalists saw as the pattern of the world as a whole and which some contemporary astronomers have seen as a pattern in the universe. Pressed hard by hostile forces around it, the covenant idea contracts in upon itself (what the Kabbalists called *tzimtzum*), until what is left are a few points in which it is densely concentrated. Then it begins to spread again beyond those points of concentration in ever widening circles around each that, in the past, have come in many cases to connect with one another to influence great parts of humanity and thereby reconstitute the world.

Now we appear to be at the moment of greatest contraction and concentration. Will the way of covenant expand once again?

Notes

1. On seventeenth-century covenantalism, see Patrick Riley, "Three Seventeenth-Century German Theorists of Federalism: Althusius, Hugo, Leibniz" in *Publius*, vol. 6, no. 3 (Summer, 1976); Donald Lutz and Jack D. Warden, *A Covenanted*

People: The Religious Traditions and the Origins of American Constitutional-ism (Providence, R.I.: John Carter Brown Library, 1987).

For Althusius's works in the original and in translation, see Carl J. Friedrich, ed., *The Politica Methodice Digesta of Johannes Althusius* (Cambridge, Mass.: Harvard University Press, 1932) and Frederick S. Carney, ed. and trans., *The Politics of Johannes Althusius* (Boston: Beacon Press, 1964).

2. Cf. Lutz and Warden, *A Covenanted People: The Religious Traditions and the Origins of American Constitutionalism* (Providence, R.I.: John Carter Brown Library, 1987); Donald Lutz, ed., *Documents of Political Foundation Written by Colonial Americans* (Philadelphia, Pa.: Institute for the Study of Human Issues, 1986); and Charles Hyneman and Donald Lutz, eds., *American Political Writing During the Founding Era, 1760–1805* (Indianapolis, Ind.: Liberty Fund, 1983).

3. On the American Founding, cf. Daniel J. Elazar and John Kincaid, *The Declaration of Independence: The Founding Covenant of the American People* (Philadelphia: Center for the Study of Federalism, 1982); Daniel J. Elazar, *The American Constitutional Tradition* (Lincoln: University of Nebraska Press, 1988); Hyneman and Lutz, *American Political Writing During the Founding Era, 1760–1805*; and Lutz and Warden, *A Covenanted People: The Religious Traditions and the Origins of American Constitutionalism*.

4. J. David Greenstone, "Lincoln's Political Humanitarianism: Moral Reform and the Covenant Tradition in American Political Culture," in *Covenant in the Nineteenth Century,* Daniel J. Elazar, ed., (Lanham, Md.: Rowman and Littlefield, 1994).

5. *Ibid;* John Anderson, *Calhoun: Basic Documents* (State College, Pa.: Bald Eagle Press, 1992).

6. On Abolitionist thought, see Austin Willey, *The History of the Antislavery Cause in State and Nation* (New York: Negro University Press, 1969). For a collection of essays on the topic, see Hugh Hawkins, ed., *The Abolitionists, Means, Ends, and Motivations* (Lexington, Mass.: D.C. Heath, 1972).

7. On Lincoln's convenantalism, see Daniel J. Elazar, "The Constitution, the Union and the Liberties of the People," *Publius,* vol. 8, no. 3 (Summer, 1978); Harry V. Jaffa, *Crisis of the House Divided: An Interpretation of the Issues in the Lincoln-Douglas Debates* (Seattle: University of Washington Press, 1973); and J. David Greenestone, "Covenant, Process, and Slavery in the Thought of Adams and Jefferson" in *Covenant in the Nineteenth Century,* Daniel J. Elazar, ed., (Lanham: Rowman and Littlefield, 1994).

8. On Francis Lieber and his group, see H.B. Adams, *The Study of History in American Colleges and Universities*, Bureau of Education, Circular of Information, no. 2 (Washington, 1887), p. 21 and Daniel W. Hollis, *University of South Carolina* (Columbia: University of South Carolina Press, 1951), vol. I, pp. 120–23.

9. Cf. Woodrow Wilson, *Congressional Government* (Boston: H. Mifflin, 1913) and "The Study of Administration" in *Political Science Quarterly,* vol. 2 (June, 1887), pp. 197–220. See, in particular, the analysis of Wilson, his ideas, and their impact by Vincent Ostrom in "Can Federalism Make a Difference" in Daniel J. Elazar, ed., *The Federal Polity* (New Brunswick, N.J.: Transaction Publishers, 1974); *The Intellectual Crisis in American Public Administration*, 2nd ed., (Tuscaloosa: University of Alabama Press, 1989); and *The Political Theory of a Compound Republic: Designing the American Experiment* (Lincoln: University of Nebraska Press, 1986). Of all the Reformed Protestant churches, Presbyterianism was the most covenantal and federal in doctrine and governance.

10. On social Darwinism, see Edward Osborne Wilson, *On Human Nature* (Cambridge, Mass.: Harvard University Press, 1978); Josiah Royce, *The Spirit of*

Modern Philosophy (Boston: Houghton Mifflin, 1920); and Herbert Spencer, *The Evolution of Society: Selections from Herbert Spencer's Principles of Sociology*, edited and introduced by Robert Z. Carneiro (Chicago: University of Chicago Press, 1974).

On racism in the late nineteenth century, see John Higham, *Strangers in the Land: Patterns of American Nativism, 1860–1925* (New Brunswick, N.J.: Rutgers University Press, 1955).

11. Loren Beth, *Politics, the Constitution and the Supreme Court* (New York: Harper and Row, 1962); Samuel Krislov, *The Supreme Court in the Political Process* (New York: Macmillan, 1965); and Robert Brent Swisher, *American Constitutional Development*, 2nd edition (Westport, Conn.: Greenwood Press, 1978).

12. George Mowry, *The California Progressives* (New York: Quadrangle, 1976) and Russell B. Nye, *Midwestern Progressive Politics: A Historical Study of the Origins and Development, 1870–1958* (East Lansing: Michigan State University Press, 1959).

For an eastern exception, see Richard Abrams, *Conservatism in a Progressive Era* (Cambridge, Mass.: Harvard University Press, 1964).

13. Daniel J. Elazar, "Toward a Revival of Progressivism," in *The Ripon Forum* (October, 1972).

14. For histories of the early twentieth century, see Ray A. Billington, *The United States: American Democracy in World Perspective* (New York: Rinehart, 1947); Abraham S. Eisenstadt, *American History: Recent Interpretations* (New York: T.Y. Crowell, 1966), vol. 2; and Arthur M. Schlesinger, *New Viewpoints in American History* (New York: Macmillan, 1948).

15. Cf. Richard Hofstadter, *The Age of Reform: From Bryan to F.D.R.* (New York: Alfred A. Knopf, 1956). On southern progressives and the race issue, see Stanley Coben, ed., *Reform, War, and Reaction: 1912–1932* (New York: Harper and Row, 1972).

16. See, for example, Charles E. Harvey, "Congregationalism on Trial, 1949–1950: An Account of the Cadman Case," *Journal of Church and State* (Spring 1970):255–72.

17. Richard J. Neuhaus, *The Naked Public Square: Religion and Democracy in America* (Grand Rapids, Mich.: Eerdmans, 1986); Harvey Cox, *The Secular City*, (New York: Macmillan, 1971); Robert Bellah, *The Broken Covenant: American Civil Religion in Time of Trial*, second edition (Chicago: University of Chicago Press, 1992).

18. *Public Policy and the Impact of the New Right*, Grant Jordan and Nigel Ashford, eds. (London: Pinter Publications, 1993); Dexter Whitfield, *The Welfare State: Privatisation, Deregulation, Commercialisation of Public Service* (London: Pluto Press, 1992).

19. William Johnson Everett, *Religion, Federalism, and the Struggle for Public Life: Cases from Germany, India, and America*, (New York: Oxford University Press, 1997).

14

Toward a World Covenantal Network

From Statism to Federalism: A Paradigm Shift

In one other arena, the covenant idea has become more assertive and influential then ever before. The world as a whole is in the midst of a paradigm shift from a world of states, modeled after the ideal of the nation-state developed at the beginning of the modern epoch in the seventeenth century, to a world of diminished state sovereignty and increased interstate linkages of a constitutionalized federal character.[1] This paradigm shift actually began after World War II. Future historians may yet conclude that the "package" of agreements developed by the Allies of World War II, such as the Bretton Woods agreement in 1944 establishing the beginnings of a new international economic order, and the United Nations, founded in San Francisco in May 1945 as a league of politically sovereign states with the elevated goal of maintaining world peace, were the first institutional steps toward this paradigm shift in the globval arena.

In the broadest sense, federalism involves the linkage of individuals, groups, and polities in lasting but limited union in such a way as to provide for the energetic pursuit of common ends while maintaining the respective integrities of all parties. It does so by pact and constitution grounded in some shared set of commandments that ultimately rest on some moral principles and sufficient mutual trust. Federal principles are concerned with the combination of self-rule and shared rule.

As a political principle, federalism has to do with the constitutional diffusion of power so that the constituting elements in a federal arrangement share in the processes of common policymaking and administration by right, while the activities of the common government are conducted in such a way as to maintain their respective integrities. Federal systems do this by constitutionally distributing power among general and constituent governing bodies in a manner designed to protect the existence and authority of all. In federal systems, basic policies are made and implemented through negotiation in some form so that all can share in the system's decision-making and executing processes.

Parallel to them was the movement for European integration which after a slow start came to surpass all others. As the Italian federalist scholar Andrea Bosco has said, "The central problem of our time is no longer a question of achieving a high degree of freedom, democracy or justice, but how to organize peaceful constitutional relations among nations." In Western Europe this idea became a matter of urgent reality among the resistance agianst Nazi Germany in World War II. It was to be the great postwar project of a group of individuals whose first major public involvement was in the resistance and who saw in a federal union of the peoples of Europe the only remedy for the evils of national sovereignty.

The developments in Western Europe in the intervening years led to the diminution of the political sovereignty of the member states of the European Union through confederal links. Similar developments appeared in other parts of the world, particularly Southeast Asia (the Association of Southeast Asian Nations—ASEAN) and the Caribbean. Still, it was not until the collapse of first the Soviet empire and then the Soviet Union itself between 1989 and 1993, that the extensive and decisive character of this paradigm shift became evident to most people, even (or perhaps especially) those who closely follow public affairs. Most of the latter were, and still are, wedded to the earlier paradigm that the building blocks of world organization are politically sovereign states, most or all of which strive to be nation-states and maximize their independence of action and decision. While there are a few who have been aware of this paradigm shift as it has been taking place and some who have advocated it as a major political goal, for most it has seemed to have crept up unawares.

U.S. Ambassador Max Kampelman, who has taken account of the shift, presents it in the following terms:

> The interdependence of the world and the globalization of its economy does not imply or suggest the disappearance of the nation-state, which is showing resilience as an important focus of national pride and ethnic preservation.

> For hundreds of years, international society has been organized on the basis of separate sovereign states whose territorial integrity and political independence were protected and guaranteed by an evolving international law.

> Into this principle, Woodrow Wilson...introduced in the early 20th century a new principle, that of self-determination of peoples, intended as a blow against colonialism. Its effect, however, introduced mischievous consequences in many parts of the world. Increasingly, violence associated with ethnic conflicts has been justified with assertions of the right of self-determination. What has been misunderstood is the fact that the right of self-determination of peoples certainly does not include the right to secede from established and internationally legitimized nation-state borders.

> We are brought up to believe that necessity is the mother of invention. I suggest the corollary is also true: invention is triumph over necessity. Science, technology

and communication are necessitating basic changes in our lives. Information has become more accessible to all parts of our globe putting totalitarian governments at a serious disadvantage. The world is very much smaller. There is no escaping the fact that the sound of a whisper or a whimper in one part of the world can immediately be heard in all parts of the world—and consequences follow.

But the world body politic has not kept pace with those scientific and technological achievements. Just as the individual human body makes a natural effort to keep the growth of its components balance, and we consider the body disfigured if the grows of one arm or leg is significantly less than the other, so is the world body politic disfigured if its knowledge component opens up broad new vistas for development while its political and social components remain in the Dark Ages.[2]

Let us understand the nature of this paradigm shift. It is not that states are disappearing, it is that the state system is acquiring a new dimension, one that began as a supplement and is now coming to overlay (and, at least in some respects, to supersede) the system that prevailed throughout the modern epoch. That overlay is a network of agreements that are not only militarily and economically binding for de facto reasons but are becoming constitutionally binding, de jure, as well. This overlay increasingly restricts what was called state sovereignty and forces states into various combinations of self-rule and shared rule to enable them to survive at all. Kampleman again:

Abba Eban [in], a recent analysis of the prospects for confederation between Israel, the West Bank, and Jordan, commented on the apparent contradiction of a politically fragmented world existing alongside an economically integrated one. He suggests that regional confederations may harmonize the contradiction.[3]

The implications of this paradigm shift are enormous. Whereas before, every state strove for self-sufficiency, homogeneity, and, with a few exceptions, concentration of authority and power in a single center, under the new paradigm all states have had to recognize their interdependence, heterogeneity, and the fact that their centers, if they ever existed, are no longer single centers but parts of a multicentered network that is becoming increasingly noncentralized, and that all of this is necessary in order to survive in the new world.

At first these seemed to be simply extensions of modern constitutionalism into larger arenas, first, in connection with decolonization and the efforts to introduce modern constitutionalism into former colonies as independent states. Then some independent states sought to federate with others in their region, at least for certain purposes, while still others leagued together in alliances that were more than simply traditional interstate treaties, having as they did constitutional dimensions, even if very limited ones. All started out with these by now traditional or conventional ways.

The United Nations was the first of these, dating back to 1945 when the wartime alliance of the same name was transformed into a quite limited but still constitutionalized form to promote and maintain world peace, and a vehicle for pursuing that end. From the first, the United Nations was limited under the terms of its charter to minimal peacekeeping efforts and noninterference in the internal affairs of member states, a limitation very broadly defined and controlled by institutions which protected the member states: a General Assembly paralyzed by the weaknesses of its mass membership and a Security Council paralyzed on the other side by great power tensions. Cold war hostilities soon brought the U.N. almost to a state of paralysis, useful only in providing an arena for backstage discussion of issues as well as public grandstanding about them.[4]

The U.N. leadership strove valiantly to prevent that and simultaneously extended the work of the organization as a vehicle into concrete fields of action that overtly were less political, such as education and culture (UNESCO), labor standards (ILO), agricultural standards and worldwide pest control (FAO), human rights (UN Covenant on Human Rights), and genocide (UN Covenant on Genocide). None of these was able to do more than its members or signatories found it advantageous to do and each member signatory state could make that decision for itself. Some, especially those dealing with more technical matters, were quite successful in this context; others were considerably less so.[5]

As decolonization of Africa and Asia progressed, the ex-colonial "third world" emerged as a third bloc. They found it useful to use the U.N. and those U.N. agencies as means to gain additional aid from the major powers and wealthier states and to give employment with great personal benefit to members of their political elites. Neither enhanced the constitutionalization of those agencies or the United Nations itself. Rather, they led to a certain disgust on the part of the Western world with the corruption inherent in this system and further cynicism on the part of the Communist world which sought to exploit the opportunities it offered.

In the end, the U.N. was reduced to being a forum where various member states could talk and negotiate with one another. It was especially useful with regard to contacts between member states otherwise not willing to recognize one another through normal diplomatic channels. Only a few "breaks" permitted the U.N. to function as a rubric on occasion and thereby retain sufficient usefulness in the eyes of the Great Powers to bring them to continue their support, obviously very necessary for the U.N. to survive. One such "break" was the Soviet bloc walkout just prior to the Korean War that enabled the U.N. to formally furnish the umbrella for United States-led resistance to North Korean aggression in 1950.[6] Others involved the necessity to have a neutral framework through which to send peacekeeping forces to various trouble spots around the world where it was perceived by every member state, or at the very least every powerful one, to be worth doing so, as in Cyprus, Palestine, and Kashmir, but not in Northern Ireland or southern Africa or the East Indies where the powers on the ground opposed any such move.[7]

Among its other activities, the U.N. did negotiate worldwide pacts to try to promote the ends for which it was constituted in various fields from atomic energy to human rights. The U.N. even used the term "covenant" to describe some of these agreements, especially those that embodied high moral purposes and required moral commitment but really were no more than morally binding, a recognition, intentional or unintentional, of the moral basis of all covenants. Although in the real world, this moral basis was without teeth, it was not the less real or important for that. In the existing world situation, those seeking protection had to rely on the moral sensibilities of the signatories to make those covenants work.[8]

Other worldwide agreements began to take form within a few years, outside of the U.N.. The General Agreement on Trade and Tariffs (GATT), the International Monetary Fund (IMF), and the World Bank were organized to establish a more stable world economic order so as to avoid catastrophes like the Great Depression which contributed so much to bringing dictatorships into power and led to war.[9] Using modifications of traditional methods of economic linkage, whether through agreements which could be enforced by the stronger parties through state economic measures, or through the establishment of new frameworks that acquire a life of their own, including a measure of economic power, these rapidly acquired a constitutional position beyond that of treaties, cautiously recognized in the terminology used to describe most of them, as "international organizations." Unlike the United Nations, these organizations were led by experts who could make decisions with a minimum of purely political distortion, primarily because of the great economic power of the United States which backed them.

Other similar organizations appeared on a regional basis. The North Atlantic Treaty Organization (NATO), for example, formalized the U.S.-led military alliance against the Soviet bloc that established what Karl Deutsch referred to as a "security-community," for North America and Western Europe, something that also was more than a treaty but constitutionally less than a confederal arrangement.[10] The Soviet bloc replied in kind with the Warsaw Pact. Whole networks of regional agencies and organizations were developed, as well as various high-sounding bodies embracing Europe or at least Western Europe (the Council of Europe, the Western European Union) and Latin America.[11]

Then in the 1950s, after the failure of the movement for a full-blown United States of Europe which foundered on the rock of state sovereignty, a more modest approach was initiated in Western Europe. The failure of the avowed federalists led to the victorious emergence of the "functionalists" who were determined to bring about greater Western European unity on a task-by-task basis.[12] They were successful in securing the establishment of the first "communities" for coal and steel and the commonmarket through the treaties of Rome in 1958.[13] All of this was at the interstate level and its beginnings were presented as deliberately devoid of moral purpose, although its founders saw in Western European union a high moral purpose, namely, the containment of Germany, the reconciliation of Germany and France, and thus the peace of Europe.

The suggestion that we are witnessing a major paradigm shift does not mean to suggest that the outcome will be perfect or even work in every case. Indeed, the potential for excess and worse remains great. Humans are still humans and their conflicts are very real. For example, federalism has probably received most attention as a suggested means to solve ethnic conflicts in a world that has rediscovered the harsh realities of ethnicity and has lost its confidence that modernization will bring about the desuetude of ethnic identification. But students of federalism have already recognized that ethnic demands are among the most exclusivist in the world and that the same ethnic consciousness that makes federalism in some form necessary makes it all the more difficult and less likely to succeed. Perhaps the solution lies in the extent of the federal bonds as much as in their depth.

The old state system was the product of the modern epoch, given practical form by the new nation states of Western Europe such as France in the late Middle Ages or Prussia in the nineteenth century. These states rested on the idea that by (1) concentrating power in a single head or center, the state itself could be sufficiently controlled and its environment sufficiently managed to achieve (2) self-sufficiency or at least a maximum of self-sufficiency in a world which would inevitably be hostile or at best neutral toward each state's interests and in which alliances would reflect temporary coalitions of interests and which should not be expected to last beyond that convergence. The old maxim, "No state has friends, only interests," typified that situation.

The third defining element of the nation-state was its striving for homogeneity. Every state was to be convergent with its nation and every nation with its state. Where people did not fit easily into that procrustean bed, efforts were made to force them into it.

In the end, none of these three goals could be achieved. In many cases they were not achieved at all; in others they were achieved temporarily until those disadvantaged by them succeeded in revolting. In still others they proved to be unachievable by any sustainable means, usually with a combination of all three factors that prevented their attainment. As the late Ivo Duchacek, himself a Czech and thus exposed to the futility of these efforts in Middle Europe between World Wars I and II, pointed out in the early 1970s, of the then-existing states in the world, 90 percent contained minorities within their boundaries embracing 15 percent of their population or more and of the remaining 10 percent, almost all had large national minorities living outside of their state boundaries. Since he documented that fact, matters have gotten more complex, as we see by the great resurgence of ethnic conflict in one form or another throughout the world, a factor that has become one catalyst for the new paradigm in its search for ways to overcome those conflicts. There are some 3,000 ethnic or tribal groups in the world conscious of their respective identitiess. Of the over 180 politically "sovereign" states now in existence, over 170 are multiethnic in composition.

Self-sufficiency, in reality was never achievable. It is well to recall that modern economic liberalism which was essentially based on the principle of free trade emerged shortly after the emergence of modern statism with its economic basis in mercantilism which sought self-sufficiency because of the problematics of that idea brought to the brought to the fore, inter alia, by the American coalition against Great Britain. When that policy failed, imperialism replaced it as the means to the end of self-sufficiency. Imperialism failed by the middle of the twentieth century, not only because the subjugated peoples rejected it, but because a democratic moral sensibility came to affect the subjugators. Nor was free trade in the nineteenth-century liberal sense the answer since it was an extension of the nineteenth-century conceptions of the "automatic society" (that is, that government could be replaced by the market or the march of history, or the unshackling of humans' original goodness) and suffered from the same defects.

By the mid-twentieth century, after attempts to achieve laissez faire capitalism led to social and economic injustice and the Great Depression and the other attempts led to one or another form of totalitarianism and the *gotterdammerung* of World War II, most of the world was disabused of the idea of the automatic society. Free trade, too, ran afoul not only of illegitimate interests of different peoples and polities but of their legitimate interests, and while its value was increasingly recognized, so, too, was the need to harness it within some kind of framework that provided for those regulations and encouragements necessary for free trade to be most advantageous.

Moreover, the World War II *gotterdammerung* had itself clarified several points: one, that states potentially powerful militarily had to be somehow harnessed to one another to prevent further all-out catastrophes, and, two, that peoples would not submit to rule by others whom they did not see as linked to them in some meaningful way.

All of this was topped off by the introduction of nuclear energy into the equation. The atomic bomb and its successors made it clear to all but the world's crazies that absolute sovereignty was no longer possible, that even the strongest power in the world was limited in what it could do to make its power felt without generating a catastrophic reaction. The "balance of terror" of the cold war years generated by Soviet imperialism but restrained by their nuclear realism, was an effort to harness the old state system to new realities.

Obviously a balance of terror could only be a temporary device. As both great powers and many lesser ones feared, others less interested in maintaining a balance would acquire the same weapons of terror in due course with unforeseen but not very hopeful consequences. So within the balance of terror, especially outside of the very oppressive Communist bloc which tried to use new versions of old imperialist techniques to preserve the power of its leading state and ruling class, small efforts began to go beyond the old system to find new ways to gain control of the situation to everyone's mutual satisfaction.

Thus was born the European Community, now the European Union, initially a network of treaties establishing functional linkages between the various states of Western Europe, anchored on the effort to bring the two great European rival states, France and Germany, together on a peaceful basis so as to prevent future wars between them. In due course the European Community evolved from joint functional authorities established by international treaty to confederal arrangements to, with the adoption of the European Union Treaty of Maastricht, confederation. Soon similar efforts were underway in other parts of the world, not necessarily directly influenced by the EC experience but stimulated by the same recognition of similar needs.

Simultaneously, the two great cold war power blocs under the leadership of the superpower dominant in each, tried to build ostensibly looser but equally binding links in the realms of economics and defense. Those fostered by the Soviet Union were old fashioned imperial ties in a new ideological guise. Hence, it was not surprising that they collapsed with the collapse of the Soviet empire in the late 1980s and early 1990s. Fortunately, those developed for the free world were those developed by the United States which had the generous view that it was in its interest to rebuild Europe and make its components into partners, even though that might bring with it moments of heartburn for the U.S., because in the long run it would be better for everyone. So after World War II the United States rebuilt both its allies and its former foes in Europe and the Far East, generously providing its own resources in order to do so.

In a real sense, the postwar world backed into the new paradigm and did not seek it per se. Their first task after World War II was to resurrect the old state system with a minimum of modifications, that is to say, reconstruction of the former Axis powers on a rehabilitated basis so that they could be readmitted to the family of nations, reconstruction of the wartorn Allies so that they would be able to function again as equal members of the world community of states, and a minimum of collective security arrangements to try to insure world peace, of which the United Nations was one. As a result of the beginning of the cold war, the U.N. became more symbolic than effective, although it was fortuitous that the USSR and its satellites had walked out of the Security Council before the outbreak of the Korean War which left the U.N. free to take a one-time stand on an issue of that magnitude and to throw its support and cover behind the U.S.-led defense of South Korea.

In the meantime, NATO had been established as a Western collective security pact which, in retrospect, we can see as a major step toward the new paradigm. On the other hand, while efforts to establish federations or decentralized states in West Germany, Japan, and Italy successfully served as part of the rebuilding process and a small number of federations succeeded in surviving decolonization in countries such as India, Pakistan (more on paper than in practice but still surviving), Malaya-Malaysia, and Nigeria, efforts to federalize aggregations of preexisting states as federations such as the abortive United States of Europe or in the Balkans did not succeed at all.

In the 1960s, however, in addition to the functional solutions to the problems of union of the Western European countries, parallel efforts were begun in the Caribbean. First, Britain, the ruling power in the region tried to establish a West Indies Federation but it failed. Nevertheless, confederal arrangements uniting most of those same islands emerged out of the wreckage. Islands are by definition insular, hence federation was too much for them but, although they sought independence, they also perceived that they needed to share certain functions such as a common market, a common currency, higher education, and a common supreme court.[14] Thus without in any conscious way abandoning the state system, the federal paradigm was extended in the international arena, in confederal form through binding constitutional pacts among states.

All of this was much enhanced by new economic realities which led to constituent states of existing federations having to insert themselves in the international system as states for purposes of economic development, a drive that has only gained momentum since.

Thus the new paradigm began to emerge slowly without conscious planning and gained momentum as time passed. In the mid-1970s even the European Community looked like it would not survive. Then in the 1980s it picked up momentum along with all these other forms of federalism, while the growing weakness of the Soviet empire and the Soviet Union itself contributed to the growing transformation of worldwide international treaty arrangements such as the General Agreement on Trade and Tariffs (GATT) and the then newly established Council on Security and Cooperation in Europe (CSCE) to more constitutionalized leagues of nations that had become dependent upon membership within them. Each of these is a story in itself, a story that needs to be told to better understand the full dimensions of the paradigm shift.

As the dust settles in the 1990s we find the following: one, more federations than ever before covering more people than ever before. These can be seen as the foundation stones of the new paradigm. At present there are twenty-one federations containing some two billion people or 40 percent of the total world population. They are divided into over 350 constituent or federated states (as against 180 plus politically sovereign states).

Attached to those federations are numerous federal arrangements of one kind or another, usually asymmetrical (federacies and associated states), whereby the federate power has a constitutional connection with a smaller federal state on a different basis than its normal federal-state relationships, one that preserves more autonomy for the small federated state or is based on some relationship between a Westernized federation and its aboriginal peoples. The United States, for example, has federacy arrangements with Puerto Rico (recently reaffirmed by the people of Puerto Rico in yet another referendum) and the Northern Marianas.[17] The U.S. has recognized Native American (Indian) tribes within it as "domestic dependent nations" with certain residual rights of sovereignty and certain powers reserved to them that now are gaining some real meaning, whether through tribal self-government or the opening of gambling casinos in tribal hands.[18]

While the ideology of the nation-state itself remains strong, the single nation-state itself is rare enough. Over one-third, approximately 80, are involved in formal arrangements or are utilizing federal principles in some way to accommodate demands for self-rule or shared rule within their boundaries or in partnership with other polities.

Indeed, one of the manifestations of the new paradigm is the way in which federalism has played a role in restoring democracy in various states. Spain has already been mentioned. Federalism was also reflected in the restoration of democracy in Argentina and Brazil. Indeed, in Brazil the existence of federalism even preserved a modicum of free government during the military dictatorship through the state governors who could remain in power and even have limited elections because of their strength, both political and military (the state police). It has been a means of trying to further extend democracy in Venezuela where the state governors recently were made elected officials, played a crucial role in protecting democracy during the last attempt to oust the president, and seems to be an instrument in slowly transforming Mexico from a one-party into a multiparty polity.

Even more dramatic was the way in which federalism was used to reunify Germany after the collapse of the German Democratic Republic. The territory of the latter first was redivided into five federated laender (federated states). Then those five states joined with the eleven federated laender of the German Federal Republic plus Berlin (previously an associated state) to form the expanded federal republic.

Beyond this circle of federations there emerged new confederations such as that the European Union embrace smaller federations, unions (such as Great Britain), and unitary states (such as France) in new-style federal arrangements. Many of the states within these new confederations have developed federacy and associated state relations of their own or have decentralized internally as part of the spread of the new paradigm. Take, for example, Portugal and the Azores or Monaco and France.

Beyond those federations and confederations, there are looser league arrangements such as the CSCE in Europe and NATO for the North Atlantic community which have moved beyond their standing as groups of states linked by standard treaties to acquire certain limited but nonetheless real constitutional powers, the first in the area of human rights and the second in the area of defense. In the 1990s, these began to be supplemented by regional free trade areas. The oldest, linking Belgium, the Netherlands, and Luxembourg as the Benelux nations, essentially has been superseded by the European Union. The newest, the North American Free Trade Area (NAFTA) offers all sorts of promise for the future for its members and possibly for future expansion.

Last but hardly least are similar-type arrangements on a worldwide basis. Despite the fact of GATT being merely a treaty, the world's leading industrial nations have discovered that they could not live without it so they had to resolve the serious difficulties among them whether they liked it or not. The result was a much strengthened system and agreement in the last round of negotiations that it would be transformed into the World Trade Organization (WTO) as of January 1, 1995. The transformation reflects its strengthened character and give it the institutional mechanisms to deal with that new strength.

If we look at a map of the world from this perspective, we can see a number of overlapping circles. Moving from the smallest to largest or from the more limited to the more comprehensive, we see the following pattern:

1. Fully covenantal polities.
2. Other federations or confederations that link polities from various models which function in a covenantal manner.
3. Formally federal polities in which the federal ties are in practice, minimal but serve in some way the interests of their constituents.
4. Asymetrical arrangements, both internal and external.
5. Regional or interregional leagues.
6. Worldwide leagues united through mechanisms that have acquired constitutional status, either *de jure* or *de facto*.

Thus, at the threshold of the third millennium of the Christian era and in the second generation of the postmodern epoch, the paradigm shift seems to be well advanced and moving right along. Indeed, even the most troubled spots of the first generation of the postmodern epoch seemed to be choosing federal paradigms as ways to get out of their presumably "insoluble" conflicts: the Commonwealth of Independent States embracing most of the former Soviet Union, the new near-federal constitution in South Africa, the Israel-Palestinian Declaration of Principles and subsequent agreements which rest upon the ability of the two sides plus Jordan to establish a network of joint authorities as well as to further develop their separate integrities either as states or in the manner of states and the British-Irish declaration on Northern Ireland which opens the door to peace negotiations for that troubled area, also along lines that will combine self-rule and shared rule, though still very vague ones.

Much remains before this new paradigm has become as rooted as the old one. Included among what has to be done is for scholars and public figures to recognize the new paradigm for what it is, to seek to understand it and to promote their understanding, each group in its own way. For what can be said about this new paradigm is that while the old state paradigm was a recipe for war more often than not, the new federal one is equally a recipe for peace, if it works.

Federal Accommodations of Cultural Cleavages

In pursuing that paradigm, humanity finds itself confronted with a number of political problems whose sources lie deep in cultural cleavages which, in turn, are manifested in conflicting national, ethnic, linguistic, racial and perhaps other claims arising out of historical experiences. Some of these problems are headline material almost daily, others are less visible but consistently influential, while still others have been temporarily submerged but only await the appropriate moment to reappear.

The expression of the covenant idea through federal arrangements and institutions offers one possible resource for dealing with these problems within the framework of the paradigm shift, utilizing one or another of the models for the application of federal principles. This is possible because the essence of federalism is not to be found in a particular set of institutions but in a particular kind of relationship among the participants in political life. Consequently, federalism is a phenomenon that provides many options for the organization of political authority and powers; as long as the proper relations are developed. And surprisingly, then, a wide variety of political structures can be and have been developed expressing federal relationships.

There are those uses of federalism that are deliberately built upon or anchored on federal principles and that are intended to be federal in the fullest sense. On the other hand, there are those arrangements which the outside observer will note as being federal although they are not so labelled and may not even be seen as such for reasons that are either deliberate or mistaken, but nonetheless reflect enough of the elements of federalism to be recognized as federal. As it has been said, "if it quacks like a duck, waddles like a duck, and has feathers like a duck, then it's a duck."

Where federal principles are involved, sooner or later these are extensions of the covenantal tradition. Where only federal arrangements can be identified, the likelihood is that there is not only little or no conscious recognition of the covenantal tradition but a deliberate effort to reject that tradition for reasons adhering to the peoples or polities involved. What is happening is the emergence of that natural tendency for establishing political arrangements through pact that the political philosophic founders of modernity emphasized as the grounding of their teachings. Whereas federal principles can only be consciously applied, federal arrangements can develop from human psychology and remain unrecognized as such by those who apply them. In that sense they are "of nature."

In modern and postmodern times, federalism has emerged as a major means of accommodating the spreading desire of people to preserve or revive their cultural distinctiveness within larger combinations developed to better mobilize and utilize common resources. Consequently, federal arrangements have been widely applied, on one hand, to construct new polities while preserving legitimate internal diversities and, on the other, to link established polities for economic advantage and greater security.[18]

To summarize, the variety of means for translating the federal idea into practice has been greatly expanded. Whereas in the nineteenth century federalism was considered particularly notable for the rigidity of its institutional arrangements, in the twentieth it has come to be particularly useful for its flexibility when it comes to translating principles into political systems. Premodern Europe knew of only one federal arrangement, *confederation*. Two centuries ago, the United States invented modern federalism and added *federation* as a second form, one that was widely emulated in the nineteenth century. In the twentieth century, especially since World War II, new forms have been developed or federal elements have been recognized in older ones previously not well understood. *Federacies*, or *associated state* arrangements, *consociational polities, unions, leagues*, and *common markets* represent postmodern applications of the federal principle to a greater or lesser degree. New *regional arrangements* represent more limited application of federal mechanisms. There is every reason to expect that the postmodern world will develop new applications of the federal principle in addition to the arrangements we already know, including *functional authorities* and *condominium*. Thus, reality itself is coming to reflect the various faces of federalism.

Federal accommodation of cultural cleavages has taken two forms: either the structuring of polities to cut across those cleavages and thereby dilute them or structuring unions of polities to give each culture group a primary means of expression through one of more of its constituent polities. These two dimensions are parallel to the two faces of territorial democracy, the one neutral, whereby any population that occupies a territory gains appropriate representation through it, and the other specified, whereby particular territories are designed to give representation to different groups.

Examples of the two forms of accommodation can be found among each of the several species of federalism, as Table 14.1 reveals. The assignment of each federal issue is based upon its predominant tendency since, of necessity, both must be present to some degree.

Even as Western Europe moves toward a new-style confederation of old states, its federalist revolution is taking yet another form in the revival of even older ethnic and regional identities in the internal political arenas of its neighbor states. As a result, Belgium, Italy, and Spain have constitutionally federalized or regionalized themselves. Even France is being forced to move

TABLE 14.1
Species of Federalism and Form of Accommodation

	Polities That Crosscut Cleavages	Polities Used to Express Cleavages
Federation	United States	Ethiopia
	Mexico	Canada
	Switzerland	Belgium
	Venezuela	Russia
	Brazil	
	Argentina	Nigeria
	German Federal Republic	India
	Austria	Pakistan
	United Arab Emirates	
	Malaysia	Papua/New Guinea
	Australia	Spain
	Yugoslavia	
	Comoros	
Confederation	Nordic Union	Carribean Community
		Commonwealth of Independent States
		European Union
		ASEAN
Federacy		U.S.-Puerto Rico
		U.S.-Northern Marianas
		Netherlands-Curacao
		Switzerland-Liechtenstein
		U.K.-Isle of Man
		Finland-Aaland Islands
		India-Bhutan
		New Zealand-Cook Islands
		Italy-San Marino
		Denmark-Faroe Islands
		U.K.-Channel Islands
Regional/National Union	Columbia	United Kingdom
	Solomon Islands	Burma
	Italy	
	Portugal-Azores	Philippines
		Belgium
		Netherlands
		Denmark-Greenland
		Sudan
		Republic of South Africa
		Tanzania
		China
Condominium	Andorra	
Consociation	Netherlands	Namibia
		Lebanon
		Fiji

a bit in that direction in connection with Corsica and its overseas territories. Portugal is devolving power to its island provinces as the Netherlands and Denmark have long since done. Switzerland, Germany, and Austria are already federal systems.

Most of the new states of Asia and Africa much come to grips with the multicultural issue, whether nominally through the recognition of local cultural autonomy as in the USSR and China or through formally federal systems as in India, Malaysia, Nigeria, and Pakistan. It is an issue that can be accommodated only through the application of federal principles that will combine kinship—the basis of ethnicity, and consent—the basis of democratic government, into politically viable, constitutionally protected arrangements involving territorial and non-territorial polities.

On the other hand, in the older, more established federal systems of North America, the reemphasis of ethnic and cultural differences has challenged accepted federal arrangements. In Canada this challenge has taken the form of a provincial secessionist movement and in the United States, an emphasis on non-territorial as against territorial-based sub-national loyalties. Traditional federalism is being strengthened in Mexico and all three have a new link through the North American Free Trade Area (NAFTA). The latter, while ostensibly confined to limited economic purposes, has already had political repercussions, at least on Mexico as it strives to become a full North American partner.

The Middle East and Balkans area is no exception to this problem of cultural diversity. Indeed, many of its current problems can be traced to the breakdown of the Ottoman Empire which had succeeded in accommodating communal diversity within a universal state for several centuries. The intercommunal wars in Yugoslavia, Cyprus, Iraq, Lebanon, and Sudan, not to speak of the minority problems in Turkey, Egypt, and Syria and the Jewish-Arab struggle, offer headline testimony to this reality. Unfortunately the intensity of the ethnic conflict for the entire area of the former Ottoman empire is such that there seems to be little room for federal solutions or for any other resolution of those conflicts.

Some Intransigent Problems

The new thrust toward ethnic, racial, religious, and national, and cultural self-assertion has generated a number of extremely difficult problems of political accommodation of group aspirations within the same territory which to date have proved to be intransigent when conventional solutions (including conventional federal ones) are proposed. Every one of these problems will require some kind of pact or set of pacts and some constitutional arrangement for its resolution. All will require an appropriate moral basis and new levels of trust, hitherto absent, between the parties involved. In at least that sense all will have to draw upon the covenantal tradition, in one form or another, for resolution.

These problems or others like them have been with us for much of human history, however today they are being reshaped by at least three new developments.

One, the worldwide spread of these problems is not only apparent to all; the irresolution also requires an engagement with the incipient world community in one way or another. No longer can such problems be resolved in isolation or even separate from the world community. Take the example of Russia and Chechnya. In an earlier time their conflict would have been seen as an exclusively internal Russian problem and the rest of the world would have kept hands off, even if the sympathies of some were with the Chechens. In the 1990s, it almost immediately became a matter for the CSCE which was given the mandate to actively intervene to try to stop the fighting between the two parties. The fighting stopped in part because of pressures on Russia from the outside and even then for the Russians to maintain forces around Chechnya they had to obtain the approval of the signatories to the treaty establishing what forces the Russian army could maintain west of the Ural mountains including the approval of the U.S. Senate. Or take the example of the Zapatista revolt in Chiapas against the Mexican government. Ingeniously, it was timed to begin on the day that NAFTA went into effect, on the correct assumption that from that time onward, American media attention would be sufficiently focused on Mexico, not, as in the past, viewing it as a local uprising that went unnoticed in the United States.

Two, we are now in a democratic age and any resolution of those problems must fit with the principles and demands of contemporary democracy. This means that hierarchical control or elite accommodation can only be temporary vehicles for resolving these problems. The consociational arrangement which had worked in Belgium until after World War II no longer accomodated the popular demands of the Flemish-speaking population for greater autonomy so Belgium had to adopt a more democratic form of federalism, transform the country into a territorial federation.

Three, it is more than likely that any resolution of these problems will take place within larger federal frameworks. Thus the European Community was formed and was able to move to confederal union within the context of NATO which provided the member states with a defensive umbrella, thereby enabling those that govern to avoid the very difficult problem of developing a common defense for the community before sufficient reconciliation with Germany. Puerto Rico, the Northern Marianas, the Federated States of Micronesia, Palau, and the Marshall Islands were able to gain appropriate self-governing status sufficiently according to their citizens' wishes because the United States already existed as a federation. In the same way, the CSCE made possible the transformation of the USSR into the CIS and for further transformations of the former Soviet states in light of their own internal cleavages. GATT/WTO and the regional economic arrangements such as NAFTA are providing new frameworks within which previously intransigent problems may be resolvable. The influence of the European Community/Union on the resolution of the struggle between the Flemings and the Walloons in Belgium, the Protestants and the Catholics in Ireland, and the various peoples of Spain has already become evident. Since all are embraced by the EU, their incentives to fight over every resource are substantially diminished when the opportunity for collectively increasing their resources has become so apparent.

We may expect more such "end-runs" around intransigent problems that may lead to greater internal peace than was possible when every polity had to confront its problems essentially alone. In the process, we will undoubtedly find the use of derivations of the covenantal tradition for their constitutional arrangements.

Federalism and the Development of Appropriate Publics and Polities

Without covenantal dimensions, federal structures often have been introduced unsuccessfully to accommodate cultural cleavages, either failing entirely to hold a particular polity together or serving as mere window dressing. The degree of success or failure in this regard depends not simply on the erection of structures but on the creation of appropriate *publics* as well. Here is where federalism most clearly becomes a matter of building relationships and not simply institutions.

Here the distinction between peoples and publics becomes crucial. A people may be defined as a multigenerational collectivity based upon kinship or some combination of kinship and consent whose existence has a prior biocultural character and which holds its members together whether or not the means for civic life and political expression exist. A public is a community which also is multigenerational, but which is inevitably characterized by its civic character and political expression, based on consent rather than dependent on a sense of kinship. Not every polity serves a separate people but in order to survive, every one must have a public that supports it. Conversely, not every public is a people. Indeed, a people may be divided into several publics or a public may embrace several peoples or parts of peoples.

For example, we may question whether the United States is home to the American people or the American public. At the time of the American Revolution, the Americans used covenantal devices to establish the American people. Subsequent immigration increased the diversity of the inhabitants of this land and virtually all of them became part of that people and to accept the American way of life, however nuanced. With the rise of the new ethnicity in the late 1960s and the subsequent development of multiculturalism, it may be that the inhabitants of the United States have ceased to be a people but were transformed into a public, almost all of whom are deeply commited to the maintainance of the United States and its institutions because, in the last analysis, those institutions serve them well in spite of their chronic discontents.

Or to take another example, the European Union commands the loyalty of a broad public which consists of a number of separate peoples identified with the member states of the Union. An E.U. without a public could not mobilize the trust and moral support necessary for it to survive and thrive. But the development of a European public supporting the E.U. does not need—and should not expect—to eliminate the various peoples who comprise it.

In some cases there may be differences of opinion or disputes within states as to whether the state serves a people as well as a public, perhaps not phrased in that terminology. In Spain for example, its strong territorially based minority populations see themselves as separate peoples, but they also see themselves as part of a larger Spanish public.

Ethnic and cultural cleavages most frequently reflect the existence of separate peoples, each of which is clamoring for its place in the political sun. Under certain circumstances, federalism, because of its covenantal foundations, offers the possibility of creating publics that transcend the divisions among peoples and thereby make possible the establishment of civil society and political order. Here is where federalism transcends pluralism. Pluralism involves the recognition of legitimate differences; federalism the building of relationships that permits the groups bearing those differences to function together within the same political system.

The polity formation and maintenance function of federalism is well known. Indeed the study of federalism in its various forms has focused on that function almost to the exclusion of all others. The function of public formation and maintenance has not been recognized as yet but is of first importance. A proper study of the degree of success or failure of federal accommodation of cultural cleavages must focus on this public building and maintenance function.

Building a Covenantal World Order

Our age more than any other in history is preoccupied with the problem of forging a world order. Other societies in other ages have sought to create universal orders—the Hellenistic attempt has become almost paradigmatic in contemporary discourse, the Roman efforts are well known, and the Catholic Church made an effort in the same direction on a religious basis during the Middle Ages—but our age lends a particular and unprecedented urgency to the task as well as a particular and unprecedented condition. Needless to say, the urgency lies in the problem of nuclear holocaust and the condition is the technical possibility of creating a fully world-wide social order for the first time in history.

Most people concerned with the problem of world order agree that the problem before humankind is not simply the control of nuclear weapons for survival's sake but the creation of a just world order based upon decent and proper relationships between people and communities as well as between nations and power blocs. At the height of the Communist threat, there were some who argued, "better Red than dead" and others who would respond with an equally cliched answer. Most of us, however, would rather spend our time seeking ways to be neither enslaved by totalitarianism nor cremated by nuclear weapons. Moreover, we know now that there are other problems that confront the world; the population explosion, the division of the world into "haves" and "have nots," the softening influences of affluence, AIDS and other diseases, the problem of moral purpose in a secular age, the urban challenge to old virtues, the breakdown of old moral standards—that must be considered in any effort to achieve a just and harmonious world.

The air is filled with proposals for meeting those problems. Curiously, all the "respectable" ones are apparently based on the notion that the ideal solution would be the creation of a single universal society in which people are educated to their fullest capacities in the methods of contemporary science and in the values of contemporary art, where a universal government plans for the wise use and equitable distribution of resources, where people's bellies are filled to meet their material needs and their creative powers stimulated to satisfy their spiritual hungers, where the things that divide humans—by accepted definition artificial and trivial—are reduced to impotence in an environment where every individual is free to make his or her own choices.

Stated thus, the vision at first seems a good one, subject to criticism only because it seems too utopian. Many are compelled by the vision. But we must recall the terrible evils that have accompanied efforts to establish universal societies in the past, usually based on the self-same or similar values contained in that vision. The Jews, for example, have felt the pressures of both benevolent and malevolent universal societies and know what they mean from their experiences with the Seleucid Antiochus and Rome, in medieval Europe, in Nazi Germany, and most recently with the Soviet Union. At their worst those universal polities sought the extermination of those who were considered unassimilable within them but even at their best they have represented a terrible mixture of repression of legitimate differences and tolerance of gross evils.

While the horrors of Fascist or Communist universal societies should need no introduction to any citizens of our age, it may be necessary to remind some of the allegedly more benevolent attempts to achieve similar ends. Rome is perhaps the grandest example of an attempt to create a universal society based on high principle and universal citizenship. Yet it could not tolerate any independent nations outside of its ken. Because some nations—among them the Gauls and the Britons and the Armenians and the Jews—had the impertinent audacity not to agree with its conception of the universal order or wished to pursue their own ways of life independently, Rome had to constantly commit itself to imperialistic wars on behalf of its ostensibly high principles.

Moreover, although Rome's rulers tried to submerge legitimate differences among nations and communities, they insisted that all constituent parts of the empire be broadly tolerant of every kind of individual appetite, whether in religion or in morality. What was one more god (or a dozen more) in an already crowded pagan pantheon? Who could say what was moral or not with so many gods offering so many moralities? When one people—the Jews— and, later, one religious community—the Christians—rejected this increasingly unlimited catering to human appetite, the Romans persecuted and sought to destroy them as subversive elements.

The Romans repressed real communities and fostered radical individualism in the consumption of pleasures because they wished to secure complete citizen attachment to their universal empire while at the same time keeping the citizens from any interest in the moral issues that abounded in imperial politics. This policy of "bread and circuses" fostered, not a great universal civilization, but a corrupt and demoralized mass society that, in time, fell under the weight of its corruption.

Fascist, Communist, and Roman attempts to build universal order have embraced all or most of the major elements of the seemingly attractive vision outlined above. All three rested their legitimacy on belief in the absolute character of certain ostensibly scientific principles—the fascists, "scientific racism"; the Communists, "scientific socialism"; and the Romans, the pagan science of their day—while denigrating the existence of any moral standards not in keeping with their scientific understanding. All three have fostered the arts as a means to distract people from moral concerns, hoping that cultivation of aesthetics would so preoccupy them that they would not be concerned over the lack of justice in the society around them. All sought to fill people's material desires and passions to keep them satiated. The more liberal ones raised the notion of private creativity into an end in itself without considering the purposes or directions of creative actions. They have fostered freedoms which have been used to stimulate individualistic pursuit of every kind of pleasure in the name of creative experience. All have sought to abolish differences labeled "artificial" by state order.

Just because the totalitarians have perverted their meaning is no reason to condemn science, arts, or freedom, or to in the least denigrate morally the human importance of full stomachs or experience that leads to human growth. None of the elements included in the vision is bad in and of itself. Science has been a great liberator. Art has enriched society in every age. People need full stomachs and the exercise of our intellectual and artistic powers are major ways in which we express our humanity. Some differences between people are artificial (in the common sense use of the term) and harmful.

But, the totalitarians' misuse of these tools should teach us that attempts to raise them to the level of principles instead of understanding them as tools is idolatry. Reliance on science to provide a vision for humanity rather than as a tool for use in the implementation of a vision derived from more appropriate sources is a reliance on false gods. The elevation of art to a level of importance that surpasses all external moral considerations is exactly the kind of idolatry banned in the commandment against "graven images." Untempered concern with material prosperity and recognition of virtue in any and every expression of creativity is pure paganism. And the rejection of all differences between humans as artificial makes it impossible to discriminate between good and evil, promoting self-destructive tolerance of bad things to the detriment of good ones.

Until humans themselves are changed, it appears that the aforementioned perversions are inevitable concommitants of the very attractive universalistic vision with which we began. We see the signs around us. While fighting Fascism and Communism, the West, too, took long steps down the road toward mass society in the name of universalism. We have elevated science and art to ends in themselves, materialism and private creativity have been raised to the level of ultimate purpose; while, for the sake of individual liberation, we seek to do away with legitimate communal differences. Our ways of doing these things are softer and perhaps the end result will be more benevolent, but one still sees paganism at the end of such roads; only a step beyond the mass society and only a step before the corrupted one.

Though this kind of vision and the universal society it is trying to shape may be wrong, the problem of world order remains. What is needed is a different vision.

The Covenant Vision

This series has focused on another vision which, while offering no short cut to final solutions and even hedging on any promises of utopia, has already demonstrated a real measure of value in moving humans along the road toward a better world. As a vision and a plan of action, it is potentially more serviceable to humans because it is more in tune with what the Bible calls "the way of man." This is the vision of a covenanted world order composed of covenanted communities. If we were to construct a picture of the good world order as presented in the Bible for the "end of days," we would see a vision of the whole world bound by interrelated and generally equal covenants into a "covenant system" with each covenanted party bearing specific responsibilities toward God, the natural universe, and humans. While there may be inequalities in the level of holiness, in this vision, there is no hierarchy of authority among humans except as covenanted.

All covenants are based on the moral law—on the recognition of the sovereignty of God and the values embodied in the great value concepts of the Bible—so that the activities of all societies and all aspects of society are measure din moral terms first and foremost. Thus they are moral limits placed on

human behavior—including science, the arts, and "creativity" generally—
and moral requirements directing human behavior in specific ways. As it is
stated in *Proverbs*, "The beginning of wisdom is awe of the Lord."

A covenanted world order of this kind is neither collectivist nor individu-
alist. It is certainly not based on a universal state serving a society that does
not recognize distinctions since proper distinctions are of the utmost importance to it. (One of the deepest problems of the modern world is the indis-
criminate erasure of distinctions, good or bad—distinctions between men and
women, adults and children, and ways of life.) It *is* based on the continued
existence of strong communities formed by consensus of their members, who
give their consent through covenants that strengthen them as persons because
they have ceded certain rights to the community. Beyond that, the success of
the covenant system depends upon each community's diligent cultivation of
its own integrity insofar as it conforms to the moral demands of the covenant.

The covenant vision walks a close line between linking individuals and
communities together and allowing them space in which to be free. The ambiguous origins of the Hebrew word *b'rit* tells us much about this fettered
freedom or liberating bondage. Of its two Akkadian root words, *biritum* means
"space between" while *beriti* means "fetter" or "binding agreement." The tension between the two makes it possible for the covenant idea to stand as a
potential antidote to both the mass society and the jungle.

The modern translation of the covenant idea into practical political terms
was accomplished through the medium of federalism. The first modern use of
federalism in a covenantal way was through modern federation which generally worked where homogeneous polities were involved or at most ethnic and
religious cleavages did not follow the federation's territorial boundaries. In
the postmodern epoch various other species of federalism have been applied
on a case-by-case basis to accommodate more complex situations. The success of many of these has widened the scope for the application of federal
principles in an operational manner beyond the original federative nucleus of
federalism in appropriate ways.

In the past, the covenant idea has flourished in periods similar to our own,
when people found themselves faced with the problems of reconstituting
masses into communities and societies into commonwealths. Disregarded at
times, its principles did not die when the Bible was exiled from its land. Nor
was its vision buried in the traditions of a persecuted minority ignored or
oppressed in the midst of communities which boasted new dispensations tenu-
ously covenanted. After a strange half-sleep of some 1,600 years, it rose again
from the very pages of the Bible to confront the people of the West at the very
outset of the modern era. As seventeenth-century Calvinists and Puritans pon-
dered their Bibles for guidance in building the holy commonwealth, they found
the covenant idea a compelling guide. From them Dutch, English, American,
and Jewish philosophers took and translated the idea into a secular political

theory used as the basis for the development of modern democratic government generally and American constitutional federalism in particular. Within the framework of the federal principle one perceives the old covenant of the twelve United Tribes of Israel with Moses before the Mountain of the Lord and with Joshua in the Land of Promise.

But the age of reconstitution passed and the covenant idea ran into difficulties. Because it had been secularized, its vision was clouded and because it had been brought to earth it had become entangled with other theories used to exploit men rather than liberate them. By the mid-nineteenth century, very different theories linked to another vision emerged to assault the covenant idea—laissez-faire capitalism, socialism, Marxism, fascism, and collectivism. While their failures were to become manifold in our century, their echoes remain to haunt us all—and to plague us with a vision of world order than can only lead to destruction.

Means and Ends

In light of the covenant idea, what can we suggest as the proper vision of good world order:

1. A society of individuals (people, families and communities) who are freely bound to each other and to the moral order by covenant; a covenant based on federal liberty that encourages them to maintain their diverse integrities but does not confuse the legitimate search for individuality with the idea that they can follow their own stars without limit. Covenant implies law and law sets forth guidelines and limits.
2. A world community of substantially self-governing nations composed of substantially self-governing communities bound by interlocking covenants. Political covenants that encourage partnership, cooperation, and forbearance among nations and communities to allow each to act correctly by its own choice and will.
3. A constant search for individual and social integrities in each nation and a constant striving for *hesed.*
4. Ultimately a world-wide covenant society of individuals, communities, and nations but not a world-state based on a single universal society.

The foregoing is indeed a utopian vision, fit for the "end of days" and far removed from the immediate possibilities of our own time. Yet its very utopianism is useful—it makes us aware of what real solution is and how difficult it is to achieve it, thereby preventing us from seeking easy answers that will lead us into dangerous paths. At the same time, it is a vision so structured that we can reach out for it without destroying ourselves in the process.

What steps can we suggest to start reaching out for it?

1. A revival of the covenant idea as an operating principle as part of a renewal of the search for basic principles in the world.
2. The construction of covenant relationships among individuals and peoples who are willing to accept the binding obligations of covenant-law and *hesed.*
3. The extension of meaningful political covenants in as many ways and directions as they can be extended.
4. The recognition of different orders of relationship among people and nations based on their respective relationships to the basic principles of the covenant and the development of appropriate policies to deal with each.
5. The constant effort to stimulate the cultivation of diverse integrities within a shared moral vision while promoting greater equality of material conditions throughout the world.

The practical difficulties posed by the covenant idea are no doubt apparent by now. It is not an ideology, hence it can only offer a vision and the outlines of a pattern. The covenant system may be based on unity without uniformity but it is also predicated on a common conception of truth. It is not simple pluralism—far from it. Not every interest "goes." Rather the good world order will be based on federal liberty and embrace only covenantal diversity. Still, the covenant vision is not a call to the fanaticism of a self-righteous crusade. It simply says that humans will achieve the good society on earth when every nation cultivates its own moral integrity under its own covenant and when people will relate to each other through *hesed*, acknowledging that the road to that goal will be long and arduous.

In the meantime, the vision of the covenant gives us some guidelines to follow and some standards by which to judge our situation. It can help us from confusing necessary tolerance of those who move away from the right path with acceptance of their ways as equally legitimate and from the equally dangerous problem of confusing the necessary intolerance of evil with the bigotry of self-righteousness. It can help us select our steps along the way and to understand the inevitable setbacks. Perhaps some day this will bring us within striking distance of the goals we seek. Beyond that, it is up to Heaven.

Notes

1. Here, as elsewhere in this book, I use the term "federal" in its larger historical sense, not simply to describe modern federation but all the various federal arrangements including federations, confederations and other confederal arrangements, federacies, associated states, special joint authorities with constitutional standing, and others.
2. Max Kampelman, "Negotiating Towards a New World: The Art of Conflict Resolution Through Diplomacy," Speech to B'nai Brith, Jerusalem, October 13, 1993.
3. Ibid.

4. Leland Goodrich, *The United Nations* (New York: T.Y. Crowell, 1959); Evan Luard, *A History of the United Nations*, 2 vols. (New York: St. Martin's Press, 1982–1989).

5. Yves Beigbeder, *Management Problems in United Nations Organizations* (London: Francis Pinter, 1987); Douglas Williams, *The Specialized Agencies and the United Nations* (New York: St. Martin's Press, 1987); H. Ameri, *Politics and Process in the Specialized Agencies of the United Nations* (Aldershot: Gower, 1982).

6. John George Stoessinger, *The United Nations and the Superpowers* (New York: Random House, 1970); Tae-Ho Yoo, *The Korean War and the United Nations* (Louvain: Desbarax, 1965).

7. Philippe Manin, *L'Organisation des Nations Unis et le maintien de la Paix* (Paris: Librairie Generale de Droit et de Jurisprudence, 1971); James M. Boyd, *United Nations Peace-Keeping Operations* (New York: Praeger Publishers, 1971).

8. Hans Kelsen, *The Law of the United Nations* (New York: Praeger, 1951); Benjamin V. Cohen *The United Nations: Constitutional Development, Growth and Possibilities* (Cambridge Mass.: Harvard University Press, 1961).

9. Joel D. Singer, *Financing International Organization: The United Nations Budget Process* (The Hague: M. Nijhoff, 1961); John Stoessinger, *Financing the United Nations System* (Washington, D.C.: Brookings Institute, 1964).

10. Nicolas Henderson, *The Birth of NATO* (London: Weidenfeld and Nicolson, 1982); Werner Feld, *NATO and the Atlantic Defense: Perceptions and Illusions* (New York: Praeger, 1982).

11. Brian Hunter, ed. *The Statesman's Yearbook 1994–95* (New York: St. Martin's Press, 1994).

12. Michael Burgess, ed. *Federalism and Federation in Western Europe* (London: Croom Helm, 1986).

13. Derek Urwin, *The Community of Europe: A History of European Integration Since 1945*(London: Longman, 1991); David Weigall and Peter Stirk, eds. *The Origins and Development of the European Community* (Leicester: Leicester University Press, 1992).

14. Robert D. Crassweiler, *The Caribbean Community* (London: Pall Mall Press, 1972).

15. Truman R. Clark, *Puerto Rico and the United States* (Pittsburgh: University of Pittsburgh Press, 1975).

16. Stanley Steiner, *The New Indians* (New York: Harper and Row, 1968); Vine Deloria, *The Nations Within: The Past and Future of American Indian Sovereignty* (New York: Pantheon Books, 1984).

17. Daniel J. Elazar, *Exploring Federalism* (Tuscaloosa, Ala: University of Alabama Press, 1987); Daniel J. Elazar, *Federal Systems of the World*, 2nd ed. (London: Longman, 1994).

15

Covenant, Republicanism, and Democracy

The contemporary traveler boarding a plane at Ben-Gurion Airport in Israel, thirty-five minutes from Jerusalem, to fly to the United States, soon finds himself winging his way over the Aegean along the coast of Asia Minor, the Balkans, and the former Austro-Hungarian empire to Switzerland, from there northward to the Low Countries and then across the English Channel to Britain. If the weather is a little off normal, his plane crosses northern Britain, that is to say, Scotland, and if it is even more off normal, it may even go further north to Iceland, but in any case it crosses the Atlantic until it reaches the Maritime Provinces in Canada, Newfoundland and Nova Scotia in particular, from there to the United States, perhaps landing in Boston, the first international aviation port of call in the U.S. and the principal city of New England. In that flight of less than twelve hours duration, our traveler has crossed the most important manifestations of frontiers, borderlands, and covenantal societies in the world.

The Land of Israel was the first frontier of Western civilization, part of the interior Asian migration to Western Asia. More specifically it was one of the first two culturally decisive frontiers of the West, along with the Hellenic frontier in Asia Minor. The Israelite frontier even produced a recipe for frontier initiation and development which can be found in the Bible in the record of the migrations presented in Scripture from prior to Abraham's migration from Haran in northern Syria to Canaan and through the Israelite exodus from Egypt and their resettling of Canaan.

The Israelites were part of a general West Asia/Middle Eastern oasis culture. Even when Israel's core was secure, its peripheries were parts of boundary regions, subject to fluctuation and to maintaining peace through negotiated pacts both to advance its frontier and organize its borderlands.

The Israelites took the older idea of vassal treaties between imperial and local rulers and transformed it into the theo-political idea of covenant. There were pacts among equals or those equal to the tasks at hand, who, by assumed obligations through their pacts, whether those of international comity as *baalei brit* (masters of the covenant) or in even closer connections as *bnai brit* (sons of the covenant) via covenants that established separate peoples.

The ancient Israelites developed the idea of covenant, a covenantal ideology to support it, a network of institutions incorporating those ideas, a political culture to sustain those institutions, and appropriate political behavior flowing from that political culture. As they were transformed into Jews, all of this was retained as part of the deep structure of Jewish life, both religious and political.

Switzerland was the next great covenanted commonwealth, emerging as a frontier society nearly three millennia after the Israelites did. Helvetians, Celts, and Alemanni settled in or around mountains considered too infertile or fearful for others to be willing to penetrate. In the mountains they were joined by others who fled from lowland empires in search of freedom. The mountains became the setting for their initial frontier of development and they, too, had to live with borderlands under indeterminate control. They also adopted a system of oaths, pacts, and covenants to organize the people settling in both, using them to form the basis of a free and independent confederation. Their greatest moment in history came with the Protestant Reformation, some three millennia after the great biblical covenants, when they gave the world Reformed Protestantism and Calvinism and its greatest political product, the covenanted republic, which in due course gave birth to modern democracy.

The religious and political dimensions of Reformed Protestantism engulfed Switzerland and flowed northward through the Rhine River Valley, broadly defined, the main borderlands of Western Europe where Roman and Germanic civilizations had met centuries earlier, to reach the Low Countries that had also given refuge to people seeking freedom because they, too, were on the periphery of settled Europe, under water rather than above the clouds. Particularly in the Netherlands, another covenantal culture was developed. In the process of reclaiming land from the sea, its people found the drive to achieve political independence and religious reformation. It became the first covenanted polity to achieve world power status and plant colonies influenced by covenant in the Americas and Southern Africa.

Our airplane continues over Scotland, a great covenantal country and community in earlier times that transformed its culture into a complete example of covenantalism by embracing and redefining Reformed Protestantism, to build a strong covenantal basis under the influence of John Knox. After its union with England, the Scots carried covenantal theory and practice throughout the world and became leading pioneers in the British empire. Their covenantalism was particularly instrumental in the new societies developed by Britain in North America and the South Pacific where Scottish religion, commerce, and politics were decisive if not dominant in shaping the configurations of those newly settled lands throughout the modern epoch.

If we have been fortunate enough to fly over Iceland, the jewel of the Scandinavian oath societies, we have had a glimpse of the one exception to biblical covenantalism. Hardy people from Scandinavian countries and the northern British Isles migrated to Iceland to find freedom on a covenantal basis some 1,200 years ago. They established an oath society that remains to this day a fragment of what Scandinavia once was.

Our next sighting is of Canada, including those portions predominantly settled by Scots and those portions settled by Bretons, the French Canadians who came from a similar Celtic background who were turned in a different direction by their historic experiences but did not have difficulty in developing a covenant with the British after resistance to them proved futile and out of the necessity to insure French Canadian survival. Canadians from various covenantal backgrounds settled the whole northern half of North America and brought it under their version of covenantal political institutions, culture, and behavior.

Finally we land in the United States, the greatest of all the modern covenantal civil societies, born out of the Reformation as it manifested itself in Puritan England, Presbyterian Scotland, Calvinist Netherlands, Huguenot France, and the Reformed Protestant Rhineland. All of these various streams and currents met and mixed in that part of British North America that became the United States where, modified by the influence of British Whigs and the eighteenth-century European Enlightenment, particularly in its Scottish form, they founded the United States of America and its institutions. Dominated and shaped by New England, America's covenantal core, the United States not only settled the southern half of the North American continent to establish a covenantal society from coast to coast, but became the great power that in the twentieth century successfully led the world in the great war against totalitarianism and for democracy, a war which is closer to being won as we reach the end of the twentieth century than any of us could have expected even a few years earlier.

Republican institutions are the mainstays of all of the covenantal societies and their constituent parts. Indeed, the demand for republican institutions (which was inextricably linked with the demand for constitutional government) was one of the great political reasons for founding them in the first place. In this light, republicanism properly focuses on the character of the political institutions and the relationship between one structure of these institutions and their functioning, within the framework of polities which demand that they be representative of the people they serve.

The representativeness (or republicanism) of political institutions is to be measured both in terms of the actual distribution of power and the formal allocation of authority within the polity. In democratic republics, the political norms tend to favor the wide dispersal of power. The pressures for dispersal are tied to involvement of different elements in the policy—political and economic interests, socio-economic groupings, and reference groups (e.g., cosmopolitans and locals)—with different governments or governmental agencies, many of which are established as separate entities in response to just such group demands. The network of tie-ins that tends to develop from this often makes serious concentration of power (particularly executive power) impossible. When this is so, government often follows the classic "congressional" pattern whereby the executive and administrative functions are in the hands of independent or loosely linked boards or, alternatively agencies controlled by a committee or committees of the legislative body (or bodies) which, over time, come to speak for the relevant special constituencies.[1]

Whether it began that way or not, republicanism in the modern covenantal societies soon became democratic republicanism, committed to making representative institutions popular ones as well. The contemporary manifestations of democratic republicanism emphasize the participation of the people as a whole, in groups or as individuals, in the processes of government in their polities, through elections, associational and interest group activity, individual involvement, and the like.

The role of socioeconomic variables in determining the character, scope, and forms of popular participation in the decision-making process is generally accepted. These variables are particularly important in polities with important class divisions (particularly those with large working-class populations or the equivalent). Even more important is the division in frame of reference and activity between those who are extensively involved in the decision-making processes in the community (cosmopolitans) and those whose involvement is constricted by choice and interest to their own localities, neighborhoods, or groups, particularly in community conflict situations (locals).

The ramifications of the cosmopolitan-local division extend beyond electoral alignments and into the structure and functioning of governments, government agencies, and public nongovernmental bodies in the polity. Since the "power structure" of covenanted polities is fundamentally pluralistic, government (insofar as it involves decision-making) rests upon the mobilization of concurrent majorities developed from among the strongest group and individual interests represented in the polity. This means that a wide variety of groups and individuals hold the power of tacit veto over given issues, by preventing the formation of the requisite concurrent majority. The strength of their tacit veto power varies by group and by issue. Some groups and individuals have wide powers of tacit veto. The power of others is confined to limited areas where it may be great. The determination of which groups and individuals have what degree of tacit veto power provides the best basis for identifying the community's "power structure."[2]

Democracy in covenanted polities tends to have a strong ideological basis, in the sense that to be a full citizen one must share the moral vision and commitments of the covenanted community which at times become near-doctrinal in character. One consequence of this is that true covenanted communities are almost invariably new societies founded by people who have chosen to be bound by the same vision, commitments and way of life. In the natural history of things, in the course of a generation or two—at most three—those new societies settle in. Their members are members by virtue of being born into the new order, not by having chosen it. Some, indeed, are moved by the vision, commitments and way of life of their forebears and become assenting members of the covenanted community. Others simply go along, and still others reject the covenantal consensus.

This natural phenomenon leads to the necessity of adapting the original covenanted community to these new conditions. This is the essence of the transition from ideological to territorial democracy. Since the adaptation has to do with the relationship between parents and children, both parental and covenant love (*hesed*) are involved in making the transition work. In the process, some originally covenanted communities become almost-covenanted polities as they seek to accommodate those who are entitled to citizenship by other criteria, but do not accept the covenant in the same way as their forebears. Ironically, that is which brings about the weakening of the covenant itself. But that is only human.

This indeed points to one of the great weaknesses of the covenanted community. The more pure and uncompromising it is, the less it is able to cope with human frailty. The expectations from its members are impossible of achievement even by those most devoutly committed to its covenant. The insistance of its leadership on the undeviating maintainance of the covenant ultimately leads to the development of a large group of disaffected members who, in time, combine to overturn the very fundaments of the covenanted community itself. That is why if we look upon the diluted covenanted community as a failure in the abstract, in fact the only way to preserve a reasonable amount of the covenant tradition over the generations is to intermix its covenantal foundations with others that allow greater flexibility in matters of human weakness. Needless to say, the proper balance is very difficult to achieve. Several situations are indicative of the problem.

"The Law of the Land" and "The Law of the Group"

Where the community persists in holding to its own law and excluding all those who refuse to accept it, the law of the group never becomes the law of the land, rather one's legal status, standing and allegiance are determined by one's group. Essentially, there is no law of the land under such conditions. Here we have a great contrast between the Anglo-American and the Middle Eastern approaches to law.

In all likelihood, the concept of "the law of the land" developed in England as a result of the pluralistic nature of the English population at the time of the earliest formulations of English law. We often forget that in that period England was subject to a whole series of invasions and migrations which brought Britons, Anglo-Saxons, Danes, Norwegians, Normans, and who knows what else, to English shores. Each group brought with it its own law, but for some reason, perhaps one akin to the melting pot to become characteristic of the United States a millennium later, the various peoples of England in effect opted to become Englishmen or were forced to do so. Since, once they became Christians, they shared a common religion this was possible. Thus, what was needed was not the disparate or separate laws of the various peoples but a common law which of necessity had to be defined "neutrally" as the law of the land rather than that of any one of the particular peoples.

This is in great contrast to the situation in the Middle East where the peoples, separated by different religions or religious traditions, as well as ethnically, chose to remain separate and, as a result, developed their own laws regardless of the lands in which they were located. Consequently, in that region, until the rise of the modern states in the twentieth century, there was no such thing as the law of the land, only the laws of particular peoples. We may summarize by suggesting that these represent two polarities in the formulation of basic law—the law of the land designed to apply to any resident of the land; the law of the people designed to apply only to those who are accepted within a particular people. Each allows for its own kind of pluralism but each kind of pluralism is very different.

The Social Contract

The potentially successful extension of the covenant tradition has its source in the contractarian character of contemporary civil society which may serve as a jumping-off point for going beyond contractarianism. There is no democratic polity, perhaps there are not even any less than democratic republics, that does not rest in some important respects on a basic social contract among its members and between rulers and ruled, explicit or implicit. The modern epoch began in the mid-seventeenth century with the demise of notions of divine right of rule, however phrased or developed. The postmodern epoch began in the mid-twentieth century with the failure of the idea of the nation state. This double collapse left some sense of political compact or social contract as the glue holding the body politic together.

Virtually all of the world's polities are essentially heterogeneous, whether individualistic or collectivist in character. In some way their members must see themselves as consenting to be part of the political whole. In those polities where what passes for consent is essentially a matter of compulsion, wherever possible the inhabitants vote with their feet and, by leaving, withdraw whatever consent was implied. Contemporary political leaders, then, devote a major share of their political resources to fostering, maintaining and, if necessary, renegotiating the social contracts that bind their polities. This task has now become necessary even in those few polities that can be considered homogeneous nation states, since individualism is so much part of the contemporary spirit that even people who see themselves as members of the same nation by kinship give priority to their individual interests and implicitly or explicitly give or withhold consent from the polity accordingly.

The proof of all of this is to be found in those cases in which the social contract has unraveled or has been violated by rulers. This is easily demonstrated in democratic regimes, but it is equally demonstrable in less than democratic ones. Take the Philippines. There the basic social contract, or perhaps better, the political compact was essentially negotiated among the notable families of the islands who have both competed for power and cooperated in its exercise over the generations. It provided, inter alia, that while the ruling party could exile and even imprison members of these notable families, it could not kill them.

Ferdinand Marcos maintained this unwritten rule and accordingly retained power even after his popularity had substantially diminished. Then his army chiefs arranged for the assassination of Aquino, his rival, violating this norm and setting off a chain of events that within a short time brought down the Marcos regime. Even not so keen observers of the Philippines could see that once Tomas Aquino had been assassinated, a process had been set in motion that could only have one conclusion because the very fabric of the social contract had been torn. The fall of the Marcos regime may or may not have brought better government to the Philippines but it did restore the unwritten rules of the compact and the trust vested in them.

A similar process can be seen in South Korea, another regime with no serious claim to being popularly based. Nevertheless the social compact provided that there would be a certain ritual relationship when it came to demonstrations whereby students protesting against the authoritarian regime could be dispersed through use of nonlethal methods, but were not to be killed. Once this got out of hand and a few students were killed, the fabric of the social compact was shredded and a similar process of change was set into motion. Clearly the situation is far better in democratic regimes where there are regularized procedures for ratifying or reaffirming compacts and contracts, and changing governors and even regimes.

Political Association versus State

This is not to suggest that a social contract or even a political compact is the same as a covenant. The differences have already been pointed out, but their similarities also need to be noted. Covenantal politics go beyond contractarian politics. Yet both require a reconceptualization of the nature of the polity as a political association, away from the idea of the state. By conceiving of the polity as a state, it is given a separate and special status emphasizing its coercive powers and opening the door to its reification. A gap is created between state and society, making each too independent of the other, thereby hampering the development of a proper politics of self-government.

Covenantal thinking, on the other hand, brings us to see polities as associations, the most comprehensive associations, but still associations, part of the network of associations that constitute the commonwealth or civil society in all its facets. The association is the greatest instrument of human liberty, the device that transforms abstract principles of liberty, equality, and rights into concrete realities. That is why advocates of popular government have always emphasized freedom of association as its foundation stone.

Two of the most important discussions of the importance of associations and freedom of association are to be found in the works of Johannes Althusius and Alexis de Tocqueville. Althusius presents us with a systematic picture of the network of associations, from the family through the body politic and the theory of how they are, perforce, interrelated, while Tocqueville presents us with a discussion of the importance of freedom of association. He makes the point that, by understanding the state as no more or less than a comprehensive political association established by the people to serve their own ends, the people are encouraged to form other more limited associations as well, thereby emphasizing both the legitimacy and vitality of the power of association.

Hesed and Covenant Morality

Each of these strands leads in its own way to the great question implicit in the concept of *Hesed*. We have here been concerned with three dimensions of *Hesed*: (1) *Hesed* as the dynamics of loving covenant obligation, that is to say, that which prevents covenantal relationships from becoming merely contractual ones by requiring performance beyond the letter of the law. (2) *Hesed* both as a means of judgment and redemption, whereby being a party to a proper covenant not only offers special relationships but places the partners under special judgment, yet offers them the possibility of return and redemption; (3) *Hesed* as the dynamic element in federal liberty as distinct from natural liberty.

While Hebrew has a rich vocabulary for different kinds of sin, for the most part, sinning is viewed in the biblical worldview as erring, departing from the right path, which is something that all humans do from time to time. Covenant shows us the right path or way. It ensures human freedom to proceed down that way if we so choose.

Yet those bound by covenant accept the concomitant element in the bargain that they will be under judgment based upon how well they measure up to the standards established by the covenant. Covenanted individuals and peoples can be under the judgment of the transcendent power that serves as guarantor for the covenant or can place themselves under their own judgment based upon covenantal criteria. Being under judgment is the basis for self-correction and reform, the latter a semisecular effort to find an equivalent of redemption.

Covenantal redemption is not so much a matter of Divine grace as of human return, that is to say, return to the proper way of the covenant. Perhaps in a paradoxical way it is this possibility of return that enables humans to make progress down the path of history since, at least on occasion, we are likely to depart from the path that, in biblical terms, leads to the messianic era and the final redemption of the end of days.[3]

The rejection of natural liberty in favor of federal liberty is of the essence in the covenantal way. Among peoples committed to liberty, natural liberty is a perennial temptation, just as in human nature as a whole, idolatry is a perennial temptation. It is all too easy to assume that all liberty is natural liberty, the absence of all human or Divine restraint, and that federal liberty is a set of golden chains in disguise. Natural liberty is in fact license, tolerable only in the kind of environment where nature can exact easy retribution from those who do not play by her rules. Thus the North American mountain men of the early nineteenth-century west could live in a state of natural liberty because they knew what self-discipline was required of them to survive. Today, death from drug overdosing is an example of the limitations that nature places on those who take license from the moral law.

Federal liberty is a category of political as well as other morality and there can be a federal liberty bound by secular political bonds. Indeed, that is one of the tasks of covenants and constitutions, to make explicit the bonds of contemporary federal liberty for particular peoples and polities.

A subject needing further exploration is that of the relationship between covenant and fraternity. In a certain sense fraternity involves a step beyond covenant. It involves an attempt to make out of social and political relationships a relationship that is essentially interpersonal and has to do with kinship rather than simply consent. That is to say, under normal circumstances kinship is a prerequisite to brotherhood or fraternity (or sisterhood). It is true that kin can reject each other. Even with kinship a measure of consent is required. It is also true that sometimes people who are not kin by blood become kin by adoption in various ways. But the norm for fraternity is kinship and it provides the model for its variants.

Fraternity may be more than any set of ideas or tradition may be able to successfully demand from its adherants. Indeed, it may put forth impossible demands that lead people to reject the whole system because they recognize the impossibility of a major part of it. Moreover, implicit in the idea of fraternity is not only connection but also exclusion. One has fraternal relations with one's kin or with those whom one chooses to consider as kin based upon that sense of kinship, but that implies that there are others who are not kin with whom one does not have that kind of relationship, even if one has other kinds of good relationships with them.

Biblical covenantalism recognized this so it set *hesed* as the minimal demand for all *bnai brit*. Beyond that, it established a higher demand in the form of *re'ut* or neighborliness, as in *veahavta l're'eha kamoha* (love thy neighbor as thyself; the positive version of the golden rule). While these are difficult demands, they are not impossible of achievement. They are also not the demands of fraternity which cross the line into impossibility for many. *Re'ut* is a critical yet much neglected biblical value concept. Much of Jewish law is devoted to trying to translate neighborliness and the golden rule into practical terms, at times successfully and at times in a manner that limits more than it advances, but part of the realistic character of covenant is its recognition that there is a difference between neighborliness and fraternity that must be recognized and preserved if we are to have the benefits of neighborliness.

Shalom, the Completeness of Covenantal Peace

Just as the Greeks had their ideal polity in which *harmonia* reigned, so too does the political theology of covenant posit an ideal commonwealth existing under a *brit shalom*, the completeness of covenantal peace. In the first volume of this series we discussed the way in which shalom was a covenantal term, related to *shalem* or completeness, the coming or binding together of the parts to make a proper whole. While shalom is used in Hebrew as a prosaic as well as a messianic term, it properly belongs in the latter category as the projection of an ideal, perhaps one impossible for humans to attain by their own effort, but one to be sought and worth striving for.

As the Greek philosophers saw in the description of the *harmonia* of the ideal polity, a way to learn to make our ordinary political lives better, so, too, is the effort to understand the completeness of the *brit shalom* a means to illuminate and improve the ordinary life in the commonwealth. Thus understanding the covenant idea and the tradition that flows from it can give us the principles by which humans should seek to live, a set of practices by which to live, criteria for judging how well we live according to those practices, and an ideal to pursue.

In our times, Martin Buber, perhaps more than any other political theologian, captured the essence of this in his concept of "I and thou" which, when lived, forms the basis for a perfect covenant of peace. Buber, indeed, was a covenantal political theologian par excellence, applying his biblically grounded principles of covenantal relationships to individuals, communities, and polities. One need not accept every detail of the Buberian formulation as guidance to practical living to understand their greatness. Buber's thought, formed as it was in that age of optimism which marked the end of the nineteenth century, did not sufficiently take into consideration human capabilities for departing from the path of peace and doing evil, something which more sober federal theory does, as witness the Puritans and the United States Constitution.

As the very terms "I and thou" suggest, Buber saw true covenantal peace as demanding intimacy, or, at the very least true neighborliness (re'ut). The American federal founding fathers were satisfied with a covenantal peace that was less than complete, based upon comity and partnership. The one represents a vision for the end of days, the other, a recipe for surviving in these days. We need to draw upon covenant for both.

Is Covenant Primordial?

This book began by suggesting that covenant was one of the three ways by which humans established their polities. Evidence can be mustered to identify the workings of each of those three ways in practice, yet the question remains: is covenant, along with kinship, a primordial way for linking humans beyond the family and, at times, in the formation of families as well, as in the case of marriage? This takes us back to the question of contractarian theory. Exponents of the primordial political compact or social contract would argue that, indeed, this is the case. While that question cannot be answered definitively, there is sufficient evidence to suggest that covenanting is so much part of the human way (whether connected with its natural or its cultural dimensions) that is has such primordial character.

For example, the pygmies and the Bantu of Central Africa have developed a symbiotic relationship over the years whereby the larger Bantu enable the small and very primitive pygmies to survive in return for services rendered. The relationship between the two is sealed for every member of each tribe through initiation rites of young boys from both. At the age of puberty the boys of each tribe join to take part in the ceremony of blood exchange which establishes a contractual obligation to maintain reciprocity. The pygmies who are hunters renew their obligation to supply the Bantus with meat while the Bantu who are traders and farmers renew their obligation to provide the pygmies with iron, salt, hunting dogs, and the like.[4]

Since all life involves some combination of force, accident and choice, even in cultures where covenant is not a prevailing concept friends will enter into covenantal relations with one another, often solemnizing their pact through some religious act. In China, burning incense together before some popular idol; in the Islamic world by visiting together a holy shrine; and among Christians by partaking together of Holy Communion.[5]

What we do know is that covenantal or proto-covenantal forms are widespread in tribal societies albeit in ways that are quite limited in comparison to our later understanding and use of the concept and mechanism. Thus in those societies that are most closely linked by kinship, the other primordial form of social organization, one finds covenantal forms and processes abundant. Further, we know that by the third millennium BCE, covenants as vassal treaties were already well-developed as political instruments in Western Asia. Finally, we know that the first enduring system of human thought, that of the Bible, is covenantal through and through.

The first ordered written covenants were products of Western Asia and the structure of covenant documents which still endures was established by them at that time. It includes a preamble, historical prologue, stipulations, provisions for deposit and public reading, witnesses, and, usually, formulary curses and blessings.

In the last analysis, most of the model polities of the West were built at least partially on these foundations—the Greek and most particularly the Hellenistic *polis*, the Roman republic and empire, the more constitutionalized feudal societies of medieval Europe, Anglo-Saxon England, and the Germanic and Scandinavian tribal and territorial republics. In many cases, this is true despite political philosophies which developed in those same political systems which negated and rejected their contractual foundations. As we saw in the case of the Bible, it was not the idea of covenant or compact alone that was important, but the doing, the reality of polity building as distinct from the theorizing about how to build proper polities.

What the experience of those polities teaches us, among other things, is that while it is true that there are three ways in which polities have come into existence and developed, the most successfully legitimate of those ways remains through political compact. There are two implications regarding the relationship between political theory and polity building which are to be drawn from all this. First, is that what European civilization has defined as political theory, namely, abstract and systematic political conceptualization, is not the only way to do political theory, nor is it always the most useful if political theory is to teach us something about political systems. It is equally important to develop an inductive political theory, derived from political behavior and elucidated by the efforts to direct and comment authoritatively on political behavior so that there can be a dialogue between the two forms in light of the realities of human life, especially political life. Thus, U.S. Supreme Court decisions and medieval Jewish rabbinical rulings on political matters may tell us as much or more about political life between theory and practice than many other sources, especially when looked at in connection with the very life of the political systems in which they were embedded and to which they were addressed.

This is not to denigrate systematic deductive political theory but only to put it in its proper place. The study of covenantal polities should introduce a measure of testing of both theory and practice not easily found in other forms of political study precisely because the idea of covenant involves both theory and practice. The test of every theoretical question in the study of covenant is whether it works in practice and the test of every practical aspect of a covenantal polity is whether it is consistant with covenantal theory. Thus each side is held up to a rigorous test by the other and both ideas and behavior must pass through these rigorous measures.

The other implication has to do with the perennial reemergence of compacting and bonding as the basis for any political system that emphasizes liberty or liberties, equality, and fraternity. What we have before us throughout history is the interaction of two related but still separate sources of bonding and pacting: the covenantal and the contractual. Both stand together as systems requiring reflection and choice rather than force (conquest) and accident (organic development). Indeed, each is separate from the other. As separate approaches to bonding and pacting they may interact or they may conflict. Perhaps the most successful of all polities are those in which they have interacted, with the covenantal dimension establishing the polity's vocation and emphasizing its moral aspirations, while the contractual has been particularly useful in establishing its mechanisms of governance and in defending the immediate interests of its citizens.

According to the Bible, Issachar and Zebulun were two of Jacob's sons and ancestors of two of the twelve tribes (Genesis). In Jacob's blessing to his sons Zebulun is described as a seafaring tribe and in the allocation of land to the individual tribes after the conquest of Canaan, is located on the Galilean coast. Issachar is portrayed as a pastoral tribe located inland from Zebulun. In subsequent rabbinic literature, Issachar is portrayed as a community devoted to the study of Torah, the sacred texts of biblical and post-biblical Judaism, while Zebulun is a community devoted to commerce. In what came to be called, much later, the Issachar-Zebulun transfer, Zebulun provides the economic wherewithal for Issachar to continue its studies while the merit earned by Issachar's studies generates Divine grace for both. The implications of this for our discussion are not difficult to see. Both covenants and contracts are necessary, especially when they are used to supplement and balance each other.[6]

Reform and Renewal as Covenant Themes

Covenantal thinking accepts the all-too-human reality of both backsliding and redemption and provides means to bring back a people which has departed from its covenantal ways through a covenantal renewal. The political implications of this are enormous. People in covenantal systems are not only bound by the constitution but by the covenantal spirit of the constitution. However, people being people, they will from time to time, and perhaps with some frequency, fail to live up to that spirit and, through that failure, come to violate the constitution itself.

According to Scripture, at the time of the flood, God's response to human backsliding was virtually to destroy the human race and start again, but with the Noahide covenant He gave up the notion of mass destruction, a result of His recognition of the realities of human weakness, and promised to use His destructive powers only selectively and to seek other ways to deal with backsliding humans. For people who have entered into a covenant with God, then, there must be ways of covenantal renewal. Thus, one of the inventive elements of true covenantal systems is the possibility they provide for reform and renewal within the context of an established constitution, that is to say, change for the better short of refounding, which in other systems often is the only means of renewal.

This aspect of covenanting can be traced right on through the Bible, to wit: the promise of covenant in Ex. 6, the covenant itself in Ex. 19 and 20, the full threat of Divine retribution for violating the covenant, Lev. 26; the redrawing of the covenant in political terms in Deut. 4; the renewal of the covenant in the land, Josh. 23 and 24; the introduction of the monarchy in I Sam. 5; the regime reforms of Jeremiah and Josiah, the call for massive covenant renewal in Jeremiah, chap. 11; the restatement of the covenant vision by Ezekiel, and the final covenant renewal by Ezra and Nehemiah in Nehemiah 8–10.

One of the best examples is in the Book of Leviticus, chap. 26 beginning with verse 3 to the end:

(3) If you follow My laws and faithfully observe My commandments, (4) I will grant your rains in their season, so that the earth shall yield its produce and the trees of the field their fruit. (5) Your threshing shall overtake the vintage, and your vintage shall overtake the sowing; you shall eat your fill of bread and dwell securely in your land.

(6) I will grant peace in the land, and you shall lie down untroubled by anyone; I will give the land respite from vicious beasts, and no sword shall cross your land. (7) You shall give chase to your enemies, and they shall fall before you by the sword. (8) Five of you shall give chase to a hundred, and a hundred of you shall give chase to ten thousand; your enemies shall fall before you by the sword.

(9) I will look with favor upon you, and make you fertile and multiply you; and I will maintain My covenant with you. (10) You shall eat old grain long stored, and you shall have to clear out the old to make room for the new.

(11) I will establish My abode in your midst, and I will not spurn you. (12) I will be ever present in your midst: I will be your God, and you shall be My people. (13) I the Lord am your God who brought you out from the land of the Egyptians to be their slaves no more, who broke the bars of your yoke and made you walk erect.

(14) But if you do not obey Me and do not observe all these commandments, (15) if you reject My laws and spurn My rules, so that you do not observe all My commandments and you break My covenant, (16) I in turn will do this to you: I will wreak misery upon you—consumption and fever, which cause the eyes to pine and the body to languish; you shall sow your seed to no purpose, for your enemies shall eat it. (17) I will set My face against you: you shall be routed by your enemies, and your foes shall dominate you. You shall flee though none pursues.

(18) And if, for all that, you do not obey Me, I will go on to discipline you sevenfold for your sins, (19) and I will break your proud glory. I will make your skies like iron and your earth like copper, (20) so that your strength shall be spent to no purpose. Your land shall not yield its produce, nor shall the trees of the land yield their fruit.

(21) And if you remain hostile toward Me and refuse to obey Me, I will go on smiting you sevenfold for your sins. (22) I will loose wild beasts against you, and they shall bereave you of your children and wipe out your cattle. They shall decimate you, and your roads shall be deserted.

(23) And if these things fail to discipline you for Me, and you remain hostile to Me, (24) I too will remain hostile to you: I in turn will smite you sevenfold for your sins. (25) I will bring a sword against you to wreak vengeance for the covenant; and if you withdraw into your cities, I will send pestilence among you, and you shall be delivered into enemy hands. (26) When I break your staff of bread, ten women shall bake your bread in a single oven; they shall dole out your bread by weight, and though you eat, you shall not be satisfied.

(27) But if, despite this, you disobey Me and remain hostile to Me, (28) I will act against you in wrathful hostility; I, for My part, will discipline you sevenfold for your sins. (29) You shall eat the flesh of your sons and the flesh of your daughters. (30) I will destroy your cult places and cut down your incense stands, and I will heap your carcasses upon your lifeless fetishes.

I will spurn you. (31) I will lay your cities to ruin and make your sanctuaries desolate, and I will not savor your pleasing odors. (32) I will make the land desolate, so that your enemies who settle in it shall be appalled by it. (33) And you I will scatter among the nations, and I will unsheath the sword against you. Your land shall become a desolation and your cities a ruin.

Then shall the land make up for its sabbath years throughout the time that it is desolate and you are in the land of your enemies; then shall the land rest and make up for its sabbath years. (35) Throughout the time that it is desolate, it shall observe the rest that it did not observe in your sabbath years while you were dwelling upon it. (36) As for those of you who survive, I will cast a faintness into their hearts in the land of their enemies. The sound of a driven leaf shall put them to flight. Fleeing as though from the sword, they shall fall though none pursues. (37) With no one pursuing, they shall stumble over one another as before the sword. You shall not be able to stand your ground before your enemies, (38) but shall perish among the nations, and the land of your enemies shall consume you.

(39) Those of you who survive shall be heartsick over their iniquity in the land of your enemies; more, they shall be heartsick over the iniquities of their fathers; (40) and they shall confess their iniquity and the iniquity of their fathers, in that they trespassed against Me, yea, were hostile to Me. (41) When I, in turn, have been hostile to them and have removed them into the land of their enemies, then at last shall their obdurate heart humble itself, and they shall atone for their iniquity. (42) Then will I remember My covenant with Jacob; I will remember also My covenant with Isaac, and also My covenant with Abraham; and I will remember the land.

(43) For the land shall be forsaken of them, making up for its sabbath years by being desolate of them, while they atone for their iniquity; for the abundant reason that they rejected My rules and spurned My laws. (44) Yet, even then, when they are in the land of their enemies, I will not reject them or spurn them so as to destroy them, annulling My covenant with them: for I the Lord am their God. (45) I will remember in their favor the covenant with the ancients, whom I freed from the land of Egypt in the sight of the nations to be their God: I, the Lord.

(46) These are the laws, rules, and directions that the Lord established, through Moses on Mount Sinai, between Himself and the Israelite people.

This text makes manifest the links between constitutional enactments, commandments, and ways. Here we have the blessing and the curse stated in completely covenantal terms.

The covenantal process in the Bible includes several dimensions. One is the promise of the covenant, the second is the covenant itself, the third is the threat of sanctions with regard to breaking the covenant, fourth is the call to return to covenantal ways, and fifth is the renewal of the covenant. The possibility of return and renewal is carried through in one form or another, in every other covenantal polity or people. From the Reformed Protestants of the Reformation to the civil ideas of reform in the modern United States, it is an integral part of the covenantal process, critical to its vitality.

In short, not only does the Bible understand covenants as having a dynamic as to their implementation, but given the way of humankind, there is also a dynamic process with regard to the maintenance or restoration of covenantal commitments.

Covenant and Partnership

This brings us back to the issue of partnership with which we began, focusing now on human partnerships. In the simplest human terms, a partnership is created by a pact among its members. In Roman law, the Latin word *societas* literally meant an associated interest arising from contract (as distinct from *communitas*, associated interest arising out of testamentary disposition and in other ways). A partnership is a form of *societas*. The modern use of the term society implicitly and specifically describes a contractual association and is a modern adaptation of that Roman principle.

Thus the civil society/partnership that is the United States is established through the Declaration of Independence and Constitution of the United States, which is built around the federal government and the states as the principle partners. The contents of the constitution reflect the definition with which we began. First of all, it establishes a lasting yet limited union in which the partners must cooperate but through which they preserve their respective integrities. Second, it divides the powers of government of that union in such a way that each partner either has the right and obligation to act unilaterally or the right and obligation to participate in the common action of the partnership so as to help shape it. In fact, the federal constitution leans toward the fostering of the latter more than the former and American history has borne out the necessity for that kind of sharing rather than for a division of powers and functions. Partnership is both the goal of sharing under the constitution and the means by which sharing is effectuated.

The Pervasiveness of Covenant

Although the covenant idea, like all great ideas, has gone through cycles of influence; at times the regnant political theory and at times virtually ignored, like all great ideas its power has been such that it has never been totally obscured. The pervasive power of Scripture alone has prevented that. It has been easier to misunderstand the covenant idea than to ignore it. That, too, is not extraordinary in the course of human events.

Consequently, most of what has been written in this book is not new, nor does one have to delve deeply to uncover it. So much of the covenantal teaching is there for all humans to see and learn. If this book has made a contribution, it has been to systematize and order some of the history and expressions of the covenant idea in relation to political life and thought and perhaps to probe it a little more deeply in parts. What should emerge from this is a recognition of how eminently practical the covenant idea is, even as we note its transcendent and ideal dimensions. Federal relationships and arrangements not only make a life of liberty possible but, by doing so, make life worth living in the best sense.

Hence the principle of organizing civil societies through covenants among the people who form them is as valid today as it ever was. In the past, these were periodic opportunities for people to come together to covenant with one another and form a commonwealth. Now more often than not people come as individuals (or in family groups) to covenant with existing civil communities or civil societies.

This covenanting usually involves an implicit contract only. People move to a new civil community and become part of it without consciously affirming the contract—they vote, pay taxes, etc. all acts that bind them contractually to the community. In a mobile social order, this is the only way that people can come together in communities or societies.

Granted, these are not organic communities or societies—only civil ones, constituted for political (in the largest sense) purposes but these are the societies we have built to serve our needs as "free individuals." Now we must create an ethic and justification that will enable us to live in them as best we can. This ethic and justification can be found in the covenant idea which can motivate people to replace living-in-the-mass with living-in-community in a way that does not negate individual freedom but enhances it.

While here we have dwelt on the continuation of covenantal possibilities, we must also note the reality of the differences between these forms of political-social organization. Earlier uses of covenant were directed toward establishing holy communities or at the very least commonwealths. From the time of the Reformation, reality dictated that polity builders should seek commonwealth in recognition of circumstances that, despite the fervent hopes of the Protestant divines, the populations they had to deal with were too heterogeneous in their religiousity to expect holy communities. A commonwealth in this sense was a community that, while heterogeneous in the character and degree of religiousity of its inhabitants, was at least committed to certain public standard of behavior and action whose maintenance and even observance was required of all permanent inhabitants.

It goes without saying that citizenship was linked to being of an appropriate character and belief and that even permanent residents who were noncitizens were expected to follow certain patterns of public observance. Commonwealth, then, was already a step toward recognizing the legitimacy of the private sphere and the need to separate it from the public sphere. But still the public sphere remained powerful and could "trump" the private.

The seventeenth-century political philosophers introduced the idea of civil society to compete and, they hoped, to replace the idea of commonwealth. (Of course in their writings and speech they often used the terms interchangeably to reach their larger audiences.) In the civil societies they proposed, the private sphere was not only strengthened but the public sphere was limited. As the architects of the liberal civil society they sought to make religion and matters of belief generally a private concern, if not exclusively then overwhelmingly. They proposed civil societies of this character as replacements for what they saw as overrestrictive commonwealths and developed the term "political compact" to replace that of covenant for their more secular grounding.

Since the seventeenth century, throughout the modern era in the West and in parts of the world continuing today, the struggle for liberty and democracy is not simply a struggle between republican and nonrepublican ideas and regimes but, within those who embrace republicanism, also a tension between those who seek commonwealth and those who seek civil society. If the answer regarding the first struggle is by now clear, at least for the partisans of liberty and democracy, the verdict on the second is not. Each form has its virtues, not only recognized by philosophers but by ordinary people who simply observe the world around them and its discontents.

If the late medieval period was a period of struggle between hierarchy and commonwealth, and the modern epoch between commonwealth and civil society with the latter embodying the new wave, at least the early generations of the postmodern epoch may involve the renewal of that conflict in connection with the conflict between civil society and mass society which is presently threatening the very foundations of the civilizations that the world has known until now. Because of technological changes, mass society is unavoidable in some way. It may be that both commonwealth and civil society will have to provide answers to the problems of mass society for different populations.

Generations of students of political thought have recognized that Western civilization rests upon a synthesis of biblical and Greek thought and the messages of two great cities: Jerusalem and Athens. Political science has its origins in Athens, while political hope has its origins in Jerusalem. Political science is vital for us to understand and analyze regimes. It gives birth to political philosophy which is one means of evaluating them. Political hope is vital if we are to make regimes serve humanity. It gives rise to political theology, another valuable but volatile means for judging regimes because it claims links with the Divine. In one way or another, many political philosophers and political theologians have come to recognize that the covenant idea and its tradition offer the last, best hope for humanity; that they constitute the foundations of our political hope; that they can only do so if they also constitute the foundations of our political science.

What Then are Preferred Covenantal Regimes Today?

In *Covenant and Polity in Biblical Israel*, the first volume in this series, it was shown that God or the Bible did not specify any particular regime as absolutely necessary for the Israelites or any other covenanted people. Rather, the Bible sets down a series of relationships that are required to make a regime legitimate and that different regimes can meet the biblical test. The Bible does this because it recognizes that different peoples—or even the same people at different times and in different situations—require different regimes. To better illustrate its point, the Bible itself poses two alternative classic regimes for Israel. The first and probably the preferred is the Mosaic polity, *(Adat Bnai Yisrael)* the tribal federation as designed (according to the Bible) in the Sinai desert immediately after the Exodus from Egypt and modified by the Book of Deuteronomy, which adapted that regime from the nomadic life of the desert to the rooted life in the Land of Israel.

Deuteronomy, indeed, opens the door to a legitimate regime change that brought about the Israelite federal kingdom instituted by David and Solomon ten generations later as the alternate classic regime. Human kingship and the regime change that it brought were made necessary by the Philistine invasion of Israelite territories and their subordination of the Israelite tribes. The confederal character of the Mosaic tribal federation, therefore, had to be replaced by a more institutionalized and centralized political system that could wage war effectively against Israel's enemies to keep Israel free or to restore its freedom so that it could be God-fearing according to its covenants.

Both regimes are legitimate. Indeed, the Bible and subsequent Jewish political tradition are, in certain ways, a dialogue involving various arguments between partisans of one or the other to this day. If this writer, clearly a partisan of republicanism, were to sum up that dialogue, I would conclude that the Bible prefers the former but finds the latter acceptable given the realities of the world, provided the appropriate covenantal laws and relationships are maintained by each.

In late medieval and modern times, after the revival of biblical covenantalism by Reformed Protestantism, the Western world also was confronted with two choices of appropriate regimes. The idea for the first of these regimes was developed at the height of the Reformed Protestant covenant revival and given its finest expression by Althusius. It called for a polity which, in the covenantal manner, was to emphasize liberty and equality based on a free self-governing citizenry who would be essentially homogeneous both in matters of religious faith and in political order so that they might be treated as one community, as in the case of biblical Israel.

This regime, despite its ideally fine characteristics from a covenantal perspective, became impossible of achievement in many places, this time for internal reasons, because the internal diversity of ideas and of society itself, became too great to enable the achievement of the necessary homogeneity and to still preserve liberty and equality. Therefore, an alternative regime was developed later in the seventeenth century by the founders of modern political philosophy—Hobbes, Spinoza, and Locke—who argued on behalf of a civil society based upon a political compact. A civil society would recognize the new heterogeneity and provide for its maintenance in a manner that would be compatible with the political order by dividing the polity into public and private spheres and further dividing the public sphere into governmental and nongovernmental ones, and thereby reducing the impact of the conflicts potential in any heterogeneous society by either removing them from the public sphere (as in the case of religion), neutralizing them (as in the case of economics), or managing the conflicts between them (as in the case of politics).

In time, the idea of civil society was modified to become the idea of liberal democratic society which further strengthened its private sphere and simultaneously further weakened the power of the public sphere to intervene into the private, even on behalf of recognized public goods. The very term "civil society" fell into desuetude under the pressure of ideologies advocating automatic societies and refusing to recognize the essential place of government—even properly limited—in the scheme of things, or, conversely, the importance of the non-governmental realm, whether private or public.

In late modernity, liberal democratic society was brought even further in the direction of the private. The last third of the modern epoch devoted to denigrating the public nongovernmental sector in favor of a much strengthened and expanded governmental sector with attendant bureaucratic organization and elements of collectivism. The discrediting of collectivism in the early postmodern epoch led to a great denigration of the governmental sector particularly during the epoch's second generation. Thus, questions of virtue and interest were transformed from questions of public virtue and private interests to questions of an entirely private character with a concomitant effort to build up an ideology of private virtue to make the public dimension seem even less necessary.

This, in turn, led to a communitarian reaction, both conservative and liberal. The former sought to restore public virtue through restoration of a sense of the great tradition while the latter sought to build a new communitarianism based on the transformations of the past two generations and their consolidation whose character, scope, and content was not entirely clear.

Thus, while many speculate about the best regime an either explicitly or implicitly advocate commonwealth in their speculations, most of the major polities in the world serve civil societies and indeed "civil society" has become the rallying cry for those fighting for human freedom in the late twentieth century. Nevertheless, both kinds of regime can and perhaps must be derived from covenantal principles broadly understood and there needs to be room in the world for both.

In the first generations of the modern epoch, both commonwealths and civil societies were threatened by authoritarian systems. During the first half of the twentieth century that threat was transformed into a totalitarian one. Both of these overt and open threats were destroyed, in due course.

With the opening of the postmodern epoch after World War II a new and more subtle, or insidious, threat emerged in the threat of the mass society, held together neither by the communal covenants of commonwealth nor by the modern covenants of civil society but by the shared sensations provided by mass culture and its purveyors. On the one hand, these were managed by an ostensibly democratically chosen but actually quite self-selected core of professionals who chose the increasingly detached public sector within which to pursue their careers and accordingly were increasingly detached from the public they served. They were freed, as it were, within broad limits, to pursue those interests and occasionally principles that they found useful or desirable. The extreme forms of these mass societies have been described by the dark utopian writers of the twentieth century: H.G. Wells, Aldous Huxley, and George Orwell foremost among them.[7] If the world has not yet reached the horrors that these writers portrayed, the essence of their vision is far closer to us than many of us perceive.

Mass culture is entirely anticovenantal. First of all, it influences people by sensation rather than reflection and choice and in order to do so it raises the sensual to the highest level of good. Moreover, it communicates even those matters involving reflection and choice by translating them into sensations. One need only watch the political campaigns of mass democracy and the kind of candidates who are successful in the mass democracies to see how this is so.

This also is so in the way that news is even reported. Rather than being designed to give the receiver the information necessary to make educated judgements through reflection and choice (as the mass media claim in defense of their almost unrestrained freedom), newscasting is designed to provoke one sensation or another through "stories" (their term) that sacrifice depth and often accuracy for the sake of awakening sensations through the story line.

The last remaining place in the media where information is provided and must be in a way in which the advocates of modern civil society saw the free press as working to promote reflection and choice, is with regard to sports. Ironically, there the intense interest of sports fans demands a kind of reporting which provides serious information on a comparative basis, alongside of straight news reports and stories, enabling the audience to exercise considered judgements where such are called for. This is no doubt one of the reasons why sports are more attractive to the average person than public affairs. Reporting on sports is considered trustworthy as are the activists involved, while that is not so in either case when it comes to public affairs. Lately, however, even sports is beginning to undergo a change embrace the deficiencies of mass society as money begins to corrupt its activists.

The emergence of mass society does not eliminate the need for governance or the existance of drives for power on the part of humans. Thus a third element of its impact is a shift in the bases for the achievement of power back from publicly selected to self-selected individuals. Obviously, even the most democratic system in any community beyond the most intimate tribe or village where people know each other so well that they can select those whom they think best for the task, based on personal knowledge whether the selectees seek power or not, there always is a measure of self-selection as to who seeks power and a governance role. In modern democracies, that self-selection was filtered through public processes through which the citizenry made decisions. As long as those public processes were kept close enough to the citizens who did the choosing, there still could be a real measure of reflection involved in the choice, although it is always true that people who are more attractive to the public (according to whatever criteria of attractiveness used) had a better chance to be selected. That was one of the strongest and most real justifications for federalism in the modern epoch. Moreover, when government was smaller, the gap between those selected by the citizenry to lead it and those hired to administer it was not too great.

This can no longer be true in contemporary mass society, if only because of its size and scope. That is to say, there is no way that in polities with tens, if not hundreds of millions of inhabitants, citizens can get to know either the candidates or the situation well enough to make choices that are not simply manipulations. Moreover, with the vast increase in the velocity of government in the twentieth century, most of its work has to be entrusted to people who never appear before the public to be chosen but are hired by "the system" to administer "programs." The public must rely upon their good intentions and good will as to the way those programs are administered. In most cases, even if they as individuals have those good intentions and good will, the programs are so complex that they are but cogs in the machinery and subject to regulations severely limiting their discretion on these matters in the name of equity, efficiency, and honesty.

During the beginning years of this change, federalism served to modify it, entrusting only limited tasks to the widest arenas of government and keeping as many tasks as possible in smaller arenas closer to the people. This also had its problems of equity, efficiency, and honesty but when it worked well, as it usually did in democratic republics, federalism did provide a built-in corrective by allowing alternative channels of appeal on critical issues. But since modern federalism essentially involved federation and federation was based on the premise that the largest arena was the principal custodian of the "supreme law of the land," the need for increasing the velocity of government and the desire to correct the distortions in the smaller arenas (which in all likelihood occured only in some rather than all of them, but were treated by those seeking change through centralization as if all suffered from the same distortions) led to centralization which brought about the same problems of mass society and government referred to above.

In time, the larger federations and even some of their constituent units grew too large to be what they were intended to be. (What does one do about constituent states of the size of California, with over 30 million population, not to speak of those the size of Uttar Pradesh with 150 million population.) So far, no adequate solution has been advanced for these problems which daily become a greater threat to both commonwealths and civil societies.

In the meantime, the idea of civil society was being revived first in Eastern Europe and then in the former Soviet Union itself by the dissident leaders of the revolt against Soviet and Communist domination. They quite properly recognized that the human freedoms that they sought were included, indeed encapsulated, by the idea of civil society which provided for public and private, governmental and nongovernmental power-sharing, as against monolithic totalitarianism which placed everything in the hands of the state. Not only did the Communist empire collapse as a result of their efforts, but they succeeded in reviving the idea of civil society in the West as well, albeit in somewhat inchoate form. We in the West have just begun our journey to publicly explore the meaning of civil society for our times as a result of observing that revolt.

In the last analysis, we are left once again with two alternative regimes: commonwealth for those societies sufficiently homogeneous with regard to their public purposes to achieve it, and civil society for those societies that are too heterogeneous for that. As in ancient times, both regimes are acceptable within the covenantal tradition although one or another may be preferred because of circumstances. What is not acceptable are the kinds of regimes that since the early twentieth century have been coming out of mass society, regimes which destroy or oppose all true community, true individualism, true liberty, or true equality.[8] In other words, we are back to a situation whereby the test of which regime is right for a particular people or population depends upon the relationships it fosters. As always, in the covenantal tradition those are relationships of federal liberty.

Notes

1. See Martin Diamond and Winston M. Fisk in Herbert Garfinkel, ed., *The Democratic Republic* (Chicago: Rand McNally, 1966), introduction and chapter 3 for a brief exposition of democratic republicanism with particular reference to the United States and "Power and Community Structure" by Peter H. Rossi, *Midwest Journal of Political Science*, IV, no. 4 (November 1960):390–400 for examples of the influence of local "republicanism" in the sense used here.
2. See Norton Long, "The Local Community as an Ecology of Games," *The Polity* (Chicago: Rand MacNally, 1962); Edward C. Banfield, *Political Influence* (New

340   Covenant and Civil Society

York: The Free Press, 1961); and Arnold M. Rose, *The Power Structure* (New York: Oxford University Press, 1967), part three for three exemplary theoretical statements, the last two based on important case studies.

3. Leo Strauss, *The Rebirth of Classical Political Rationalism* ed. and introduced by Thomas L. Pangle (Chicago: University of Chicago Press, 1989).
4. Colin Turnbill, *The Forest People* (New York: Simon and Schuster, 1961), pp. 219ff.
5. Cf. H.C. Trumbull, *The Blood Covenant* (New York: 1865) or *Friendship: The Master Passion* (Philadelphia: 1892), p. 71.
6. Mordecai Rotenberg, *Dialogue with Deviance* (Philadelphia: Institute for the Study of Human Issues, 1983) explicates this phenomenon at length.
7. H.G. Wells, *The Invisible Man* (New York: Scholastic Book Services, 1963); *idem, Men Like Gods* (London: Cassell, 1923); Aldous Huxley, *Brave New World* (Harmondsworth, Middlesex: Penguin Books, 1972); George Orwell, *1984* (New York: New American Library, 1961).
8. Leo Strauss recognized a trend in this direction early on. He attributed much of it to the transformation of the premises of political philosophy from the theleological premises of pre-seventeenth century political philosophy to the naturalistic ones of the modern era, suggesting that the results of that transformation were, while classical political philosophy or for that matter classical biblical religion that sought the end of man as the highest good, naturalistic political philosophy and religion focused on the beginnings of man, in other words, on the lowest common denominator. The result was that while the first tended to bring humans to concentrate on their higher natures, the second brought humans to concentrate on their lower ones with the consequences that we have described above. See Kenneth Hart Green, *Jew and Philosopher: The Return to Maimonides in the Jewish Thought of Leo Strauss* (Albany: State University of New York Press, 1993).

16

Where Does This Bring Us?

Covenantal, Organic, and Hierarchical
Modes of Political Organization

We have now had the opportunity to explore the covenant idea, the tradition it generated, and the political behavior that it produced from its biblical origins to the present in the political life of the Western world, with excurses into Islam, Asia, and the lands of modern and postmodern Western settlement or influence. At the beginning of this series we described the three models of polity building that have served as the "mothers" of all political foundings and subsequent developments in every polity: hierarchical, organic, and covenantal. While presented as models or ideal types, from the first it was pointed out that in reality the models are rarely applied exclusively or in pure form, at least not for any length of time, but that in the end just about all polities draw from all of three of them, in some combination suitable to their situation and that the longer lasting a polity is, the more likely it is to draw from more than one model at different times.

What is critical, however, is the model on which they are founded. While successful covenantal societies may also have a strong organic dimension, the covenantal dimension must be able to trump the latter if it is to succeed. This is true of human culture and society altogether. Every human culture or society is in some respects a combination of all three, but what determines the true character of that culture or society is which one has the power of "trumps."

In that sense, while all three models are "natural," that is to say, there are human beings and human societies that tend to one or another on the basis of their primordial being (which undoubtedly reflects some combination of nature and culture that is lost in the earliest times), the first two are more likely to rely upon nature while the last is already a product of human design. As the authors of *The Federalist* noted by describing it as "accident," the organic model is the least likely to be affected by any overarching human design. Rather, human design comes in small increments in response to "accidental" or organic developments. The hierarchical model may flow naturally from the human drive for power but to be implemented requires at least a modicum of design, more in a technical than in a constitutional way, in other words, not so much as to what should be done, which seems to flow from nature, but how it should be accomplished, which requires some design.

It is the covenantal model that, while occurring among some peoples "by nature" (or so it seems), is a model requiring design, at the very least to overcome the recalcitrance of people interested in preserving their own independent ways and control over them. There is much irony in this. Covenantal polities by design require humans to be "federal men" (in the Puritan terminology), to surrender their natural liberty and replace it with federal liberty, that is to say, the liberty to live up to the terms of the covenant or pact which they make with one another to establish the commonwealth or civil and political society. They come to the conclusion that they must make such a pact at the very least because necessity brings them to a recognition of human weakness and the resultant inability either to live morally better lives or to prevent the stronger from taking over the weaker through either conquest and its resultant hierarchy or through accident and its resultant oligarchies. But they accept that human fate reluctantly so they seek to embody the elements of order and control inherent in civil society on as equal a basis as possible. While they perforce cease being as free as natural men, they are able to better protect their freedom in civil society as federal men.

Quite the reverse happens in organic polities. Originally they were probably congeries of natural men or people who strove to maintain a life of liberty by nature, but either natural difficulties required them to cooperate or individuals among them who were more gifted in matters of leadership emerged to take command, which they did organically, that is to say, as if it just happened. Left to their own devices, organic societies will develop under the iron law of oligarchy and the dominant elites that emerge from them come to rule naturally. In this way organic societies, left to their own devices, either become hierarchical or acquire characteristics that are the equivalents of hierarchy. In this way natural men surrendered their liberty but rarely, if ever, were able to organize their new political societies so as to preserve as much of it as possible within the framework of political and social life. Wanting too much, they ended up with too little, while in covenantal polities by accepting the realities that there could not and should not be that much, they were able to keep more.

Of hierarchies little more need be said. There, those natural men with an impulse for conquest and the strength and talent to realize it acquired the power to do so and, with rare exceptions, were not concerned about the preservation of either the natural or the federal liberties of others. They wanted to conquer and rule and they did, modifying their rule only insofar as it was absolutely necessary in order to maintain it.

What we have tried to do in this study is not to present a unidimensional covenantal doctrine but rather to examine how the covenant idea and its tradition present one general ideational matrix subject to different interpretations based on the common raising of the same questions. There is not a simple straight line of covenantal thought and, far more than could be presented here, there are varying interpretations of the covenant idea and its tradition.

From a philosophic and perhaps even a cultural perspective, covenantal thinking is dialectic while hierarchical and organic thinking is monistic. The difference has extraordinary implications. In the first case, covenant offers the world a dynamic model to relate to real life in which change and flux are expected and proper balance the desired goal. In the latter, change and flux represent interference with the ordered path in the pursuit of a single unity.

Both dialectic and monistic urges or inclinations are present among humans. The Bible reconciled this problem by rejecting a world in which the gods were dynamic, changing, and in flux and introducing the monotheistic idea of one God and one alone who created and managed the change and flux humans see all around them. Seen in this context, it is not difficult to understand what the great biblical scholar Yehezkel Kaufman meant when he said "monotheism was and is not a matter of arithmetic" but a profound revolution, since by transferring monism from human society to one God, human life and history can be dialectic and left to a dynamic understanding yet remains within bounds.[1] The covenantal tradition institutionalizes the results.

Except for those interpretations which try to denature the fundamental concept and remove covenantal thought from its general ideational matrix, all covenantal political understanding revolves around similar questions of obligation and consent, free will, self-government, and political order—in other words, how are the relationships of humans one to another and to this universe and its transcendent power established and maintained so as to preserve both order and freedom, equality and opportunity, neighborliness and distinctiveness, liberty and law?

Humans have wrestled with these questions since they began to raise their thoughts above the level of sheer survival. Early on, so early that we cannot even know exactly when, those thoughts were established in three general ideational matrices: one hierarchical, another organic, and a third covenantal. Each has made its contribution to political philosophy and, more than that, to political life.

The covenantal ideational matrix has at least contributed its share and, we would argue, has been even more useful than the other two in articulating and stimulating a world of constitutionalized human freedom, of democratic republican liberty anchored in law—federal liberty, if you will.

Covenant: The Theopolitical Basis of Liberty

These, then, are the three models with which we began and which have accompanied us throughout our exploration. We have focused on the covenantal model in which humans sacrifice aspects of their human impulses by design in order to preserve what they can and also in that way gain a better life, however defined. We have seen different definitions of that better life broadly within the covenantal tradition and we have noted that in covenantal societies most of those definitions were and are religious or at least have a strong religious base.

Hence constitutional design among covenanted peoples and polities begins more often than not with a theopolitical foundation. Even if there are subsequent changes, some of that foundation remains. I would posit that if and when none of it would remain, the people, the civil society and its polity would cease to be covenantal, cease to enjoy federal liberty, and, in the end, cease to enjoy liberty at all. There is an ancient Hebrew expression: *"Tafasta merubeh, lo tafasta,"* roughly translatable as "If you reach for too much, you end up with nothing." That is true in the case of the other models as well, of course, since it is a human failing in all spheres of human life. Prudent partisans of each model seek to prevent that from happening, if necessary by modifying the model they use or its application. In hierarchical models they do so by granting limited liberties and more benefits to the people who live within them. They also do so in organic models but seek to anchor them in tradition.

In covenantal models it seems that it is not necessarily some set of rulers who seek too much but rather those who comprise the publics, at least some of whom consistently confuse federal and natural liberty and reassert their claims for the latter. This is natural enough, since the people are also the governors in the last analysis. That, in turn, opens the doors for the political leaders to respond to them, ostensibly to protect liberties and provide benefits but actually for political advantage. The end result is the same, but while it may be the same it is even more painful to friends of liberty and equality, not to speak of true religion, because, in time, the people throw away all of their liberty by their own actions rather than being compelled to do so by the actions of others as in the other models.

In the eighteenth century, Rousseau and others could write that while liberty was the natural human condition, everywhere humans were in chains, because he and others saw a world around them built on hierarchical and organic models. In time their words succeeded in arousing enough people in the Old World to bring about the age of revolutions which ostensibly destroyed or at least subordinated those models and replaced them with some offshoot of the covenantal model, usually a secularized and weakened version based on a political compact or social contract expressed through some form of modern constitutionalism. However, where hierarchical or organic models were ingrained in the political culture, those constitutional efforts were rejected or substantially modified in favor of one or another form of centralized control not particularly friendly to democratic or even republican government.

In the mid-twentieth century there was a second wave of revolutions, this time totalitarian. Those were seen as the counterrevolutions of the early twentieth century. They, in turn, provoked a new wave of democratic revolutions designed to restore constitutionalism which, on the face of it, succeeded. These last, whether because of human nature or as a result of earlier traditions, rested upon the kind of voluntary associational basis associated with the covenant tradition in politics, sometimes in an overtly religious manner and sometimes on the basis of secular ideas of civil society. This was a two-stage process. Initially the people who made the revolution came together on that basis, often invoking older covenantal traditions of liberty, in East Germany for example, or turning to the seventeenth century secular adaptation of those traditions through the idea of civil society, as in Czechoslovakia and the other Eastern European states, using one or the other or in some cases both as the ideational anchor for their revolutions against totalitarian regimes. Subsequent to that, the people as a whole through their representatives came together in a covenantal manner to adopt democratic constitutions or, as in the case of East Germany, to accede to the German Federal Republic on both a covenantal and a constitutional basis.

Liberty, Covenantal Society, and the New Enslavement

Now, however, as we approach the end of the twentieth century, we see people throughout the world enchaining themselves again, this time not to external rulers but to their own passions and appetites. Those passions and appetites have always existed in humans. As long as there were external social controls of whatever kind or the natural controls that harnessed natural men whereby human excesses of passion and appetite had very detrimental physical consequences and often led to early death, the world or most of it could maintain itself on something of an even keel and survive. In the late twentieth century not only have we eliminated most of the earlier external societal chains on humankind but have acquired the technologies necessary to eliminate many of the physical restraints on humans as well, thus opening the door for people to enchain themselves and even get away with it for awhile. Still, nature has a way of taking care of its own and reasserting itself. We are already seeing signs of that.

Covenantal society, which included built-in moral restraints as part of the very essence of the covenant, gave way in the modern epoch to civil societies based on political compacts which had fewer moral restraints built in but which relied upon the existence of the prior moral restraints derived from earlier covenants or sources derived from them. As those earlier covenants and sources were rejected by those who benefited from the political compact, the moral restraints began to disappear and the political compacts were transformed. Federal liberty or its equivalent was rejected for a new experiment, the effort to maintain natural liberty within the framework of civil society, the political and sociological equivalent of squaring circles.

This transformation has taken two forms. One is the decline of the public order (or the public square, as Richard J. Neuhaus has put it). We have noted that one of the characteristics of the modern epoch has been to reduce the scope of the public square to allow more space for private life. Still, the idea that individuals as well as civil society as a whole had a public dimension was a concept shared by covenantal peoples, whose concepts of community membership (citizenship) included popular participation in a variety of ways. Where there was no covenantal tradition, "public" all too often became synonymous with the state, a reified rather than a popular institution which, even when made responsible to the public, did not necessarily seek to involve them beyond the most limited ways. In such states, the people gained greater recognition for their private liberties than for their public participation. Those who chose what in covenantal polities was called public life essentially chose to pursue professional careers in the service of the state. They did not become public servants and only the few at the top acquired some celebrity by their choice to serve the state.

The idea that all people had public responsibilities, even if most of their lives were devoted to private pursuits was uniquely associated with the modernized covenantal tradition as it had been with that tradition in premodern times in different ways. The idea that individuals and not only society can and should have, ipso facto, significant public responsibility without losing their primarily private character represents a major democratic advance. It was taken to heart by millions of people who accepted positions for voluntary service on boards and commissions of all kinds, who became local officers in their towns and rural governing bodies, thereby involving themselves in the democratic government of their polities, learning of the problems of governance first hand and acquiring the kind of responsibility that such knowledge and experience brings.

This idea of the individual as a public as well as a private person was undercut in the latter part of the nineteenth and throughout the twentieth centuries by "reform" movements seeking toward greater governmental "efficiency." From their managerial and usually hierarchical vantage point, those "reformers" could only see the "waste" of having many amateurs involved instead of a few professionals. Spreading their ideas of efficiency, they systematically undercut the older covenantal ideas just as in the seventeenth and eighteenth centuries the idea of professional armies undercut the responsibilities of premodern local militias. In the last analysis, for the most part, they have won, subverting the covenantal system, damaging the covenantal tradition, raising the costs of government to inordinate heights, and leading to the establishment of a governing class who end up pursuing their private careers within government and its machinery, not as public servants in the old sense, despite their occasional protests to the contrary.

Ironically, the end results of this were quite predictable based on earlier experiences with military "reform." The move away from raw or semitrained militias to small professional standing armies was designed to relieve the burden on "private citizens" as well as to improve the efficiency of warfare. Instead it led to more wars and the need for mass conscription of all of the eligible young males, and later females as well, in the state for military service in professionally run armies, not as a matter of sharing public responsibility for fighting which also gave the militamen a say as when to fight, but more often as cannon-fodder for the ambitions of rulers and professional soldiers.

In the postmodern epoch, especially since the late 1960s, the balance has entirely shifted towards the private trumping the public in almost every sphere. The most visible is the way in which private rights have trumped public concerns in two ways.

First, interest in public things has declined immensely. Virtue, once associated particularly with the maintenance of the public square, has now become almost entirely privatized. While there are new discussions of how to anchor a civil society in private rather than public virtue, the difference is palpable. Public regard has fallen even further. A new celebrity has replaced the old heroism. Unlike heroism, celebrity celebrates people's private rather than public behavior, first by erasing the distinction between the two and then by discounting the public dimension.

More recently, the doctrine began to develop in the West that public and private people had different rights. If one did somehow become a public personage, one abandoned one's rights to privacy. Anything could be written or said about "public" people, including the most private things, on the grounds that public celebrity involves a waiving of privacy. This further discouraged ordinary people from choosing to accept their public responsibilities. Only those who relished celebrity or craved power were willing to pay that price.

The second way is that the private has become dominated by a kind of hedonistic individualism. This is probably a natural outgrowth of the coincidence of an exponential expansion of the redefinition of liberty as natural liberty along with a denial of the relevance or even the existence of public standards. As a result, anyone can do what comes naturally and not even be considered as deviating from some (no longer existent) public norm.

Alexis de Tocqueville was in all likelihood the first to identify this problem from the perspective of a friend of democracy. He left us a classic description of it in *Democracy in America*, written in the 1830s and first published in 1835.[2] Slightly more than 100 years later, Erich Fromm examined the question from another, more psychological, angle and wrote *Escape from Freedom* to explain the rise and success of the new totalitarianism.[3] Today we can appreciate Tocqueville's analysis even as we note an added dimension of hedonistic individualism that even he could not anticipate.

Covenant and Democratic Self-Government

How do we respond to this turn of events? If all three of our models are real, the last is almost unequivocally best for democratic self-government, but it must rest more fully on the covenantal model than on the compactual or contractual ones that have attempted to supersede it. The covenant model requires the sense of commitment to public purposes and the acceptance, or at least the search for, public standards in those critical areas that are civilization-defining.

The covenantal idea and tradition in its purest form were originally based on a series of covenants with God in which the Deity was a direct partner; at the beginning, the actual initiator of the covenants and, by the end, a respondent to human initiation, but always a partner. After God ceased to be a direct and active covenant partner, humans continued to make covenants among themselves "under God." These covenants, both religious and civil, while not directly involving the Deity as a partner, had Him as a guarantor or witness and were made according to terms of reference that it was believed fell within His mandates to humanity.

In our own time, not only have political compacts and social contracts ceased to be made under God, but in the process there has been a division in covenanting between method and purpose. Some people have adopted the covenantal method of oaths, pacts, and consent without covenantal purpose or spirit. Covenantal legitimacy is retained only insofar as the method provides for a free people to freely enter into agreements after reflection and choice. While there may be some virtue in retaining the method, the lack of moral purpose involved in its use unquestionably reduces its covenantal significance. To the extent that this is the case the question can be raised in regard to the degree of covenantalism involved even if we conclude that the method itself is more noble for humans than any other. Other pacts, even though more secularized, still have a sense of covenantal purpose in that they are designed to achieve moral ends. However, detached from God, the morality of some of those ends would be questionable to those who see themselves as remaining within the earlier tradition. Nevertheless, all of these are manifestations of the covenantal idea and its tradition, but they should be viewed as a series of concentric circles with the first at the core and the last representing two sides of the periphery.

The sense of moral obligation and moral purpose, whether in the polity or in the human environment into which the polity is embedded, must be restored or regenerated. This is not necessarily a call for a return to "the old-time religion" however defined. Rather, it is a call to understand what brought about the old-time religion in the first place and what gave it its compelling character for so long, so that those of us who are alive today may reinvent our civil societies and their polities on an equivalent basis.

In this series we have traced the emergence and reemergence of covenant and the movement from covenant to constitutionalism, where we are today in our political life, and how these have been great political achievements. We need to understand this for the next stage, the melding of covenant and constitutionalism, through the restoration of federal obligation as the basis for federal liberty, which will allow us to enjoy the fruits of both.

Federal Liberty: Covenant vs. Hierarchy and Anarchy

Let us return to the three models of polity, the hierarchical, the organic, and the covenantal. Throughout history, humans have been struggling for freedom, that is to say, to get out from under the hierarchical model or hierarchical impositions on the other models to be free (and hopefully, to be responsible for their own acts). True, that has not been the only human goal, but it has been a great, if not *the* great, human goal. It became the great goal of the modern epoch when the modern situation made it possible for the desire to be substantially realized. After realizing it, humans began to discover that, while the destruction of older hierarchies took place, new ones crept in by the back door so that the struggle for freedom was and is a never-ending one.

Humans also began to discover that freedom per se is not enough. Taken alone, freedom will only mean natural liberty. Freedom is a great thing but it must exist for a purpose. Freedom combined with purpose constitute federal liberty.

While covenantal societies have not had untroubled histories, relative to others they have been indeed fortunate, able to develop their covenantal heritage and the federal liberty that they have built on it for themselves, or at least to fight others who would take that heritage away from them. For those others, the fortunate among them have had to struggle to introduce a sufficient measure of covenantalism at least into their politics, but also into their lives if they want those politics to succeed. The less fortunate have not even been able to do that much. They have remained mired in hierarchies or in organic societies and polities that emphasized the hierarchical.

Hierarchical structures are most effective for certain kinds of mobilization of populations, particularly military ones. Organic structures have, in a sense, guided the overall flow of history by enabling the rise and fall of peoples and structures, allowing some peoples to assimilate among others, to acquire the characteristics of their conquerors, to migrate to new lands and establish new structures and identities.

While organic forms provide the flow, hierarchical and covenantal ones provide the direction. The direction provided by hierarchical ones is antithetical to the striving for freedom. Only through covenantal forms is there both a striving for freedom and for compatible meaning. All in all, only the polities, cultures, and societies molded in covenantal forms have been able to even approximate the appropriate synthesis that can bring together freedom and meaning. In a sense, this was what Tocqueville was referring to when he described the felicitous success of the United States as of the 1830s as the result of the spirit of liberty and the spirit of religion marching hand in hand.

Hierarchical societies can offer meaning but they cannot be free. Organic societies can be free or at least can be at certain periods in their history, but cannot offer meaning because meaning would require more commitment than those within them would be willing to make if they still sought to preserve the organic flow of life. Humans must have covenantal societies to provide them with both freedom and meaning and they can only have those societies if they are willing to work at them, to develop their reflections in that direction and then to make the right choices, including choosing to accept not only rights but obligations and then choosing to live up to those obligations.

Covenant: Vision or Dream?

The covenantal tradition requires a certain degree of political and social self-consciousness and self-criticism. That is essentially the reflection dimension in reflection and choice. That is why covenantal polities and societies must be animated by a vision and are not content simply by being. That vision must be a moral one as the term "vision" implies and it must provide a set of measurements against which the members of the polity or society can measure themselves, collectively and as individuals, from time to time with greater rather than less frequency.

In the covenantal system being conscious of the vision makes one self-conscious of one's shortcomings in reaching it, whether the one is collective or individual. It also provides the grounds for self-criticism which, as we have seen, are built in to the covenantal tradition. The covenantal tradition must also make it possible to "return," that is, to rediscover that vision, make what adaptions are necessary for the times, and force the polity, society, and individuals within it to return to that vision as best they can.[1]

As already pointed out, a vision is not the same as a dream. A dream is more self-centered, more concerned with self-gratification and usually material or pleasure-seeking, whereas a vision seeks higher moral ends. Indeed, it has been one of the perversions of the twentieth century, especially in the postmodern epoch, for Americans and for that matter much of the rest of the world to emphasize the pursuit of "the American dream" or its variants in other countries and to refer to that dream as "the good life," rather than concentrating on pursuing the American vision.

The so-called "good life" is indeed pleasurable and often materially satisfying. It allows one to enjoy comfort, recreation, and pleasant sensation. That is the hedonistic life and, valid as it is to a point (few, if any, of us seek to live in hair shirts), as a target of human endeavor it should not be confused with the truly good life embodied in an appropriate vision.

The American founders apparently knew the difference when they discussed the pursuit of happiness and included that phrase in the famous triad of the Declaration of Independence. The more we understand it, the more it seems that the founders themselves believed that government could not promise anything more than the pursuit of happiness as self-defined which generally would be more materialistic and hedonistic than otherwise. But perhaps because they were close enough to classical thought, they referred to that as the pursuit of happiness and not the pursuit of the good.

Paradoxically, for humans to be able to take matters into their own hands and give them due reflection and make proper choices, they need to recognize the true Sovereign Power of the universe who under normal circumstances is hidden from them in its majesty. Politically this has the advantage of removing ultimate sovereignty from any human agency and locating it outside of the sphere of human authority except insofar as God delegates sovereign powers to the people through covenant. According to the Bible, He delegates those powers as a necessary aspect of the governance of the universe. At the same time, the discovery of those universal laws and divine commandments necessary for life and for the right life also become possible through covenant and, more important, exist in human reflection and choice, providing what humans cannot (have not been able to) provide on their own.

Covenantal Societies Take the Lead

These special abilities of covenantal societies have enabled them to take the lead in the advance of human civilization over the course of time. Sometimes they have done so both as covenantal societies and through covenantal polities as in the case of ancient Israel. Israel gave the world Christianity, a further modification of the covenantal form capable of reaching out to tens and hundreds of millions rather than to a few hundreds of thousands and millions alone.

Christianity began by making its adjustments to the exigencies of the time. Whereas Judaism combined theological and political models, making both covenantal, early Christianity separated the two, confining the covenantal to its theological models and allowing its political models to go in other directions. Even its theological models modified the rather pure covenantalism of Israel. Still, there were pockets in Christendom that preserved more fully the covenantal spirit and ways in both the political and theological fields and in time a large part of the Christian world fell under their influence through the Protestant Reformation.

The search for freedom advanced by the Reformation led beyond the intentions of the reformers and brought about a new separation even beyond the covenantal tradition, one that reduced once religiously grounded covenants to political compacts and opened up great new spaces for private decision making. Originally instituted in a world that still saw humanity as under God in a meaningful way, in time the political compacts became more secular and more emancipated from that conception as did the system of private contracts. The latter, in fact, followed organic directions in the name of serving individual interests and forced the polities established by political compact to separate themselves from the search for meaning and redefine themselves as congeries of private interests that could compete in the marketplace like all other interests.

Under such circumstances it is not surprising that the proper search for meaning which required reflection and choice, commitment and obligation, invariably lost out to pseudo-answers. Humans could not and cannot avoid the quest for meaning. They need it in order to survive. But when an answer comes along that suggests that they can have all their natural liberties and pleasures, while at the same time finding meaning in life, they grabbed for those answers. All proved false because in truth, as the first bearers of the covenantal tradition quickly found out, the only way that meaning can be achieved is through acceptance of the obligations of a certain life discipline which are hard to fulfill and in which all of us fall short at some point, but nevertheless which must command us and direct our behavior even against our passions and sometimes our short term interests for the sake of larger rewards. Still, why these obligations may command us, we are free to hearken to them or not, taking the consequences either way.

The Bible knows no word for obedience. *Shamoa*, the word the Bible uses in place of obedience, means hearken. Thus according to the Bible, humans hearken to commandments. They choose whether or not to accept and act on them; it is a matter of consent freely willed and not obedience with its connotations of subordination. The Bible makes regular reference to the fact of man's ability to choose, indeed God or His representative are often in positions of posing the choice before the people. The only necessity is the necessity to choose.

This concept of hearkening is linked to the fundamental premise of Biblical thought, namely the premise that relationships, including the relationship between man and God, are covenantal in nature, that is to say, are based on morally sustained compacts between partners, each of whom has an integrity that is preserved through the covenant. Given that integrity, a partner does not obey a command even from his senior, but hearkens to it by virtue of his recognition of his commitment under the covenant. The word "hearken" today has an antique ring about it and indeed is apparently considered obsolescent. It was the word used for the term "*shamoa*" by the scholars who translated the King James version of the Bible in between the sixteenth and seventeenth centuries. Those scholars were principally Puritans, men from within the covenantal tradition. For them, the difference between obeying and hearkening was critical to their whole conception of the human relationship to God and to each other. Hence they carefully chose the correct term, seeking to capture the biblical meaning as accurately as possible. In our time, when translators of the Bible are less interested in precise accuracy on these matters and more interested on rendering the Bible understandable to our generation, which seems to be more limited linguistically, several translations have abandoned the term "hearken" in favor of the more familiar term "obey." Not only is that a gross distortion of the biblical text that loses one of the most important of its essences, but it is a sign of the times.

Covenant and Text

Perhaps it is for this reason that, in most cases, covenantalism also rests on faithfulness to a text. It is no accident that the most covenantal of peoples were referred to by the Muslims as "the People of the Book." Obviously the text they must be faithful to is the covenantal text, either the covenant itself or, more likely, the covenant, its elaborations, commentaries and perhaps its renewals as well. That faithfulness to the covenantal text provides people with what they need in the way of an anchor against the anticovenantal forces often associated with power.

These covenantal texts become part of the sacred record of each covenantal people and their tradition, the foundation of their sacred history and the touchstone of their moral vision. Since we humans cannot avail ourselves of direct contact with God on every or even most matters, we have God-given or God-inspired morally grounded texts to serve as our anchors and guide. That, too, is part of the humanness of humans because if we have our texts we are fixed with regard to the texts but free with regard to our interpretation of them. It becomes our problem to reflect and choose wisely on what must be fixed and what can be more freely interpreted.

To the extent that the covenantal tradition has penetrated the world, it has done so through a series of compromises from its original core and expectations. These compromises have had both an enlarging and a restrictive effect, enlarging the sphere influenced by the covenantal tradition but narrowing the scope of that tradition's application. The modern shift from covenant to political compact represented another such widening and narrowing.

Covenantal Expansion and Contraction

In the modern epoch, first through the idea of a political compact and then through constitutionalism, the sphere of the covenantal tradition was further widened, expanded in its core and out beyond that core to vast and broad peripheries. In order to do so, the tradition's scope had to be limited politically to the organization of political authority and power while freeing the rest of civil society for private pursuits, religiously by confining religious pursuits to the private or at best the public nongovernmental sphere, and further reducing the scope of what was deemed the legitimate scope of religious concerns. To a certain extent, this was like the old joke about the religious leader who sought to preach on the social and political problems of the day and upon the demands derived from religious principles in relation to those problems, only to be told by his congregants that he should "stick to reli-

FIGURE 16.1
Circles of Covenental Authenticity

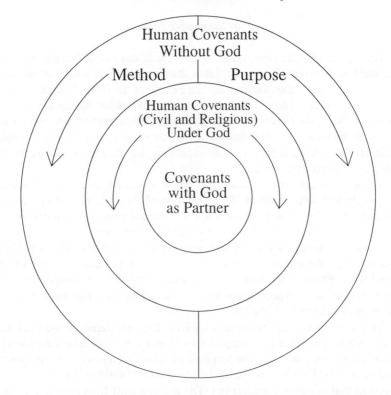

gion," a topic then defined to exclude everything of meaning except plati-
tudes about peace and harmony.

In this sense the covenantal tradition has not expanded but rather has con-
tracted. While its periphery has grown, its core has shrunk. It may be that
some humans are beginning to recognize the consequences of that and wish
to expand that core without doing violence to the covenantal tradition in its
various legitimate manifestations, but their efforts necessarily run afoul of
the reigning pursuit of passion and interest. To reconcile these contradictory
forces and solving the problem that they pose is a task in and of itself and a
truly major one at that.

Fortunately, the covenantal tradition was originated in Western Asia, an
area of oasis cultures, and the first bearers of covenantal ideas originated in
ancient Israel where oases and rectilinear regions met. What characterizes
oases and the cultures that spring from them is that the oasis is centered around
a common core, where the source of the water—the wellspring—is, and goes
out from there until it reaches the limits of the still watered peripheries and

then fades into areas to which the water does not carry. The size of the peripheries ebb and flow depending upon the amount of water available, that is, in good years and bad, while the core always is preserved, stronger or weaker depending on good years and bad but always as long as the oasis survives.

What characterizes rectilinear regions is that they are extensive fertile areas, adequately watered throughout, large areas that do not go through the processes of expansion and contraction and therefore can be divided by boundaries established by humans. In oases, the idea is to control the core, thereby insuring control over the peripheries. In rectilinear environments, the idea is to control the boundaries so as to control what is inside of them.

The same is true culturally. Some peoples think in terms of oases and some in terms of boundaries. Some strive to establish a solid core and to keep control over that core and how it is defined, thereby having a greater say in controlling the peripheries, while others think in terms of boundaries and seek to control the boundaries so that they have a better chance to control what is inside of them. In the covenant tradition, the tradition can be spread informally within a set of boundaries as in a rectilinear environment, but failing that, the covenant tradition can be preserved through control of a core in relationship with changing peripheries as in the oasis environment.

Can Covenant Serve the Contemporary World?

This volume begins by describing the transition in thought and action from the covenanted commonwealth of the Protestant Reformation to the civil society of the modern epoch rooted in a more secularized political compact. It first examines the work of the seventeenth-century political philosophers in transforming the ideas behind the commonwealth into ideas of civil society. Then it looks at early modern England as an example of the movement from Puritan commonwealth to Whig commonwealth to civil society and finally to liberal democracy and how in the process the very idea of covenant or even political compact was lost and in its place there arose a new organicism with its concomitant elite domination of the polity.

While the nineteenth century retained that organic model which came to be dominated by a view of Westminster parliamentarism that gave it full play, already by mid-century the organic model, although remaining dominant in theory, was giving way in practice to the new hierarchy of the administrative state. Parliaments were increasingly controlled by the cabinets that nominally were subordinate to them, and the cabinets built increasingly elaborate administrative structures to gain monopolies over information and action, leaving the parliaments to be mere debating societies with a few formal tasks to ratify cabinet proposals. Part I concludes with the reemergence of federalist thought out of earlier modern organic theories in twentieth-century Europe. At the same time, their American counterparts added a social dimension to the ideas of federal democracy handed down to them from their eighteenth-century federalist forefathers, thereby adding a different kind of organic dimension to federalist thought. In a certain sense both sets of theories remained deficient in two ways until well after World War II. They accepted the premises of organic thought rather than articulating sufficiently separate federalist principles because they had lost or abandoned the covenant principle, in most cases the former. Only in the 1950s was there a rediscovery of the covenant idea in theology and the federal principle in politics and the beginnings of a synthesis of both as a few students of philosophy and politics began to see federal democracy as a form of democracy in its own right, distinct from organic and hierarchical models, one derived from covenantal principles.

Part II explores the role of covenant in the second half of the modern statist epoch, looking at how attempts were made to translate covenant principles into revolutionary theories and the limits on the use of those principles and practices within the context of modern statism. Those limits become particularly apparent when contrasted with Swiss exceptionalism in Europe. There in the Helvetic Confederation, federal principles and practices survived and flourished to offer the Europeans a model, usually ignored, of what modern federal democracy could be like, with its strong sense of individual liberty and integrity within a framework of communal solidarity based on federal principles and rooted in the willingness of the Swiss to take on the obligations they needed to for self-defense and self-improvement.

Part III examines modern constitutionalism, the synthesis between the covenant- and compact-based theories of early modernity and the organic statism that challenged them. Constitutionalism, indeed, became the most practical application of the covenant principle in the modern epoch, embodying the ideas of free political association grounded in public moral commitment expressed through agreed-upon rules of the game accepted by all citizens of the body politic. Obviously, not every constitution embodied this kind of constitutionalism. Some would remain paper documents and still others were sham, but in those polities that became the leaders of modern democracy, far more often than not, that kind of constitutionalism played a leading role.

Initially, modern constitutions differed from ancient ones in that they were designed to be frames of government, no more, but in order to be real and not merely paper documents, they had to reflect the other two dimensions of the polities they served—the socioeconomic distribution of power and the moral demands of the people. In some, these were even built into the constitutional document itself, especially into the bills and declarations of rights. It should not be surprising, then, that as the structures and institutions of constitutional government were consolidated, whatever the balance achieved in this respect in the nineteenth century, concern with them gave way in the twentieth to an expanded emphasis on individual human rights. This concern often came at the expense of the other dimensions of the constitution and even as part of the revolution against them, made possible by ignoring the obligational dimensions of constitutional life in favor of the rights dimensions.

In a sense, this was a natural outgrowth of the republican revolution of the seventeenth century that laid the foundations for modernity. Ideas of civil society were transformed into those of liberal democracy. The lack of need to be attentive to the frames and institutions of government made possible under this system by the consolidation of governmental gains in the realm of structures and institutions, made possible the new concern for individuals and their rights, leading to great achievements on behalf of individual liberty and social justice but also to the disfunctionalities and discontents of the late twentieth century in a world in which in many of the "best" polities communal solidarity has disappeared, to be replaced by hedonistic individualism.

All this brings us to the present and the future, discussed here in Part IV. The present state of covenantal thought, culture, and behavior seems to be based on two contradictory trends: First, in the political arena, globalization of economic and political organization on a federal basis, indeed, through a return to confederal arrangements. This revival of confederalism emerged on a global basis out of the Bretton Woods Agreements of 1944. It was first transformed into political union on confederal lines in Europe beginning in the 1950s and has spread rapidly throughout the world from the mid-1980s onward. The European Union may well be for it and the postmodern epoch what the United States was for the theory and practice of federation in the modern epoch.

Second, in the local and private arenas there is a revival of the covenantal spirit among those leading the fight against hedonistic individualism and its discontents through voluntary organization to reintroduce communal solidarity on a postmodern basis through a variety of local and private initiatives, many of which are religious. Indeed, religious fundamentalism, found in every religion, is often explicitly based upon covenantal principles, particularly among Protestants and Jews, and the effort to translate those principles into practice.

Both of these developments are complex and in some ways even contradictory. In that sense, they fit into the dialectical pattern of the covenantal tradition and, one may assume, will find the necessary reconciliation and synthesis in due course if they flourish at all. There is every chance that they will. Whenever humans have encountered the kind of cultural and institutional crisis that is now afflicting civilization, they have, it seems, of necessity turned to covenantal principles and practices to find a way out because only free human beings freely associating for common purposes can make the changes necessary to do so.

In the last analysis, covenantal behavior at some level has penetrated into just about every corner of Western society and at least in symbolic ways into world society in the form of modern constitutionalism. To some extent that has also brought with it a degree of covenantal behavior, although true covenantal behavior seems to be confined to those societies and polities where there is a covenantal political culture. Even after this exploration we are unable to discover the origins of that political culture. The most we can do is go back to its earliest recorded manifestations.

We have been able to review how that political culture has been reinforced through historical experience and the ideas and behavior that have emerged from it. By contrasting those covenantal cultures in which the political culture has been reinforced by historical experience and those in which it has not, we have seen how necessary historical reinforcement through life experience is. We have also seen how long-lasting those political cultures can be, whether we consider the Jews and their ancient Israelite ancestors, or the Swiss, or those who live along the borderlands where the Roman empire and the German tribes met whose covenantal political culture received reinforcement throughout the Middle Ages through the kingdom of Lothar, son of Charlemagne, and its successors.

The most important borderlands experience was along the Latin-Germanic borderlands which stretched from northern Italy to the North Sea. Whether we look at Robert Putnam's recent study of social capital formation in the cities of northern Italy or the studies of the European Union that have pointed to the cultural origins of its leaders in the Lotharian borderlands region, we are reminded of this cultural continuity which has received different kinds of political expression under different circumstances, many of which overtly reflected hierarchical or organic models, but in the end when the opportunity presented itself, reemerged as covenantal ones.

We may also note in this connection that covenantal political cultures seem to be especially prominent where borderlands and frontiers in the Turnerian sense are involved, that is, where humans have to organize themselves to go out and develop the wilderness or where cultures clash and humans have the opportunity to choose to organize themselves for peaceful coexistence rather than for perpetual conflict. The greatest example of the latter is the great frontier opened by Europeans at the end of the fifteenth century and most especially its North American component. While far from the only example, it was there that covenantal expressions have flourished essentially uninhibited and, fostered by the explorers and especially the pioneers of that frontier who also pioneered modern constitutionalism and federal democratic republicanism, spread from there, especially from the United States, to the rest of the world in various degrees including spreading back to Europe itself.

As we have already suggested, the modern federal idea is a product of the felicitous collaboration of both frontiers and borderlands, especially where reenforced by the ideas and experiences of the Protestant Reformation, a borderlands product if there ever was one. Transplanted to the North American frontier where it was able to blossom and take concrete form, those ideas gradually became the greatest political product of the covenant tradition, involving the form, processes, structures, and spirit of contemporary political life in an increasingly greater share of the world.

We have yet to see the full extent of this transformation or of its meaning. For the moment, it seems that much of it has to do with the collapse of twentieth-century totalitarianism under the pressure of the greatest covenantal society of all time and its allies, and the spread of federal arrangements even into areas where other statist or other hierarchical models had dominated for so long.

Yet, in the pattern of human affairs, there seems to be no positive development that does not have its negative aspects. The covenant tradition, which is essentially optimistic in its assumptions about human nature, is no exception. As always, the choice between good and evil, life and death, stands before us. Let us hope that we will choose life.

The rather denatured pact-making that represents the covenantal tradition in most of the world today is undoubtedly a step forward. It may well be a way to preserve peace in a world as diverse in its ideas, expectations, and cultures as ours. Nevertheless, it cannot go beyond that. In order to build a world whose character is of a higher order, however, people must return to covenant in its original meaning; that is to say, as the voluntary commitment to a moral order freely chosen by those within it who accept the obligations of decency, individual and social justice, and piety embodied in the covenant idea and the tradition spawned from that idea.

In the jargon of contemporary public administration, the latter would be maximizing while the former merely satisficing. As such, the latter may be impossible of achievement. It may remain in the realm of a vision only. It may be that humanity as a whole cannot do better than to satisfice and that to attempt to maximize is to attempt to achieve too much.

There are those who argue that holding out for the best often prevents achievement of the good. Nevertheless, if humans cannot strive for the best or at the very least have a vision of it, they often are hard-put to know what is good. There is an aspect of classical Jewish covenant theory that encompasses this problem, the Kabbalistic theory of the breaking of the vessels. According to that theory, when God created the world, the world was in effect a clay vessel into which God poured some of His essence. The power of the impact of God's essence on the vessel shattered it, thereby introducing imperfection and evil into the world. Hence, the task of humanity, working together with God to fulfill His will, is to repair the broken vessel and make the world whole as it was intended to be. God's covenant with humanity establishes the fundamental way to do so. Humans must strive to live up to the terms of the covenant, but the repair can only be made when God does His part as well, something which only the right human striving can bring Him to do.

The breaking of the vessels not only poses a challenge for humanity but points to the tragic dimension of human existence, namely, that it is precisely the entrance of God's essence into vessels too frail that leads to their shattering. Thoughtful people know all too well how ultimately tragic life is, in the sense that humans never seem to be satisfied, that they are just as likely to undermine the good as they are the bad in their restlessness, to destroy as much as to build in their endless pursuit of change and, in any case, they never get out of their predicament alive.

While in our modern or postmodern way of thinking we may seek other than traditional ways to repair the vessels, the insight that the tradition gives us into the difficulty of the problem of how to construct vessels capable of the best without destroying the good remains as valid as ever. Utopian effort after utopian effort has run aground on this problem, often with terrible consequences for those caught in the web of the effort. The covenantal tradition with its emphasis on relationships, on *hesed* as well as *brit*, attempts to safeguard us from such consequences. Even as we continue our striving, effectuating the combination is the essence of the great experiment of humanity, an experiment made in heaven, if you will.

Today the wider sphere of the covenantal culture follows the rectilinear pattern of bounded civil societies while the true covenantal tradition with its scope and depth has had to retreat to a core from which, hopefully, it again can expand its peripheries in due time but, in the interim, at the very least can preserve itself. It is a cliche to say that this is both a challenge and an opportunity. Understanding both the powerful reality of the covenant tradition in politics and its limits constitutes a necessary first step in meeting both.

Notes

1. Yehezkel Kaufman, *The Religion of Israel*, trans. and ed. by Moshe Greenberg (Chicago: The University of Chicago Press, 1960).
2. Leo Strauss, *The Rebirth of Classical Political Rationalism* (Chicago: University of Chicago Press, 1989); and Robert A. Licht, "Communal Democracy, Modernity, and the Jewish Political Tradition," *Jewish Political Studies Review*, vol. 5, nos. 1 and 2 (Spring 1993).
3. Alexis de Tocqueville, *Democracy in America*, J.P. Mayer and Max Lerner, eds. (New York: Harper and Row Publishers, 1966).
4. Erich Fromm, *Escape From Freedom*, (New York: Holt, Rinehart and Winston, 1964).

Excursus 1
The Language of Covenant

One key to understanding any tradition is the language of discourse used by those who share in it among themselves; the recurring basic terminology that creates the conceptual and perceptual frameworks for considering and dealing with their affairs. It is well recognized that language is the "program" through which humans give shape to their universe. This truth, first stated in the Bible in the first two chapters of Genesis where Adam is given dominion over the animals by virtue of his power to name each species (1:28 and 2:20) and reiterated in the Babel story (Genesis 11) has long been reaffirmed and reinforced by contemporary behavioral science. Since this is the case, it is reasonable to expect that, if covenant is truly an organizing principle of human society, the worldview which it encapsulates should be reflected in the languages of those communities shaped by it.

The exploration of this dimension of a tradition is best undertaken through the identification and explication of *value concepts*, in this case terms and phrases bearing political content and meaning.[1] In this respect, a language informed by a covenantal vocabulary should indicate a covenantal culture and political tradition. Thus the exploration of the language of covenant has two primary purposes: (1) to serve as a tracer to help determine the extent to which a particular culture, people or polity is covenantal and (2) to help probe the deeper structure and meaning of the concept as it works in human society.

The Presence of Covenantal Language

Most, if not all, languages are likely to have at least a term for covenant and perhaps even for other covenant-related concepts, just in the course of things. Hence, it is important that a distinction be made between the existence of mere terms and a full vocabulary. For example, many languages may have a term for covenant simply because they have to describe a phenomenon which the cultures they serve have encountered, but that is not integral to them. On the other hand, if a language has an extensive covenant vocabulary, it is likely that the culture it serves has a covenantal dimension. If the covenant vocabulary is used to provide basic metaphors and concepts for the culture, even in matters in which the covenantal aspect is not stated explicitly, then the culture is covenantal in character.

Here it is possible to suggest a continuum:

1. Some languages may have *no terms for covenant* and related matters, or even equivalencies. Consequently, there may be no way to properly translate covenant or any related concepts into those languages (in the same way that Chinese has no real word for republic but must develop a compound to try to express the idea or classical Hebrew, being covenantal, has no word for "obey" and uses "hearken" instead).

2. Some languages may have *equivalency terms for covenant* and covenant matters, but basically as translations from other cultural concepts. They may demonstrate an awareness of the concept; but it has no particular rootedness or importance in the cultures served by those languages.

3. Some languages seem to have *sectoral covenant terminologies*, suggesting that the culture does entertain and have a place for covenant ideas along with others.

4. Some languages seem to have *extensive covenant vocabularies*, indicating that the culture makes wide use of covenantal concepts.

5. In some languages, *most basic concepts dealing with human relations and organization are expressed by a covenantal vocabulary or have their roots in such a vocabulary*, indicating that the entire culture is permeated with covenantal forms, which are pervasive in the culture, even if there is little conscious or explicit recognition of them in many of the fields in which the terms are used. For example, seventeenth-century English seems to have produced the term "Whig" in this manner. According to the *Webster's English Dictionary*, the term is probably a shortening of *Whiggamore*, a term referring to an adherent of the Presbyterian covenanters in mid-seventeenth century Scotland in their opposition to the succession of a Catholic to the Scottish throne. From thence it was adopted by the English in 1689 to reflect a parallel party in that country. Several generations later, the revolutionary party in America acquired the same designation.[2] In the process, its covenantal origins were obscured as it acquired a specialized meaning of its own, but not only is it traceable to covenantal roots but those parties that adopted it were founded on covenantal principles which were basic to their political ideologies.

The sixteenth-century Netherlands had a set of covenantal concepts even before its provinces revolted against the Spanish. Seven in particular deserve mention. They will be given in their English equivalents. The first is *joyous entry* (in Dutch, *elijdinkomst*), whereby the sovereign must swear the traditional oath to uphold local liberties before being invited to enter the city. This term dates back to the mid-fourteenth century. Two, the *compromise* or common oath. This was the term used to describe the covenant among the lowlands nobles in 1566 to initiate serious resistance to Philip II. Three, *lovingkindness*, a term used to characterize relationships within the Netherlands, apparently taken from the Bible in Dutch translation. Four, *contract, league, and privilege*, a phrase applied to the agreement between sovereign and subject. Five, *liberties and privileges of the country*. Six, *oath*. Seven, *confederation and alliance*, a pact among equals, including such subsidiary terms as *confederates* and *confederation*. Eight, *community*. Nine, *commonwealth*. Ten, *treaty and confederation* (*traité* and *confédération*).

Similarly, the Talmud, though it does not often use the term covenant relies upon a whole series of covenantal terms in Hebrew and Aramaic such as *haver* (i.e., partner-through-association) and *kayemah* (i.e., oath-as-covenant) and their derivatives to express central ideas and describe vital institutions.

The placing of particular peoples or cultures along this continuum can be enhanced by adding a historical dimension including three of four (depending on the people in question) elements:

1. The present situation.
2. The situation at the founding.
3. The situation in previous periods of stability.
4. The situation during refoundings, if any.

Figure Ex 1.1 classifies the major languages of covenantal and other European societies by this framework.

The reasons for delineating the present situation are obvious. Delineation of the situation at the founding is particularly important because of the special role of the covenant idea in the founding of peoples and polities. Moreover, it is well known that great events, especially formative or transformative ones, generate languages or terminologies of their own. Thus covenant ideas and language may have a greater influence as parts of a founding than if introduced subsequently. Hence the founding situation must be given special weight compared with subsequent periods of stability. Conversely, lack of same at a founding will usually be decisive in keeping such ideas and language from becoming of central significance later. In some situations, refoundings, especially revolutionary ones, have introduced (or tried to introduce) covenantal concepts into non-covenantal cultures or revive such concepts where they have weakened. Thus, if refoundings have occurred, they must be examined as well.

The Character and Content of Covenantal Vocabularies

What follows is a useful paradigm of expected terms for a covenantal vocabulary. Through it, it is possible to build terminological matrix which can be filled in for each language to the extent that the language is covenantal. The elements which comprise the paradigm include:

FIGURE Ex. 1.1
Occurrence of Covenantal Language

	No Covenantal Terms	Equivalency Terms Only	Sectoral Covenant Terminology	Extensive Covenant Vocabulary	Pervasive Covenant Vocabulary
Present Situation		French Spanish	German	Hebrew English	
Founding Situation	French	Spanish	German	English	Hebrew
Periods of Stability		French Spanish	English German	Hebrew	
Refoundings		French Spanish	German	Hebrew	English

Historical Location

Structure	Process
Root Term	Principal Operative Terms
Synonyms/Parallel Terms	Participants
Covenantal Metaphors	Initiating Mechanism
Related Terms/Idioms	Response Mechanism
Specialized Political/	End Result
Governmental Terms	
Other Specialized Terms	Other Specialized Usages

Figure Ex. 1.2 portrays them in matrix form. The matrix has two axes, one essentially nominal and the other essentially dynamic. The root term straddles both axes of the matrix since it usually is both nominal and denominative, that is, it includes both nominal and dynamic dimensions. The other divisions relate the nominal to the dynamic dimensions of the matrix. The matrix suggests the range of terms necessary and sufficient for a covenant vocabulary to exist. Thus it offers a way to measure the comprehensiveness of covenant vocabularies in any particular language.

What is required here is more than simply listing terms found by reviewing the dictionary. Rather, it is the exploration of the subtleties and nuances of linguistic usage, making connections which require understanding of the historical principles which shaped the language's development and its idiomatic expression. It is vital to understand how, in truly covenantal systems, so much of the covenantal idiom is lost to view. "Whig" is an excellent example of that, one which can be further developed by examining the deep structure of covenantal thinking that animated all those who made use of the term from the seventeenth through nineteenth centuries and how abandonment of that line of thought led to abandonment of the term in favor of some other ("Liberal" in the United Kingdom, "Republican" in the United States where the abandonment was only partial.

Covenantal Vocabularies

A language with a proper covenantal vocabulary will have a widely used root term, several synonyms or parallel terms, and an extensive number of related terms and idioms. It should also have a full range of specialized political and governmental terms and full ranges for other special purposes as well. Moreover, it should have clearcut ways of reflecting covenantal dynamics linguistically. These include a special term that reflects the dynamic dimension of covenant and terms that identify the participants in a covenantal relationship, the means for initiating and responding to such a relationship or actions derived from it, and the covenantal expression of the end result. There also should be various specialized usages that have developed specifically within the context of the people and culture which the language serves.

FIGURE Ex. 1.2
The Terminological Matrix of Covenantal Vocabularies

Process	Principal Operative Term(s)	Participants	Initiating Mechanism(s)	Response Mechanism(s)	End Result(s)	Other Specialized Usages
ROOT TERM						
Synonyms/ Parallel Terms						
Covenantal Metaphors						
Related Terms/ Idioms						
Specialized Political/ Governmental Terms						
Other Specialized Terms						

No complete mapping of any language for this purpose has been undertaken to date. What follows are basic but still partial maps for Hebrew and English, two of the foremost languages with extensive covenantal vocabularies. The Hebrew map is shown in figure Ex. 1.3 and the English map in figure Ex. 1.4.

Hebrew

The Bible is rich in political terminology, as any close reading of the text in context reveals. Indeed it remains the prime source of Hebrew political terms, many of which have been transmitted with minimum change in meaning over the millennia. The terminology as such and in context has substantial implications for understanding the sources of the Jewish political tradition and deserves full treatment on its own.[3] Among those terms and phrases are several that are of special importance because they give and continue to give meaning to fundamental political relationships and the regimes they shape. In essence, they are the Hebrew equivalents of the classic political terminologies of ancient Greek and Latin. The classic character of this political terminology can be illustrated through the device of the "mapping sentence" as devised by Louis Guttman as the basis for hypothecation in social research.[4] The language of the Biblical political worldview can be summarized as follows:

The family of tribes (*shevatim*) descended from Abraham, Isaac and Jacob which God raised up to be a nation (*goy*) became the Jewish people (*Am Yisrael*) through its covenant (*berit*) with God, which, in turn, laid the basis for the establishment of a Jewish commonwealth (*edah*) under Divine sovereignty (*malkhut shamayim*) and hence bound by the Divine constitutional teaching (*Torah*). The *am* so created must live as a community of equals (*kahal*) under the rule of law (*hukah, hok*) which applies to every citizen (*ezrah*), defined as a partner to the covenant (*ben-berit*). Every citizen is linked to his neighbor (*rea*) by covenant obligation (*hesed*). Within these parameters there is wide latitude in choosing the form of government or regime as long as the proper relationships between the various parties referred to above are preserved. That, in turn, requires a system of shared authorities (*reshuyot*)— what today would be termed "checks and balances." Moreover, since the full achievement of its religio-political goals requires redemption (*geulah*), the Jewish political view is messianic in orientation, looking toward a better future rather than a golden past.

American English

Figure Ex. 1.4 reveals the extensiveness and pervasiveness of covenant-related terms in the language of American political discourse. The American political worldview can be summarized as follows:

FIGURE Ex. 1.3
Hebrew Covenantal Vocabulary Map

	Process	Principal Operative Term(s)	Participants	Initiating Mechanism(s)	Response Mechanism(s)	End Result(s)	Other Specialized Usages
ROOT TERM BRIT	Likhrot Brit	Hesed	Bnei-Brit Hassid(im)	Zakhor (God) Dabber (God) Emor (God) Za'ak (Humans)	Shamoa (Humans) Zakhor (God)	Brit Shalom	Reshut
Synonyms Parallel Terms Edut Alah Amanah (Kayameh)		Arevut	Haver(im) Shutaf(im) Edah	Tzavo (God) Va-ye'etar (Humans)	Haskama	Hevrah Mitzvot	
Covenantal Metaphors Masoret HaBrit		Arevah		Devarim		Shalom Arevah	
Related Terms/ Idioms Shevuah Masoret Edut Emet		?	Anshei Shlomenu ? Rea(im) Ezrah(im) Ed(im)			Segulah	
Specialized Political/ Governmental Terms Agudah Vaad			Kahal Ohavim Baalei-Brit		Askamot	Hitagdut Hevrot Yashar Brit	Agudah Vaad
Other Specialized Terms Shtar Mesharim							Brit Milah Brit Olam

FIGURE Ex. 1.4
American English Covenantal Vocabulary Map

ROOT TERM	Process	Principal Operative Term(s)	Participants	Initiating Mechanism(s)	Response Mechanism(s)	End Result(s)	Other Specialized Usages
COVENANT	to Covenant	Federal Partnership	Partners	Covenant	Covenant	Covenant Partnership	
Synonyms/Parallel Terms Articles Bond Pact	to pact to bond to write articles	comity share	confederates covenanter	promise pledge	bind hearken	consociation society	
Covenantal Metaphors Symbiotic						symbiosis	
Related Terms/Idioms Compact Contract Oath League	to compact to contract to take an oath to league	association		ban communication convene		consent community	
Specialized Political/Governmental Terms Articles of War	to federate to confederate	federate confederate	Whig Congress	initiative		confederation federation commonwealth	
Other Specialized Terms Conventicle	congregate	congregate	congregate	grace		congregation	covenant of Grace covenant of works

The various *emigrants* or *colonists* who settled the New World and established their *commonwealths* as part of British North America became the *American people* through the process of establishing their independence from Britain. The Declaration of Independence adopted by the representatives of the *United States* in *Congress assembled* was their *covenant* with each other affirming that peoplehood before "nature and nature's god." The Declaration, in turn, laid the basis for the establishment of the *United States of America* on the principles of *popular sovereignty* and *consent*, first under the *Articles of Confederation* and then, after a struggle between *Whigs* and *Federalists*, under the *Constitution* of the *United States* which restates the terms of the *covenant* to establish a *federal union*. The American federal union is based upon the twin principles of *liberty* and *equality* which the Constitution tries to reconcile through tacit acceptance of the idea of *federal liberty*, that is to say, the liberty to do what is constitutional under the common covenant. The whole is grounded in the *rule of law* which applies to every *citizen*. Citizens are linked to one another as partners ("pardners" in the language of the cowboy the archetypical American folk figure). The system of government created under the federal and state constitutions is based upon the principle of *partnership* expressed concretely through various federal-state-local and public-private partnerships. Governmental power is disposed among many *governments* or *authorities* and different branches within the principal governments. The whole is pointed toward the attainment of *life, liberty*, and the *pursuit of happiness*.

Yet another dimension of covenant language is uncovered by *Covenant Modifiers* listing terms that are commonly used as modifiers of covenant within covenantal vocabularies. The following terms in dyads or triads, suggested by Gordon Freeman, are appropriate for such a list:[5]

unilateral/bilateral/multilateral
grace/nature/works
mutual/reciprocal
conditional/unconditional
single/double/triple
social/civil/political

Part of the significance of these terms rests with their occurrence in triads or dyads.

Freeman has also suggested that covenantal vocabularies include sets of dialectical terms which pose what might be called covenantal issues, to wit:

voluntarism-discipline
fellowship-exclusivity
nature-covenant
mass-elect

old-new
freedom-authority
individual-corporation
consent-coercion

Other Languages

This model can be applied to other great classical languages, Akkadian, Greek, Latin, and Sanskrit; the languages of other identified covenanted people, such as Scottish Gaelic, Dutch and Afrikaans, Swiss-German and German, and languages of possible covenanted peoples such as the Iroquois and Cheyenne. The great world languages such as Arabic, Chinese, French, and Spanish should also be examined for their treatment of the concept of covenant. Beginnings for several of these linguistic maps are to be found in figures Ex. 1.5 (Akkadian), Ex. 1.6 (Greek), and Ex. 1.7 (Latin).

It is important to note at the outset that Greek, for example, gives all the signs of being an utterly non-covenantal language. Even *diatheke*, the accepted Greek term for covenant, makes its first appearance late in the history of Greek thought and then in the translations the *Septuagint*, the first translation of the Hebrew Bible into Greek in the third century before the Common Era, after the classical age of Greek thought. It is clearly a Hebraism in concept.

Notes

1. Max Kadushin, *The Rabbinic Mind*, second edition (New York: Blaidsell Publishing Co., 1965), and *Organic Thinking: A Study in Rabbinic Thought* (New York: Jewish Theological Seminary, 1938).
2. *Webster's Third New International Dictionary* (Springfield, Mass.: G. and C. Merriam and Co., 1981, pp. 2603–2604.
3. See terminological lists by epoch in Daniel J. Elazar and Stuart A. Cohen, *The Jewish Polity* (Bloomington, Ind.: Indiana University Press, 1984).
4. Louis Guttman, "An Additive Metric from All the Principle Components of a Perfect Scale," *British Journal of Statistical Psychology*, vol. VIII, part I.
5. Cf. Gordon Freeman Communication, *Covenant Letter*, no. 4 (Fall 1980):5.

FIGURE Ex. 1.5

Akkadian Covenantal Vocabulary Map

	Process	Principal Operative Term(s)	Participants	Initiating Mechanism(s)	Response Mechanism(s)	End Result(s)	Other Specialized Usages
ROOT TERM(S) RIKSU (bond) SALIMOM (peace)	šarisdabnbi	riksuu' mamitu twbh/twbwt damigta/dingate	ra'imka	awate	sm'	riksuu mamitu šalmn tabûtu	
Synonyms Parallel Terms rikistu biruru (m) rikilltu ade be-ri-ti		ra'amuta remutu ademamite mamitu (oath)				salimu sulum tubtu/tablu abbutu/athatr	
Covenantal Metaphors nksuumamitu alimamite							
Related Terms/ Idioms kittu	haiarum qatalum		sheba			sikiltu	
Specialized Political/ Governmental Terms			ra'amu ra'amutu			tuppinis ilani mesharum nišilim riksatim	
Other Specialized Terms							ade mamit or ade u mamite (binding oath)

FIGURE Ex. 1.6
Greek Covenantal Vocabulary Map

	Process	Principal Operative Term(s)	Participants	Initiating Mechanism(s)	Response Mechanism(s)	End Result(s)	Other Specialized Usages
ROOT TERM	harmozein (to bind)	SYMBOLION KOINEN HARMONIA	symbiotes				
Synonyms Parallel Terms	synthesin synemosyne	syntheke					
Covenantal Metaphors		horkoskui syntheke					
Related Terms/ Idioms	pistia poietin (to make a c.) eispistneithein (to entr a c.) pistin didonai (to give a c.)	diathike pistis					
Specialized Political/ Governmental Terms		symmarchia	philia				
Other Specialized Terms							

FIGURE Ex. 1.7
Latin Covenantal Vocabulary Map

	Process	Principal Operative Term(s)	Participants	Initiating Mechanism(s)	Response Mechanism(s)	End Result(s)	Other Specialized Usages
ROOT TERM	FOEDUS	foedarare	?	foederae	?	?	foederatio
Synonyms Parallel Terms	testamentum pactum fides	convenir vinculumfidei	comutatum	confederare	paciscere pactus		pax societas symbiosis
Covenantal Metaphors	symbiotica			symbiotes			symbiosis
Related Terms/ Idioms	lega articulus compactum contractus	associatus ad-sociare					associationem
Specialized Political/ Governmental Terms	sacramentum	confoederare		amicita			res publica confederatio foederationem confoederationem
Other Specialized Terms	conventiculum						

Excursus 2

The Biblical Covenant as the Foundation of Justice, Obligations, and Rights

The Three Dimensions of Covenant

The Bible describes how God sets Israel aside for His religio-political purposes through covenant.[1] Covenant is not just a device but shapes the whole worldview of the Jewish people. In part it does so through the very idea that humans establish partnerships with God, even if they are the junior partners, in order to reinforce this idea.

As the Puritan theologians of the sixteenth and seventeenth centuries pointed out, the whole idea of covenant is a most daring one. The omniscient and omnipotent God, creator and ruler of the universe, chooses to limit Himself through a pact with his creatures, human beings, to both enable and to require them to take more control over their lives and the world created for them. In a sense, the biblical story can be read as the progressive transfer of power and responsibility in this world from God to humanity in such a way that humans assume that power and responsibility only after they have assumed their obligations to Him, but still the transfer is made.

The covenantal worldview and mindset are reinforced by an extensive terminology and language of covenant (Excursis One). That terminology enables us to introduce nuances and subtleties in the use of concept, for example, to distinguish between kinds of covenants, especially constitutional covenants that create new partnerships (*bnai brit*, literally sons of the covenant) or limited covenants between entities that remain separate (*baalei brit*, literally, masters of the covenant), such as international covenants; or *hesed*—loving covenant obligation—which provides for covenantal dynamics, and *shalom*, which defines peace as a covenantal coming together into completeness (*shalem*).[2]

There remains much to be explained in understanding the meaning for this now-conventional view of Scripture and its application in the Bible and in the Jewish political tradition. One critical question that must be asked is whether *brit* also is the foundation of justice, with its concomitant obligations and rights, according to the biblical worldview, or is justice built in to the world from its creation, that is, natural. Is there a natural law of justice in the biblical worldview? This excursis begins the examination of the multidimensional character of the biblical idea of *brit*, especially as it relates to issues of *tzedakah u'mishpat*, best translated as acting/doing justly through law, or what moderns refer to as obligations and rights.

Biblical covenants have three dimensions. They contain a theological dimension, either a direct connection with God or with God as a witness; a national-political dimension relating to Israel as a people (*am*) or an organized body politic (*edah*); and a normative dimension dealing with foundation or maintenance of justice, either *tzedakah u'mishpat* or *hok u'mishpat* (law and justice) which includes within it a framework of obligations and rights.[3] This is particularly true of those covenants which establish new frameworks, in Hebrew the covenants of *bnai brit*. It is somewhat less true but still frequently true of those covenants which regulate international relations, where the covenant remains subordinate to its partners, that is, covenants of *baalei brit*.

One may find in the Bible references to three possible positions. In Genesis, chapter 4, the story of Cain and Abel suggests that there is such a thing as natural justice built into the world. Verse 10 is the proof text. After Cain asks God whether he is his brother's keeper, God turns to him and says: What hast thou done? The voice of thy brother's blood cries to me from the ground" (*Kol damai akhikhah tzoakim elai min ha-adamah*). This is by far the most significant biblical passage speaking on behalf of the existence of natural justice and has been quoted to that end by generations of commentators.[4]

Far more ambiguous are passages such as that beginning in Job, Chapter 38, Verse 4, when God, speaking out of the whirlwind, asks Job the famous question: "Where were you when I founded the world," and then proceeds to set forth a description of God's creation and systematization of the natural order. However, the upshot of God's answer is to suggest that while there is a natural order, there is no natural justice; that God behaves according to His own will in ways that may seem to humans capricious in meting out justice. The closing verses of Ecclesiastes (especially *Kohelet* 12:13) suggests the same but in a more positive tone, that God has ordered the world and therefore has redeemed humanity from the desperately cynical conclusion that all is vanity, presented throughout the rest of the book.

Apparently refuting the claim that the Bible rests on natural law is Genesis 9, which describes God's first explicit covenant, with Noah and his descendents after the flood.[5] That covenant sets down the basic rules that God expects humans to live by and provides for the establishment of means of enforcement of those rules.[6] It binds all humans forevermore.

One can conclude from the foregoing that while there may be natural justice built into the universe, there is no natural law; that law is entirely a product of God's commandments, which, except for a few basic commandments that God gave Adam such as to be fruitful and multiply, to be His steward in the Garden of Eden, and not to eat of the fruit of the forbidden trees, are all mediated through God's covenants, first with all humanity through Noah and then through segments of humanity beginning with Abraham. Thus *brit* is required for the ordering of the world (for humans) in matters of *tzedakah u'mishpat*. This, indeed, is the conclusion in Kohelet 12:13, referred to above.

From reading the first chapters of Genesis one can theorize that it is possible that God tried natural justice before the flood and found that it did not work, that human nature itself included too much egoism, appetite and self-interest for humans to act justly without the necessity to do so, and that, prior to His covenant with Noah, God had to intervene personally in every instance to assure just behavior or to punish injustice. In order to eliminate the necessity for such massive personal Divine intervention, God acted, through His covenant with Noah, to establish an order that included requirement for human enforcement of *tzedakah u'mishpat*. This would make God's initiation of His covenant the first major step in the transfer of His active authority in this world to humans, essentially providing that in matters of ordinary law humans would be responsible, with His involvement confined to extraordinary situations or where human institutions failed to perform according to the terms of the covenant and God's justice.

Covenanting is a most appropriate instrument for this transition. The putative covenant with Adam refers to him as God's *shomer* (steward) in the world (Genesis 2:16) and the covenant with Noah (Genesis 9) where the specific terms are not used, examples of the retribution necessary to maintain justice are given. In the first covenant with Abraham (Genesis 15) the term *tzedakah* is used. The second covenant (which does use the word *shamor*) is followed immediately by the story of Sodom (Genesis 18) in which one of the most famous justice-related verses in the Bible is presented: Abraham's query of God, *Hashofet col haaretz lo ya'aseh mishpat* (Will the judge of the whole world not do justice?) The culmination is in the Sinai Covenant which provides the details of what constitutes *tzedakah, hok u'mishpat*. This pattern continues in Joshua's covenant (Joshua 24) which refers to *hok u'mishpat* and David's (I Chronicles 16:7–43), in which David refers to *mishpatay piv*, the justice or just judgements from God's mouth.

Every *brit* is an agreement that requires from both parties *shmiya* (hearkening) and *shmira* (observing). Hearkening, a good English word now unfortunately considered obsolete, expresses in a single word the act of hearing and responding, implying consent, while observing involves taking action. The combination of *shmiya* and *shmira*, hearkening and observing, is the way that humans are expected to respond to God's *mitzvot* (commandments). The Bible holds that human being are free to hearken to God or not, and to observe or not, which is why covenant is needed to bind them by sworn promise to do so. Since every *brit* includes the obligation to justice through law (or just judgment), in Hebrew *tzedakah u'mishpat*, whether there is natural justice or not, becomes a moot question after God's covenant with Noah.

Three Forms of Justice, Obligation, and Rights

Elsewhere, this book has described three models or archetypes of political organization (constitution or regime) in the world governing political (including social) behavior—hierarchical, organic, or covenantal.[7] Each can be said to establish a different basis for justice and obligation and source of rights. In hierarchies, one is obligated to those senior to oneself in the hierarchy and ultimately to the person or institution at its top. Under such circumstances one's rights are derived from one's place in the hierarchy. Feudalism is an excellent example of constitutionalized hierarchy where both obligations and rights are clearly demarcated.

In organic polities, one is obligated to one's primordial group, which has developed organically out of kinship over time and one's rights are based on one's standing in that primordial group. Tribal societies are excellent examples of the organic model, with tribal custom fixing one's obligations and rights. We are more familiar with medieval English society, an organic polity that pioneered in the development of individual rights in Europe. In its view, this meant the development of the idea of the rights of Englishmen, rights that the English and other Europeans understood adhered to Englishman because they were Englishman and were different than the rights, say, of French men or Germans, if such existed.

In covenantal polities, justice is determined by the moral principle upon which the covenant is based. One's obligations are to one's covenant partners and one's rights are derived from and defined by the covenant itself. Thus all humans have obligations to each other through the Noahide covenant and derive rights from those obligations unless they reject the terms of that covenant, in which case they are essentially outlaws. Smaller groups of humans have obligations and rights that derive from covenants subsidiary to that first one, as in the case of the Jews who are bound by God's covenants with Abraham and with the Assembly of Israel at Sinai.

While each of these models can be seen as an ideal type, in the real world models are often, perhaps usually, mixed. Thus, the Bible presents Israel as a combination of kinship and consent, beginning, if you will, with God's covenant with Abraham, to produce a family of nations which would be blessed through him. Abraham's immediate descendants form such a family, with Israel emerging out of the line of his grandson Jacob and his twelve offspring who are reunited around a common commitment to God's justice and moral law through the Sinai Covenant, which provides the specifics missing from the Noahide Covenant.

In keeping with the organic character of the twelve-tribe kinship group, before Sinai the tribes were governed by customary law. Through the Sinai Covenant God changes the moral basis of the Israelites' obligations and rights as much as He changes their content.[8]

In general, covenants are pervasive in the Bible. The major ones are multipurpose, providing for a connection between God and the relevant human group, a just ordering of relationships between the covenant partners. They are also dynamic, not mere contracts or agreements designed to be as minimally interpreted as possible, but embodying *hesed*, which requires the partners to behave generously toward one another, beyond the more letter of the *brit*, and having as their end *shalom*, itself a dynamic state.

Spinoza, for example, implicitly if not explicitly following the teachings of the Hebrew Bible, saw the foundations of true religion in justice and charity, *iustitia* and *caritas*, which gives every indication of being a Latin translation of *tzedakah v'hesed*, a prepolitical formulation of the covenantal framework within which justice belongs.[9]

The biblical history of the covenants between God and humans suggests a trend from hierarchical to fully covenantal relations between God and man. At first, God takes the lead in initiating His covenants, establishing His covenant with the patriarchs, perhaps Adam, certainly Noah and Abraham.[10]

It is clear from the biblical account that Abraham's role as father of multitudes includes Israelites and others, for example, the Ishmaelites, descended from his son by Hagar. But the Bible carefully distinguishes between the *brit* that Isaac is to reaffirm and continue, and the *brakhah* (blessing) that Abraham confers on Ishmael and the other peoples (or religious communities) descended from him. The book of Genesis describes such covenants.

In the second stage God seeks to gain popular consent to covenants that He initiates through His designated servant (*Eved Adonai*) who is the principal leader of the people. God's first attempt to do this can be found in Exodus, Chapter 6, where He has Moses approach the governing elders of the Israelites enslaved in Egypt to renew the covenant of their forefathers, a step which they reject.[11] This technique is successful at Sinai where God initiates the covenant but through Moses requires the popular consent of the Israelites expressed three separate times before the pact is made (Exodus 19:9, 24:3–8).

In the third stage, the principal leader turns to God and to the people to covenant or recovenant. Moses is present as initiating this process in the Plains of Moab at the end of his tenure (Deuteronomy 28:69–33:47). Joshua's initiative is of this type in Joshua, Chapter 24. Indeed, it may be an older account of that type of initiative than the one we have in Deuteronomy. David does the same after he brings the Ark of the Covenant to Jerusalem (I Chronicles 16), as did Hezekiah after the destruction of the northern kingdom (II Chronicles, Chapters 29–31), and Josiah in the seventh century (II Kings).

In the fourth stage the people themselves initiate a covenant renewal. This occurred in the days of Ezra and Nehemiah, as described in Nehemiah, chapter 8. They turn to their leaders who simply act as organizers of the act. While God is the object, the description of the even does not involve His direct intervention as it does not in any of the covenants after Sinai. Applying the themes of our initial model, we see that the Bible portrays God's initial covenants with humans in a hierarchical mode. God initiates and acts through patriarchs. Covenanting then enters an organic mode; God covenants with a kith, presented as descending from common ancestors, that becomes a people through the combination of kinship and consent. Only in the final stages does covenanting itself become fully covenantal, that is to say, initiated by all of the partners. Thus, even within the covenantal model there are echoes of the other models.

Covenantal Justice Based on Obligation

Sinai, the culminating covenant, makes clear what has been the critical primal element of covenantal partnerships from the first, namely that covenants establish justice through mutual obligations, indeed, systems of mutual obligations, from whence are derived (in modern terms) the partners' rights. Under the covenantal system there are no rights that are not derived from obligations. As I have discussed elsewhere, covenantal obligations are those of being holy and being just.[12] Hence they are excellent sources of what moderns define as rights, but covenant also keeps rights conditional on one's maintaining one's covenant with God which establishes basic morality, justice and law, at the very least, transforming natural justice into law.

Just as covenants establish different levels of obligation, so, too, they make possible differentiation in rights among those who are covenant partners or those who are partners to different covenants or covenants of different scope. As in the case of the biblical view of covenant obligation, this is not designed to invidiously discriminate among humans but to allow humans to decide for themselves by which covenants they are bound, which obligations they take upon themselves, and hence, what rights are available to them.

In the biblical worldview, all humans are expected to be bound by the Noahide covenant which obligates them and also endows them with all the basic human rights. Those who refuse to be bound by accepting the obligations of the Noahide covenant are thereby not entitled to those basic human rights because they have proclaimed themselves outlaws. But it is their choice. Although they can be punished for violating the terms of the covenant, as humans, they cannot be outlawed by others except perhaps for the most blatant causes (what contemporaries would describe as seriously "inhuman").

All human beings can also accept the covenant of Abraham, that is to say, join one of the monotheistic faiths and accept its obligations and gain certain rights thereby. They may also accept the Sinai Covenant and become Jews, thereby taking on even greater obligations and winning the right to be numbered among God's singular people (*am segula*), that is to say, to have the full *brit* and not merely benefit from Abraham's *brit* and *brakhah*. These are all matters of individual human choice.

In sum, the Bible sets forth a comprehensive covenantal system, establishing a framework for both justice and rights in this world, one that offers the civil and social protections of contemporary rights theory without succumbing to the excesses of that theory. It does so by providing constitutional means for guaranteeing rights and controlling the demand for rights by tying them to obligations.

Notes

1. Moshe Greenberg, *Understanding Exodus* (New York: The Jewish Theological Seminary, 1969); Albrecht Alt, *Essays on Old Testament History and Religion,* Trans. R.A. Wilson (Garden City, N.Y.: Doubleday, 1968); Martin Noth, *Exodus: A Commentary,* trans. J.S. Borden (Philadelphia, Pa.: Westminster Press, 1974); *idem, The History of Israel* (New York: Harper and Row, 1960); Harry M. Orlinsky, *Ancient Israel* (Ithaca, N.Y.: Cornell University Press, 1954).
2. Norman Snaith, *The Distinctive Ideas of the Old Testament* (New York: Schocken Books, 1964).
3. Moshe Greenberg, *Understanding Exodus.*
4. Walter Brueggemann, *Genesis* (Atlanta, Ga.: John Knox Press, 1982); Umberto Cassuto, *A Commentary on the Book of Genesis,* trans. Israel Abrahams, Vol. 1 (Jerusalem: Magnes Press, 1961); Klaus Westermann, *Genesis: A Commentary,* trans. John J. Scullion (Minneapolis, Minn.: Augsburg Publishing House, 1984–1986), 3 vols.
5. There are those, especially Christians, who argue that God established an implicit covenant with Adam, which is only reaffirmed by the covenant with Noah. They base their argument on Genesis 2:16, but that conclusion must be derived by heavy interpretation of the verse in question. It would, of course, moot the question of natural justice since all other references come after Adam.
6. The requirement that thereby human mechanisms for the punishment of murderers is embodied in the plain text (Genesis 9:5–6). The sages of the Talmud concluded from these verses that God required institutional mechanisms, that is, the establishment of courts of justice. They derived from this chapter the seven Noahide commandments, holding that God's covenant with Noah bound all humanity to a set of basic Divine commandments, ranging from the practice of monotheism to the prohibition of theft and the establishment of a just polity. See Sanh. 56–60. A good discussion of the Noahide commandments can be found under the entry of that name in the *Encyclopedia Judaica.*
7. Daniel J. Elazar, *Exploring Federalism* (University, AL: University of Alabama Press, 1987).
8. The Bible indicates that the beginnings of the process of the transformation from customary to covenantal law are to be found at Marah (Exodus 16:23–26). See Verse 25: *sam lo hok u'mishpat* (there He made for them a statute and an ordinance), cf. Nachmanides Commentary on Exodus 16:25).
9. Douglass J. Denuyl, "Power, Politics and Religion in Spinoza's Political Thought," *Jewish Political Studies Review,* Vol. 6, No. 1.
10. In general, God's chosen patriarch rather quickly understands the purpose of the covenanting. Where a patriarch does not, as in the case of Jacob, who sees God's first initiative at Beth-El as contractual rather than covenantal (see Genesis 28:10–28), God works him over through a series of tests covering many years, culmi-

nating in Jacob's wrestling with Him, until Jacob understands the difference (Genesis, Chapters 29–33).

11. Here God also introduces a dimension of popular involvement in the initiating by indicating that He is responding to the people's groaning (*Shamati et naakat bnai yisrael...v'ezkor et briti*—I will remember by covenant, Exodus 6:5). In other places in the Bible, God's response is triggered by the people's *zaakah* or crying out, whereupon God remembers His covenant and comes to their aid.

12. Daniel J. Elazar, "Deuteronomy as Israel's Constitution," *Jewish Political Studies Review*.

Index

Aargau, 185

The Abduction from the Seraglio (Mozart), 242

Abel, 378

Abortion, 250

Abraham, 34, 44, 177, 244, 317, 367, 377–380

Abravanel, Don Isaac, 61, 67

Absolutism, 21, 60, 117–119, 122, 146–147, 208

Achean League, 23

Act of Mediation (1803), 185

Act of Union of England and Scotland, 68, 70, 137, 208, 220

Acton, Lord, 19, 64, 74–75, 77

Adam, 44, 361, 376–377, 379

Adams, John, 63, 269

Adat Bnei Yisrael (The Congregation of Israel), 243, 335

Addams, Jane, 271

Adenaur, Konrad, 147

Adriatic, 122, 154

Aegean, 317

Africa, 2, 122, 227, 294, 305; central, 327; southern, 294

African National Congress (ANC), 219–220, 254

Afrikaners, 219–220

Agape, 108

Age of Revolutions, 142, 169, 344

Agreement, 19

AIDS, 309

Alapide, Ripolitus, 25

Algeria, 145

Alientation, 276, 279

Allemani, 179, 318

Alliance, 363

Alps, 130

Altgeld, John Peter, 271

Althusius, Johannes, 2, 20–21, 22, 25, 27–28, 46–49, 53, 70, 90, 92, 106, 150, 324, 335

Am (people), 376

Am segula (God's singular people), 244, 380

Am Yisrael (Jewish people), 367

America, American(s), *See* United States of America

The American Commonwealth (Bryce), 75

Ammon, 133

Amsterdam, 37, 151

Anarchism, 88, 168

Anarchy, 187

Ancien regime, 142, 149, 228, 241, 268

Andalusia, 219

Anglicans (Church of England), 65, 74, 94

Anglo-American law, 321–322

Anglo-Boer War, 74, 219

Anglo-Saxon, 270, 321

Anglo-Saxon Model of politics, 145

Anglophilism, 270

Anschluss of 1938, 165

Antinomianism, 59

Antistatism, 133

Aosta, Italy, 90

Apartheid, 219

Appenzell, 182, 186

Aquino, Tomas, 323

Arabs, 106

Aragon, 155

Aram, 133

Arbitration, 180–181

Argentina, 121, 300

Aristocracy, 131, 147, 167, 181

Aristotle, Aristotelian thought, 25–26, 47, 53, 215, 256, 277–278

Ark of the Covenant, 379

Articles of Confederation, 14, 55

Aron, Robert, 28, 89

Art(s), 310–311, 312

Aruba, 152

Arumaeus, Dominicus, 24

Aryans, 148
Asia, 2, 121, 294, 305, 317, 341; Asia Minor, 317; Western, 327–328, 354
Assemble Constituatente, 143
Associated State arrangements, 300, 303
Association(s), 162, 187, 323–324, 356
Association of South East Asian Nations (ASEAN), 292
Athens, 334; political thought of, 19
Atomization, 89–90, 150
Austin, John, 75
Australia, 204, 222; federalism, 76
Austria, 23, 96, 119–121, 124–125, 146–147, 154–155, 158, 165, 166, 178, 182, 205, 305; political thought, 96
Austro-Hungarian Empire, 121–122, 147, 158, 317
Austro-Prussian War of 1966, 120
Authoritarianism, 132, 142, 170, 227, 234, 240, 337; France, 69, 144, 145; Hapsburgs, 123; Latin America, 122
Authority, authorities, 23, 41, 83, 85, 89, 117, 170, 188–189, 204–206, 221, 267, 285, 291, 293, 301–302, 311, 351, 353, 370; ecclesiastical, 95; governmental, 88
Autocracy, 119, 142, 146–147,170
Autocratic, 132, 155, 156
Automatic society, 297, 336
Autonomy, 88, 126, 163, 168, 186, 217, 221–223, 231, 299, 305–306
Axis powers, 298
Azores, 300

Baalei brit (masters of the covenant), 317, 375–376
Babylonia, 131
Bacon, Sir Francis, 70
Baker, Newton, 235
Balkans, 129, 299, 305, 317
Bantu, 327
Baptist(s), 73
Bargain, 19
Barker, Sir Ernest, 76–77
Barth, Karl, 89
Basel, 182, 184, 186
Basic law, 226, 322
Basques, 126, 155, 218
Bastille, 143–144
Bavaria, 24

Beatitudo (blessedness), 41
Begin, Menachim, 226
Belgium, 121, 146, 150, 152–154, 158, 217, 220, 230, 301, 303, 306–307
Bellah, Robert, 110
Ben-berit (my covenant partner), 367
Ben-Gurion, David, 208
Ben-Gurion Airport, 317
Benelux Customs Union, 152–153, 301
Bentham, Jeremy, 75, 81
Berit (covenant with God), 367
Beriti (binding agreement), 312
Berlin, 149, 300
Bern, 180, 182, 184
Besold, Christop, 25
Bible, 7–8, 12, 18, 20, 31–32 35, 41–43, 56, 62, 66, 69, 84, 105, 124, 133, 135, 185, 187, 200, 211–212, 225, 243–244, 267–268, 276, 311–312, 317, 328–332, 334–335, 343, 351–352, 361, 363, 367, 376–381; biblical criticism, 31; Hebrew Bible (Old Testament), 18, 34, 44, 48, 62, 67, 134, 180, 225, 244, 379; King James version, 352; and political philosophy, 38–39
Biblical, model, 133; thought, 102, 334, 342; political tradition, 105
Biblical Israel, 7
Bildung, 71
Bill, 189
Biritum (space between), 312
Bismark, Otto von, 92–93, 95, 120, 147, 269
Blitzer, Charles, 63
Bluntschli, Johann Kaspar, 96
Bnai brit (sons of the covenant), 317, 325, 375–376
Bodin, Jean, 2, 21–23, 25, 27–28, 118
Boer Republics, 219
Bohemia, 165
Bolshevik Revolution, 126, 134, 167–168
Bolshevism, 50, 119, 121, 142, 167–168, 272
Bonaparte, Napolean, 59, 142, 144, 146, 149, 155–156, 164–165, 167, 172, 185
Bonaparte, Louis, 149
Bonapartism, 268
Bonding, 329
Bonn, 149

Bordeaux, 144
Borowitz, Eugene, 111
Bosco, Andrea, 292
Boston, 317
Bourbons, 142, 145
Bourgeois (citizen), 157
Brakhah (blessing), 244, 379–380
Brazil, 121
Bretons, 319
Bretton Woods Agreement, 291, 357
Brit (covenant), 35, 244, 312, 360, 376–377, 379–380
Brit shalom (covenantal peace), 326
British Isles, 13, 170, 198, 267, 319
British North America, 10, 58, 72, 84, 119, 197, 211–212, 267, 319, 370
Britons, 309, 321
Brotherhood, 170, 325
Bryce, James, 75
Buber, Martin, 28, 89, 91, 101, 104–107, 326
Bulgaria, 121
Bullinger, Heinrich, 10
Bundesbrief (those bound by a federal document), 178
Bundesrat, 149
Bundestat (federal state), 92
Bundestreu (federal comity), 149
Burger (citizen), 157
Burgess, Michael, 76
Burke, Edmund, 73
Byelorussia, 227

Cain, 376
Calhoun, John C., 269
California, 224, 339
Calvin, John, 10, 50
Calvinism, Calvinist, 1, 38, 95, 108, 150–151, 312, 318–319
Cambridge University, 75–77
Canaan, 317, 329
Canada, Canadians, 76, 204, 222, 229, 254, 305, 317, 319; French, 319
Cantons, 144, 178, 184, 228
Capitalism, 88, 110, 250
Caribbean, 230, 292, 299
Caritas (charity), 42, 108, 379
Carolina, 63
Carpzov, B. C., 25
Castille, 155
Castro, Fidel, 206
Catalans, 126, 155

Catalonia, 218
Catholic League, 93
Catholics, Roman, 18, 37, 59, 91, 93–94, 134, 144, 150, 152, 157, 161, 163, 165, 184–185, 189, 286, 307–308, 362
Cattanco, Carlo, 97
Caucasians, 148
Caucasus, 167
Celebrity, 347
Celts, 318–319
Center for the Study of Federalism, 90, 97
Center-periphery model of politics, 2, 131
Centralization, 86–87, 90, 117–119, 121, 155, 157, 170, 230, 279, 339; administrative, 87; French, 143; Prussian, 4; South Africa, 219, 220
Centre European pur Culture, 90
Centre International de Formation Europeanne (CIFE), 90–91
Chamberlain, Joseph, 76
Chamberlain, Neville, 166
Champs du Mars, 142
Charity, 42
Charlemagne, 122, 211, 358
Charles I, 61, 164
Charles II, 61, 63
Charles River Bridge Case, 249
Charter(s), 19, 111, 146, 200, 222, 226, 249; civic, 287
Charter system, 200
Chechnya, 306
Checks and balances, 136, 189, 270
Chemnitz, Philipp Bogislas von, 25
Chiapas, 306
China, 206, 327
Christian(s), 35–36, 39, 41, 45, 53, 93, 108, 154, 163, 285–286, 310, 322, 327; Arminians-38; fundamentalist, 285–286; theology, 11;
Christian Democrats, 148
Christianity, 1, 37, 102, 142, 162, 164, 351
I Chronicles, 379
II Chronicles, 379
Churchill, Winston, 77
Citizens, 117, 132, 151, 157, 162, 179, 186, 206, 211, 228, 241–242, 277–278, 284, 309–310, 320, 335, 338, 370

Citizen-state, 129
Citizenship, 94, 103, 119, 128, 132, 157, 283, 309, 321, 333, 346; democratic republican, 282
Civil religion, 110, 132, 142
Civil service, 251
Civil society, societies, 16–19, 59, 81, 89, 97, 112, 141, 166, 170, 188, 193, 218, 220, 242, 247–248, 254–256, 259, 273–274, 276, 280, 282–284, 287, 308, 322, 324, 333–334, 336–338, 342, 344–346, 353, 355–356, 360; American, 15–16, 55, 135, 189, 253, 271, 286, 332; British, 64; and Buber-106; Calvinist, 151; commonwealth, 13; covenant-based, 9, 286, 319; federal republican, 56; France, 142; Hobbes, 34; Hume, 72; Jacobinism, 52; Locke, 44–45, 66; matrix of civil society, 280–283; and mediating institutions, 285; modern epic -16, 54, 87; Montesquieu, 47; Netherlands, 150; in personalistic thought, 90; secularized -10; and social contract, 57; South Africa, 219; Spinoza, 38, 39, 41, 43; Western, 246
Civility, 97
Civilization, contrast between old world and new world, 83
Cleveland, 235
Code(s), 203, 204–206, 210, 212, 225
Code Napolean, 144
Codification of law, 180
Coercion, 103, 203, 248, 284, 323
Coke, Chief Justice, 250
Cold War, 294, 297
Collectivism, 91, 150, 170, 312–313, 322, 336
Collectivity, 307
Collegium, 26
Colonialism, 148
Colonization and statism, 2
Columbia, 122
Columbia University, 270
Combourgeoisie treaties, 182–183, 185
Comenius, 165
Comity, 327
Commandments, 330–331
Committee of Public Safety, 144
Common law, 71, 208, 249
Common markets, 303

Commonwealth(s) 16–17, 38, 44, 53, 63, 65, 107, 120, 170, 312, 324, 326, 333–334, 336–338, 342; American colonies, 63; ancient Israel, 49, 62; Britain, 61; in Buber's thought, 106; Calvinist, 151; civil, 16; of communities, 106; covenantal, 149, 170; covenanted, 15, 21, 34, 271, 318, 355; and Francis Bacon, 70; Mosaic, 62; in personalistic thought, 90; Puritan, 13–15, 62; Reformed Protestant, 16; second Jewish Commonwealth, 225; in Tocqueville's thought, 83–84
Commonwealth of Independent States, 168, 199, 301, 306
The Commonwealth of Oceana (Harrington), 61–64
Commonwealthman, 64–68
Communalism, 178
Communes, 144, 179, 181, 185
Communism, 54, 88, 126, 134, 257, 311
Communist Party, 121, 126
Communists, 145, 149, 166–168, 205–207, 227, 268, 287–288, 294, 297, 309, 310, 339
Communitarianism, 46, 112, 170, 336
Communitas, 332
Community, communities, 91, 94, 105–106, 109, 112, 131, 132–133, 172, 179, 190–191, 247, 277, 307, 309–310, 312–313, 320, 329, 335, 338, 346, 361, 363; autonomous, 217; breakdown of modern community, 273; civil, 278, 333; covenantal, covenanted, 271, 311, 320–321; cultural, 220; ideological, 123; moral, 97; nonterritorial, 277; organic, 150; political, 189, 260, 274; power structure of, 320; religious, 123; security community, 295; self, governing ethnic, 153; territorial, 277;
Compacts, 3, 19, 75, 190, 198–199, 226–229, 323, 328, 348, 356; Act of Union of England and Scotland, 68; civil, 85, 188; compacting, 65, 329; coronation oath, 67; covenantal, 87; defined, 8–9; European Union, 257; France, 143; Lockean, 12, 44, 50; Mayflower, 84–85; Montesquieu, 47; and moral obligation, 9; politi-

cal, 17, 22, 26, 31, 45, 49, 52, 55–
57, 66–68, 72, 74, 81, 92, 107, 135,
141–142, 146, 153, 155, 188, 198,
212, 231, 246, 251, 254, 267–268,
270, 322–323, 327–328, 334, 336,
344–345, 348, 351, 353; public, 285;
secular compact theory, 72–73, 267,
269; social, 110, 142, 323; southern
compact theory, 269; Spanish heritage, 217; Spinozean, 12, 39–40, 43
Compromise, 362
Compte de Paris, 129
Conciliar Process of Justice, Peace and
the Preservation of Creation, 288
Condominium, 303
Confederacy, confederation, 22, 24, 26–
27, 46–47, 52, 92, 105, 119, 299–
301, 303, 306, 318, 357, 363; all
German, 120, 146–147, 154;
Canada, 229; Commonwealth of In-
dependent States, 168; European
Union, 298; Graubunden, 156;
Middle East, 293; Netherlands, 123;
North German, 147; post World War
II, 230–234; Swiss, 122, 156, 177–
186, 356; United Netherlands, 149;
United States, 158, 230
Confederal links, 292
Confederatio, 19, 26
Conference on Security and Coopera-
tion in Europe (CSCE), 257
Congregation, 19
Congregational(ism), 19, 20, 65, 73
Congress of Vienna, 120, 154, 156
Coniuratio (those bound by a shared
oath), 178, 198
Connecticut, 85, 212
Connecticut Code of Laws of 1650, 85
Conquest, 143, 170, 228–229, 329
Conring, Hermann, 25
Consent, 40, 65–68, 81, 86, 90, 124–
125, 130, 170, 181, 197, 200–202,
204, 215, 226, 228, 234, 236, 248,
258–259, 305, 312, 322–323, 325,
343, 348, 370, 377
Consensus, 179, 208, 218, 227, 229,
233–234, 312; covenantal, 321
Conservatives; American, 269–272,
286; British, 67, 268–269; com-
munitarian, 326; European, 146,
268, 271; French, 149; German, 95
Conservative Party (Britain), 208

Considerations on Representative Government (Mill), 74
Consocentio, 19
Consociation, 20–21
Consociationalism, 3, 158, 161–162,
174, 220, 272, 303, 306; Belgium,
153; Dutch, 150–152; Kuyper, 150–
152; Swiss, 157
Constant, Benjamin, 28, 52, 54
Constituent Assembly, 67
Constitutions, 19, 105, 118, 130, 136,
154, 187, 190, 195–212, 215–236,
291, 307, 325, 329–330, 344–345,
356; amendment, 224, 228; as instruments of social control, 219–
221; as adaptation of traditional
constitutions, 207–211; Australian,
204, 222; Belgium, 217, 220–221;
California, 224; Canada, 75, 204,
222, 229; changing constitutions,
201–202, 205, 223, 227, 276; as
code, 204–205; Communist countries, 205–206; Connecticut, 85;
Czechoslovakia, 206; declarations
of rights, 240–242; Denmark, 163;
Dutch, 120, 123; England, 64–66,
137, 199, 208–210, 219–220, 222,
227, 229, 242; (Magna Carta, 208,
220, 227; 1689 Bill of Rights, 208,
220; 1832 Reform Act, 208); federal,
16, 75, 221–225; federal republican,
206; as frame of government, 203–
204; France, 143–145, 228–229;
Germany, 148–149, 225, 345;
Helvetic Confederation, 183; Iran,
210; Israel (modern), 208–210, 226;
Italy, 217, 221; Japan, 210; Jews,
131; Locke, 44; models of, 203–211;
Mosaic, 48–49; Norwegian, 163;
Poland, 166; as political artifacts,
203; as political ideal, 206–207;
premodern, 199; ratification and
consent, 200–201; reconstitution,
218, 227, 313; referendum, 224,
228, 231; as revolutionary manifes-
tos, 205–206; South Africa, 204,
219–221; Spain, 155, 205, 217–218,
220–221, 229; Swiss, 156, 185, 224,
228; three dimensions of, 215–236;
Torah as constitution, 208; United
States, 14, 54–55, 75, 93, 120, 202–
203, 212, 221, 228, 241, 248–249,

270, 272, 313, 326, 332; United States—amendments, 249, 252; Venetian, 61; Western Europe, 204–205; Yugoslavia, 206
Constitution-making, 146, 202–203, 215, 218, 227, 234
Constitutional choice, 122, 202–203, 218–219, 234
Constitutional commissions, 200
Constitutional conventions, 200, 219, 224, 227
Constitutional courts, 202, 205, 280
Constitutional design, 226–229, 233, 265
Constitutional enactments, 331
Constitutional government, 142
Constitutional law, 24
Constitutionalism, 2–3, 7, 62, 130, 135, 137, 161, 163, 170–171, 197–212, 218, 223, 225, 233, 259, 265–267, 283, 305, 344–345, 348, 353, 356; ancient, 14; American, 270; defined, 8; Denmark, 163; English, 66; federal, 76, 87, 211, 313; France, 144–145; Italian, 156; liberal, 94; medieval, 181; modern, 16, 54–55, 70, 162, 164, 166, 170, 210–212, 223, 225, 234, 239–240, 254–255, 257, 260, 266, 293, 356–358; modern variants of, 174; new, 14–15; and nineteenth century Germans, 93; pre-modern, 210; relation to covenant, 9; republican, 54; in Spinoza's thought, 40,41; United States, 215
Constitutionalizing globalization, 284
Constituent Assembly, 143–144
Contracts, 19, 72, 91, 93, 111, 141, 169, 180, 186–187, 251, 269, 323, 329, 333, 348, 363; constant, 53; defined, 8–9; federative, 89; freedom of, 271; and Hobbes, 32; morally based, 89; original contract, 67, 70; Proudhon, 88–89; right of, 251; Rousseau, 51; social, 17–18, 32, 36, 50–51, 54–57, 81, 85, 89, 141–142, 246, 268, 287, 322–323, 327, 344, 348
Contractarianism, 111–112, 322
Contractual system, 169
Contractualism, 73, 287
Contractus, 19
Convention, 19

Cooperative movement, 88, 163–164, 174, 272
Cooperative work, 103–104
Cooperatives, Scandinavia, 162
Cooperation, 158, 162, 174, 188, 222, 271, 313
Corporations, private, 249
Corporatism, 117–119, 122, 246
Corsica, 231, 305
Cosmopolitans, 320
Cosmos Club, 236
Cotton, James, 63
Council of Europe, 295
Council on Security and Cooperation in Europe (CSCE), 299–300, 306
Counterrevolution, 134, 142, 170
"Countries" (land, pays) -221
Coup, 206
Covenant, 75, 81, 87, 93, 107, 111, 125, 130, 169, 170, 174, 178, 181–182, 184–185, 187, 190, 198–199, 201, 209, 211–212, 215, 225–229, 243–244, 251–252, 265–288, 274, 295, 302, 312–314, 318–319, 321, 323–325, 328–331, 333, 335, 348, 356, 359, 370, 376–380; and commonwealthmen -67; in communitarian thought, 112; and constitutionalism, 65; covenantal morality, 41; Declaration of Rights of Man and Citizen (as a French covenant), 143; defined, 8; and democracy, 317–339; and democratic self government, 347–348; and federalism, 87; Germany, 146, 148–149; of grace, 19; Hobbes, 32–37, 259; Hume and Burke on, 72; Kant, 55; in Kaplan's thought, 109–110; and Kuyper, 150–151; and language, 361–371; League of Nations as covenant, 81,107–108; and liberty, 343–350; Locke, 45; marriage, 189–190, 275, 286; and moral obligation, 9; Mosaic, 49; Noahide, 150, 243–244; and partnership, 332; and personalistic thought, 91; political, 26, 314; preferred covenantal regimes, 335–339; and primordialism, 327–329; and Rawl's thought, 112; reemergence of, 283–288; reform and renewal, 329–332; republicanism, 317–339; secularization of, 46, 117;

Sinai, 243–244; Spinoza, 39–43; success of covenantal societies, 351–353; and text, 353; theology, 19, 356; theopolitical, 16, 73, 107, 265–266, 317; and Tocqueville's thought, 82–83; transition from to compact, 12, 17–18, 68; and United Nations, 257; and United States, 110; vocabulary of, 363–371; voluntary nature of, 59, 284; and Whig Party, 63

Covenant and Commonwealth (Elazar), 134

Covenant and Constitutionalism (Elazar), 271

Covenant and Polity in Biblical Israel (Elazar), 44, 335

Covenant of 1291, 180, 182

Covenant vision, 311–313

Covenantal culture, 131, 318–319, 357–358, 360–361

Covenantal diversity, 314

Covenantal ideology, 9, 318

Covenantal networks, 181; world covenantal networks, 291–314

Covenantal process, 226

Covenantal redemption, 325

Covenantal synthesis, 126, 130–131

Covenantal thought, 70, 102, 111–112, 357

Covenantal tradition, 7, 16, 59, 68–69, 81–82, 92, 94, 101, 106–107, 118, 130, 132–136, 145–146, 152, 163, 165, 168, 170, 174, 177, 197, 199, 211, 219, 225, 233–234, 252, 254–255, 258–259, 265–266, 273, 274, 284, 286, 302, 305, 307, 322, 326, 343–346, 349–355, 357, 359–361; Althusian, 23; Belgium, 153; Britain, 65, 73; elements of, 3; and English Civil War, 64; Germans, 141; and Isaac Newton, 70; Italy, 156; and James, 104; and Jews, 111; and Kuyper, 150–151; Luxembourg, 154; and modern nationalism, 117–138; in New England, 84; and Personalistic thought, 91; and Proudhon's thought, 89; Puritan, 269; reformed tradition, 14; and revolutions, 141; and Rights, 239–260; and Tocqueville's thought, 86

Covenantal world order, 308–312; means of achieving, 313–314

Covenantalism, 1–3, 59, 65, 70, 73, 98, 101, 109, 124, 131, 158, 162, 170, 185, 197, 212, 223, 239, 270, 308, 318, 325, 341–343, 348, 353; anti-covenantal, 272, 337; American, 269; Biblical, 243; collapse of, 97, 246; corporate, 253; decline of 265–288; and federalism, 211; France, 144; liberal, 146; modern, 60; Puritan, 64; Swiss, 186

Covenanters, 68

Covenants of Helvetic Confederation, 182; Covenant of Sempach, 182, 183; Covenant of Stans, 182, 183; Priests Charter, 182, 183; Treaties of Defensional, 182

Crawford, William Sharman, 77

Cuba, 206

Culture, 124–125, 127, 130, 162, 167, 173, 193, 216, 221, 234, 239, 271, 303, 318, 327, 337, 341, 358–359, 361–363, 365; contractual, 156; covenantal, 265–266; geo-cultural areas, 210; mass, 273–275, 281; nonterritorial, 157

Cultural cleavages, 302–305, 307–308

Curacao, 152

Custodianship, 151

Cyprus, 294, 305

Czechs, 125, 206, 296

Czechoslovakia, 166, 287, 345

Darwinism, 70, 267, 270

David, 335, 377

Day of the Covenant (France), 50

Decentralization, 86, 153–154, 163, 218, 220, 300; constitutional, 156, 217; regional, 230

Declaration, 189

Declaration of Independence (Israel), 209–210

Declaration of Independence (United States), 198, 246, 252, 269, 272, 332, 350, 370

Declarations of independence, 130

Declaration of Principles (Israel-Palestine), 301

Declaration of Rights of Man and Citizen, 143, 198, 241, 254

Decolonialization, 121, 293–294, 299

Delegated power, 120
Deliberation, 179
Delors, Jacques, 154
Democracy, 51–52, 70, 86, 88, 102, 110, 132–133, 142, 185, 191–192, 205, 240, 277, 292, 300, 306, 313, 317–339, 344; American, 83; American federal, 82, 270; collective, 179; communal, 187, 190–193; constitutional, 60; cooperative, 162–163; federal, 171–172, 272, 356; and Germany, 96; guided, 144; and Henry James thought, 103; individualistic, 187–190; Jacobin, 268; liberal, 17, 148, 187–191, 193, 355, 357; people's democracy, 168; and Puritans, 85; representative, 277; Spain, 155; and Spinoza, 40, 43; territorial, 151, 163, 277, 303, 321
Democracy in America (Tocqueville), 82–83, 347
Democratic Party (United States), 271
Democratic-Republican Party (United States), 268
Democratization, 132
De Jure, Naturae et Gentium (Samuel Pfendorf), 22
De Ratione Status en Imperio Nostro Romano, Germanico, 25
Denmark, Danes, 147, 161–164, 305, 321
Departments, 144
Despotism, 87
De Statu Region um Germaniae (Ludolph Hugo) -23
Detroit, Michigan, 101
Deuteronomy, 85, 200, 330, 335, 379
Deutsch, Karl, 295
Dewey, John, 101–102, 107, 109
Diaspora, 210
Diatheke (covenant), 371
Dicey, A.V., 75
Dictatorship, 148, 168, 170, 227, 300
Diderot, 22
Discursus Academici de Juro Publico, 25
Disestablishment, 94–95
Disputationum Politicarum Liber, 25
Districts, 144
Divine right of kings, 46
Doctrine of Subsidiary, 94
Duchachek, Ivo, 215, 296

Due process, 249–250, 271
Dworkin, Ronald, 255, 259

Earl of Shaftesbury, 63
East Indies, 294
Eastern Europe, 124
Eban Abba, 293
Ecclesiastes, 376–377
Ecumenism, 134, 272
Edah (Jewish Commonwealth), 367
Edom, 133
Egalitarians (ism), 60, 112
Egypt, 305, 317, 335
Eidgenossen (federal partner), 157
Eleemosynary reforms, 249
Elijdin komst (joyous entry), 362
Endogamy, 127
England, 1, 15, 39, 60, 62, 64–65, 68, 75, 94–95, 118, 131, 134, 137, 200, 208, 220, 222, 242, 253, 267, 318, 319, 321–322, 328, 355, 378; Bill of Rights of 1688, 247; civil war, 10, 134, 188, 208; covenantal tradition in, 7; Cromwellian Period, 61; political thought, 55, 60, 69, 74, 312; Revolution, 60, 141
English (language), 362
English Channel, 317
The Enlightenment, 267, 269
Entitlements, 255–256, 259
Epicurious, 256
Epochs, medieval, 3, 20, 64, 161, 334–335; modern, 2–3. 7, 9–10, 16–17, 20, 53–54, 60, 68, 70, 87, 101, 107, 118, 124, 126–132, 138, 146, 150, 154, 158, 161, 162, 165, 169–170, 172–173, 185, 189, 193, 200–203, 210, 216, 226, 230–231, 239–240, 246, 248, 254–256, 258, 260, 265–279, 288, 291, 296, 303, 312, 318, 322, 334, 335–338, 341, 345–346, 349, 353, 355–357, 360; and philosophic theories, 11, 53; pre-modern, 7, 37, 53, 128, 132, 137, 172, 192, 202, 243, 248, 256, 258, 346; postmodern, 3, 7, 16, 54, 101, 111, 124, 126–127, 152–153, 155–156, 173, 190, 193, 202–203, 205, 211, 240, 246, 248, 253, 255–256, 258–259, 265–266, 274, 276–277, 279–280, 283–284, 301, 303, 322, 334, 336, 341, 350, 357, 360

Equal protection, 250
Equality, 46, 86, 88, 107–108, 142, 170, 221, 283, 324, 329, 335–336, 339, 343–344, 347, 370; and cooperatives, 162; and covenantal model, 82; in France, 83; Reformed tradition, 11; and United States, 83, 85, 131
Erasmus, 18
Erastianism, 95
Eros, 108
Escape from Freedom (Fromm), 347
Estates, 131, 172, 227
Ethnic(ity), 126, 130, 165, 167, 296–297, 302–303, 307–308, 312
Etzioni, Amitai, 112
Eulau, Heinz, 26
Eurasia, 270
Europe, 17, 21, 38, 86, 90, 94, 98, 101–102, 107, 118–119, 122, 124, 128, 135, 142, 146–147, 150, 152–153, 157–158, 161, 163, 171, 174, 177–178, 181, 189, 197, 202, 210–211, 230, 242, 244, 251–252, 254, 257, 267–268, 272, 278, 282, 287, 296, 298, 303, 309, 318, 328, 355–358, 363; Age of Revolution, 118, 270, 344; Central, 166–167; covenantalism, 59; Eastern Europe, 270, 287, 339, 345; Mediterranean Europe, 154–156; Northwest, 270; political traditions, 1–3; United States of Europe, 90, 97; western, 13, 129, 204–205, 231, 282–283, 292, 295–296, 298–299, 303, 318
European Community/Union, 28, 53, 91, 94, 111, 129, 145, 152–154, 230–231, 257, 259, 292, 298–301, 306–308, 357–358
European Constitutional Court -257
European Declaration of Rights, 257
European Integration, 291
Eved adonai (designated servant), 379
Everett, William Johnson, 110
Exodus, 44, 85, 105, 198, 225, 330, 335, 379
Expression, 256, 257
Ezekial, 331
Ezra, 331, 379
Ezrah (citizen), 367

Facism, 54, 134, 141, 166, 170, 172, 240, 272, 309–311, 313; ethno-religious, 170; French, 89; Italian, 156
Fackenheim, Emil, 111
Families, 313; in civil society, 21
Far East, 298
Fealty, 226
Federacies, 300, 303
Federal relationships, 333
Federal theologians, 19–20
Federal theology, 16–19
Federalism, 14–15, 27–28, 46, 70, 75, 77, 81, 85, 87, 90, 107, 165, 171, 181, 197, 202, 208, 212, 217, 219, 221, 230–231, 272–273, 278, 283, 291–314, 338, 359; American, 62, 72, 75, 136; anarchistic, 104–105; Argentina, 121, 300; asymetrical, 299, 301; Australian, 76; Austrian, 23; Belgium, 303; Brazil, 121, 300; British thought and, 73–77; and Buber's thought, 104; Columbia, 122; Constant, Benjamin, 53; constitutional, 87; and designing constitutional systems, 211–212; dual, 271; economic, 161, 174; European, 76, 97–98; formalistic federalism, 218; German, 23, 92–96, 120, 149; in German Confederation, 147; Harrington, James, 62; Herder, 48; imperial, 25, 26, 72, 74; India, 122; integral federalism, 28, 89–92, 105; Irish thought on, 77; and Italian thought, 96–97; Italy, 303; and Jacobins, 51; and William James, 102; Kant, 55; Mexico, 300; Mill, 74; modern, 170, 178; modern variants, 174; Montesquieu, 46; morality, 40; national federalism, 53; Netherlands, 123; new age federalism, 93; New Zealand, 76; nonterritorial, 150; in opposition to statism, 117, 118; Pakistan, 122; paradigm shift to, 291–314; and personalistic thought, 90; political, 288; polyvalent federalism, 90; and Proudhon's thought, 88, 89, 91; Rousseau, 52; Scandinavia, 161; social federalism, 93–94, 161, 174; South Africa, 301; South America, 121; soviets, 168; Spain, 155, 217, 300, 303; Swiss federalism, 96, 120, 156–157, 181; territorial federalism,

220, 306; theological, 59; and Tocqueville's thought, 82, 86; transnational federalism, 31; United States federalism, 119–120; utopian federalism, 106; Venezuela, 121

The Federalist , 14, 20, 36, 41, 47, 51, 55, 83, 135, 199, 225, 249, 341

Federalist Party (United States), 268, 370

Federalists, 156, 355

Federation, 26, 76, 105, 174, 277, 299–300, 303, 306, 312, 338–339, 357; aristocratic, 166; Belgium, 153; centralized, 95; France, 144; German, 92–93, 120; political, 88, 89; in North America, 121; tribal, 336; West Indies, 299

Federation of Evangelical Churches, 287–288

Feminism, 60

Feudal, 133; body politic, 117

Feudalism, 179, 378; decentralized, 154

Fichte, Johann Gottlieb, 56

Filmer, Robert, 44

First Treatise on Government (John Locke), 12

Flemings, 153, 307

Fletcher, Andrew, 71

Foedus, 19, 26, 27, 187

Ford, Gerald, 229

Foundations of Sovereignty and other Essays (Laski), 77

Fox, George, 69

fragmentarische staatsgewalt (fragmentary state power), 93

France, 1, 28, 50, 69, 77, 82–83, 87, 117, 123, 125, 128–130, 132, 141–147, 152, 154–156, 166, 172–173, 178, 184, 197–198, 212, 223, 228, 231, 241, 251, 254, 267–268, 296, 298, 300, 303, 319, 378; Fifth Republic, 145; French Resistance (World War II) -89; Huguenots, 10, 69, 82, 95, 267, 319; political thought, 70, 82–89

Franco, Francisco, 134, 155

Franco-Prussian War, 147

Frantz, Constantin, 93

Fraternity, 142, 325–326, 329

Free church councils, 73

Free market, 145, 258

Free trade, 73, 297

Free trade areas, 301

Free will, 343

Freedom, 85, 108, 151, 185, 292, 310, 312, 318, 324, 333, 335–337, 339, 342–343, 349–351; economic, 258

Freedom of expression, 256

Freedom of speech, 256

Freeman, E.A., 75

Freeman, Gordon, 370

French Revolution, 48, 52, 119, 123, 141–144, 149, 157–158, 161, 172, 197–198, 270

Fribourg, 182, 184

Friedrich, Carl, 20, 27

Friuli-Venezia Giulia, 156

Froebel, Julius, 94

Fromm, Erich, 347

Frontier, 317–318, 358; urban, 271

Fueros (feudal charters of rights), 155, 217–218

Functional authority, 303

Functionalism, functionalists, 295

Galacia, Galicians, 126, 218

Galilea, 329

Gambling casinos, 300

Garden of Eden, 376

Garrison, William Lloyd, 269

Gasterbeiter, 128, 129

Gaulle, Charles de, 145, 172, 231

Gauls, 309

Gemeinshaft, 92, 256

General Agreement on Tariffs and Trade, 233, 295, 299, 301, 306

General will, 50, 52, 136–137, 142–143, 170, 268

Genesis, 44, 124, 134, 329, 361, 376–377, 379

Geneva, 50

Genocide, 148

Gensler, 177

George, Lloyd, 77

Germanic-Teutonic, 270

Germany, 1, 10, 20, 23, 25, 27, 60–61, 75, 77, 89, 101, 104, 119–120, 123–126, 128–130, 146–149, 151, 153, 157, 165–166, 178, 225, 235, 251, 269–270, 292, 296, 298, 305–306, 328, 378; First Reich, 93; German Democratic Republic, 120, 149, 166, 287–288, 300, 345; German Federal Republic, 96, 120, 148–149, 205,

288, 298, 300, 345; immigrants, 125; Imperial Reich, 147; political thought, 49–50, 55–56, 92–96; reunification, 288; Rhineland, 10; Second Reich, 95; Third Reich, Nazism, National Socialism, 27, 50, 54, 89, 94, 98, 105, 110, 134, 147–148, 170, 172, 240, 272, 292, 309; Weimar Republic, 95, 120, 146–148

Gersau, 181

Gesellschaft, 92, 256

Geulah (redemption), 367

Gierke, Otto von, 20, 23, 25–26, 77, 92, 106

Gironde, 144

Girondists, 144

Gladstone, William, 74, 76

Glarus, 180, 182

Glorious Revolution of 1688, 43, 63, 66, 134, 208, 247

God, 15, 18–19, 21, 37, 42, 47, 65, 83, 85, 92, 102–104, 109, 133, 150, 192, 200, 226, 246, 248, 255–256, 258, 311, 313, 329, 334, 343, 351–353, 375, 379–380; and covenants, 9, 34, 44, 184, 186–187, 225, 243–244, 265, 286, 329, 348, 359, 376–378; and covenantal morality, 41; -fearing, 134; and Jews, 48, 93, 109; and sovereignty, 105, 135

Golan, 209

Golden Rule, 35, 325

Goldie, Mark, 64

Gorbachev, Mikhail, 168

Governance, 77, 91, 95, 123, 143, 172, 190, 192, 219, 225–226, 277, 338, 346, 351

Goy (nation), 367

Goyi (nations), 134

A Grammar of Politics (Laski), 77

Graubunden Confederation, 156, 185

Great Britain, 71, 75–76, 94, 134, 161, 198, 229, 268, 287, 297, 299–301, 317–319; constitution, 208, 210, 219–220, 227; politics, 63; Great Depression, 77, 89, 164, 295, 297

Greece, 18, 121, 325, 328; philosophy, 38, 334

Greenberg, Irving, 111

Greenstone, David, 289

Gresham's Law, 274

Grey, Earl, 76

Grotius, Hugo, 47, 69

Grundlage des Natureichts (Fichte), 56

Guilds, 131, 172

Gustavus I, 164

Gustavus II, 164

Guttman, Louis, 367

Hagar, 379

Halakhah, 127, 225

Hamas, 276

Hamilton, Alexander, 41, 249

Hampden, John, 64

Hapsburg Empire, 122–123, 146, 154, 165, 177–178

Haran, 317

Harrington, James, 60–64, 68, 188; agrarian model, 62, 63

Hartman, David, 111

Harvard University, 101

Harvey, William, 61

Hassidism, 104

Havel, Vaclav, 166, 287

Haver (partner through association), 363

Hebraism (17th Century) , 68–70

Hegel, 56, 81, 93

Hegelians, 92–94, 104, 270

Heimmat (original home), 186

Helvetians, 318

Helvetic Confederation, *see* Confederations, Swiss

Helvetic Republic, 185

Helvettii, 179

Herder, Johann Gottfried, 48–50

Heroism, 347

Herzl, Theodor, 49

Hesed (loving covenantal obligation), 42, 104, 108, 313–314, 321, 324–326, 360, 367, 375, 379

Hierarchic(al) model, 82, 136, 279

Hierarchy, hierarchies, 1–3, 117, 131–133, 138, 146, 154, 163–164, 168, 170, 174, 198–199, 211–212, 221, 223, 226, 228, 239, 242, 251, 254–255, 267, 269, 271–273, 283, 287, 311, 334, 341–344, 346, 349–350, 355, 358–359, 378–379; democratic, 251; Denmark, 163; and France, 83, 87; Germany, 146, 148; Hapsburgs, 123; and imperialism, 98; Luxembourg, 154; principles of, 117; and Proudhon, 88; synthesis with contract, 186

Hillel the Elder, 35
Himalayas, 186
Historicism, 92
History of Federal Government in Greece and Italy (Freeman), 75
Hitler, Adolf, 77, 120, 147–148, 165–166
Hobbes, Thomas, 11–12, 18, 21, 24, 31–37, 39–40, 42–43, 45–46, 55–56, 61–62, 66, 68, 72, 112, 188, 245, 259, 276, 336
Hoenonius, P.H., 25
Holiness, 311
Holland, 38
Holocaust, 105
Holy Roman Empire, 22–24, 26, 56, 92, 120, 146, 154, 165, 178, 179
House of Hanover, 65
House of Orange, 65
Hukah, hok (rule of law), 367
Hugo, Ludolph, 22
Huguenots, 10, 69, 82, 95, 267
Hull House, 271
Human nature, 39, 345; theories of, 11
Humanism, 126, 267
Hume, David, 47, 71–73
Hungary, 121, 124, 166
Huss, Jan, 165
Huxley, Aldous, 337

Iberian Penninsula, 144, 154, 217
Iceland, 317–319
Idealism, 104
Idolatry, 311
Illinois, 271
Imperial Federation League, 76
Imperialism, 74, 76, 287, 298, 309, 310; Bonapartist, 145; cultural, 130; ecumenical, 134
India, 122, 186, 210, 299, 305
Individualism, 17, 45, 52, 89, 91, 105, 191–192, 245, 312, 322, 339; atomistic, 187, 274; hedonistic, 347, 357; methodological, 188; modern, 264; radical, 310
Initiative, 204
Inkatha Freedom Party, 220
Integrationism, 154
Integrities, 313–314, 332, 352
Interest groups, 87
Intergovernmental cooperation, 136
Intergovernmental relations, 91, 223, 273

International Association of Centers for Federal Studies (IACFS), 90
International Labor Organization (ILO), 294
International Monetary Fund (IMF), 295
Internet, 273
Iran, 210, 227
Iraq, 305
Ireland, 75–77, 134, 208, 301, 307
Iron law of oligachy, 46, 87, 342
Isaac, 44, 367
Ishmael, 379
Islam, 341
Israel, ancient (biblical), 19, 61–62, 133, 198, 200, 210, 318, 335, 351, 354, 375; Declaration of Independence, 209, 210; kibbutz, 106; Knesset, 208–209, 226; modern, 101, 104, 147, 208–209, 226, 293, 301, 317; United tribes of, 313
Israelites, 38–39, 42, 44, 84, 105, 225, 243, 334, 358, 378, 379; exodus of, 317, 335
Issachar, 329
Italy, 1, 96–97, 119, 121, 123–125, 154–157, 164, 211, 217, 221, 230, 298, 303, 358; emmigrants, 125
Iustitia (justice), 379

Jacob, 44, 329, 367, 378
Jacobin (ism), 32, 50–52, 68–69, 89, 118, 123, 132, 136–137, 142, 144, 147, 149, 155, 157–158, 161, 170, 172, 268, 270
Jacobites, 68
James II, 65–68
James, Henry, Sr., 102–103
James, William, 101–104
Japan, 210, 298
Jaurourt, Chevalier des, 2
Jefferson, Thomas, 131, 268, 269–270
Jeremiah, 330
Jerusalem, 209, 226, 334, 379
Jesus Christ, 108
Jews, 32, 37–39, 48–49, 93, 95, 101, 106, 112, 124, 127, 157, 177, 208–210, 225, 286, 309–310, 312, 318, 325, 329, 335, 351, 357–359, 375–380; anti-Semitism, 93, 286; chosen people, 109; covenantal tradition, 101, 111, 131; Eastern European,

104; Marranos, 37, 144; national character, 48; nationhood, 125; nationalism, 127; political tradition, 66, 225, 335, 367, 375; Rabbinical rulings, 328
Jewish Agency, 209
Jewish-Arab struggle, 305
Jewish Theological Seminary (New York), 101, 109
Jim Crow, 271
Job, 376
John XXIII, Pope, 286
Johnson, Hugh, 234–235
Johnson, Lyndon B., 285
Johnson, Samuel, 64
Jonson, Ben, 69
Jordan, 123, 293, 301
Joseph, 44
Joseph, Franz, 147
Joshua, 313, 330, 377, 379
Josiah, 330, 379
Judaism, 18, 40
Judges (Book of), 105
Judicial review, 226
Judiciary Act of 1789, 249
Junkers, 147
Junto (Whigs), 63, 68
Jus Publicum Imperii Romani Germanici, 25
Justice, 42, 108, 110–112, 243–244, 292, 310; and the Bible, 375–381; civil, 33; individual, 359; natural, 33; social, 110, 357, 359

Kabbalah, 70, 103
Kabbalists, 288, 354
Kahal (community of equals), 367
Kalmar Union, 164
Kant, Immanuel, 23, 54–56, 88, 89
Kampelman, Max, 292–293
Kaplan, Mordecai, 101, 107, 109, 111, 133
Kashmir, 294
Kaufman, Yehezkel, 343
Kayemah(oath as covenant), 363
Kerensky, Alexander, 167
Kerr, Phillip (Lord Lothian), 77
Khrushchev, Nikita, 206
Kibbutz, 106–107
Kierkegaard, 34
II Kings, 379
Kingship of God (Buber), 105

Kinship, 125, 127, 307, 323, 327, 335, 378; and consent, 21, 48, 109, 124, 305, 307, 325, 378, 380
Kinsky, Ferdinand, 91
Knox, John, 318
Korean War, 294, 298
Kosciusco, Thaddeaus, 197
Kronstadt Revolt, 168
Kuyper, Abraham, 150–151, 158

Labor unions, 249
Labour Party, 208
Laender, 149, 300
Lafayette, Marquis de, 143–144, 197
Laissez-faire capitalism, 297, 313
Laissez-faire theorists, 112
Lake Lucerne, 177–178
Lake Uri, 177
Lampadius, J., 25
Landesgeminden (republic), 179
Laos, 206
Laski, Harold, 20, 77
Lasserre, David, 180
Latin America, 2, 121, 206–207, 212, 270, 295
Law of land versus law of group, 321–322
League(s), 19, 168, 182, 299–301, 303, 363; Achean, 23; confederal, 23
League of Nations, 81, 107–108
Lebanon, 305
Legalism, 59
Legislative Assembly (France), 144
Legislatures, 249, 253, 280
Legitimacy, 200–202, 207, 284, 310; consensual, 203; covenantal, 348
Leibnitz, Gottfried Wilhelm Baron Von, 22–24, 55
Lenin, Vladimir, 167–168, 206
The Leveller (Wildman), 67
The Levellers, 62, 64
Leviathan (Hobbes), 35, 37
Levinson, Henry S., 102
Leviticus, 85, 225, 330–331
Liberalism, 52, 54, 60, 93–94, 95–97, 147, 161, 167, 185, 192, 212, 267, 336; British, 73–74, 76; Czechoslovakia, 206; Dutch, 149–150; economic, 297; French, 145; German, 146, 148; individualistic, 91;realistic, 101; Spain, 155
Libertarians, 60, 112

Liberty, 46–47, 53, 85, 89, 120–121, 131, 142, 179–180, 186, 192, 247, 249, 256, 258, 268, 324–325, 329, 333–336, 339, 343–344, 347; absolute, 148; communal, 178–179, 187, 192; constitutional, 187; cooperative, 103; and covenant, 343–345; democratic republican, 343; federal, 16, 34, 85, 87, 107, 244, 248, 260, 265–266, 275–276, 313–314, 324–325, 339, 342, 344–345, 348–350, 370; human, 265, 324; individual, 16, 179, 192, 244, 356, 357; local, 123, 143, 161, 178, 244, 362; natural, 85, 87, 107, 148, 151, 187, 244, 248, 253, 275, 276, 324–325, 342, 344–345, 347, 349, 352; in Reformed tradition, 11; republican, 51
Liberties, 118, 242–244, 247, 252–253, 255–256, 260, 344, 346, 363
Lieber, Francis, 270
Liechtenstein, 165
Likud Party, 226
Limnaeus, Johann, 25
Lincoln, Abraham, 131, 248, 252, 269–270, 272
Lincoln-Douglas debates, 248
Lipjhardt, Arend, 123, 150
Littell, Franklin, 111
Lituania, 101
Local government, 87, 209, 211, 222–223, 230
Locals, 320
Locke, John, 11–12, 18, 21, 31–32, 39, 43–46, 49, 55–56, 62, 66, 69–70, 112, 188, 245, 247, 336
Lombard, 125
Lothar, Kingdom of, 122, 211, 358
Louis XVI, 144, 172
Louisiana legislature, 286
Love (in Christian Theology), 108
Lovingkindness, 362–363
Low Countries, 149–154, 174, 318
Lucerne, 180, 182
Lutheran (ism), 94–95
Lutz, Donald, 198, 247
Luxembourg, 153–154, 165, 301

Maastricht Treaty, 298
McCarthy, Bill, 286
Machiavell, Nicoli, 18, 31
McCoy, Charles, 111

MacIntosh, James, 71
Madison, James, 47, 55, 249
Madrid, 155, 217–218
Mafia (as contractual system) -164
Magistratates, 211
Magna Carta, 208
Magnalia Christi Americana (Mather), 85
Maimonides, 39, 67, 69
Majestas, 25
Major, John, 287
Malaya, Malaysia, 299, 305
Malkhut shamayim (divine sovereignty), 367
Mao Zedong, 206
Marc, Alexandre, 28, 89–91
Marcos, Ferdinand, 323
Maritain, Jacques, 89
Market economics, 168, 173
Marranos, 37, 144
Marshall Islands, 306
Martinich, A. P., 37
Marx, Karl, 82, 87, 171, 206
Marxism, Marxists, 68, 77, 82, 87–88, 91, 104, 107, 170–171, 208, 252, 313
Masaryk, Tomas, 166
Mass culture, 336, 337
Mass media, 240, 274, 277–279, 337
Mass society, 336–339
Massachusetts, 84
Massachusetts Bay Colony, 212
Massachusetts Body of Liberties, 247
Massachusetts Constitution of 1780, 9, 63
Materialism, 311
Mather, Cotton, 85
Matrix model, 84, 193, 226, 280
Mayflower Compact, 84–85
Mediating institutions, 285
Mediterranean, 130, 154–156, 167
Mercantilism, 297
Meritocracy, 145, 280
Mesopotamia, 8
Methodist(s), 73–74
Methodological individualism, 11
Metternich, Prince, 146
Mexican Revolution, 141
Mexico, 234–235, 300, 305–306
Michel, Robert, 46
Micronesia, 306
Middle Ages, constitutionalism in, 3
Middle East, 305; law, 321–322

Migration(s), 127–129, 189
Militarism, 147, 148
Militias, 132–133
Mill, John Stuart, 74–75
Milner, Alfred, 76
Milton, John, 64, 69
Mirabeau, Comte de, 143
Mishpatay piv (justice from God's mouth), 377
Mitzvot (commandments), 243, 377
Moab, 133
Mohl, Robert von, 93
Monaco, 300
Monarchy, 88, 117, 120, 137; absolute, 69, 164, 170; constitutional, 149, 165; Denmark, 162; French, 143, 172; hierarchical, 154; liberal, 145; military, 144; mixed, 66; Napoleonic type, 123; patriarchal -12, 67; Scandinavian, 161; unitary, 156
Monarchists, 145
Monism, 103, 343
Montesquieu, 28, 46–48, 53
Morality, covenantal, 41; federal, 40; natural, 41
Moravia, 165
Morgarten, 179
Moses, 42, 44, 48, 313, 379
Moses (Buber), 105
The Mountain (French political movement), 144
Mozart, Wolfgang Amadeus, 242
Muckrakers, 252
Multiculturalism, 307
Munich, 166
Muslims, 154, 210, 327, 353
Mussolini, Benito, 156
Mutualism, 162
Mutuality, theory of (Proudhon), 88

Napoleanic Wars, 119–120, 146, 161, 180–181, 185
The Nation, 270
Nation-state, 117; defining elements of, 296
National Council of Evangelical Free Churches, 73
National Guard (France), 143
Nationalism, 48, 52, 97, 101, 117–138; cultural, 130; hierarchical, 133; liberal, 146; modern, 167, 178; organic, 133, 271

Nationhood, 110, 124–125
Natural Law, 18–19, 45, 60, 66, 70, 246–247, 258, 376
Natural Right, 18, 40, 60, 66, 240, 245–248, 258; modern natural right, 259
Naturalization, 128
Navarre, 155
Nazism (National Socialism), 27, 50, 54, 89, 94, 98, 105, 110, 134, 147–148, 170, 172, 240, 272, 292, 309
Negotiation, 227
Nehemiah, 330
Neighborliness, 343
Nelson, Ralph, 88
Netherlands, 1, 10, 22, 24, 37, 59, 61, 65, 117, 119, 123, 149–153, 158, 162, 220, 230, 267, 301, 305, 318–319, 362, 363; covenantal tradition -7
Netherlands Antilles, 152
Neuhaus, Richard John, 286, 345
Neutrality, 153, 156, 164, 185
Neville, 64
New England, 10, 15, 82, 84–85, 101–102, 212, 222, 247, 317, 319
New Foundland, 317
New Haven, Connecticut, 85
New Jersey, 63
New political science, 31–58
New York City, 270
New Zealand, 76, 137
Newton, Isaac, 70
Nice, University of, 90
Niebuhr, Reinhold, 101, 107–109, 111, 174
Nigeria, 222, 299, 305
Nimrod, 177
Nixon, Richard, 229
Noah, 44, 376, 377, 379
Noahide Covenant, 150, 243–244, 329, 376–378, 380
Noahide principles, 70
Nobility, 144
Nomocracy, 48
Noncentralization, 86, 94, 121, 157, 219, 230
Nonconformists, 73–74, 95
Nonhierarchy, 163
Nonterritorialism, 123
Norman conquest, 208
Normans, 321
North Africa(ns), 128, 129

North American Free Trade Agreement (NAFTA), 301, 305–307
North Atlantic Treaty Organization (NATO), 295, 298, 300, 306
North Carolina, 55
North Korea, 206, 294
North Sea, 122, 358
Northern Ireland, 220, 294, 301
Northern Marianas, 300, 306
Northwest Ordinance of 1787, 246
Norway, Norwegians, 161, 163–164, 197
Nova Scotia, 317

Oasis culture, 317, 354–355
Oath(s), 154–155, 162, 178–179, 183, 318, 348, 362–363; common oath, 362
Oath society, 163–164, 318–319
Obedience, 352
Obligation, 112, 132, 242–244, 246–247, 253, 256, 258, 260, 275, 327, 332, 343, 348, 350, 352, 356–357, 359; and the Bible, 375–381; contractual, 327; federal, 260
O'Connell, Daniel, 77
Oligarchic, 123, 131, 192
Oligarchy, 149; patrician, 185
Opportunity, 343
Order, 108
Organic (model), 130, 138, 198, 221, 223, 228–229, 248, 251, 254, 269, 341–344, 349–351, 355, 358, 378; development, 124, 329; polities, 199, 220, 226–227, 239, 242; republics, 136; societies, 54, 73, 75, 82–83, 90, 92–94, 146, 251–252, 255, 271, 333; states, 81, 158, 254, 269; theory, 81, 111, 146, 155, 270; thought, 27, 252, 356
Orwell, George, 337
Ostrom, Vincent, 35, 107, 112, 202
Otis, James, 63
Ottoman Empire, 121, 305
Oxford University, 60, 75, 76

Pact(s), 19, 154–155, 162, 169, 181–182, 211, 227–229, 269, 285, 295, 305, 317–318, 327, 329, 332, 342, 348, 359, 363, 375; confederal pacts, 182; mutual defense pacts, 182
Pact of Rutli, 178–180

Pactio, 19
Pactum, 19
Pagan(ism), 163, 180, 310, 311
Pakistan, 122, 227, 299, 305
Palau, 306
Palestine, 106, 294, 301
Papacy, 155
Paris, 142, 143
Parliament (Britain), 67
Parliamentary model, 279
Partnership, 327, 332, 370, 375
Paths in Utopia (Buber), 91
Patriotism, 133
Peace of Westphalia, 25
Peirce, Charles, 101–102
Pennsylvania, 63
Peoples, peoplehood, 126–127, 131, 212, 234, 307–308, 325, 363, 365, 370; covenanted, 346, 361
Pepys, Samuel, 69
Pershing, General John J., 234
Personalism, 28, 89–91, 104, 105
Persuasion, 103
Phalange, 134
Philadelphia, Pennsylvania, 90, 241
Philip II, 362
Philippines, 323
Philistines, 335
Philo of Alexandria, 11
Piedmont, 156
Piety, 359
Pilgrims, 84–85, 198
Pittsburgh, 166
Plato, Platonic thought, 278
Pluralism, 77, 102–103, 110, 123, 308, 314, 322; American, 189; group, 191; humanistic, 105; lifestyle, 191; modern federal, 118; structural, 122; territorial-based, 179
A Pluralistic Universe (James), 104
Plymouth Colony, 212
Plymouth Combination, 85
Plymouth Rock, 84
Poland, 24, 124, 146, 165–167, 197
Politica Methodice Digesta (Althusius), 20
Political culture, 8, 14, 59, 149, 173, 180, 215, 216, 239, 344; ancient Israelites, 318; covenantal, 8–9, 138, 146, 152, 154, 219, 358; Dutch, 123, 150, 152; elitist, 278; European, 287; federal, 186; French, 143; Ger-

man, 148; hierarchical, 164; Iberian, 217; Italy, 123; liberal democracy, 189; moralistic political culture, 239; oath society, 162; Swedish, 164; Swiss, 119, 181
Political parties, 279
Politics, new science of, 13–16
Political philosophy, new, 11–13
Political Tractate (Spinoza), 39
Polity, 17, 19, 64, 66–67, 91, 103, 118, 133, 136, 143, 148, 163, 167, 170, 172, 192, 200, 203–204, 207, 212, 215–216, 220, 222–223, 226–227, 229, 233, 239–240, 242–243, 246, 251, 254, 269, 276, 278–279, 285, 291, 300–301, 303, 307–308, 312, 319–320, 322, 325, 328–329, 333, 335–337, 344, 348, 350–351, 355, 357–358, 361, 363, 378; almost covenanted, 321; authoritarian, 234; and Buber, 105; *civitas composita* (compound polity), 25; constituting or reconstituting the polity, 198–199; and constitutional design, 226–229; covenanted, 131–132, 137, 177, 186, 272, 301, 318, 332, 346, 351; Davidic, 105; designing the polity, 199–200, 204; Dutch, 150; federal, 221, 224, 301; Harmonia of, 326; Hellenic polis, 328; Latin America, 207; methods of founding, 226; Mosaic, 62, 105, 335; multinations, 121; non-territorial, 305; as political association, 323–324; Swiss, 192; territorial, 305; Third World, 207; Tocqueville and American polity, 86
Polity building, 3
Populism, 271
Portugal, 121, 154, 212, 300, 305
Power, 119–120, 205, 293, 302, 319–320, 338, 353, 356, 375; federal, 21, 291
Power maps, 215
Pragmatism, 101–102
Praxis, 90
Predestination, 108
Presbyterian, 19–20, 64, 73, 81, 95, 108, 270, 362; Scottish, 65, 68, 319; Southern, 286
Presbyteries, 95
Presidential government, 145, 202

Primordial groups, 256
Primordial ties, 158
Print media, 278–279
Privacy, 250, 256–257
Privatism, 52
Privilege, 363
Progressivism, 271
Promise Keepers, 286
Property, 256; private, 250–252
The Prophetic Faith (Buber), 105
Protestants, 18, 59, 93–94, 101, 157, 166, 307, 333, 357; Reformed, 1, 7, 10, 19–20, 32, 39, 46, 50, 56, 65, 69, 71, 94–95, 107–108, 112, 151–152, 165–166, 184, 211, 272, 318–319, 332, 385; Reformation, 1, 7, 38, 60, 94, 108, 123, 149, 163–165, 181–182, 185, 211, 318–319, 333, 351, 355, 358
Proudhon, 28, 77, 82, 87–89
Proverbs, 312
Providence, Rhode Island, 85
Provinces, 221
Prussia, 24, 93–95, 118, 120, 130, 146–147, 149, 296
Public(s), 126, 135, 234, 284, 307–308, 344
Public Square, 286, 345–347
Puerto Rico, 230, 300, 306
Pufendorf, Samuel, 22, 47, 70
Puritan(s), 15–16, 19, 32, 34, 44–45, 64–65, 69, 85, 102, 112, 208, 244, 247, 269, 271, 312, 319, 326, 342, 352, 355, 375
Puritanism, 10, 39, 59, 65, 84, 97, 141; and Locke's political thought, 12
Putnam, Robert, 156, 358
Pygmies, 327
Pyrenees, 129

Racism, 81, 148, 219, 270–271; scientific, 310
Radicalism, 60–61, 68, 145, 167
Rappard, William E., 183, 184
Rashi, 67
Rawls, John, 112
Rea (neighbor), 367
Realpolitik, 234
Rechstslehre (Kant), 54
Reciprocity, 246
Recovenanting, 142
Redemption, 106

Referendum, 204, 300
Reformed Protestants, 7, 20, 27, 32, 39, 56, 69, 71, 95, 101, 107–108, 112, 165–166, 184, 211, 272, 318–319, 332, 335; and American federal democracy, 82; and covenantal idea, 1, 19–20, 46, 50, 94, 151–152; Dutch, 65; Netherlands Reformed Church, 150; Swiss, 187
Regionalism—Belgium, 303; Italian, 96, 123–124, 156, 221, 303; Spain, 121, 155, 218, 303
Regional arrangements, 303
Reign of Terror, 144
Relativism, 274
The Religion of Ethical Nationhood (Kaplan) -110
Religious dissent, 65
Religious naturalism, 109–111
Du Renouvellement des Pactes Confederaux (Rappard), 183
The Republic (Plato), 277
Republics, compound -136; covenanted, 318; city republics, 50; confederated, 185; democratic, 134, 255, 319, 322, 338; federal, 71, 104, 121, 144; Israelite, 49; Jacobin, 120, 123; res publica, 120, 134; res publica composita, 25; res publica simplex, 25; territorial, 328; tribal, 328; united indivisible, 144
Republican constitution, 54
Republican party, 271
Republicanism, 13–14, 17, 32, 133, 136, 172, 186, 202, 267–268, 317–339, 344; American, 135, 143; civic, 71, 156; democratic republicanism, 86, 143, 154, 170, 174, 179, 212, 216, 277–278, 320; English Civil War, 64; federal democratic republicanism, 82, 358; federal republicanism, 20, 102; Jacobin, 136–137; Jewish people, 209; liberal, 154; medieval, 244; modern, 136–138, 174; parliamentary, 145; secular civil democratic, 46; Swiss, 192, 244; tribal, 132; village, 132; Westminster system, 136–137; Republicans, 60, 119; Whigs, 64
Reshuyot (shared authorities), 367
Responsibility, 246
Restoration, 149, 185

Restraint, 103
Re'ut (neighborliness), 326–327
Revolutions, 132–138, 141–158, 207; aquarian, 151; cybernetic, 273; ideological, 171; modern European, 2–3, 270; totalitarian, 173
Rhine, 149, 158
Rhine Valley, 174, 318
Rhineland, 149, 319
Rhode Island, 85, 212
Rougement, Denis de, 28, 89–91
Rights, 15, 83, 112, 132, 155, 205, 212, 324, 332, 357, 378; and the Bible, 244, 375–381; bills of rights, 253–254; civil, 225, 252–253; constitutional, 248–249; of contract, 251; and covenantal tradition, 239–260; declaration of, 215, 240–242; groups, 128, 166, 256–257; human, 170, 209, 225, 240, 244, 246, 252–253, 257–258, 300, 356; individual, 73, 166, 189–191, 240, 242, 245–246, 249–250, 252, 255–257; natural, 240, 245–248; property, 250–253, 259; social, 241
Risorgimento, 96
Rome, 18, 134, 309–310
Roman Empire, 22–23, 122–123, 179–180, 308, 318, 328, 358
Roman Philosophy, 38
Romania, 121, 124, 166
Romanticism, 69, 74; German, 93
Rota Club, 61, 64
Roundheads, 64
Rousseau, Jean-Jacques, 9, 32, 50–53, 55, 89, 112, 142, 344
Rule of law, 370
Russia, 50, 119, 141–142, 164–167, 169, 197, 206, 306
Russian Empire, 121, 164, 167, 270
Russian Revolution, 141, 167–168, 268
Rutli, Pact of, 177–178, 186

Saadia Gaon - 131
Sahara, 227
St. Gotthard Pass, 178
Saint-Simon, 88
Samuel I (Book of), 105, 330
Samuel II (Book of), 105
San Francisco, 291
Sanctions, 332
Sandel, Michael, 112

Salus (salvation), 41
Salvation, 41–42, 102–103
Sardinia, 156
Saxony, 24, 93
Scandinavia, 74, 161–164, 174, 318–319, 328
Schaffhausen, 182, 184
Die Schecksalsstuden des Foederalismus (Lasserre), 180
Science, 310–312
Scientific management, 251
Schmira (observing), 377
Schmitt, Carl, 27
Schwyz, 177, 180–181
Scotland, 15, 64, 68, 71, 75, 95, 134, 179, 208, 220, 253, 267, 317–319, 362; covenantal tradition, 7; political thought, 55, 77
Scots, 10, 319
Scottish Enlightenment, 70–72
Secularism, 12–13
Secularization, 38
Seeley, John, 76
Sefer Ha Brit (Book of the Covenant), 225
Segregation, 219
Selden, John, 69–70
Seleucid Antiochus, 309
Self-determination, 122, 292
Self-government, 153, 163–164, 170, 191–192, 198, 218, 277, 313, 324, 335, 343; democratic, 347–348; tribal, 300
Self-rule, 126, 218, 239, 291, 293, 300
Self-sufficiency, 296–297
Separation of church and state, 95
Separation of powers, 87, 136–137, 145, 202, 205, 216, 221, 280
Serbia, 121
Shalem (completeness), 326, 375
Shalom (peace), 35, 326–27, 375, 379
Shamoa (hearkening), 41, 352
Shared-rule, 126, 218, 239, 291–292, 300
Shared values, 222
Shavuol, 40
Shevatim (family of tribes), 367
Shomer (steward), 377
Sicily, 125, 156, 169
Sidgwick, Henry, 75
Simmel, George, 92, 106
Simon, Yves, 88
Sin, 108, 324

Sinai, 40, 243–244, 335, 377–380
Six Books of the Republic (Bodin) -118
Slaves, slavery, 250, 252, 269
Slovakia, 124, 167, 206
Smith, Adam, 71
Social contract(s), 50–51, 54–57, 81, 85, 89, 141–143, 246, 268, 287, 322–323, 327, 344, 348
Social Contract (Rousseau), 142
Social Darwinism, 270–271
Socialism, 54, 60, 87, 106, 110, 126, 164, 167, 205, 208, 313; guild, 88; libertarian socialism, 91; scientific, 310
Societas, 26, 332
Society of Friends (Quakers), 69
Sodom, 377
Soloveitchik, Joseph, 111
Solomon, 335
Solothurn, 182, 184
Some Remarks Upon Government (Wildman) -67
Sonderbund War of 1847, 185
South Africa, 74, 76, 204, 219–221, 254, 301
South Carolina, 55, 200
South Korea, 298, 323
Sovereignty, 23–26, 52–53, 55, 75, 77, 85, 92, 102, 105, 117–120, 135–137, 179, 187, 200, 230, 271, 276, 284, 291–292, 295, 297, 300, 370; sphere sovereignty, 150
Soviet Bloc, 294–295, 301
Soviet Union, 126, 166, 168, 199, 206, 284, 292, 297–299, 305–306, 309, 339
Spain, 1, 37, 65, 117–118, 121–122, 126, 154–155, 157, 205, 212, 217–218, 220, 229–230, 300, 303, 307, 308, 362
Spinoza, Benedict, 11–12, 18, 31, 37–43, 49, 188, 336, 379
Squatters, 152
Staatenbund (confederation), 92
Stackhouse, Max, 111
Stalin, Joseph, 168
State-building, 117–118, 121, 270
State of Nature, 33, 45, 276
Statehood, 254
States-General, 143
Statism, 1–2, 22–23, 27, 28, 74, 77, 96–97, 119, 121, 124, 272, 284, 297, 323–324, 356, 358
Steffans, Lincoln, 271

Stevens, Alexander, 269
Stewart, Dugald, 71
Stuarts, 68
Studies in the Problem of Sovereignty, 77
Sturm, Douglas, 111
Style, 173
Sudan, 305
Susser, Bernard, 106
Sweden, Swedes, 161, 163–164, 167
Switzerland (Swiss), 10, 22, 52, 59, 75, 118, 124–125, 128, 156–158, 165, 177–193, 198, 204, 220, 224, 228, 244, 305, 317, 318, 356, 358; confederation, 48, 86, 122; covenantal tradition -7, 82; federation, 86, 96, 120
Sydney, Algernon, 66
Synods, 95
Syria, 305, 317

Talmon, J. L., 50
Talmud, 363
Tarbell, Ida, 271
Taylor, John, 112
Television, 278–279, 282–283
Tell, William, 177
Temple University, 90
Territorialism, 118, 128
Territoriality, 130
Terrorism, 167
Teutonics, 164
Texas, 285
Thailand, 197
Thatcher, Margaret, 154, 208
Theism, 37
Theocracy, 106
Theology, federal, 59; political, 101
Third Estate, 143
Thirty Years War, 60–61, 120
Thomasius, Christian, 26
Ticino, 185, 186
Timosoara, 166
Tocqueville, Alexis de, 15, 28, 82–87, 178, 186, 258, 324, 347, 349
Toennies, Ferdinand, 92, 106, 256
Tokes, Lazlo, 166
Toland, John, 63
Tolerance, 189, 310, 311, 313; in Netherlands, 151–152
Torah, 35, 40, 131, 200, 208–209, 225, 329, 367

Tories, 72
Totalitarianism, 27, 68, 81, 94, 105, 122, 134, 168, 170, 257, 272, 285, 297, 309–310, 319, 337, 339, 345, 347, 359
Tower of Babel, 134, 361
Tractatus Theologico Politicus (Spinoza), 38
Treaties of Rome (1958), 295
Treatise on Civil Government, 43
Treaty(ies), 19, 111, 183, 298, 300, 317, 363; interstate, 293
Treaty of Paris, 185
Treaty of Utrecht, 117
Treaty of Versailles, 166
Treaty of Westphalia, 38, 59, 230
Trentino-Alto Adige, 156
Treuhandelstalt, 149
Trotsky, Leon, 168
Trust, 169, 235–236, 284, 305
Turkey, 132, 305
Turks, 128
Turner, Frederick Jackson, 358
Tuscany, 125
Tyranny, 44
Tzedakah u'mishpat (acting/doing justly through law), 376–377
Tzedakah v'hesed (covenantal framework of justice), 379

Underdoggism, 112
UNESCO, 294
Unio, 26
Union(s), 132, 300, 303, 332; confederal, 306; federal, 370
Union Theological Seminary (New York), 101, 108
Unitarians, 269
Unitarists, 156
Unitary states, 300
Unitary systems, 221–222, 230–231, 233
United Nations, 111, 257, 291, 293–294, 298
United Nations Covenant of Human Rights, 294
United Nations Covenant on Genicide, 294
United Nations Declaration of Rights, 256
United tribes of Israel, 313
United States of America, 27, 125, 130, 132, 165, 167, 171, 179, 181, 186,

197–198, 222, 229–230, 235, 250–
255, 257, 259, 267–272, 278–279,
282, 284, 294–295, 297–298, 303,
305–308, 312–313, 319, 321, 332,
349–350, 355, 357–358, 362, 370;
almost chosen people, 252; Articles
of Confederation, 14, 204, 230, 370;
Bill of Rights, 240–241, 246–247,
249; blacks, 128, 252; civil religion,
110; civil rights revolution, 110;
Civil War, 103, 131, 235, 249, 252–
253, 269–270; colonies, 72, 131,
198, 200, 267; confederation, 158;
Congress, 241; constitution, 202–
203, 212, 221, 226, 228, 241, 248–
249, 267, 269–272, 326, 332, 370;
constitutional federalism, 313; constitutional convention, 200; constitutionalism, 197, 215, 222–225, 270;
covenantal ideology, 9; as covenantal nation, 110, 131, 273; covenantal tradition, 101; Democratic party,
271; democratic republicanism, 143;
democracy, 110; federal democratic
republicanism, 82; federal democracy, 172, 270, 272; federalism,
119–120, 158, 162, 230; Federalists,
241; Founding, 7, 63, 119, 131;
Founding Fathers, 81, 102, 202, 282,
327, 350; Gilded Age, 103; Great
Society, 251, 285; Jim Crow, 271;
as model liberal democracy, 189;
nationalism, 125, 128, 133, 271;
Native Americans, 128, 300; patriotism, 285; polity, 86; Populism, 271;
Progressives, 252, 271; Republican
party, 271; Revolution, 63, 71, 72,
131, 141, 143, 173, 200, 212, 223,
242, 247, 267, 307; Selective service
in World War I, 235–236; Senate,
306; and sovereignty, 135; Supreme
Court, 187, 189, 202, 204, 225, 248–
252, 271, 328; theopolitical tradition, 51; and Tocqueville, 82–87;
and Tocquevillian studies, 82
United States of Europe, 90, 97, 231,
295, 299
Universal Covenant of Human Rights,
111
Universal Declaration of Human
Rights, 257
Universalism, 311

University of Colorado, 286
Unterwalden, 177, 181
Ural Mountains, 306
Uri, 177, 178, 181
Uttar Pradesh, 339

Valais, 185–186
Valle d'Aosta, 156
Varieties of Religious Experience
(James), 102
Vaud, 185
Veahavta l're'eha komoha (love thy
neighbor as thyself), 326
Velvet Revolution, 206
Venezuela, 121, 300
Venice, constitution, 61
Versailles, 143
Veto, 320
Vichy France, 89
Victor Emmanuel, 156
Victorianism, 97
Vietnam, 206
Vietnam War, 110
Vikings, 162–163, 167
Villa, Francisco (Pancho), 234
Virginia, 270
Virginia Declaration of Rights, 246
Virtue, 71, 151, 162, 311, 336, 347;
civic, 86; moral, 124
Voluntary associations, 87, 162, 345
Vom Geist der Ebraischen Poesie
(Herder), 48

Waldstatte (forest states), 177, 181
Wales, 65, 75, 77, 94–95, 137, 208
Wallonia, 153
Walloons, 153, 307
Walzer, Michael, 112
Wandervogel Youth Movements, 104
Washington, DC, 235–236, 286
Washington, George, 143
Watergate, 110, 229
Ways, 331
Webster's English Dictionary, 362
Weimar Republic, 95, 120
Welfare, 256–257
Wells, H.G., 337
West Bank, 293
West Indies Federation, 299
Western European Union, 295
Westminster Parliamentary model, 137,
355

Westphalia System, 230, 233
Whigs / Whiggism, 44, 60, 63–68, 70–
    73, 141, 208, 215, 240–241, 247,
    253, 355, 362, 365, 370
Wildavsky, Aaron, 44, 112
Wildman, Major John, 64, 67
Wilhelm I, Kaiser, 147
Wilhelm II, Kaiser, 147
Will, human, 81
William the Conqueror, 208
William III, 63, 65, 67
Wilson, Woodrow, 81, 107–108, 235,
    270, 292
Winkelbach, Karl Georg, 93
Winthorp, John, 85
Wolf, Arnold, 111
Workshop in Covenant and Politics of
    the Center for the Study of Federal-
    ism, 91
World Bank, 295
World Trade Organization (WTO), 233,
    301, 306
World Zionist Organization, 209

World War I, 77, 89, 95, 96, 98, 105, 110,
    122, 126, 147–148, 153, 164, 166,
    252, 270, 278, 281, 283, 296, 337
World War II, 81, 89–91, 98, 105, 120,
    148–149, 153, 156, 163, 165–168,
    206, 210, 230, 252, 281, 291–292,
    296–298, 303, 356
Writs of habeous corpus, 242, 265

Yankee, New England, 101
Yugoslavia, 121, 167, 206, 222
Yugoslavs, 128

Zapatistas, 306
Zebulun, 329
Zionism, 49, 101, 104, 110
Zollverein, 120, 146
Zuckert, Catherine, 51
Zug, 180, 182
Zulu, 220
Zum Ewigen Frieden (Kant), 54
Zurich (Switzerland), 10, 180, 182, 184
Zwingli, Ulrich, 10

GENERAL THEOLOGICAL SEMINARY
NEW YORK

DATE DUE

APR 0 4 2000			
			Printed in USA

HIGHSMITH #45230